Gender, Culture and Society

DATE DUE

Gender, Culture and Society

Contemporary Femininities and Masculinities

Máirtín Mac an Ghaill
and
Chris Haywood

First published in 2007 by
PALGRAVE MACMILLAN
Houndmills, Basingstoke, Hampshire RG21 6XS and
175 Fifth Avenue, New York, N.Y. 10010
Companies and representatives throughout the world.

PALGRAVE MACMILLAN is the global academic imprint of the Palgrave Macmillan division of St. Martin's Press, LLC and of Palgrave Macmillan Ltd. Macmillan® is a registered trademark in the United States, United Kingdom and other countries. Palgrave is a registered trademark in the European Union and other countries.

ISBN-13: 978–0–333–98783–4   hardback
ISBN-10: 0–333–98783–7   hardback
ISBN-13: 978–0–333–98784–1   paperback
ISBN-10: 0–333–98784–5   paperback

This book is printed on paper suitable for recycling and made from fully managed and sustained forest sources.

A catalogue record for this book is available from the British Library.

A catalog record for this book is available from the Library of Congress.

10 9 8 7 6 5 4 3 2 1
16 15 14 13 12 11 10 09 08 07

Printed in China

For Eilís Ní Dáley
Susan, Michelle and Jade Haywood

Contents

List of Tables

Acknowledgements

A number of people have contributed to the writing of this book. Our thanks to those who have helped us think through the issues that arose during the writing of the book: Liviu Popiviciu, Deborah Chambers, Tony Purvis, Santokh Singh Gill, Claire Worley, Po-Wei Chen, Bruce Carrington, Christine Skelton and Jayne Goble. Special thanks to the students on the B.A Applied Communication / B.A Media, Communication and Cultural Studies at the University of Newcastle for their thoughtful and engaging debates. Thanks also to those at Palgrave Macmillan, particularly Sheree Keep, Sarah Lodge, Emily Salz and Vidyha for their support. We are particularly grateful to the two external reviewers, who provided us with critical comments on the text.

Introduction:
Gender Relations in Context

What is This Book About?

Fundamental transformations in men's and women's lives are taking place in western societies (Hennessy, 2000, Walby, 1997). Empirical studies are beginning to detail how traditional 'gender roles' no longer look the same, mean the same or feel the same. Popular media commentaries have taken up these changes and characterized them as simple gender confusion and loss: 'Who's wearing the apron?', 'When men were men and knew it', 'Men lose out to women's touch at work'. Part of the difficulty in discussing these questions is that gender relations are one of the most contested areas of human behaviour. It is also an area that intersects individually and collectively across a range of cultural arenas that includes, for example, politics, family, employment, leisure and schooling. However, such discussions of gender tend to remain disconnected from the complexity of contemporary social relations. In response, *Gender, Culture and Society* provides a systematic investigation and evaluation of how we might make best sense of social change and contemporary femininities and masculinities.

Confronted by the lack of consensus about these much-debated issues, it is easy to overlook the fact that a fundamental transformation in social theory has occurred. Perhaps the most important advance in feminist theory is that gender relations have been problematized. In other words, gender can no longer be seen as a simple, natural fact (Flax, 1990). This book is about continuing to problematize, contest and interrogate current popular understandings of femininities and masculinities by engaging with a range of feminist, sociological and cultural studies frameworks, bringing together main theories, key concepts and major debates. This book is also about a social imagining. Consequently, the book may be read as an attempt to jostle the imagination of the reader, by providing some more metaphors for living life, some more complexities to disturb old routines, some more politics to disrupt the functions of the past, some more views to punctuate the now crumbling view of a unified social order (Plummer, 1992: xviii–xix). Thus, resulting from the following inquiry is an evaluation

1

of past understandings and analysis of implications for contemporary political practice. Informed by our own reading of existing studies and our own empirical research, we offer a critical yet constructive diagnosis of the origins and development of current conditions and controversies enveloping gender relations (Mac an Ghaill, 1996).

We set out to make a conceptual intervention in existing studies of masculinities and femininities. This book does this by situating the discussion of contemporary femininities and masculinities within three main aims. These are as follows:

1.   To explore how changes in gender relations are linked to wider social and cultural transformations in late modernity (see below).   Connections between social change and gender are evident at a number of different moments in social and cultural history. However, it is important to consider how currently gender is an increasingly visible category that has contextually specific meanings attached to it.

2.   To explore the theoretical and conceptual tensions that become apparent by exploring approaches to gender relations *alongside* each other, including feminism, studies on masculinities and post-structuralism (see below).   Central to our examination of femininity and masculinity is identifying the possibilities involved in the connections between gender and social change.

3.   To recognize that the struggle for gender and sexual equality is occurring at a time of rapid global change in which there is criticism from the political right and left of the limits of feminist politics and the emergence of men's movements in the west.   Furthermore, there are alternative responses from developing countries highlighting the limits of western accounts that depend upon specific US or European-based concepts, while claiming universal application.

The Sex/Gender Category as a Cultural Flashpoint: Mobilizing Gender in the New Modernizing Project

B.L. Marshall (1994: 6), in her text, *Engendering Modernity*, critically explores the history of gender in contemporary societies. She begins:

> Against the backdrop of the Enlightenment, modernity is associated with the release of the individual from the bonds of tradition, with the progressive differentiation of society, with the emergence of civil society, with political equality, with innovation and change. All these accomplishments

are associated with capitalism, industrialism, secularization, urbanization and rationalization.

In other words, the concept of modernity here does not refer to a simple description of contemporary societies. Rather, it suggests a theoretical model based on the interaction of four major deeply structured processes – the political, the economic, the social and the cultural – developing over long periods of time, in response to major changes (Hall, 1992; Hall and Gieben, 1992; Hall, *et al.*, 1992).

Presently, in response to recent major transformations, social theorists have offered a range of contrasting accounts of contemporary western societies, in an attempt to capture the suggested defining features of what they refer to as late modernity. These defining features include globalization, risk, individualization and reflexivity (see definitions below; Beck and Beck-Gernsheim 1995; Giddens, 1992; Smart and Neale, 1999). Theorists of late modernity suggest that individuals (or modern subjects) in detraditionalizing western cultures are intrinsically linked to social and cultural transformations, involving processes of fragmentation, dislocation and mobility (Beck, 1992; Giddens, 1991; Laclau, 1990; Urry, 2000). More specifically, for Marshall (1994), a key current task for theorists of gender is how to respond to claims that the project of modernity has exhausted itself. The starting point of this book is that our specific location is within late modernity and each chapter explores what this means in relation to gendered lives. Of particular importance has been the effect of globalizing forces on gender relations (Altman, 2001; Bauman, 1992). At a general level, globalization may be understood as referring to the economic, cultural and political processes, procedures and technologies underpinning the current 'time – space' compression that is producing a sense of immediacy and simultaneity about the world (Brah *et al.*, 1999).

Placing ourselves within late modernity, as we explain below, signals a wish to hold onto a synthesis between theories of gender developed within modernity, for example, early feminist and gay/lesbian accounts and more recent critiques of these positions, for example, post-structuralism and queer theory.[1] We argue that there is much explanatory value in emphasizing the interpenetration of old and new social and cultural representations and practices and how gendered relationships are undergoing a series of fusions, conflicts, amalgamations and contradictions. For example, we wish to address the limitations of theorists working within older static theoretical frameworks based on industrial models of society (Bruegal, 1996). More specifically, the gendered dualism of male breadwinners and female homemakers have been projected as defining cultural images, exemplifying a naturalized social order, functional to the prerequisites of western, industrial capitalism. We suggest that this old modernist language is not able to grasp the generational specificities of emerging femininities and masculinities. A late modernity framework helpfully suggests that consumption can now be seen as a key dynamic move away from production (paid labour) in shaping contemporary identities, meanings and self-expression – in short, how we enact contemporary lifestyles (Baudrillard, 1988; Bocock, 1993). At the same time, processes of regendering are central to this move, with media-led projections of young men, within traditionally defined female space, refashioning masculinities (Nixon, 1996).

A key argument of this book is that we are experiencing a shift from the establishment of the social constitution of gender associated with modernity politics to the gendering of society that has an intensified resonance among (heterosexual) men and women in late modernity. We suggest that at this current historical juncture the category gender has become a lens to make sense of wider social transformations. We refer to this as a *cultural flashpoint* that we see as operating at two levels (Mac an Ghaill *et al.*, 2003; O'Sullivan, 1999).[2] First, at an immediate level, this intensified gendered awareness is intimately about the politics of transforming social relations and attendant changing structures and subjectivities between (heterosexual) men and women.[3] From different political positions, this is spoken through the rather vague notions of a *masculinity crisis*, a *backlash against feminism* or a *politics of recuperative masculinity*. (These powerful discursive constructs operating across a wide range of sites are further explored at different points in the book.) There is a sense of a transition in which the old cultural stories of gender identity formation, which are caught up in redrawing of the boundaries between men and women, are no longer making common sense (Carter *et al.*, 1993: x). For example, during the last few decades, gender shifts have been identified within high profile current public controversies, most notably such issues as the work–home balance, 'underachieving' male students and post-divorce childcare custody. Such shifts across western societies may be read as a search for a new gender settlement between women and men within conditions of late modernity.

At a second level, this is not directly a crisis of men's and women's social practices and interactions but rather the category *gender* provides the lens through which the assumed crisis is perceived and mediated. In short, the crisis has increasingly come to be spoken through gender. Hence, a gendered sensibility is no longer the preserve of political minority of political activists, such as feminists and pro-feminist men. Rather, it has become naturalized at a collective subjective level, as an epistemological organizational theme. In other words, the language of gender is increasingly used as a central means by which men and women articulate their understanding of being subjects in and objects of a world in flux (Berman, 1983). For example, the notion of gender as a lens is illustrated through the interpretative framing (that is, how we make sense) of the changing structure and meaning of paid labour.

One of the major effects of global changes on local urban sites is the collapse of regionally based manufacturing industries and expansion of the service sector, resulting in changing forms of incorporation, social division and spatial mobility of labour. These cumulative effects include new patterns in the international division of labour, the changing nature of the nation-state and the associated assumed crisis in Anglo-ethnicity, new labour processes and local labour markets within the context of deindustrialization and deregulation, new educational and work technologies, increased state regulation of youth, advanced global communication systems and diverse family forms (Appaduri, 1991; Giddens, 1990; Harvey, 1989; Jameson, 1991). Thus, the changing structure and meaning of paid work needs to be located within the context of these diverse, interconnecting social relations at a time of rapid change (Altman, 2001; Bauman, 1992). However, this restructuring of paid work is reductively read through the lens of gender, with sustained media attention declaring a 'sex war', marked by the projected feminization of the workplace and the collapse of stable masculinities. Hence, late modernity gender is circulated as a container in which contemporary western societies' complex fears, tensions and anxieties are seeking resolution.

In *Gender, Culture and Society* we argue that within western societies, in the twenty-first century, gender and sexual identities have come to speak a wider sense of social (dis)location in globally-based, post-colonial, (de) industrializing societies (Altman, 2001; Bhatt,1997).[4] The long history of the interplay between social change and shifting notions of masculinity and femininity currently has a specific cultural meaning within the late modernity of the risk society, marked by uncertainty, flux and ambivalence (Bauman, 2002, 2003). As examined in later chapters, in exploring contemporary social and cultural transformations, late modernity theorists, such as Giddens (1991) and Beck (1992), have identified gender as a central element of the narrative of change within detraditionalizing western societies. They suggest that shifting gender relations are dynamically involved in the move away from the rigidity of the structural determinants of class-based industrial societies to the new modernizing project of late modernity. Furthermore, it is suggested that the effects of the deregulating of individuals from the normative demands of established social categories is that late modernity subjects (or individuals) are compelled to forge their own identity as part of a highly reflexive making of a Do-it-yourself (DIY) biography. They argue that one effect of this is that women have now become *late modernity beneficiaries or winners* in response to the barriers established through gender during industrialization being challenged and overturned.

Critics from a range of theoretical positions have questioned this universalizing and overly optimistic picture of women as late modernity winners. They point to the underplaying of structural constraints, thus failing to address the question of power in relation to systemic inequalities that impact upon subordinated groups of women (and men) (Adkins, 2000; Harris, 2004; Lash, 1994). An important effect of this writing out of an increasingly highly differentiated allocation of material conditions, social capital and cultural resources is to see the 'failing female individual' as personally responsible for her own lack of achievement. However, as Harris (2004) argues in her critique of accounts of young women who are positioned as benefiting from the late modernity economy, nevertheless, contemporary young women are of central importance to the global demands of capitalism, both as workers and consumers (p. 37). As Weeks (1995: 4–5) makes clear with reference to a changing sex/gender order:

> The anxiety about the sexual, like mysterious creatures scuttling under the floorboards, implicitly shaped many of our public debates for a long time, from the fear of national or imperial decline at the end of the nineteenth century to the structuring of the welfare provision from the 1940s to the present.[5]

However, as he finely illustrates, what is new is the intense public anxiety in which changing sexual behaviour, emerging gender/sexual identities and fragmenting femininities and masculinities are explicitly linked to 'debates about the current shape and desirable future of society'. Hence, whatever the empirical evidence about the changing social realities of women's and men's lives, the question of gender is currently centre stage in terms of how we make sense of the world.

Working from within a wider explanatory framework, Epstein (1988: 232) has noted that no area of social life, 'whether the gathering of crops, the ritual of religion, the formal dinner party, or the organization of government – is free from the dichotomous thinking that casts the world in categories of "male" and "female" '. In turn, there is a long history of shifts in sex/gender and racialized ethnic relations being read as a barometer of social and cultural transformations across western societies. This interdependent relationship is particularly visible at times of real or imagined crisis in society. In the United States, for example, Kimmel (1987a) has illustrated how a notion of *masculinity crisis* appears at moments of wider disturbances in the social order. The history of British sex/gender relations is littered with changing gendered images in which national internal political discontents were displaced onto gendered minorities. Historically, this has been exemplified through the State's production of a range of regulatory representations, such as the 'single mother' and more recently that of the 'career woman'. These representations are projected as the cause of family breakdown, which in turn is connected to the assumed breakdown of the moral order of society (Hughes, 2002; Lawler, 2000). The production of these categories and their circulation through the media serves to illustrate an interesting temporal and spatial shift from the universal demonization of the 'single mother' (in the private sphere of the home) during the 1970s, to the more ambiguous current deployment of the term 'career women' (in the public sphere of paid work). The latter has occurred as more females are encouraged into the labour market in an expanding service sector, with which women have traditionally been associated (Bradley, 1996). In short, at a time of projected crisis in society, gendered minorities are coerced into carrying the gender majority's sense of moral disorder. This involves complex processes of social exclusion and psychic (unconscious) expulsion of social groups who are represented as a threat to the maintenance of social and symbolic borders.

Knowing Possibilities: Social Change and Theories of Gender

Throughout this book, we engage with issues of social change and how we make sense of gender relations. Of key importance is an underlying tension surrounding what we mean by social change and the impact that it has on gender relations. One approach suggests the need to correlate social practices with patterns of behaviour. Thus, social change can be measured, for example, by the number of women participating in the labour market. As participation rates increase, the impact on gender can be calculated. A similar argument is based upon documenting how men and women's roles have changed. In this way, men's changing roles can be measured by how far they identify with the notion of fatherhood. This is in contrast to an approach where gender and social change are intricately connected. From this position, researchers become interested in how such processes in themselves *are* gendered. This position, in effect, collapses the notion of change and gender as disparate variables that can be measured. What becomes important is establishing how processes of social change are constituted, how social practices can be understood as gendered categories. At various moments throughout this book this tension is the dynamic for our engagement with gender and social change. Thus, in many ways, the source of the tension is epistemological. In other words, what becomes important are the reasons (or theory) we use to argue why some knowledge counts and other knowledge does not. The position taken up in this book is that both perspectives offer valuable insights into how we might connect – epistemologically – gender and social change.

The centrality of social change, at both global and local levels, is a dynamic device allowing theories of gender relations to be historically

situated and socially, culturally and politically contextualized. At the same
time, gender theorists have done much work in explaining the connections
between gender and social change. Earlier feminist theories have provided
the social sciences with a language with which to make sense of 'structured
inequality', such as the operation of institutional gender stratification, for
example, within family life and the labour market. More recently, new
ways of thinking, including post-structuralism, post-colonialism and queer
theory have made available ways of understanding gender that are not tied
to notions of patriarchy. (Patriarchy is commonly understood as a social
organization that structures the dominance of men over women.) Uneasily
situated alongside and within these frameworks are studies of masculinities. In response, this book explores these current theoretical and empirical
uncertainties, providing a critical synthesis or mixture that brings together
feminist frameworks, sociology and cultural studies. As an inclusive text, it
uses the above approaches to social change to emphasize the social organization of gender and the active cultural production of competing images
and social practices of femininities and masculinities within specific
contexts. This enables us to understand gender relations as being central
to more traditional concerns with conceptions of structural power,
domestic–occupational stratification and sexual violence, alongside more
recent questions of consumption, the body, desire and subjective identity
formation (Butler, 1993; Cronin, 2000; Harris, 2004; Scott, 2000; Smith, 1987).

   Cross-cutting such approaches to gender is the need to move away from
the notion that social change has always impacted upon gender, towards a
recognition that gender has become a major constituent of contemporary
understandings about masculinity and femininity. What is distinctive
about this position is that it does not simply suggest that social change and
its impact upon gender is a recent phenomenon. For example, gender and
social change have been historically seen as mutually constitutive.
However, we suggest that such connections between gender and social
change are currently resulting in the formation of designated ways of
knowing. Such knowing has circumscribed how we might make sense of
gender and social change; they provide a form of closure around what can
be known. As Spanier (1993: 329) suggests:

   A formalised knowledge system functions as an institution – like the law,
   the family, capitalism, motherhood etc – that plays a particular role in
   sustaining and reproducing dominant beliefs about gender and sexuality,
   justifying them with the power of the objective and rational academy.

Throughout this book, we suggest that theoretical and conceptual
arguments can operate in regulative ways, endorsing and delegitimating
particular ideas, understandings and meanings. Therefore, it is important

to provide a critical understanding of the relative adequacy of different theoretical accounts through a series of contrasts but also to encourage a view of these theories as alternative explanations which make different assumptions about men and women, and associated processes of gender relations.

Theoretically, we are in a fortunate position and this book builds on earlier work in sociology and cultural studies, which suggests that gender relations are problematic, negotiated and contested within frameworks at individual, organizational, cultural and societal levels. Importantly, we have a range of tools with which we can analyse systematically and document coherently these levels by exploring the material, social and discursive production of gender relations. In short, gender relations can be seen as a crucial point of intersection of different forms of power, stratification, desire and subjective identity formation. A main argument of this book is the need to hold onto the productive tension between these different sociological/cultural studies explanations of gender relations (Haywood and Mac an Ghaill, 1997a). Recent texts reveal a tension between what are referred to as *materialist* and *post-structuralist* critiques of gender identity formation. In this book, the term *materialist* refers to social movements that perceive the organization of gendered identities as deriving from fixed bases of social power. Such bases of social power are seen to work logically and predictably, often being illustrated through an individual's occupation of fixed hierarchical positions, such as dominant/empowered (men) and subordinate/oppressed (women). This position is clearly illustrated by early feminist studies that located the source of women's oppression in the male body. In contrast, post-structuralist theorists (as outlined in the Notes to this chapter) have emphasized that the living of gender categories and divisions is more contradictory, fragmented, shifting and ambivalent than the dominant public definitions of these categories suggest. Most importantly a post-structuralist account of gender relations suggests that we cannot simply read off social behaviour from a pre-existing male–female oppositional binary structure of 'victims' and 'oppressors'. In short, *post-structuralism* explores such issues as the limits of the way that gender identity categories are portrayed in terms of social groups, such as men and women, how to make sense of the interconnectedness between multiple relations of power, such as gender, class, sexuality and disability, and the making of subjective identities.

Throughout the book, we shall highlight the need to engage with both *materialist* and *post-structuralist* approaches, in order to generate more comprehensive accounts of gender relations. We argue that rather than hold up a 'straw wo/man' to argue against, there is a need for approaches to be considered as a critical synthesis that brings together feminist frameworks with that of studies of masculinity. *Gender, Culture and Society* provides an authoritative profile and critique of recent developments in sociological and cultural theories of gender relations. As we demonstrate, this is a complex area, increasingly conscious of the complicated relationship between theoretical frameworks, methodological strategies and the phenomena subject to examination. It is important to hold these relationships in a critical synthesis which seeks to preserve a materialist core from earlier feminist accounts focusing upon patriarchal relations, while incorporating insights from more recent reflection on representation, identity and cultural difference with reference to women's and men's social experiences. In other words, notions of what are referred to as decentred forms of performing genders and hybrid (mixing of) sexualities are being constituted within a wider arena of late modernity, which in turn they are helping to shape (Jameson, 1991). From the theoretical investigation emerges an evaluation of past understandings and analysis of implications for contemporary political practice. In social relations, people occupy certain positions simultaneously. We need to think about not the ways social categories accumulate but the ways that they inflect. When we talk about the notion of power, we have to think about it relationally, thinking about powerful in relation to whom. In this way, we do not look at power as an either/or division but as being much more relational. We can say power is shaped relationally: one group is both powerful and powerless.

Understanding Social and Cultural Change: The Collective Political Subject and Pluralized Identities

The final aim of this book is to preface our discussion of social change and gender relations by highlighting the importance of the political context of gender and social change. Throughout *Gender, Culture and Society*, sociological literatures on gender and sexuality reveal highly divergent theoretical and conceptual positions that have been adopted across western societies, within the context of rapid social and cultural transformations. However, even within such a context of rapidly shifting explanations, the representation of sexual politics appears as an intensely contested terrain. The last two decades have seen unprecedented transformations in social relations of gender across Britain, much of Europe and the United States. For example, Phillips (1998a: 1) in her edited collection *Feminism and Politics*, writes of these:

> transformations that can be measured in the global feminization of the workforce, the rapid equalization between the two sexes (at least in richer

countries) in educational participation and qualifications, and a marked increase in women's self-confidence and self-esteem that is probably the most lasting legacy of the contemporary women's movement.

Segal (1999: 203), while acknowledging such changes, notes the continuities of sexual divisions, including women's average earnings being less than that of men's throughout the world; women having less leisure time than men, with housework and childcare still the primary responsibility of women and the increased reporting of men's violence against women and children since the mid-1980s, while conviction rates have decreased. Segal raises the question about these 'radically contrasting configurations', suggesting that how we respond politically depends upon which feminist position we take up (p. 5).

By the early 2000s, with an intensified awareness of how we live with difference, and the identification of various interconnecting forms of sexual politics marked by fusions, hybridity and body ambiguities, we might add, or which other political positions we take up, for example, those emanating from men's studies or queer activism. The former projects *a crisis masculinity* across western contemporary societies that is marked by bitter debates about the assumed changing social location of men and accompanying threatened male subjectivities (see Kimmel and Messner, 1989). The latter's antiassimilation stance suggests a reconceptualization of what we understand by the political. This involves a shift away from challenging structural inequalities and power relations between relatively given or fixed sexual/gender categories to deconstructing the categories themselves – 'their fixity, separateness or boundedness' and a move 'towards seeing the play of power as less binary and less uni-directional' (Epstein and Johnson, 1998: 38). At the same time, such a move sensitizes us to the tension between the mobilization of the collective political subject (for example, women, gays/lesbians, black community) and the pluralization of identities. The latter involves processes of fragmentation and dislocation of femininities and masculinities within the contexts of different geographies and histories of change at the local level of the nation or state (Hall, 1992; Mac an Ghaill, 1999). A post-colonial framework suggests that within the changing morphology of western urban sites, new identities are being manufactured, marked by diaspora (movement of people – dispersal), hybridity (mixing of cultures) and syncretism (pluralistic forms of cultural belonging) (Bhabha, 1990; Gilroy, 1993; Spivak, 1988a, b). Reading through the above texts makes clear the need to engage with these more sophisticated theoretical frameworks that belies easy political categorization. At the same time, they remind us that a political understanding of this field of inquiry is not simply an empirical question. As we argue throughout this book, specific conceptual and methodological limitations emanate from the undertheorization of social and cultural change. In turn, there is a difficulty in exploring the question of sexual politics at local and global levels. For Mohanty (1992), writing of the shift from the politics of transcendence to a politics of engagement, deploying non-western, cross-cultural studies serves to illustrate other potential ways of making sense of shifting gender structures, identities and practices.

Within a British context, a main political success of New Right (neo-liberal) dominance in Britain in the late 1980s was to challenge critical sociological accounts, taking up and reworking radical sociological critiques of society. These were seen by many people as making sense of their lives that were shaped by broader national anxieties and political concerns of 'new times'; that is, social transformations that mark a break with an older social order. As Hall (1988: 49) suggests in his analysis of Thatcherism, it success-fully constituted 'new subject positions from which its discourses about the world make sense'. He adds that it:

> combines ideological elements into a discursive chain in such a way that the logic or unity of the discourse depends on the subject addressed assuming a number of subject positions. The discourse can only be read or spoken unprob-lematically if it is enunciated from the imaginary position of knowledge of the self-reliant, self-interested, self-sufficient tax-payer – Possessive Individual Man; or the 'concerned patriot' or the subject passionately attached to individ-ual liberty and passionately opposed to the incursion of liberty that occurs through the state; or the respectable housewife; or the native Britain.

In other words, the New Right promoted itself as constructing a modern Britain, with a radical agenda that gained the ascendancy, occupying the high moral ground with its projected atavistic accounts of a consumer-based acquisitive individualism, the patriarchal family, the strong state and the patriotic British nation. The response of the mainstream Left to the New Right's (neo-liberalism) modernizing project was to restate 'old times' Enlightenment-based principles, involving vague conceptions of a social-democratic, welfarist and multiethnic citizenship. This included the sug-gested return to notions of community, participatory democracy and the more recent additions of empowerment and the learning society. During this period, a self-fulfilling prophecy appeared to have captured English society, with its claim that there was no real alternative to the New Right's policies. Consequently, by the early 2000s, the mainstream British Left's response can be seen to be uncomfortably accommodating the Right's rad-ical version of 'new times'. As Williams (2003: 25) points out:

> The vocabulary of choice and opportunity, of social market type justice and diversity for all, spread from the Conservatives to the SDP [Social

Democratic Party] and then infused Labour's notions of a joined-up party with a consensus across the political spectrum.

Simultaneously, the bigger picture suggests that currently the political hegemony of the US neo-conservative project is attempting globally to become all-pervasive. Luttwak (1998: 27) captures the ideological power of the shift from a post-war, state-regulated capitalism to what he refers to as turbo-capitalism. Referring to contemporary advocates of the free-market, he writes:

> What they celebrate, preach and demand is private enterprise liberated from government regulation, unchecked by effective trade unions, unfettered by sentimental concerns over the fate of employees or communities, and molested as little as possible by taxation. What they insistently demand is the privatization of state-owned business of all kinds, and the conversion of public institutions, from universities and botanic gardens to prisons, from libraries and schools to old people's homes, into private enterprises run for profit. What they promise is a more dynamic economy that will generate new wealth, while saying nothing about the distribution of any wealth, old or new.

In contrast to the political convergence between the parliamentary Right and Left in Britain, over the last 30 years, radical alternative agendas have been developed by New Social Movements, such as feminism, gay and lesbian liberation and antiracism, producing new political subjects that challenged this hegemonic socially conservative position. A significant development in the social sciences has been the impact of New Social Movements that have generated shifts in critically rethinking how we understand social institutions and cultural arenas, such as workplace, family life, education and leisure activities. By the early 2000s, questions of culture, identity and representation have moved centre stage. This shift enables us to explore the different theoretical frameworks made available by New Social Movements, namely *identity politics* and *the new politics of cultural difference*, which are two of the most dynamic contributions to current debates. (These distinctions are further explored in ch. 9). In this text, a *materialist* position is taken as underpinning a *politics of identity* and a *post-structuralist* position as underpinning *the new politics of cultural difference* (see above). Working within this framework highlights the need to connect an understanding of sexual politics, recent mobilizations and a sense of intimate belonging *with* wider social and cultural transformations as mutually constitutive. It is within this context of a complex politics of location that *Gender, Culture and Society* is placed, exploring the extent and direction of change in relation to the social relations of gender, sex/gender identity formations and subjectivities.

Structure of the Book

Thus, this book is written in order to provide a critical examination of old and new questions: What is gender? How does it differ from our understanding of natural sex differences? How are gender relations and power related? Have women's lives been transformed? How is gender linked to bodies? How are we to understand the globalization of gender formations? Is there a crisis in masculinity? What does it mean to talk about post-feminism? These questions have been answered by a growing number of popular and academic texts. Given the prevalence of gender as a cultural flashpoint, in currently making sense of our lives, we have been selective in the areas that are being examined. Areas of violence, health and crime have received much attention. In contrast, gender and social change remain relatively under-explored in the context of globalization and generation. Alongside this, the social and cultural arenas on which we have focused are those areas that reflect our own academic and intellectual biographies, which include areas such as sexuality, politics and the media.

Chapter 1, 'Approaching Gender: Feminism, Men's Studies and the Cultural Turn,' examines the main sociological and cultural studies approaches to understanding men and women within the broader context of social change. We provide a systematic overview of the field in an attempt to produce a synthesis of main approaches to gender. For example, there is a critical presentation of a wide range of theories, including sex-role theory, second-wave feminism and post-feminism, alongside approaches that draw upon post-structuralism. In doing so, it draws out the major theoretical, analytical and methodological tensions that characterize contemporary approaches to understanding masculinities and femininities. These tensions provide the major themes that will be explored throughout the following chapters.

In Chapter 2, 'Fragmenting Family Life: Beyond Maternal Femininities and Paternal Masculinities,' we explore the issue of representations of familial femininity and masculinity and women's and men's participation in the domestic arena. Beginning with a socio-historical approach, it explores earlier feminist work on the sociology of the family – emphasizing the need to see gender as primarily not a property of individuals but rather a consequence of institutions and cultural practices – from a position of recent social and cultural theory. It is suggested that earlier studies tend to understand mothers and fathers as asymmetrically positioned within absent/present, powerless/powerful, good/bad typologies. Within the context of the changing family, recent years have seen ever-increasing research and writing on men's experience of families and the personal, social and political representations of those experiences. This work, moving beyond a 'mother focused' paradigm, has addressed traditional typologies by understanding mothers and fathers as occupying, at the same time, contradictory social and emotional subject positions. The latter approach provides an analytical framework that brings together multiple levels of mothers' and fathers' experiences, and conceptualizes motherhood and fatherhood as a multi-faceted lived out experience of classed, racialized and generationally located dynamics. Finally, by re-examining the gendering of parenting we might begin to sketch out changing sex/gender relations in this arena and begin to re-imagine future possibilities of fragmenting family life.

Chapter 3, 'In and Out of Labour: Beyond the Cult of Domesticity and Breadwinners,' highlights that the shift from an industrial to a service-based economy in western capitalist countries has been marked by an experience of collapse, fragmentation and contraction. In the light of these changes and the suggested major transformation, we map men's and women's employment patterns within the context of the pervasive talk about a *crisis of masculinity*. Indeed, recent accounts have argued that a changing gendered division of labour has blurred traditional modernist understandings of men and women as homemakers and breadwinners. This chapter explores this assumption by examining recent quantitative data to highlight how the relationship between men, women and work has altered. The chapter further explores the suggested changing nature of gender relations, emerging occupational identities and the accompanying production of work-based subjects by examining a range of contemporary explanatory frameworks. These include political economy, structuration theory and theories of reflexive and aesthetic modernity. The latter, late modernity theorists often emphasize the current reconfiguration of the social division of labour and the reorganization of the gendered meaning of work. In contrast, critics maintain that we are a long way from the spatial containment of the cult of (female) domesticity and (male) breadwinners that earlier feminists identified as of central importance to the social reproduction of western industrial societies. In other words, a narrative of 'nothing but the same old story', it is claimed, remains in place.

Chapter 4, 'Interplaying Gender and Age in Late Modernity,' notes that although gender has become an established theme of young people's agency and cultural creativity (Griffin, 1993; McRobbie, 1991), there is a need for a broader analysis that develops the interrelationship between masculinities and femininities and age-related categories. For instance, gender theorists tend to unproblematically apply (adult) notions of masculinities and femininities to children and young people and use such concepts to explain experience and behaviours. Gender itself is often considered the exclusive study of men and women; children, teenagers and older people tend to be excluded or appended to 'real' theorizing. Informed by recent developments in the sociology of childhood and older age, this chapter provides existing gender theories with new ways to understand the age dynamics of masculinities and femininities. The chapter first considers how studies of masculinity in the context of schooling reveal limitations of how gender and age tend to be connected. The chapter then turns to examine the formation of femininity in the context of older age with particular reference to menopause. Finally, the chapter considers older men and how categories of age and sexuality converge to produce possibilities of ageing.

Chapter 5, 'Shifting Gender Connections: Sexuality, Late Modernity and Lifestyle Sex,' recognizes how in late modernity increasing importance is attached to gender and sexuality as a modern resource for demonstrating *who we are, what we are* and *who we might become*. It is suggested that, at a time of multiple social disruptions, including the diversification of family life, uncertainty in the sphere of employment and distrust in established public institutions, the connections between gender and sexuality are becoming more problematic. In this chapter, we address the intimate relationship between gender and sexuality and more specifically focus on rethinking this couplet within the context of transformations in sexual lives. The chapter begins by exploring the interrelationships between sexuality and gender from feminist and queer theory positions. These discussions are then contextualized by introducing the notion of the confessional society. We suggest that this has had a crucial impact on how the interrelationships between gender and sexuality are being forged. The chapter goes on to explore these connections in relation to emerging communication interfaces, sex tourism and media construction of gendered sexualities.

Chapter 6, 'Representing Engendered Bodies: Producing the Cultural Categories "Men" and "Women",' explores the diversity of work within western cultures arguing for the central location of the corporeal (the body) in the making of gender relations and sexual desire. For Connell (2000), gender is the way bodies are drawn into history; bodies, rather than being seen as determining patterns of masculinity and femininity as biological essentialists and popular psychology would suggest, are arenas for the making of gender relations. Women's bodies were a major subject of research in earlier feminist work, which was very successful in constructing a new explanatory vocabulary, in which they named men's social practices across a number of sites – the state, medicine, family life and cultural technologies – as instituting and reproducing control and exploitation of women's bodies as the locus of relations of ruling and the accompanying masculinist power (Smith, 1987). Most significantly, the scale of men's violence – within the home, on the street, within sporting arenas, inside public institutions and imperial military activities – called into question what we understood by normal masculinity (Dworkin, 1981; Hanmer and Maynard, 1987). While holding onto the continuing significance of these accounts of materialist patriarchal domination, the chapter also addresses more recent work on the body that has developed a range of productive and controversial concepts: sexed embodiment, performativity, heteronormativity, gender transgression and the third sex (Diprose, 1994; Gatens, 1996; Grosz, 1999). Simultaneously, masculinity theorists in exploring the media-led gaze on male bodily practices – technologies of looking – as spectacular performance, in response to the global fragmentation of social relations, read this new cultural trend in alternative ways. For some, it is evidence of the discursive emergence of the new (heterosexual) man. For others, it indicates the stabilization of the existing hegemonic sex/gender order. As a result, the chapter is located within the main current conceptual tensions and confusions in this field of inquiry.

Chapter 7, 'Media Masculinities and Femininities: Sporting Genders,' reviews contemporary representations of masculinities and femininities that are being made available by media technologies. Previous work on the gendered nature of these cultural technologies has established the systematic patterns of women's cultural invisibility. While assuming a passive homogeneous audience, it has tended to underplay the complex processes of popular culture, in which textual and visual meanings are produced in diverse social contexts, marked by differentiation, diversity and ambiguity. Importantly, this chapter focuses on sport and considers how masculinity and femininity are mediated by media technologies that do not convey gender but are integral to its constitution. It highlights the structural inequalities that pervade the representation of gender in the media. Alongside this, it draws attention to how such representations convey only part of the story. While engaging with the structuring of the visibility of particular femininities and masculinities, it also explores how media reporting of sport might offer alternative views of gender and sport. More specifically, it highlights how the media in the context of sport might offer new possibilities of understanding and experiencing gender relations.

Chapter 8, 'Men and Women of the World: Emerging Representations of Global Gender Relations' addresses questions that have tended to be underplayed in sociological and cultural studies texts – that of global gender relations. It begins by problematizing what gender in a global context of the development of extensive worldwide patterns of cultural, social and economic relationships across nations means. It highlights a broader concern with establishing the question of when does something become gendered. A key aspect of this chapter is the notion of cultural imperialism. There is an argument that contemporary gender relations are being produced by a hegemony that is cultivating dominant versions of masculinity and femininity. Such versions are being distributed through a range of cultural products. Cultural products are not simply reducible to consumer goods, but may also include notions of health care, education and politics.

This chapter focuses on the cultural imperialism thesis, first by demonstrating how global forces are calibrating local genders to match global forms. Second, the chapter then deconstructs this view by examining how local inflections of gender recontextualize global cultural forms. The chapter concludes by drawing upon a case study, based on our empirical work that examines the interplay between global forces, gender and ethnicity.

Chapter 9, 'Gender on the Move: The Search for a New Sex/Gender Order in Late Modernity,' explores how the central categories in the field of gender studies as unstable constructions have been constantly contested with new meanings emerging in relation to socio-economic, cultural and political transformations. Most significantly, theorists have established the dynamic presence of gendered inequalities and sexual difference, which in turn are central to the constitution of political understandings of these wider transformations. In order to gain a clearer understanding of the politics of femininity and masculinity, we locate the changing accounts of the complex interrelations between sex, gender and sexuality within the long history of sexual politics to the recent focus upon sexual citizenship (Richardson, 2000). From a contemporary perspective of talk about post-feminism, masculine backlash and new men's movements in western societies, the history of sexual politics includes the new social movements of second-wave feminism and its discontents, gay and lesbian mobilization, men's groups' protests, gendered ethnic and national visibility, transgendered voices and the more recent cultural projects such as HIV/AIDS activism and queer interventions (Bryson, 1999). In turn, this puts us in a position to explore the question of the future of sexual politics at local and global levels, using non-western, cross-cultural studies to illustrate other potential ways of making sense of shifting gender structures, identities and practices.

The last chapter, 'Conclusion', provides a brief summary of the main themes of the book by reengaging the aims that were set out above. We hope that this results in a clearer picture of some of the crucial questions and tensions that need to be addressed by future work in this area.

1

Approaching Gender: Feminism, Men's Studies and the Cultural Turn

Introduction

Major evidence of the emergence of gender as a cultural flashpoint in western societies is provided by the pervasive circulation of images of a sex-war between men and women (Mac an Ghaill *et al.*, 2003). With changes occurring across various cultural arenas and through a range of social practices, gender has emerged as crucial to understanding such changes. Therefore, from being a relatively marginal part of social and cultural analysis in the past, gender itself is now being considered a vital feature of contemporary explanations. As a result, a range of social and cultural theory is being used to make sense of gender and social change. At the same time, from a late modernity position, there is a certain cultural amnesia about the explanatory power of earlier theoretical work in opening up what we mean by gender. In response, this chapter highlights some of the main approaches in this area by focusing on the frameworks that are used to explain sexual difference that are drawn upon and further explored in later chapters of the book. Overall, this chapter provides a profile and critique of recent developments in sociological and cultural theories of gender relations. As we demonstrate, this is a complex area, increasingly conscious of the complicated relationship between theoretical frameworks, methodological strategies and the phenomena subject to examination.

An interrogation of the suggested shifting gender relations, in which contemporary women are projected as late modernity 'winners' might usefully begin by addressing the pervasive reporting of an assumed *masculinity crisis*. Here, an interesting paradox immediately emerges. On the one hand, diverse media representations are suggesting that the 'what about the boys?' narrative is a late modern(ity) phenomenon. On the other

19

hand, it draws upon rather atavistic ideas – an amalgam of common sense and scientific theories – making appeals to an earlier imaginary gendered social order, based on fixed biological differences between 'real' men and women. These essentialist images are accompanied by a nostalgic remembering of a 'golden past', when men and women occupied established gender roles in a stable social system. A popular media script is circulated to a wide audience, selecting out specific social problems: the absent father, the violent football fan or the underachieving male student. The description of the hard times that men are currently experiencing is followed by the suggestion that the increase in these 'failed masculinities' is caused by their inability to internalize appropriate models of masculinity. A major flaw in this approach is that it is tautological, with the high profile media attention to the crisis of masculinity producing a lot of information that reinforces a sense of a 'sex-war' but generating little in terms of explanatory frameworks that might begin to explore ways forward. The following chapter thus identifies some of the key theories – Sex Role Theory, Second-Wave Feminism, New Feminism, Masculinity Studies and the more recent 'Cultural Turn' – to demonstrate the variety of ways in which we can make sense of contemporary gender relations.

The Attraction of Sex Role Theory: Searching for Difference

One of the more influential accounts of gender identities is to focus on a gender polarity of fixed notions of masculinity and femininity, in which gender identity is seen as an attribute of the individual. This means that much of the recent history of our understandings of sex and gender has been regulated by psychological paradigms that perceived masculinity and femininity as naturally present in different behaviours and attitudes (Farrell, 1974; Maccoby and Jacklin, 1974). For example, such paradigms have insisted on the separation of biological sex identity and gender role. Work, such as that of Stoller (1968), disentangled the notion of biological sex, gender identity and gender role, thus depicting a more complex relationship between self-understandings and social ascriptions. Second-wave feminists often cite the research of this American psychoanalyst, because of the important breakthrough in disconnecting sex and gender. His work has helped generate the foundations of our current sensibility in making sense of a changing social world. He writes (1968: ix):

(O)ne can speak of the male sex or the female sex, but one can also talk about masculinity and femininity and not necessarily be implying anything about anatomy or physiology. Thus, while sex and gender seem to common sense to be practically synonymous, and in everyday life to be inextricably bound together, one purpose of this study will be to confirm the fact that the two realms (sex and gender) are not at all inevitably bound in anything like a one-to-one relationship, but each may go in quite its independent way.

This work, in particular, attempts to explore the discontinuities of gender within identities that may result in psychological disorders. Thus, particular methods and tests are devised that can measure the amounts of femininity and masculinity of individuals. Consequently, attitude tests, according to one strand of sex role theory, can be used to measure levels of socialization by the amounts of masculinity that males possess (See Bem, 1974). Within this perspective, gender is subject to objective and unproblematic measurement through an index of norms of masculinity and femininity. Hence, a wide range of individual men and women are seen as not having enough masculinity or femininity. For example, within the current dominant sex/gender system, gay men are represented in the media and social commentary as having *too little masculinity*, in contrast to lesbians who are projected as having *too little femininity*. Often such accounts are underpinned by a notion of science, where masculinity and femininity derive from objective quantifiable sources such as genetics, hormones or cortical variances.

Such a paradigm is driven by a search for sex difference, even though the psychological evidence points the other way, emphasizing a wide range of similarities between male and female attributes (Connell, 1987). Segal (1990: 65) maintains: '[T]he difficulty of finding significant sex differences in cognitive and temperamental capacities led some psychologists to an interest in the sociological category of sex roles.' Through socialization, sex role theorists argue, the biological basis of male and female becomes attributed to social norms and expectations that are circulating through masculinity and femininity. During the period after the Second World War, social anthropology began to point to the variability of gender roles across different societies. In her work on New Guinea society, Margaret Mead (1935) explored the different ways of being male and female. She examined different cultures – one culture where men and women shared feminine characteristics; one culture that shared masculine characteristics and one culture that inverted masculinity and biological sex. Mead's focus on the cultural construction of gender highlighted the disconnection of the social roles of gender from the biological basis of sex. This groundbreaking work provided a serious consideration of the role of nature/nurture in the shaping of gender identities. By highlighting the variability of gender, Mead's work provided many of the theoretical and conceptual precepts for contemporary studies that contest the ubiquity of femininity and masculinity.

Mead's notion of the variability of gender has provided an important critique to social analysis. Feminist research on sex roles through the work of Klein (1946), along with other sociological work, such as Parsons and Bales (1955), explored gender identities within the context of social divisions. In contrast to these more structured approaches to gender formation, symbolic interactionists, such as George Herbert Mead (1967) and Erving Goffman (1969), have provided different conceptual foundations to explore the variability of identities within particular social contexts. For Goffman in particular, the presentation of the self was central to the production of impressions. By using dramaturgical metaphors, Goffman suggests that impressions can be understood as 'performances' that are highly dependent on the individual, the audience and the particular social context. However, a more explicit formulation of a situational approach to gender can be identified by Garfinkel's (1967) introduction of ethnomethodology. During the 1940s, Garfinkel developed a means of applying rules of social engagement to events that appeared as common sense or taken for granted. In other words, rather than locating gender identity as anchored in phenomenology, Garfinkel reconfigured gender identity as something that was governed by rules rather than being simply inhabited. Therefore, he maintains that the actual sense making, meaning of social situations occurs through the negotiation of social action. This implies that the meanings that permeate everyday life are much more rule governed. In this way, we don't bring meanings in and display them, situations may actually produce the meanings, albeit through a series of social rules.

Garfinkel's approach is to understand how individuals make sense of reality and the interpersonal manoeuvres that are involved in the construction of meaning. Garfinkel's case study of 'Agnes' considers a person who was suffering from the 'disorder' 'testicular feminization syndrome'. This syndrome was a label used to describe a condition where the body is completely female such as breasts, subcutaneous fat distribution and absence of facial, body and limb hair. Alongside this, the person has a normal sized penis and testes, with a male abdomen. As a child, Agnes was raised as a boy. At puberty she suggested to Garfinkel that she began to develop these female characteristics and that culminated when Agnes left home and changed into 'female attire'. Eventually after some years Agnes had a sex change operation. Agnes rejected any claim that she was transsexual, agreeing with common sense definitions that the world is made up of naturalized genders. She made clear that she should be treated as a natural and normal female. The operation to change sex was understood as a 'corrective procedure' that removed the penis, something Agnes identified as an 'abnormal growth'. Central to her biography was the need to achieve femininity. A key element of this identity achievement, according to Garfinkel, is 'passing'. For Agnes conforming to a role was necessary in order to be a normal and natural female, but the role was met according to both private and public social rules of gender. An interesting development in the story of Agnes was that she had lied to Garfinkel about her 'natural' intersexuality. She had disclosed to one of the researchers on Garfinkel's team that she had been ingesting female hormones in order to reshape her body. Although seen as a key methodological flaw in Garfinkel's work, Denzin (1990) suggests that such a lie supports the conceptual basis on Garfinkel's perspective.

Throughout *Gender, Culture and Society*, we refer to the importance of a range of theoretical and methodological contributions to understanding gender across the disciplines, including early social constructionist and ethnomethodologist accounts, cultural anthropological interventions and the more recent late modernity frameworks. However, cutting across these disciplines, feminism as an intellectual and political project has culturally made the most significant, sustained contribution. One of the most innovative features of such work has been to suggest that gender itself is imbricated in power relations.

Second-wave Feminism and Theories of Patriarchy

There have been a range of approaches drawing upon sex roles as a concept to understand femininity and masculinity, including as Segal points out, early feminist work, such as McIntosh (Segal, 1990: 65), who writes:

> To see ourselves as players, as hapless victims of a malign scriptwriter, freed us from our past and invited us to embark on writing our own future. It also presented a way of seeing men as redeemable, if only they would break out of their sex roles.

One effect of this achievement is that within western societies, gender as a central analytical category is currently taken for granted, even though it only emerged in the late twentieth century (Scott, 1988a). Across western societies, in the 1960s and 1970s, second-wave feminism provided a pivotal cultural position and mobilizing force as a central inspiration, strategic influence and defining metaphor for a wide range of new social movements. Feminism's major political achievement was providing a new vocabulary, including notions of the personal is political, sexual division of labour, gender stereotyping and so on which enabled new conversations about women's and men's lives. Of specific significance was the conceptualizing of power around the notion of patriarchy, which uncovering the logic behind the organization of social inequalities, opened up the possibility of naming women's oppression and thus the possibility of political change. Given the pervasiveness of the subordination of women and the domination of men across public and private life, this critical interrogation inevitably employed a unitary notion (one style) of masculinity, with patriarchy attaining a universal status as the single cause of women's oppression. A central concern was to understand masculinity that is situated within a structure of gendered hierarchies, in which particular social practices are used to reproduce social divisions and inequality.

At the same time, feminist work argued for a more complex picture of male domination (Acker, 1989; Beechey, 1979; Walby, 1990). These texts stressed the need to rethink categorical theories that suggest that gender/sexual relations are shaped by a single overarching factor. Rather, they point out that there is a need to disaggregate the overinflated concept of patriarchy, maintaining that these relations are multidimensional and differentially experienced and responded to within specific historical contexts and social locations. In other words, differentiated forms of male power can only be explained by an analysis which takes into consideration the specific conditions that give rise to these situations. It is the relationship between these social structures that determines how gender relations are lived out. Such a critique of patriarchy is also suggested by Jackson and Scott (2002) who maintain that patriarchy has been a highly contentious concept. They argue that it is a concept that has never resolved the difficulties of including other social divisions such as class, 'race' or sexuality. In response, Jackson and Scott (ibid.: 11) suggest that the concept of gender itself: 'describes an asymmetrical, hierarchical division between men and women, which is ubiquitous and enduring'. As they point out, it is not that issues that early feminists brought into focus are dispensed with. Rather, material relations of inequality have to be understood within the context of intersections of inequality across other social divisions.

From a contemporary perspective, with an overconcentration on the limitations of these materialist analyses, in terms of their essentialism, functionalism and over determinism, it may be difficult to see how notions of patriarchy, class domination and social change provided major explanations that resonated with wider social concerns and anxieties of their period (MacKinnon, 1987; Smith, 1987; Stanworth, 1987). Currently, within conditions of neo-liberal ideology and the accompanying decline of the importance of social inequalities, a main strength of the materialist position has been to place on the sociological agenda such issues as the social reproduction of sexist ideology, state regulation of patriarchy and institutionalized sexual discrimination. Presently, it is important to hold onto the theoretical and political achievements of this work that raised questions of the State's control of women's bodies, violence against women and women's exclusive responsibility of childcare and housework in the sexual division of labour (Dobash *et al.*, 1998; Hearn and Parkin 2001; Hennessy, 2000). In so doing, we may address the socio-historical amnesia, which characterizes many contemporary contributions in the field of inquiry. For example, there is a strong tendency in postmodern work and converging discourses of neo-liberalism circulating across the State, new economy and media to downplay or erase such issues as that of the patri-archal state power, social class divisions, institutional structures and hege-monic cultural capital. In such texts, there is a suggestion that discourses and practices of representation have displaced the conceptual necessity of such terms as ideology and social reproduction, in making sense of the increasing polarization of multiple inequalities in contemporary western societies (Mac an Ghaill, 1999).

There are a number of accounts that continue to place the materiality of inequality at the centre of analysis. For example, in a move that integrates complex theories of identity formation and structured inequality, Cranny-Francis *et al.* (2003) argue that we need to understand the materiality of women's subordination as both men and women are subject to patriarchal discourses. Therefore, the femininities and masculinities that are inhabited simplistically work to hide the ambivalence and ambiguity that constitute contemporary gendered subjectivities. Thus, through the identification of particular patriarchally defined genders, men and women are ascribed legit-imate ways of doing masculinity and femininity. This position has also been adopted by Wharton (2005) with her attempt to bring together subjectivity and structured inequalities. She sees gender as a process not a fixed state of identity; rather gender can be found to be evident in social structures at mul-tiple levels. Importantly, the gender system not only creates distinctions, but such distinctions generate inequalities that underpin them.

From its earlier inception, second-wave feminism has been marked by diverse positions. Various classifications have been used to capture this diver-sity, perhaps the best known being that of the theoretical typology of liberal, Marxist/socialist and radical stances. Alongside this typology, other estab-lished categorizations (explored further below) have included black feminism, psychoanalytical feminism and, more recently, postmodern/post-structuralist feminisms, each with their own conceptual emphasis on contemporary representations of the interrelationship between women/femininity, gender relations, sexed subjectivities and accompanying political stances. Phillips (1998a: 17–18) summarizes the recurrent tensions within these positions in relation to feminism and politics:

> Does a feminist approach to politics lead to the conclusion that there has been too much gender in previous analyses, too much stereotyping of male and

female? Does it lead, on the contrary, to the conclusion that there has not been enough gender, not enough attention to differences between women and men? Is the implication that public notions of equality and justice should be applied equally to relations in the private sphere? Or that private notions of care and intimacy should be applied more imaginatively in the public? Should feminists see themselves as challenging male dominance by opening up politics more fully to women? Or should they consider 'women' a fictitious entity that pretends to a spurious coherence but fails to address differences by class or race? Does feminism see politics as the expression of diverse and heterogeneous identities, identities previously swept under the carpet by grand notions about the citizen or the common good? Or does it see identity as too inherently ambiguous to form the basis for any politics at all? Do we think, in the now-classic terms of the 'equality versus difference' debate, that equality is best served by denying differences between the sexes? Or do we believe that equality can only be promoted by stressing the special needs of women?

Historically, these conceptual and political tensions have been played out across a range of spaces created by women. This is the ambiguous legacy inherited by contemporary gender theorists.

Contemporary 'New Feminisms'

By the 1990s, of particular significance was a shift from community activism among women and academic interventions to that of the emergence of the global-based media as a prominent site for the mobilization of a diverse range of representations of women and femininities. These included the overlapping notions, variously branded as new feminism, power feminism and post-feminism (see ch. 9). While a multiplicity of conceptual and political engagements with the legacy of second-wave feminism emerged at this time that appears to have made a break with earlier debates, there is little consensus of how to read the past. For some, feminism as a modernist social movement has achieved its political goals of sex equality, others feel that as the social world has become more complex, it has lost its strategic purpose, while others argue for the need for women to move beyond a victim position that assumes a simple oppositional logic of female powerlessness and male power (Coppock *et al.*, 1995; Denfeld, 1995; Modeleski, 1991; Paglia, 1992; Roiphe, 1994). The concept post-feminism appears as a highly confused term due to the diverse ways that it is deployed. It includes a popular descriptive discourse of post-feminism as signalling a generational shift in understanding and perhaps a remaking of social relations between men and women. An alternative understanding of post-feminism has been developed by feminists working within a cultural politics of difference position (Brooks, 1997;

Yeatman, 1994). They locate post-feminism within a wide range of antifoun-dationalist movements, including postmodernism, post-structuralism and post-colonialism. In contrast to identity politics theorists, who interpret the concept of 'post' as a temporal term signalling what follows the completion of the feminist political project, here 'post' is understood as part of a long process of ongoing cultural and social transformations.

Walter attempts to capture recent shifts in gender lifestyles in her text, *New Feminism* and in the edited collection *Feminism for a New Generation* (see ch. 9). As the titles suggest, the focus is on a younger generation of women, from their teens to their earlier thirties, who, working against negative media portrayals of the struggle for women's equality, express their desire to refashion new styles of feminism. These new times, marked by an inter-est in 'power feminists', project inclusive discussions of Margaret Thatcher, Monica Lewinsky, Bridget Jones and the Spice Girls. This is an optimistic and celebratory picture of a confident, assertive younger generation who are reporting high levels of success across private and public sites, includ-ing family life, schooling, workplace and leisure. These high performers are compared historically to an earlier generation of women (their mothers and grandmothers) and currently in relation to underperforming male peers as evidence of a genderquake. However, alongside these changes, gender inequalities continue, as most manifestly portrayed in young women's tran-sition from being 'top of the class' at school to glass ceiling in the workplace.

In response, Walter (1998) suggests that new feminism must reclaim the early women's movement's focus on material issues of inequality. For her, second-wave feminism lost its way by shifting to an overconcentration on sexual politics and culture in the mid-1970s. Walter exemplifies this by a discussion of the urgent need to disentangle the personal from the political, which she represents as moving beyond the limitations of a mode of polit-ical correctness, with which a younger generation of women actively disidentify. Rather, she maintains that new feminism needs a vocabulary that combines social and political equality with personal freedom for the diverse constituencies of feminists across existing political and gender boundaries to include conservatives and men. In short, new feminism is making a claim for exchanging the ideological constraints and certainties of cultural feminism of the mid-1970s, for a contemporary flexible, prag-matic politics that addresses concrete political, social and economic reforms beyond reductive accounts of female victimhood.

A further major shift away from second-wave feminism can be identified. The latter as a modernist social movement is based upon collectivist mobi-lization, seeking fundamental transformations across western societies (Walby, 1990). In contrast, new feminism is located within a wider paradox of contemporary politics of forging social change at a moment marked by individualization. New feminism resonates with late modernity theorists' claims, as indicated in the introductory chapter, that shifting gender relations, including gender blurring, are an effect of western societies experiencing a surge of individuation in which globalized change is bringing an end to the constraining influences of gender and other forms of industrial society. As outlined in the introduction, modernization and detraditionalism have specific implications for women, who are repositioned as reflexivity winners, as agency is freed from the inherited ascriptions of institutional structures. It is further suggested that the effects of the freeing of individuals from the normative demands of established social categories is that late modernity subjects (individuals) are impelled to forge their own identity as part of what Giddens refers to as the 'reflexive project of the self ' (Beck, 1992; Beck and Beck-Gernsheim, 1995; Giddens, 1991). Walter (1998: 2) provides an example of this, arguing that contemporary young women

> are beginning to move somewhere without markers or signposts ... they are making up their lives as they go along. No one before them has lived the lives they lead. They are combining traditionally feminine and traditionally masculine work and clothes and attitudes.

New feminism and post-feminism have received much criticism from academic feminists for their misrepresentation of the history of feminism, their theoretical underdevelopment and their naiveté in misreading the media-led political backlash against feminism and women. For example, Faludi (1992: 14) points out:

> just when record numbers of younger women were supporting feminist goals in the mid-1980s ... and a majority of all women were calling themselves feminists, the media declared that 'post-feminism' was the new story – complete with a younger generation who supposedly reviled the women's movement.

However, operating with an empirical rather than analytical purpose, new feminism and post-feminism does attempt to track contemporary young women's experiences of the impact of gender on their personal lives. Alongside this, it explores the self-production of subjectivities within the context of competing media-led representations of diverse performances of femininity and masculinity in a rapidly changing world.

Masculinity Studies: Men as a Gendered and Political Category

It is not an assumption of the book that there is a cultural equivalence between Women's Studies and Men's Studies. It is conventionally acknowledged that to speak of gender is to name women, that is, women are marked as gendered beings. What is less understood, even though, as Kimmel (in Kimmel and Messner, 1989) reminds us that historically we have been looking at men's lives for a long time, is that to speak of men, including within much media and academic commentary, is to locate them outside wider gender relations and an accompanying sexual politics. This is a point of departure in this book for making sense of contemporary confusions about the paradox of the difficulty of identifying men as a political category. As feminists have illustrated, mainstream politics, involving the governing state, economic management and institutional regulation remains a predominantly public male space. It is served by and in turn produces dominant forms of heterosexual masculinity, through which middle-class men exercise power (Phillips, 1988a). As Brown (1988: 4), emphasizing the intimate link between formal politics and power argues:

> More than any other kind of human activity, politics has historically borne an explicitly masculine identity. It has been more exclusively limited to men than any other realm of endeavour and has been more intensely, self-consciously masculine than most other social practices.

At the same time, there is increasing understanding from cultural theorists that if women are configured through traditional representations of femininity, men are also bounded by specific masculine cultural forms. Furthermore, the messages being conveyed in the media aim to promote particular masculine subjectivities. The unravelling of this paradox is part of a larger conceptual and political problem of developing frameworks that enable us to make sense of the structural location and subjective positioning of social majorities, such as men. Analysing men as a politically gendered category removes it from its normative location as transparent, neutral and disembodied. This is part of a more general trend in culturally based theories whereby the ascendant social category in established binaries (for example, men, heterosexuals, whites and able-bodied) are becoming the new objects of critical appraisal. There is much empirical and conceptual work to be done in exploring the gendering of men.

There is a need to address the question of the narrative moment, both temporally and spatially, when western men and masculinities became culturally visible, both to others and themselves, as gendered phenomena. As Segal (2001: 237) comments:

> But here's the oddity. What men found when in the wake of feminism, they turned to survey themselves (it is no longer sufficient merely to scrutinize and reify women), provided an analogue of women's adversities: evidence of constraint, unease, misery, trying to embody the ideals of masculinity.

This soon engendered the parallel rise of men's studies, outlining men's gender specific problems. Men joined us as gender scholars.

A specific feature of *Gender, Culture and Society* in seeking a synthesis in the field is to bring together recent historical and contemporary theoretical and empirical work. We suggest that this allows a critical reflection on the relative adequacy of different perspectives on gender. This is illustrated below in theoretical work that highlights the different problematics employed in making sense of men and masculinities. Currently, at a time when earlier materialist work is often caricatured as failing to capture the complexity of a late modernity period, we need to reread the analytical input of male pro-feminist theorists, who working within a materialist perspective constitute the foundations of this scholarly work. An organizing theme of the materialist position has been to build on and expand earlier feminist theories of patriarchal domination.

Connell (1987: 183) identifying a multiple range of inequalities across public and private spheres as resulting in a pervasive pattern of male oppression of females, suggests: 'It is the global subordination of women to men that provides an essential basis of differentiation.' This global subordination is anchored into a perspective that identifies differentiated forms of masculinities and femininities existing relationally at local levels. Connell argues: 'structure is the pattern of constraint on practice inherent in a set of social relations' (ibid.: 97). Hence, looking at particular social relations in localized contexts enables us to map out the material, cultural and psychic (unconscious) practices and constraints that produce formations of masculinity. Addressing the internal dynamics of masculinity, Connell develops earlier cultural approaches to masculinity, such as that of Tolson (1977: 12), who provides a definition of gender that:

> allows us to appreciate the highly particular ways in which 'masculinity' is commonly understood ... 'masculinity' is not simply the opposite of 'femininity' but there are many different types of gender identity ... and different expressions of masculinity within and between different cultures.

In later work, Connell (1995) develops this further, arguing that masculinities are not only differentiated, they stand against one another in relations of power, and most importantly, it is the internal relations of masculinities and femininities that are the significant dynamic of continued gender inequality. He adapts Gramsci's (1971) notion of hegemony in order to describe the relationships in society's gender order. Hegemonic masculinity is established by the domination of one masculinity over others. Thus, masculinities are 'not fixed character types but configurations of practice generated in particular situations in a changing structure of relationships' (ibid.: 81). Men occupy a hegemonic masculinity or assert a position of superiority by 'winning the consent' of other males and females, in order to secure their (hegemonic) legitimacy. Men are able to position other men by what Connell refers to as their subordinated, complicit or marginalized relationships. By considering gender meanings as relatively autonomous, a diverse range of masculinities can exist in the same institution that are produced through individual life histories, involving multiple sites of family background, peer groups and other social experiences. It is in this way, Connell (ibid.: 736) argues: 'Different masculinities are constituted in relation to other masculinities and to femininities through the structure of gender relations.'

Challenging current discussion of the essentialist images of earlier work in the field of inquiry, Brittan (1989) provides an innovative framework. He locates the plurality of masculinities within a socio-historical context, enabling an understanding of the diversity of becoming male. Moving beyond a simple description of multiple masculinities, or in his terms, male signs, he holds onto a concept of masculinity that also addresses socio-economic structures of male behaviour. Brittan maintains that: 'While it is apparent that styles of masculinity alter in relatively short time spans, the substance of male power does not' (ibid.: 2). Hence, the apparent contradiction between pluralistic styles of behaviour and the predictability of patterns of male domination is resolved by redefining what is meant by masculinity, that is, different styles of self-presentation. For example, he suggests that we can compare these styles of male behaviours to fashions. Youth cultural theorists have illustrated these consumption based changes among sub-cultural groups. Presently, a changing sensibility about fatherhood is a popular masculine style across western societies. In attempting to resolve this conceptual tension, Brittan introduces the term 'masculinism'. This is translated as meaning an ideology (of patriarchy) deployed by men in their justification and legitimization of male positions of power as natural and inherently superior, which in turn serves to justify the oppression and subjugation of females. He argues that this ideological positioning of males as being naturally more powerful, competent, successful and fundamentally different from females can be traced across various historical periods. Hence, masculinism transcends reproductive and productive relations, with ideology informing and forming the nature of those relations. Interestingly, Brittan's argument inverts the classic Marxist tenet that the infrastructure determines the superstructure. Rather, he emphasizes the transcendence of ideologies over class relations. In so doing, this conceptual separation allows Brittan to posit the fluidity of male styles, while simultaneously allowing for the continuities of male oppression of females.

(Male) pro-feminist accounts have been analytically and politically central in mapping critical investigations of men and masculinities. They have also been of central significance to opening up understandings in this field of inquiry. However, they share what post-structuralists have identified as a major weakness of the materialist position, that of underplaying the importance of men's subjectivities. In response, Middleton, (1989, 1992) has critically engaged with the latter's understanding of oppression. He begins by suggesting that earlier studies of masculinity have tended to see oppression itself as a structure, rather than consider that oppression is structural practice. Furthermore, he emphasizes that male oppression of females refers not only to an infraction of a standard, but also an intention to infract, suggesting that men can change oppressions. For Middleton, this creates conceptual confusion as:

> oppression results in a double bind for those who are accused of being oppressors, because they are assumed to have intentionally violated rights which everyone can agree to, and to have constructed the system of those rights for their own aggrandizement (1989: 9).

He argues that a way forward is to conceptualize gender relations beyond the polarity of oppression and domination. For example, one way of achieving this is to rethink gender relations as dynamic forms of regulation and control, both excluding and including social inequalities.

Alongside the development of this theoretical work in the United States and Britain, the early 1970s saw the political growth of men's groups. From their conception, the constitution of these groups have tended to be placed outside a broader political framework. At the same time, men's movements tended to have little political resonance among men, who did not identify as a specific gendered collectivity. As argued above, a key argument of this book is that we are experiencing a shift from the establishment of the social constitution of gender associated with modernity politics, to the gendering of society that has an intensified resonance among (heterosexual) men and women in late modernity. However, by the early 2000s, this has not manifested itself in terms of widespread mobilization of men into political organization. Rather, we are witnessing highly fragmented responses, in which it is difficult to make sense of the structure and meaning of men's sexual politics (Pease, 2000). This fragmentation is explored in Chapter 9, in terms of male liberationists, pro-feminist men and the new men's movement. Alongside the politics of masculinity, social and cultural theorists currently have responded to the highly anxious discussions that are taking place about the social role of men and the constitution of masculinity, in response to the global fragmentation of social relations. As is illustrated throughout this book, theoretical writing across traditional institutional sites within western post-industrial societies, including family life and the workplace and more recent questions about the media, consumption and the body have been of particular conceptual productiveness in generating an analytical purchase on the contextual coding of male gender and the refashioning of masculinity. This social world of re-signified, mobile and reflexive masculinities, which is claimed as evidence of the fluid and negotiated nature of gender, has developed an expanding vocabulary of emerging paternal masculinities, 'deadbeat' dads, male fetishized and narcissistic displays, masculinized feminine performances, disembodied male subjects and the new man's non-phallic masculinity. It should be noted that in this highly contested field of inquiry, there are alternative readings of these new cultural trends. Some emphasize the discursive emergence of the new (heterosexual) man, while others maintain we are experiencing a 'variation on an old gender theme', the stabilization of the existing hegemonic sex/gender order (Edwards, 1997; Nixon, 1996).

Cultural Turn: Gender Relations in Reflexive Modernity

There have been different responses to the increasing complexity and fragmentation of the contemporary feminist project. These have included an argument for the productiveness of shifting away from the rigidity of early oppositional stances to that of an emphasis on multiplicity, diversity and inclusivity (Hirsch and Fox Keller, 1990). For example, Segal (1999: 232) in response to the title of her book, *Why Feminism?*, replies: 'Because its most radical goal, both personal and collective, has yet to be realized: a world which is a better place not just for some women, but for all women.' Early criticisms from within second-wave feminism opened up an internal debate that included a range of women's accounts of social and cultural marginalization. For example, Brah (1992: 136) has argued: 'As a result of our location within diasporas formed by the history of slavery, colonialism and imperialism, black feminists have consistently argued against parochialism and stressed the need for a feminism sensitive to the international social relations of power.'

By the 1990s, the legacy of this debate continued in relation to the politics of difference. However, alongside this, post-structuralism and post-modernism raised fundamental theoretical and methodological questions and in the process, deconstructed the foundational premises, which underpinned second-wave feminism developed in the 1970s (Barrett and Phillips, 1992). Barrett (1992) captured this analytical move, identifying a paradigm shift in feminist theory from a materialist emphasis on *Things* to a post-structuralist emphasis on *Words*. The academic ascendancy of the arts, humanities and philosophy and the accompanying decline of the social sciences is witnessed in the shift of theoretical interest from social and economic structures to linguistic, symbolic and representation systems. More specifically as Barrett (ibid.: 205) suggests:

> Feminist theory has been able to take up a number of issues outside that classically 'materialist' perspective: in particular the analysis of corporeality and the psyche. 'Post-structuralist' theories, notably Derridian deconstructive reading, Lacanian psychoanalysis and Foucault's emphasis on the material body and the discourses of power, have proved very important in this.

Barrett adds that the feminist appropriation of the above theories makes sense, given their focus upon such issues as sexuality, subjectivity and textuality that feminists have been central in placing on the academic and political map. A number of key analytical moves can be identified in this work, involving what has come to be referred to as the 'cultural turn' in social and cultural theory, including a move beyond a system of binaries, the articulation of more complex understandings of power and the centrality of identity making (Dollimore, 1991; Nicholson, 1990; Seidman, 1993).

This contemporary cultural work which claims to be sensitive to complexity and differentiation, also places at its centre a more complex analysis of power that allows an interrelation between the social, psychological and interpersonal, alongside emotional histories and future aspirations. A further element of the cultural turn is that the question of identity has emerged as one of the key dynamic concepts in the context of rethinking social and cultural change. It is suggested that socio-cultural change is marked by the disintegration of older social collectivities, such as social class, and increased fluidity of social relationships, with an accompanying interest in identity and subjectivity (Bradley, 1996). More specifically, there has been a focus on the pluralization of identities involving processes of fragmentation and dislocation (Giddens, 1991; Hall, 1992). The concept of identity is a highly resonant term that is used in a wide variety of ways in different contexts. Brittan (1989: 17) illustrates the usefulness of the concept of identity, examining three emphases, which are relevant to the theorization of masculinity, namely, the socialization case, masculine crisis theory and the reality construction model. Sociologically, the high conceptual value of identity emerges from its contribution to new frameworks, which open up innovative ways of exploring the relationship between individuals and society. Most importantly, as Mercer (1990: 43) argues with reference to social change: 'Identity only becomes an issue when it is in crisis, when something assumed to be fixed, coherent and stable is displaced by the experience of doubt and uncertainty.' This doubt and uncertainty is experienced at individual, social and psychic (unconscious) levels, circumscribed by the local–global nexus of cultural transformations. Currently, there is a wide range of critiques of earlier definitions of identity categories, with queer theory providing one of the intellectual spaces for a systematic appraisal.

Post-identity Formations: Queer Theory – Forging Dissident Femininities and Masculinities

Emerging forms of sexuality have been identified by late modernity theorists as of central significance to their linking of mobile gender relations, performing sex/gender subjectivities and wider transformations (Giddens, 1992). Social and cultural shifts such as the separation of sexual pleasure from reproduction and marriage (the sexual as plastic), the development of reproductive technologies, the increasing spacial visibility of lesbians, gays, bisexuals, transsexuals and transgendered communities, hybridized sexed subjects' performances, cybersex, the mass production of sexual products and pornography, and the emergence of HIV/AIDS have had a major impact upon globally mediated, representations, meanings and subjectivities of womanhood and manhood (Epstein and Straub, 1991; Giddens, 1992; Hawkes, 1996). However, as argued above, in relation to the erasure of second-wave feminism, a similar process is occurring among contemporary sexual theorists, of writing out both earlier social constructionist accounts of sexuality and gay/lesbian political contributions, which were informed by a radical intention of liberating all genders (Altman, 1983; Plummer, 1981; Weeks, 1977).

During the last few decades, gay and lesbian scholars and activists, in challenging legal, religious and medical discourses of (homo)sexual pathology have been one of the most dynamic contributors to sexual theorizing. These accounts have served to destabilize sociological and common sense meanings of men/women and masculinity/femininity within the broader structure of patriarchal gender relations (Bristow and Wilson, 1993). In telling sexual stories, decentred female and male gay subjectivities continue to provide concrete evidence that femininity and masculinity is not something one is born with or inherits. Rather, it involves an active process of achievement, performance and enactment (Plummer, 1995). At the same time, it might be argued that gays and lesbians, alongside other socially marginalized groups, such as migrants, anticipated the living out of the notion of cultural hybridity (mixture) and reflexive subjectivities ascribed to a late modernity condition, inhabited by queers, post-colonials and transnational migrants (Haywood and Mac an Ghaill, 2003). The changing processes of being and becoming men and women lived out by gays and lesbians, respectively, resonate with and dynamically help to constitute the bigger picture, a bigger picture of changing institutions, fluid and changeable relationships, a shifting emotional landscape and the complex transformations of intimate life. In short, the dynamic of this interrelationship serves to collapse the most troubling boundary between the private and public spheres in a global age of uncertainty (Jamieson, 1998; Rubin, 1993; Weeks, 1995).

Although the term queer has only recently emerged as a political concept, it has acquired a complex range of meanings.[1] At one level, operating from an anti-essentialist identity position, the term signifies a conceptual and political critique of the assumed assimilationist position of the established gay community, in campaigning for community identity recognition and validation by straight society (Simpson, 1996; Sinfield, 1998). For example, Dollimore (1991: 285) critiques the contemporary gay community's libratory, humanist project in its quest to establish an authentic identity within conditions of sexual oppression. He contrasts this with an exploration of cross-dressing in Early Modern England, which he describes in terms of transgressive reinscription, which he claims

> finds expression through the inversion and perversion of just those pre-existing categories and structures which its humanistic counterpart seeks to transcend, to be liberated from; a mode of transgression which seeks not an escape from existing structures but rather a subversive reinscription within them, and in the process their dislocation or displacement (ibid.: 285).

Such an understanding currently resonates with the notion of queer as a contemporary resignified transgressive political concept. At another level, queer, acting as a dynamic element of cultural politics focuses upon problematizing heterosexuality and the linking of twentieth century knowledge and sex. As Sedgwick (1991: 34–5) argues: 'the special centrality of homophobic oppression in the twentieth century ... has resulted from its inextricability from the question of knowledge and the processes of knowing in modern Western culture at large'. Furthermore, queer has also been taken up commercially, shifting from an initial association with the 'pink pound' to a mainstream sign of cutting-edge consumer style (Simpson, 1996).

There are two key elements in the development of queer theory/activism the first of which is emerging political responses to the AIDS crisis in the 1980s/early 1990s. For example, the radical activist group Queer Nation deployed forms of political activism promoted by ACT UP (the AIDS coalition to Unleash Power). The second element has been the scholarship of literary and cultural theorists working in gay and lesbian studies. They have provided a philosophically rich range of concepts that are explored throughout this book, including deconstructing the hetero/homo boundary, the heterosexual matrix and gender performativity (Butler, 1990; Dollimore, 1991; Edelman, 1994; Sedgwick, 1991) (see ch. 6). As a deconstructive project, queer theory seeks to destablize socially given identities, categories and subjectivities around the common-sense distinctions between homosexuality and heterosexuality, men and women, and sex and gender. It does this by establishing the social and historical specificity of sexual categories, linking them to processes of state and institutional control. Queer theorists also seek to collapse the boundaries that separate sexual normality and abnormality, suggesting that separate discrete oppositions are mutually constitutive rather than exclusive. For example, Fuss (1991) drawing upon Derrida's (1987) notion of the supplement, illustrates the inadequacy of the logic of a natural opposition of homosexuality/heterosexuality, with homosexuality assumed to be additional to an original heterosexuality. Rather, locating this conventional opposition on a more fundamental related opposition, that of inside/outside, she raises questions about the usefulness of this old dialectic for an understanding of contemporary sexuality. Arguing that we can never fully escape the interdependence of these assumed oppositions, she notes:

> To the extent that the denotation of any term is always dependent on what is exterior to it (heterosexuality, for example, typically defines itself in critical opposition to that which it is not: homosexuality), the inside/outside polarity is an indispensable model for helping us to understand the complicated workings of semiosis. Inside/outside functions as the very figure for signification and the mechanisms of meaning production (Fuss, 1991: 1).

Late modernity's promise of disconnecting gender identity and sexual desire has been driven by queer theory. It contests the adequacy of matching existing sexual categories to the complexity of people's lived experiences. Rather, it stresses the need to develop the possibilities of sexual being and doing outside of conventional identities and subjectivities (including gay, lesbian and bisexual identities). In other words, queer activists work against traditional sexual and gender hierarchies in which sexuality and gender as social categories of analysis act as containers that operate normatively to fix the boundaries of how we should live our lives. Rather, they emphasize the openness, fragmentation and diversity that infuse contemporary ways of being. However, as the literature makes clear, the relationship between the categories sexuality and gender remains highly contested and increasingly confused. In Chapter 9, we explore the range of criticisms of queer theory/politics and most significantly the accompanying downplaying of gender in discussion of heteronormativity (Hennessy, 2000; Kirsch, 2000; McIntosh, 1993). HHowever, queer activists celebrate the transgressive potential of the implosion of existing gender and sexuality categories, enabling us to reimagine inhabiting a range of masculinities and femininities and the full diversity of sexual desire.

Resolving the Sex/Gender Dichotomy: Performativity and the Body

Throughout this book we draw upon one of the most recent influential critiques of gender, that of Judith Butler. Her early work in *Gender Trouble* and *Bodies that Matter* has been seminal in that they reconfigured how gender has been discussed. Central to Butler's theorizing is the impossibility of frames of reference that offer dualistic understandings of sex and gender. Thus, the category of women and the shared experience of social structures are scrutinized. What coheres gender, sex and desire is the heterosexual matrix:

> I use the term *heterosexual matrix* to designate that grid of cultural intelligibility through which bodies, genders, and desires are naturalized. I am drawing from Monique Wittig's notion of the 'heterosexual contract' and, to a lesser extent, on Adrienne Rich's notion of 'compulsory heterosexuality' to characterize a hegemonic discursive/epistemic model of gender intelligibility that assumes that for bodies to cohere and make sense there must be a stable sex expressed through a stable gender that is oppositionally and hierarchically defined through the compulsory practice of heterosexuality (Butler, 1990: 151).

This heterosexual matrix deploys notions of dimorphic sex in order to sustain the authenticity and legitimacy of heterosexuality that in turn instantiates gender. The logic of this dynamic is held through an understanding that representations produce or create social possibilities. In this way, the body becomes a site for the contestation of power, control and regulation. Thus, although much gender theory argues that the body is mimetically connected to gender, Butler argues that gender representations are constantive in that the 'signifying act delimits and contours the body that it then claims to find prior to any and all signification' (Butler, 1993: 30). Therefore, rather than having the body and gender role in a representational relationship, they are in a performative relationship. Performative in that the signs that are applied to the body operate to signify/constitute the body: 'There is no gender identity behind the expressions of gender; ... identity is performatively constituted by the very "expressions" that are said to be its results.' (1990: 25). As a result, gender theorists should consider how the body is discursively constructed so that sex and gender are unstable, historically contingent and performatively enacted.

This is not necessarily to return to the early sociologists, who outlined the importance of the situational context of gender construction through metaphors of drama or game play, rather the emphasis has been the collapse of gender and sex distinction. One of the techniques for insisting on the collapse has been to argue that the biological category of sex itself is constructed. It is argued that the dimorphic understanding of the body organized by male and female is a modern construction (Gatens, 1990; Laqueur, 1986). This, it is argued, transforms how we might understand the relationship between sex and gender. Hausman (1995: 25) suggests that 'the authenticity of gender resides not on, or in the body', but by a 'particular system of knowledge, power and truth'. This position highlights what Elam (2000: 267) argues that 'either sex is privileged as a biological attribute upon which a gender ideology is imposed, or sex is denied as merely the ideological mystification that obscures cultural facts about gender'. The implication is that the relationship between sex and gender are held together by particular ways of conceptualizing the body. As a result, biological sex is a historical construct and thus is materialized through the application to the body. Halberstam (1998) suggests that Butler's (1990) contemporary theorizing on gender and sex has opened up ways of understanding gender categories and their connection to biological categories. Given that performative becomes the reiteration of norms of sexual difference, Halberstam argues that we need to develop out this idea and in particular disconnect gender from bodies. Masculinity and femininity in this way should be understood as something that cannot simply be equated with biological sex. The implications of this is that, at particular historical junctures, female bodies are able to take on and live out particular masculinities, just as male bodies are able to take on femininities. One of the areas of gender ambiguity that has been explored in much detail has been through research on intersexuality.

The notion of constructing biology through discourse opens up a philosophical tension about the status of the 'real' body. This means that the evidence of sex difference is a discursive regime that operates to speak about coherent stable biologies that do not exist. This prompts the possibility of an inversion where the coherency of biological sex exists primarily through the discursive reiteration of gender. Thus, gender is performative in the sense that it provides the conceptual possibilities of biological sex to exist. Performance is not used in a theatrical sense but rather as a form of citation. This means that the actual citing of gender produces the possibility of biological sex. In this way, the citational operates as a material presence securing and establishing the existence of gender. Hird and Germon (2001) identifies that there has been a number of versions about the nature of the relationship between sex and gender. At one time, in the classical period, there was the assumption the body contained two biological sexes and that one was dominant over the other. In the early twentieth century the predominant medical understanding suggested that people are born with one 'true sex'. More recently, there is a sense of the 'best sex' for a person to be assigned. This involves genital morphology, psychological well being and social environment. These changing definitions of gender and sex have become important frames of reference to the decision making surrounding the manipulation of the physical body. Hester (2004) suggests that rather than there being any real underlying position, decisions about sex and gender are based upon rhetoric and strategies of persuasion. According to Hester, when a child is born, if its gender is ambiguous, a 'social emergency' is declared. A team of medical professionals is mobilized, whereupon they attempt to establish the true condition. In short:

> What causes the eventual identification of intersexuality is the perceptual confusion of the attending physician regarding the morphology of the genitals of the newborn. It is only *after* the doctor finds himself or herself confused about the genitals that tests take place to identify the underlying condition (p. 25).

Medical professionals thus operationalize culturally ascribed norms about the real nature of sex and apply them to the body. Such norms are deployed, according to Morland (2001), to the genes, gonads, genital morphology and brain structures, when multiple interpretations of the physiological base of the body is available.

It is argued that 1.7 births out of every 100 are defined as intersex, suggesting that people who are born with an ambiguous gender are more prevalent than those born with Cystic Fibrosis or Down Syndrome. Although there is no physical danger to those born with an ambiguous gender, medical intervention to 'cure this condition' often ensues. Hester (2004) argues that genetic females are usually declared females if they are reproductively fertile. In contrast, if the baby is genetically male, the morphology of the baby – the size of the penis – becomes crucial. However, such approaches to gender ambiguity are culturally specific. In Europe, if a child is born with gender ambiguity and is a reproductively fertile female, it is more likely for the medical professionals to construct a female body. However, if such a child is born in Saudi Arabia, medical intervention tends to declare the baby as male. It is argued that such 'states of being' indicate the possibility of private and public contestation of the conventional understanding of sex/gender.

However, Prosser (1998) has critiqued discursive approaches to gender ambiguity. In his empirical work with transsexuals, Prosser shows that they feel as if the new organs are real and that they experience their gender not at the level of discourse but through *real* emotions. This has led to a key criticism of the discursive formation of gender identities, that regardless of whether gender outlaws are contesting the heterosexual matrix, they depend and rely upon the reinstantiation of gendered identities. For example, transgendered and transsexuals often adopt and reconstruct traditional gender etiquette in order to 'pass'. Tarchert (2002) argues for a new essentialism where the body is reconnected to subjectivity. She maintains that such a return to the centrality of the corporeal would bring embodiment back into understandings of gender. At the same time, she maintains that if we move for a 'fuzzy' notion of the relationship between sex and gender where embodiment operates in a range of relationships with the social, then the possibility of the western dimorphic understanding of gender and sex can be avoided. This is something that is supported by Dozier (2005), whose work with 18 (female to male) transsexuals, moves away from a rational logic of being and becoming: 'The interviewees challenge the underlying assumption in much of the gender literature that sex, gender, and sexual orientation align in highly correlated, relatively fixed, binary categories' (p. 297). Such a position considers a phenomenology of the body, focusing on the existential possibilities of bodily function. Owen's (2004) research on women who self-harm highlights the importance of connecting gender with the body. In exploring women's accounts of the process of cutting their bodies, Owen suggests that the body needs to be considered as a more problematic means of discursive performance: 'it seemed to me that those women to whom I spoke were literally writing the body. They were bypassing language and were expressing with and through their bodies the things they wanted to voice' (ibid.: 161).

Conclusion

Rather than offering a resolution of these debates in an ambitious, unrealizable process much contemporary theory seeks to displace the binaries that underpin the foundations of thinking. While recognizing the importance of this approach and the productive possibilities that it generates, this book often draws upon an alternative approach to making sense of gender. Rather than seek implosion and collapse gender and sex, it may be possible to understand gender without gender. In other words, the notion of gender does not simply instantiate sex, rather it can be seen as instantiating other social categories such as race/ethnicity or sexuality. Therefore, evident throughout *Gender, Culture and Society* is an epistemological twist that suggests that gender can be explored not simply as a category of biology, but rather investigated via other social categories. An important aspect of this more complex view is a critical focus on the multidimensional social subject and the suggestion that in searching for a renewal of social and cultural analysis of gender, we need to map out some of its more intricate and intimate positions as they articulate the shifting boundaries of class, gender, sexuality, ethnicity and generation. Exploring the simultaneous relationship between these analytic concepts is a significant facet of post-structuralist strategies. This suggests that in order to understand sex/gender identities, researchers need to examine the simultaneous articulations of a dispersed, localized and shifting nexus of social power.

As outlined in the Introduction, in social relations, people occupy certain positions simultaneously. A working class identity is at the same time, and implicit in it, a sexual identity and an ethnic identity. We need to think about not the ways social categories accumulate but the ways that they inflect. When we talk about the notion of power, we have to think about it relationally, thinking about powerful in relation to whom. In this way, we do not look at power as an either/or division but as being much more relational. We can say power is shaped relationally: one group is both powerful and powerless. For example, particular social relations of ethnicity simultaneously 'speak' gender and sexuality: to be a 'Paki' is also to be a 'poof', is to be a 'non-proper' boy (Mac an Ghaill, 1994b). Furthermore, the simultaneous speaking of race/ethnicity and sexuality can also be mapped out as class based, as certain styles of gay identities resonate with forms of middle-class Englishness (Mac an Ghaill, 1996). This is still a largely undertheorized area, while at the same time there is little empirical work available to illustrate how these interrelationships are lived out within local cultural arenas. It is important to note that the relationship of gendered identity formations with wider social relations currently remains unresolved, as is highlighted in postmodern accounts of gender relations that abstract practices from institutional contexts (Seidman, 1993).

2

Fragmenting Family Life: Beyond Maternal Femininities and Paternal Masculinities

Introduction: Beyond the Boundaries of the Family

We begin with a paradox. At a time of rapid social transformations, the family culturally is projected as a safe haven from a world at risk. This appears to capture the continuing centrality in people's lives of the family, albeit often idealized that is routinely reported in social surveys (Bauman, 1990). Simultaneously, there is much talk about the family in crisis, with pervasive media representations portraying men and women as trading places. These contradictory accounts are seen as defining features of late modernity, evident in current debates about the usefulness of the concept of the family as a category of analysis (Silva and Smart, 1999). Given the alternative forms of domestic organization and familial solidarity that individuals are constructing over their life course, for example, among the ever-extending kinship network of relationships among post-divorce families and stepfamilies, a key question emerges: who belongs to the family? (Allen, 2000). We seem to be a long way from second-wave feminists' rejection of the institution of marriage, with contemporary lesbian and gay activists celebrating the official acknowledgement of same-sex relationships and families of choice (Weeks *et al.*, 2001). However, it was early feminist theorizing and activism – as part of a broader New Social Movement sexual politics – that enabled a major conceptual change in the meaning of the family. As this chapter illustrates, we are witnessing a fundamental cultural shift from understanding the family in terms of traditional, blood or marriage ties to that in which it has come to signify the subjective meaning of intimate relations. Nevertheless, at conceptual, political and policy levels, the ongoing narrative of mothering and fathering is being told in an

43

old modernist language – the gendered dualism of *female homemaker/male breadwinner* – that is not able to grasp the generational specificities of emerging femininities and masculinities and an accompanying shifting semantics of gendered relations.

The main aim of this chapter is to explore how recent social and cultural transformations are impacting upon gender relations within the context of the family and how understanding of femininities and masculinities are mediated through contemporary changes in the family. Two main positions can be identified. First, a dominant quantitative approach with its focus on women's and men's participation in family life that tends to understand mothers and fathers as asymmetrically positioned within absent/present, powerless/powerful, good/bad typologies. Contemporary commentators on gender relations have suggested that the family is undergoing significant changes with a wide range of family formations now commonplace. This includes non-married cohabiting partners, non-cohabiting fathers, the increasing number of non-blood related children, ethnic minority extended families and the visibility of gay/lesbian partnerships, all emerging alongside the traditional extended family and the modern nuclear family (Weeks *et al.*, 1999). Across Europe, Australia and the United States there is more diversity in family life (Bjornberg, 1992; Kimmel, 1987b; Russell, 1983). In the early 1980s, Rapoport *et al.* (1982: 476) suggest that: 'Families in Britain today are in transition in a society in which there was a single overriding norm of what family life should be like to a society in which a plurality of norms are recognized as legitimate and, indeed, desirable.' This diversity of family life may be located within contemporary structural social transformations, as an effect of a wider restructuring of the global economy, communications networks, networks of power and capital flows (Castells, 1996). A crucial element of this recomposition is the current crisis in the welfare state and central government's response in terms of the management of collective consumption, as a new cultural landscape is constructed within deregulated markets of education, housing, health and social care and the increased dependency of young people on their family that are making an important impact on the shifting meanings of the family in the new century (Haywood and Mac an Ghaill, 1997b).

A second position is to go beyond the modernist model of family life based in industrial society. Within the context of changing family lifestyles, recent years have seen ever-increasing research and writing on women's and men's experience of families and the personal, social and political representations of those experiences. This work, moving beyond a 'mother focused' paradigm, has addressed traditional typologies by understanding mothers and fathers as occupying, at the same time, contradictory social and emotional subject positions. The latter approach provides an analytical framework that brings together multiple levels of mothers' and fathers' experiences and conceptualizes motherhood and fatherhood as a multifaceted lived experience of classed, racialized and generationally located dynamics (Hughes, 2002; Kaplan, 1992; Lawler, 2000). Theorists of late modernity provide a starting point to make sense of this second position. They suggest that contemporary changing meanings and gender blurring are an effect of western societies experiencing a surge of individuation in which globalized change is bringing an end to the constraining influences of gender and other forms of industrial society (Bauman, 2001; Beck, 1992; Giddens, 1991; Hooper, 2000). Beck (1992: 115–16) writes that, as modernization proceeds, the decisions and constraints to decide multiply in all fields of action. For example,

> Marriage can be subtracted from sexuality, and that in turn from parenthood; parenthood can be multiplied by divorce; and the whole thing can be divided by living together or apart, and raised to a higher power by the possibility of multiple residences and ever-present potentiality of taking back decisions … and gives some idea of the variety of direct and multiply nested shadow existences that are more and more often concealed today behind the unchanged and upright words 'marriage' and 'family'.

Moving beyond an understanding of the *family as an institution* to the *family as a negotiated relationship*, we are able to explore the extent and the direction of the changes in intimate relationships, within the context of wider shifts in late modernity in western societies (Morgan, 1996; Smart and Neale, 1999). At the same time, by reexamining the domestic and sexual lives of parents we might begin to sketch out changing sex/gender relations in this arena and begin to reimagine future possibilities of the self and care in family life (Rose, 1991).

This chapter complements the exploration in the next chapter of the blurring of men's and women's work and its impact upon their respective position in society. From a sociological perspective, current experiences are socially structured and differentiated with, for example, western governments actively persuading women to (re) enter the labour market, thus enabling women access to modern forms of citizenship. At the same time, while some groups of men, such as the unemployed, are being coerced into taking up increased domestic and paternal responsibilities, other men are asserting claims about the pleasures of fathering. We suggest the need to understand the concepts of women, men and family life as a gendered interrelationship, through which diverse meanings of both maternal femininities and paternal masculinities, and indeed, womanhood and manhood, are mutually constructed and maintained. This enables us to rethink the dominant modernist gendered dualism of male breadwinner – female homemaker, tracing the multiple ways of being a mother or father, by desegregating specific origins, causes and effects of gender structures in particular historical

periods and in particular geographical spaces. We begin to read through the
ideological gender work that surrounds the rigid distinctions that circulate
through notions of an active mothering and a passive fathering (Barrett and
McIntosh, 1982). Culturally, this is most clearly captured in the notion of
mothering, understood as a biological *and* a social relationship. In contrast,
until recently, as Jamieson, (1998: 45) points out, fathering has been popularly
understood simply 'to refer to the procreative process involved in becoming
a biological father'. However, she adds that 'calls for and portrayals of "the
sensitive father" are now commonplace'. A key issue is to address this reductionist position, by conceptualizing both fathering and mothering practices as
social categories within the sociology of the family linked to wider cultural
narratives. The history of the reconfiguration of fatherhood and motherhood
and the attendant changing meanings of parenting within the wider context
of a shifting sex/gender social structure enables us to trace the development
of sociology itself. A shift from a structuralist position (in which motherhood
is highly visible and fatherhood remains conceptually underdeveloped), via a
feminist intervention (naming paternal masculinity as a power relation), to
a postmodern position (with its emphasis on different styles of becoming a
social parent), allows mothering and fathering practices to be understood as
key cultural and discursive resources in the making of contemporary male
and female identities. Furthermore, as is explored below, Adkins (2000)
argues that familial relations are no longer exclusively anchored within the
private domain of the home. For example, as she demonstrates, contemporary workplace socialities reveal how the family is constituted in and through
the public domain of work.

The Family as an Institution: Political Economy and Social Change

Early work on the sociology of the family examined social processes that
shaped gender relations within the domestic arena. More specifically, there
was a concern with the social position of women in institutional areas, such
as the sexual division of labour and the social organization of reproduction
and childcare. Parsons' (1955) elaboration of structural functional theory
explained how sex-role segregation, in which the father/husband is projected as provider/protector, within the context of the nuclear family as a
socializing agency met the complex needs of an industrial society. As Cheal
(1991: 6) points out:

> The particular tasks assigned to the sexes are, in Parsons opinion, due the
> primacy of the relationship between small child and its mother. The special

nature of that relationship, he claimed, is a consequence of the unique capacities of women for bearing and nursing children.

The *visibility* of the categories women, femininities and mothers in these sociological texts can be contrasted with the *invisibility* of men, masculinities and fathers as a gendered social group.

Traditional sociological explanations of the structure and meaning of parental responsibilities have been presented in terms of the functional needs of capital in industrial societies (Morgan, 1992; Parsons and Bales, 1955). Two main models of the relationship between the home and work-place that mediated men's domestic experiences, as husbands and fathers, emerged from this earlier work. First, that a subordinated work masculinity produced a patriarchal, authoritarian masculinity within the home. Second, that the private arena of the home provided men with a space, a haven from enforced instrumentalism and alienation, within which to develop expressive qualities. Earlier feminist studies, using patriarchy as an analytical tool, challenged limitations in these models, emphasizing the under-theorization of gender identity formation, the false dichotomy of the private sphere (home) and the public sphere (work), the demonization of mothering and the social invisibility of women's involvement in paid labour (Phizacklea, 1990; Walby, 1990).

Feminist work on the family from the 1960s through to the early 1980s explored social oppression within family life as part of a wider analysis of gender relations within modern society (Gittens, 1993). It emphasized the need to see gender as primarily not a property of the individual but rather of social institutions and cultural practices (Moss, 1995; Oakley, 1972). These accounts were important in critiquing the dominant sex-role perspective. These earlier constructions of mothers and fathers relied upon concepts such as 'traditional' and 'nuclear families', 'socialization' and 'role models'. Such conceptual tools, developed in a wide range of diverse areas of sociology and psychology during the 1960s and 1970s, were important in reconsidering domestic and sexual lifestyles as socially constructed rather than biologically determined. In other words, gender differences were seen to derive from social and cultural processes that created systems of ideas and practices about gender, rather than natural characteristics, such as chromosomal differences (for example, XXY chromosomes) or hormonal differences (for example, testosterone). Such a perspective continues to be prominent in contemporary liberal accounts of motherhood and fatherhood (see Cherlin, 1988; Ku *et al.*, 1993; Moss, 1995). These studies tend to understand mothers and fathers as asymmetrically positioned within present/absent, powerless/powerful, good/bad typologies.

As Morgan (1996: 82) maintains, among the range of gendered terms associated with the family, probably the most central is that of the mother.

As he claims, it could be suggested that families are 'mothered' rather than 'gendered'. For second-wave feminism, motherhood was projected as the key constitutive element of femininity (Firestone, 1979). Some attempted to challenge the notion of motherhood as destiny; others identified the biological capacity to reproduce as an essentially feminine social practice and their main claim to sexual difference. Oakley (1979: 10), describing the direct causal link between economic social forces and the institution of motherhood within modern industrialized societies, suggests that a major reason for the subordination of women in the labour market is the institutionalization of the mother-housewife role as 'the primary role for all women'.

> The meaning of childbirth is interlocked with a society's attitudes towards women. Both reflect its economic system. Capitalism, by concentrating on production in places other than the home, altered the status of women: mothers working became The Working Mother. The production of capital requires the production of workers: thus women's role becomes not to produce but to reproduce.

At this time, the patriarchal ideology of domesticity and the notion of separate spheres that continued to operate on and within family life, underpinned the main frameworks within sociological, psychological and popular commentaries that created a familial myth in which women were assumed to be the main benefactors. Feminists were primarily concerned with critically exploring the social positioning of women as wives and mothers within marital and domestic arenas, thereby challenging the social polarization involved in women's ascribed naturalized affinity for such domestic work. In her classic text, *The Sociology of Housework*, Oakley (1974: 17–18) pointed out: 'By far the largest segment of sociological literature concerning women is focused upon their roles as wives, mothers and housewives ... Possibly family and marriage are areas in which (women's) sociological visibility exceeds social presence.' Early feminist work in this area highlighting the severe material constraints on women and limiting cultural meanings of femininity remains integral to maintaining a high profile on sociological and political agendas of such controversial questions as the redistribution of housework, child rearing responsibilities, domestic violence and child abuse (see Walby, 1999).

At this time, a main sociological assumption was that the family as an institution changed as an effect of transformations elsewhere and was particularly driven by a reconstitution of the relationship between institutions and the economy. While some early feminists worked within the limits of this unidimensional approach, others began conceptually to open up an understanding of familial change that was understood as more dynamically constituted as an interplay between what was officially constructed as the separated spheres of the public and the private. Of central importance was feminist struggles, which, as Walby (1990: 89) writes, lead to significant changes in the household and the relationships between women and men in the family:

> Women are no longer necessarily bound to an individual husband who expropriates their labour till death does them part. Instead, increasing numbers of women change husbands, have children without husbands and engage in work for an employer other than their husband. Women spend a smaller proportion of their life-time's labour under patriarchal relations of production, although while they are full-time housewives they spend many hours on this labour as did women many decades earlier. Women from different ethnic groups vary as to the extent to which they are engaged in these patriarchal production relations.

Within the wider context of the changing family, including the emergence of what Stacey (1996) refers to as the 'postmodern family', recent years have seen increasing research and writing on both women's and men's experience of families. In earlier representations of family life, the interplay between the home and the economy was seen as one of the most productive elements of British sociological explanations of gender oppression. By the 1980s, with the emergence of the New Social Movements, these earlier academic and political representations were criticized for class reductionism and economic determinism. It was claimed that such representations were conceptually inadequate in explaining the complex social and psychological processes involved in the development of changing forms of gender and sexual identity formations. Placing the capital–labour relationship at the centre of theory was seen as closing off more open analytical approaches, thus challenging the privileging of economic-based class relations, through which other categories, such as gender and sexuality, were claimed to be mediated (Bourdieu, 2001; McNay, 2000).

Understanding Family Life in Late Modernity: Reconstituting Familial Relationships

More recently, as indicated above, there has been a conceptual shift from *simple models of sex role reproduction* to the *active production of complex identity formations*. This enables us to understand mothers and fathers as occupying, at the *same time*, contradictory social and emotional subject positions, and that are sensitive to complexity, pluralization and differentiation. The latter approach provides a more complex analytical framework that brings together multiple levels of mothers' and fathers' experiences (Weeks *et al.*, 2001). In turn, this allows a shift away from an overrationalist account of sex role theory, locating family life within the context of desire, fear and imagination. Such a shift places at its centre a more complex analysis of power that allows an interrelation between the social, psychological and interpersonal, alongside emotional histories and consumer-based future life-style aspirations. At the same time, it encourages a view that takes into account the shifting patterns of gender relations and conceptualizes motherhood and fatherhood as a multifaceted lived out experience of classed, racialized and generationally located dynamics.

By the 1990s, there was a reconnection of mainstream sociology to what Morgan (1996) refers to as the marginalized sub-discipline of the sociology of the family. Particularly significant was the work of social theorists of late modernity (Giddens, 1991; Beck, 1992). In contrast to traditional accounts of the family which placed *continuity* at the centre of their analysis, Giddens and Beck locate *emerging elements* at the centre of their work. They addressed a number of limitations in the sociology of the family. Earlier concepts, such as nuclear family, socialization and role models, referred to above, fixed the field of study into a narrow position with its modernist assumption of bounded institutional sites. In contrast, Giddens and Beck developed a number of concepts, such as the chaos of love, pure relationship and plastic sexuality that marked a significant shift in opening up how we might understand changing family lifestyles and attendant new femininities and masculinities. Importantly, in connecting the family to wider concerns, they suggest the need to locate the family and intimate relations at the centre of contemporary analysis in order to make sense of late modernity. Rather than appealing to mono-causal economic explanations of change, they argue for an inclusive, multidimensional approach encompassing socio-economic, political and cultural transformations (Finch and Mason, 1993; Morgan, 1996, 1999).

Individualization and Historical Change: The Emergence of the Post-familial Family

Beck and Beck-Gernsheim's (1995) *The Normal Chaos of Love* has its theoretical roots in Beck's (1992) highly influential text *Risk Society*, which sets out a general theory of change. Beck's thesis that there has been a shift from simple modernization to reflexive modernization addresses a key problem for the social sciences at a time of rapid transformations: the relationship between social structures and social agents. He claims that western societies are currently experiencing 'a surge of individuation' (Beck, 1992: 87) in which globalized change is bringing an end to the constraining influence of social class and gender as dominant social forms of industrial society. In turn, social agents are actively reshaping the modernization process. This is occurring within the context of unprecedented risk. Ecological disasters and the AIDS pandemic are cited as evidence of a reconfiguration of temporal and spatial dimensions, as future generations across national borders experience the effects of late twentieth century hazards (Abbinnett, 2003).

Beck and Beck-Gernsheim (1995) trace the historical shift from the pre-modern family as a bounded community of economic need, underpinned by solidarity, obligation and permanence to that of an open community constituted by an elective relationship in late modernity. Industrialization marked a key moment in the dynamic development of individualization, with the emergence of employment outside the home. From a contemporary perspective, the social relations of gender during this period can be seen to have been constituted as an unfinished modernity. The industrial society, with its feudal legacy, recreated a modern hierarchy of ascribed gender roles, relegating women to the private sphere of care of the home and children, with its accompanying dependency on the male wage earner. A further stage in the history of the family and individualization began with the gradual development of the welfare state, first around the end of the nineteenth century but above all in the second half of the twentieth. Another major shift took place in the development of the logic of individually designed lives and the liberation of women from traditional gender roles through a range of social changes, including demographic freedom (an increase in life expectancy for mothers beyond the period required for children), deskilling of housework, contraception, divorce laws, educational opportunities and professional training. While Beck and Beck-Gernsheim argue that the situation for men is different, they fail to develop the impact of this shift on them.

Beck and Beck-Gernsheim (1995) explore the development of reflexive modernization within the 'private sphere' of the family, in which they argue individualization is having a major impact. For them, there is an intensification of processes of decoupling and differentiation in everyday interactions that can no longer be contained within the nuclear family. Familial relations are no longer shaped by traditional certainties in which individuals can invoke general moral precepts about how to behave. Individual paternal and maternal biographies are being forged under conditions in which the meanings of family, marriage, parenthood, sexuality and love have lost their traditional grounding in general moral laws and local community normative rules. Couples are increasingly impelled into decision-making, negotiation and individual strategies about every detail of how they live together. In short, individuals are becoming 'the legislators of their own way of life, the judges of their own transgressions, the priests who absolve their own sins and the therapists who loosen the bonds of their own past' (p. 5). However, this is not a process of simple individual choice, as is often assumed, but rather is guided by a general imperative; modernization in wealthy western industrialized countries is generating labour market freedom in which 'everyone is free to conform to certain pressures and adapt to the requirements of the job market' (p. 6). The labour market normatively projects an ideal image of the highly qualified, socially mobile and flexible worker, whose primary commitment is not to the intimate world of family and friends but to the job.

At a time when the social is increasingly projected as being constituted by and through the individual, Beck and Beck-Gernsheim's claim about the freeing of agency from structure may appear rather limited. As Smart and Neale (1999: 15) argue, they

> seem to depict women (and men) as subject to social forces beyond their understanding which are generated by wider social changes. They add that Beck and Beck-Gernsheim 'tend to give the impression that individualism has produced not a reflexive self so much as an automaton.

In contrast, for Giddens, in *Modernity and Self-identity*, the reflexive self, in attempting to secure ontological security, is a central concept in understanding the impact of global changes in late modernity.

Identity Formations, the Late-modern Self and Intimacy

A major limitation of most writing on the family is its failure to place the changing nature of parenting and accompanying diverse modes of familial relationships within the bigger picture of changing households, a shifting emotional landscape and the complex transformations of intimate life (Sedgwick, 1994; VanEvery, 1995). In what she refers to as the optimistic story of the postmodern period, Jamieson (1998: 19) captures this changing sensibility, arguing that:

> The good relationship is a relationship of disclosing intimacy, a mutual relationship of close association between equals in which really knowing and understanding each other are the crux of the relationship rather than more practical forms of love and care.

Giddens (1992), in The *Transformation of Intimacy*, has made a major contribution to our understanding of how detraditionalization unsettles inherited patterns of relationships, thus calling into question notions of the self and identity. The concept of identity, which is a highly resonant term has emerged as one of the key dynamic concepts in the context of rethinking change in late modernity. Sociologically, its high conceptual value emerges from its contribution to new frameworks, which open up innovative ways of exploring the relationship between individuals and society. It is suggested that current sociocultural change is marked by the disintegration of older social collectivities, such as social class and gender, and increased fluidity and contingency (Bradley, 1996). More specifically, there has been a focus on the pluralization of identities involving processes of fragmentation and dislocation (Giddens, 1991; Hall, 1992; Laclau, 1990). As with many terms used in social and cultural studies, identity is not easily defined. For Weeks (1990: 88):

> Identity is about belonging, about what you have in common with some people and what differentiates you from others. At its most basic it gives you a sense of personal location, the stable core to your individuality. But it is also about social relationships, your complex involvement with others.

Presently, it is claimed that individuals are impelled to forge their own identity as part of what Giddens refers to as the 'reflexive project of the self'. As Weeks (1998: 45) argues: 'This does not mean the dissolution of self, but a recognition that the task of finding an anchor for the self, a narrative which gives meaning to all our disparate potential belongings, is a task of invention and self-invention'. Here, intimate relations and family life are a key biographical location of life-planning in which an individual's sexual and gendered self and identity are enacted.

Giddens' transformation of intimacy, within the context of men and women actively fashioning their own emotional biographies, raises the possibility of the radical democratizing of interpersonal relations, 'in a manner compatible with democracy in the public sphere' (1992: 3). More specifically, he develops his notion of the *pure relationship* based upon *confluent love*. The two concepts attempt to capture a historical new form of intimacy within the spaces that have been opened up, suggesting a shift beyond the traditional claims of familial obligation and duty to a reordering of the domestic and erotic spheres, marked by egalitarianism, choice and trust. Pure relationship refers to:

> a relationship where a social relation is entered into for its own sake, for what can be derived by each person from a sustained association with another; and which is continued only in so far as it is thought by both parties to deliver enough satisfactions for each individual to stay within it (ibid.: 58).

Late-modern intimacy witnesses the disconnecting of the chain of links in the patriarchal ideology of love; that is, sexuality, marriage and family life, which were compounded in the minds, bodies and moral careers of men and women have been separated as forms of intimate social action (Quicke, 1999). In turn, confluent love refers to an 'active, contingent love, and therefore jars with the "for-ever", "one-and-only" qualities of the romantic love complex' (Giddens, 1992: 61). In contrast to the normative structures of the romantic marriage that promised a lifelong commitment between partners, the pure relationship with an accompanying ethics of reflection and open emotional communication appears highly unstable. Furthermore, as Smart and Neale (1999: 8–9) maintain:

> because the individuals who participate in this relationship are engaged in a 'project of the self' which involves personal growth, change and assessment, then it is more likely that needs and desires will change and become incompatible, or at least will be subject to renegotiation.

Recent feminist theorists, including Silva and Smart (1999) and Smart and Neale (1999), working within the sociology of the family, while acknowledging the limitations of Giddens' and Beck and Beck-Gernsheim's work on changes in family relations, generally welcome the conceptual productiveness of their contributions. The latter are seen as placing family or intimate relations at the centre of a general theory of social change, with women projected as late-modernity winners, represented as key players in this process.

Contemporary Mothering: Feminine Subjectivities, the Ethic of Caring, Heterosexuality and the Self

Hughes (2002: 59) maintains that with the reassertion of the significance of mothering in the 1980s, there was a decline in analysis of motherhood as the basis of women's social position as it had for second-wave feminism. Rather, she suggests:

> It was a concern with motherhood as an aspect of identity and as a significant part of the feminine being. Discourses within feminism have, therefore, shifted towards an examination of the connections between motherhood, identity and self-actualisation. In so doing, they turn our attention away from the oppressive nature of discourses of motherhood in shaping identity. In this, feminism provides a useful case for examining how changing

discourses give voice to a specific way of being, and, at the same time, silence others.

Hughes cites the work of Kaplan (1992) *Motherhood and Representation*, as illustrative of this development, providing a broad map of the changing cultural meanings of contemporary mothering in the United States. Kaplan locates her argument about a mother paradigm shift within the wider narrative of a postmodern cultural paradigm shift, with its focus on the self and (feminine) subjectivity. Adopting a historical perspective, she explores how our understanding of mothering has changed since 1830, making a comparison between the emergence of the modern mother within the first industrial revolution and the current emergence of the postmodern mother in an electronic age. The late 1980s/early 1990s are identified as a time of major transition, which witnessed the incorporation of 1960s subversive discourses, resulting in the blurring of established boundaries and the accompanying distinctions between those inside and outside the dominant culture. Interestingly, she acknowledges that at this time it is difficult to evaluate the extent to which structural change has taken place in North American society. Her specific focus is on 'the rhetorical mother positions that can be read from representations' (ibid.: 181). Echoing analytical work carried out on the *Risk Society*, she notes that anxiety is the common element of the diverse discourses found in contemporary popular materials. She adds:

> In searching for a paradigm shift more specific than the global postmodern one – a shift that might encompass all the different forms of anxiety – I became aware that the overall change has to do with childbirth and child care no longer being viewed as an automatic, natural part of woman's life-cycle (p. 181).

For Hughes (2002: 62), at the heart of these anxieties is the question of women's strategic responses to the absence of selflessness, that is conceptually developed in Skeggs' (1997) and Lawler's (2000) work, explored below.

Kaplan drawing upon a psychoanalytic (object relations) theoretical framework, identifies eight significant contradictory discursive positions on motherhood, which sees the displacement of 'the old negative mother-position in the patriarchal unconscious that has hitherto encompassed us all' (ibid.: 219). These discursive positions are the absent mother, the working mother, childcare responsibility, the abusive/neglectful mother, the lesbian mother, the woman who refuses to mother/the selfish non-mother, the self-fulfilled mother and reproductive discourses. For Kaplan, these discourses open up the spaces for the possibilities of new female subjectivities. The move to the conception of female subjectivities as highly dispersed, multiple and unstable, may serve to free women of their simultaneous subordination and fetishization, as lived out in their social positioning as mothers. Kaplan concludes by arguing that:

> once this position is opened up as only a part of any specific woman's subjectivity, not the all-consuming entirety of it; once any specific woman is seen to be constituted 'mother' only when interacting with her child; once mother is no longer a fixed, essentialized quality, then women may be freed from the discursive constraints and burdens (ibid.: 219).

Kaplan's work carried out in the United States provides a broad picture of changing contemporary images of mothering. Below, within an English context during the 1990s, a number of high quality empirically grounded texts, including Skeggs (1997); Lawler (2000) and VanEvery (1995), illustrate the complex processes involved in the formation of feminine identities in and around the discourse of motherhood in relation to the family as a central site of caring, heterosexuality and the self. A focus on caring has been a major concern of feminist analyses of the gendering of the family (Mason, 1996; Morgan, 1996). For Smart and Neale (1999: 20), commenting upon the work of Morgan (1996), sociological and feminist analyses on caring have transformed women, engaged in a reflexive project, into sociological agents for the first time. They add:

> No longer were they merely the 'put upon' and symbolic housewives of the domestic labour debate, nor were they simply a natural resource for other family members as implied in functionalist sociology; instead, they entered, conceptually speaking, into sociological citizenship for the first time.

There is a long history of state generated discourses about 'not-good enough/bad mothers', including that of maternal deprivation (1950s), latchkey kids (1970s), and dual workers (1980s) (Walkerdine and Lucey, 1989). A common theme linking these discourses, in which 'working-class women stand in a specific relationship to … pathologization' is a claim that women fail to care, thus imploding the family as the site of caring (Lawler, 2000: 104).

Such official categories resonate with the experiences of the young women in Skeggs' (1997) *Formations of Class and Gender: Becoming Respectable*. The text engages with a critical exploration of social and cultural frameworks examining women's social location and production of subjectivity. In so doing, she draws on a diverse range of feminist and cultural theorists, including Foucault's (1988) technologies of the self and Bourdieu's (1986) work on capital. The latter is particularly significant in

Skeggs' desire to reinstate class analysis in feminist and cultural theory. Respectability – moral worthiness – which she argues was historically central to the emergence of class as a concept is selected as a primary analytical tool which, she illustrates, continues to be a major social signifier in the formation of engendered class categorizations that are simultaneously spoken through sexuality and ethnicity (Bourdieu, 2001; Skeggs, 2004a).

This longitudinal ethnographic study was carried out with 83 white working-class women, over a period of 12 years as Skeggs followed their trajectories through the labour market, education and family. It began with the young women, who had been failed at school, enrolling on a caring course in an English college of education. From the perspective of the early 2000s, their active take-up of these low status courses may appear somewhat dated.[1] However, the specific material conditions, during the 1980s, of the construction of a casual, flexible labour force as an effect of deindustrialization and deregulation was marked by mass youth unemployment, in a north-western industrial town in England, which had a history of disproportionately high levels of female unemployment. Within this context of the young women's limited access to forms of cultural capital, the caring courses offered opportunities as an alternative to life on the dole. Equally significant, Cockburn (1987: 12) has written of the gendered two-track reality principle that infused young people's career choices at this time.

> My previous work and that of other researchers on the labour process has suggested that occupational 'choice' is governed by a strong reality principle. In particular, people know that jobs are, in a sense gendered as they themselves are. Women know full well that certain jobs are 'for' them and that if they seek to do jobs that are 'for' men they will experience, at worst, hostility and ridicule, and, at best, discomfort and persistent pressure to step back into line. Male and female act on each other, sustaining gender complementarity and difference.

More positively, being culturally marked by institutional biographies of exclusion and failure, the caring courses offered a way of making something of your self. They were actively investing in a future (self), based on their own cultural capital gained as carers in their own families. Furthermore, the study illustrates the significant regional differences in relation to labour market resources available to young women and men in the self production of their subjectivities and gendered selves. It should be added that, alongside the visibility of the current expansion of hi-tech jobs in the knowledge economy, there has been an ongoing expansion of low paid service work, though the social profile of those carrying out these jobs may change. For example, presently, new migrants and refugees are highly visible in jobs that the indigenous population does not want to do. In turn, they carry the structural constraints of a highly stratified new economy demanded by global capitalism that provides few opportunities for them individually to practice the remaking of the self as labour market successes as part of a broader biographical autonomous life project (Harris, 2004: 39).

Grounding her study in the lives of the young women, Skeggs explores the opportunities opened up by the caring courses not simply in terms of future location within the labour market, but most importantly in terms of the technological practices available to develop and monitor a caring self, in relation to respectability, domesticity and familialism. Within the context of the wider social order, she provides a sophisticated explanatory map of the historical legacies of the positioning of the working-class family and more specifically, white working-class women as both pathological and civilizing, while charting how positions of respectability emerged. Addressing current processes within the college, Skeggs identifies a range of institutional technological practices encouraged on the caring courses. These operated through an educational hierarchy premised on a sexual division of labour that circumscribed the positions occupied. At the same time, she wonderfully captures the sense making of these young women within a specific cultural world in the construction of themselves as carers – the making of themselves as 'caring women'. In our own work, we have found that while female students publicly invested in the formal technical demands of the curriculum, the way in which institutional knowledge was appropriated and utilized for their own purposes was not predictable and varied greatly (Cockburn, 1987; Haywood and Mac an Ghaill, 1996; Hollands, 1990). Confronted by the familiar exclusionary effect of the stratification of curricular knowledge, the young women in Skeggs' study creatively responded to the academic/vocational/practical divisions by inverting the institutional ascribed low status to the practical as they celebrated the practical experience provided by their work place-ments. From their own cultural field of knowing, they assessed what would be useful in producing the caring self, which is marked by the practical. Exploring how the curriculum is implicated in technologies of the self, Skeggs points out how the subject positions generated by the curricular hierarchies provide character definitions. In turn, they define personalities that are projected as naturally inhering in individuals. The historical legacies and processes of institutional differentiation referred to above are hidden, as the young women culturally inhabited a subject position in which they recognized themselves as caring. Furthermore, another element of the incitement to young working-class women to take pleasure in occupational caring is the external validation they receive in the 'real world' of work, in which their display of high levels of responsibility in caring performances is officially recognized and validated by both placement managers and their clients. For them, such legitimation enables them to return from their placements having consolidated a caring identity, while attaining respectability, high self-esteem and future employability (see Skeggs, 2004b).

At the same time, the college courses tie the young women into the notion of the family as the primary site of care. Contradictorily, although they see themselves as natural carers, nevertheless, they are inducted through an explicitly prescribed set of curricular materials on the family into a detailed catalogue of caring practices that enabled the development of an internal moral economy to self-monitor their becoming real carers. Discussing these classifications of caring practice, Skeggs notes that they have the effect of calling into question the feminine cultural capital that had sustained the young women on their placements. Anxieties and insecurities are thus generated, which in turn, enables the defining of care as an expertise which requires evidence of public displays of what it means to care. The ideal matro-focal families are resonant of Lawler's mothers (see below) who have no needs of their own and so are predisposed to meet the needs of others. Hence, Skeggs illustrates how central a display of selflessness is, in order to produce a caring self. She argues that for the young women to occupy the subject position of caring, it is not sufficient simply to acquire the right skills, whose attributes are linked to wider cultural discourses of femininity and motherhood; rather, they must become a particular kind of person. A caring person is officially defined through the conflation of two different meanings: caring *about* (displaying a social disposition that assumes a relationship between carer and cared for) and caring *for* (carrying out practices of caring). Skeggs empirically demonstrates the regulatory power of this couplet: *being* and *doing* caring. She presents a list of essential characteristics of a caring person based on her discussions with the young women. These characteristics include kind and loving, warm and friendly, reliable, understanding and so on, which most women claim to possess. In short, 'experience of the self and the knowledge of the self become organized in relation to the caring schema established by the course' (p. 68). For Skeggs, the young women, in their search for respectability, pay a big price in terms of potential economic and social exploitation, including the taken for granted unpaid caring they undertake. At the same time, in relation to the self-production of their subjectivity as women and mothers, the mechanisms of self-surveillance operated through their questioning the quality of their mothers' caring and their own capacity as real carers is underwritten by the feminine duty to be responsible by forgetting the (motherly) self. The complex processes of subjectification and accompanying subject position taken up is the main focus of Lawler's (2000) work.

Lawler (2000) in *Mothering the Self: Mothers, Daughters, Subjects*, locates her empirical work based on in-depth interviews with 14 women, examining contemporary meanings of mothers and daughters, within a wider Euro-American quest for an understanding of and search for the good/true self (Rose, 1991). In so doing, she brings together maternal and daughterly narratives, spoken by women who are both mothers and daughters, 'negotiating a maze of knowledges to forge identities within and across these often contradictory categories' (p. 15). In her discussion of mothering and gendered selves, Lawler notes that although anyone can mother, conventional assumptions about 'good mothering' are elided with ascribed feminine characteristics. Most importantly, it is suggested that women's caring natures and relational selves enables their predisposition for emotional work in the private sphere of the home, which includes mothering their male partners as well as their children. Lawler focuses upon the complex discursive interrelationship between the constitution of the childhood (daughter) and motherhood.

Drawing upon a Foucauldian framework, she critically explores how the effect of constructing maternity exclusively in relation to children's needs serves to occlude maternal subjectivity. In short, 'in nurturing the child's "self," the mother's self threatens to disappear' (p. 133). For Lawler, the specificity of the social relations of an independent (female) adult being able to provide full-time childcare is obscured by theories of child development that claim to be identifying pre-existing needs that in reality are discursively produced as natural and universal. Hence, these disciplinary-based expert knowledges/'truths' circulating in psychological and medical discourses, which promise to liberate us, serve to tie us into specific power relations of regulation, normalization and pathologization. Operating within conditions of late modernity there is a cultural imperative to intensify surveillance of the self, alongside increased technologies of surveillance emanating from the state and civil society. This is resonant of theorists of late modernity claims, referred to above, that contemporary changing meanings around gender are a global effect of western societies experiencing a surge of individuation. Across a range of sites, academic and everyday, authoritative knowledges have identified intimate relations and family life as a key biographical location of life-planning in which an individual's gendered self and identity are enacted. However, Lawler's account appears less optimistic than late-modernity theorists in terms of who can count as 'healthy' individuals or 'good' mothers, as white and black working-class mothering is often represented as 'inadequate', 'insensitive' or 'authoritarian' (p. 103).

A main focus of Lawler's text is to trace a number of interconnecting complexities and contradictions of the liberal democratic notion of autonomous subjects, which are rhetorically projected as being simultaneously self-produced by children *and* produced by the mother. Women as mothers, who have no expression of subjectivity outside the category of mother and positioned as without needs of their own to meet their children's needs are expected

> to inculcate a self which is inner-controlled within the daughter, yet they must also be sure that the daughter turns out 'well'; thus they are caught between tensions between guiding and advising, and leaving the daughter to her own devices (p. 99).

At the same time, as Lawler's accounts of daughters' critical discussions of their working-class childhood illustrates, social relations of inequality are written out of narratives that blame the mother for holding them back. Alongside this, Lawler argues that a major contradiction circumscribing the daughters' adult identity is that it is forged within the context of feminized and heterosexualized identity which, as is demonstrated throughout this text, is in opposition to the concept of autonomy. For Lawler, while discourses are central in conjoining power and knowledge, they are also shifting and unstable, including the potential for reversibility. She concludes her text with a consideration of the need to develop other ways of understanding contemporary mother–daughter relationships. Working from a different theoretical position, this is the central focus of VanEvery's work.

VanEvery's (1995) *Heterosexual Women Changing the Family: Refusing to be a 'Wife'*, a qualitative research based study of 26 antisexist living arrangements investigates how the feminist critique of the family has been translated into practice. Drawing upon feminist and sociological positions, she develops a frame of interpretation grounded in a number of themes generated by her interviewees. In exploring the social construction of gender, she particularly draws upon the radical lesbian feminist argument that heterosexuality as a practice and institution constructs gender as a power relationship of male domination and female subordination. 'Wife' is defined not simply as a descriptor, that of married women, but stresses the social relations of this position of subordination to individual men as head of household. She cites the work of Johnson (1988), who, in her text *Strong Mothers, Weak Wives: The Search for Gender Equality*, identifies subordinate status and economic dependence as defining features of being a wife. The defining feature of her interviewees' alternative lifestyle politics was the refusal to be a wife. This refusal was constituted by a rejection of the role/identity associated with the category, including a rejection of the status of head of household and the appropriation of women's unpaid labour, independent financial management and for some, the rejection of maintenance. VanEvery makes an important analytical distinction between the roles/identities of the interconnecting categories of wife, mother and worker. The oppressive nature of the making of gender within family adult relationships, as unequal power relationships, is played out in terms of women positioned as wives and men as workers. At the same time, the role of mother is subsumed under that of wife. In disconnecting mothering from being a wife, VanEvery argues that locating 'women's oppression in the social relations within which the mother allows us to begin to imagine non-oppressive mothering' (ibid.: 61).

VanEvery also explores the issue of men mothering. Locating her own work in the existing literature on fathers, she argues that the men in her study, both those in role reversals and those in relationships with shared roles, were exceptional in challenging traditional paternal roles. Interestingly, responsibility for childcare was rarely combined with responsibility for housework. She provides evidence of individual men being more knowledgeable than their partner about their child's needs, based on the father having more contact with the child. VanEvery investigates the complexity of men occupying the 'private sphere', which traditionally is associated with women and femininity. In terms of the cultural resources available for the making of male subjectivities, these men did not operate with the ideology of the good father, hence the breadwinner role was not of primary importance to the formation of their identity (Moss and Brannen, 1987). At a structural level, a range of sanctions were in place for men who refused to occupy hegemonic versions of masculinity and there were major constraints in terms of local support or sustained commitment from men and women for men mothering.

Masculinity Crisis Discourses: 'Deadbeat' Dads/'Bad Fathers'

By the early 2000s, there exists a large number of popular commentaries that have moved beyond a mother-focused paradigm to address fathers and fatherhood. However, as we argue throughout this book, conceptual understandings of men and masculinities remain remarkably undertheorized. This has a particular salience in relation to paternal masculinities, illustrative of how men as a social group continue to be thought of as existing outside gender (familial) relations. At the same time, we know more about the social histories and historical biographies of fathers in relation to the dynamics of class divisions and imperial excursions (Beynon, 2002; Roper and Tosh, 1991; Rutherford, 1997) than we do about the changing structural location and subjectivities of contemporary fathers in late modernity. As Hobson and Morgan (2002: 15) argue:

> men's agency has been a crucial component in the configurations of fatherhood. Men have organized as workers, claiming their role as breadwinners

when demanding higher wages and attacking the deskilling of their jobs in terms of their manhood. However, they have not until recently represented themselves as fathers.

In different chapters in this book, we raise the question of the narrative moment, both temporally and spatially, when men and masculinities became culturally visible, both to others and themselves, as gendered phenomena. For French (1995: 1–2), in his article 'The Fallen Idol', the cultural visibility of fatherhood as a major problem in British politics occurred at the very moment when it became, in any traditional terms, irretrievable. He notes:

> Because fatherhood has always been more than a biological relation, the authority of the father over his family has traditionally been a validating symbol of all the larger social forms of authority, of law, society and religion. And this authority in its very essence is a male.

In response, we explore the epistemological and institutional effects of that moment being grounded in a conceptual dependence on assumed crisis tendencies in notions of men and masculinity, which are currently circulating through popular cultural texts (Faludi, 1999).

Beynon (2002: 75–9) sceptically asks: 'Crisis! What Crisis?' in his introduction outlining the wide range of contradictory factors that have been identified for an ill-defined and elusive, albeit pervasive notion, as part of a new common sense. They include the changing structure of work, women breaking through the glass ceiling, the rise of feminist and gay/lesbian movements, male emotional illiteracy, higher rates of suicide among men than women, particularly among young men, men's health problems and shorter lifespan than women's, high levels of divorce and absence from their children, boys' underachievement and young men's overrepresentation in crime statistics. Such accounts which have wide currency in the discipline of psychology tend to score highly on rhetorical claims about an imploding masculinity and a sense of a loss of manhood (Horrocks, 1994). There are fundamental flaws in these populist accounts about crisis which do not engage critically with gender theorists, including the conflation of the basic concepts of men and masculinity, as well as eliding the concepts of fatherhood, fathers and fathering, which serves to occlude how familial sex/gender meanings are generated, constituted and sustained. Without this understanding, we are unable to move beyond the use of crisis of masculinity as an overarching descriptive metaphor to interrogate its analytical value – what it means, where it comes from, how it is regulated, what's driving it – that is assumed in the above texts. This is highlighted in the literature on post-divorce families, which indicates how currently the remaking of motherhood and fatherhood is premised on a move away from socio-economic to psychological explanations of the welfare of children. These accounts are built upon a reductionist deficit model of fathers as either failing to adjust to their new role or as redundant to familial relations (Furstenberg, 1988; Moss, 1995). Lacking a reflexive methodology, there is little sense in these populist texts of the rhetorical power of their interpretative frames to constitute the object of inquiry: 'deadbeat dads'/'bad fathers' (Morgan, 1999).

Elsewhere, we have argued that a major element of establishing fatherhood within a sociology of masculinity is that it is characterized by a number of social divisions or inclusions and exclusions (Haywood and Mac an Ghaill, 2003). These can be articulated through cultural representations of familial masculinity and men's participation in family life. Here we begin to explore these changing representations as one of the key elements of the history of the contemporary discourse of crisis masculinity. In other words, in attempting to interrogate the latter, we can trace one strand, that of the emergence of 'deadbeat' dads in the United States and 'bad fathers' in the United Kingdom (Dennis and Erdos, 1993; Furstenberg, 1988). For example, social theorists have outlined the changing significance of representations of the family in pre- to late-modern societies. The accounts embedded in the shifting semantics of fatherhood are historically specific in producing gendered subjects. We can trace the shift from a narrative of the pre-modern (Christian-based father figure) through the modern (economic breadwinner) to the late modern (ambiguous, domestic identity). We are able to locate the emergence of the discourse of crisis masculinity in the shift from the industrial society (masculine) to the service economy (feminine) of late modernity. In investigating the constitution of the 'deadbeat'/'bad' father, we are led to an ideological linking, during a period of a deindustrializing global economy, in which paid labour was no longer able to sustain the ideal of the single breadwinner as the primary male role within family life (Faludi, 1999). French (1995: 3), commenting upon the fracturing of this model, points out that: 'Fatherhood was part of a social and economic structure that is vanishing.'

Critical work by social historians and policy theorists enables us to disconnect the discursive associations between structural unemployment, economic authority and paternal masculine identity formation in order to challenge an assumed simple casual relationship that inevitably results in a cultural crisis of male subjectivity at the beginning of the twenty-first century (Cherlin, 1988; Gillis, 1997; Griswold, 1992; Hobson and Morgan, 2002). As they make clear, this inevitability, which is currently read through a nostalgic collective remembering of an imagined golden age of '1950s parenting', is premised on an ideological naturalizing of the eternal 'male breadwinner' as the structural foundation on which all societies are built. In reality, the normative concept of economic provider discourse (the single male breadwinner), both historically and geographically had a very short, patchy existence, emerging within the specific material conditions of the post-industrial revolution period, that resulted in the removal of fathers from their former position as central to the household.

As Gillis (1997: 187–8) powerfully argues, this male exiting from the home was not simply a physical removal but a deeply symbolic act that centrally resonates in contemporary debates.

> The world that fathers ruled would receive a seismic shock in the late eighteenth and early nineteenth centuries with the advent of the Industrial Revolution and the political revolutions that accompanied it. By the middle of the nineteenth century, the office and the factory had replaced the household as the point of production. ... This gendered division of labour effectively terminated the old notion of domesticated fatherhood. Now male generativity was associated almost entirely with the material world. In a secular scientific age, the notion of a pregnant man seemed wholly impossible, but it became increasingly common to assign men credit for giving birth to everything having to do with the economy and the polity. In the era of the market economy and the nation-state, men were imagined to father ideas, inventions, and nations. But their generativity was now confined to the public sphere; no longer the animators of family life, they were assigned the role of chief provider for the women and children who were now the family's imagined core.

Gillis, illustrating the need for a socio-historical stance, reminds us that since the early nineteenth century a recurring moral panic circulating around European and North American cultures has been the revival or revitalization of fatherhood in response to the social problem of the *absent father*. He claims that the failure of this project has and continues to be premised upon the individualized pathologization of the male sex that disconnects the liminal position of contemporary dads within households as a 'social problem' from 'the very political, economic and cultural constitution of the modern world' (ibid.: 180). Gillis summarizes his argument, paraphrasing Ann Dally (1982), that while there have always been fathers, fatherhood has never been invented. Nevertheless, ironically, despite the historical social facts about the long-standing complex factors contributing to the marginalization of fathers in the domestic domain, empiricist-based commentators continue to invoke the emergence of 'deadbeat dads' in the United States and 'bad fathers' in the United Kingdom as central evidence of the contemporary crisis of men and masculinity.

Hobson and Morgan (2002: 3) in their text, *Making Men into Fathers*, provide an analytical way forward. They argue that what is conventionally described as a crisis in fatherhood 'involves competing and conflicting social politics that revolve around the dimensions of cash and care, the obligations and rights of fatherhood'. They suggest situating 'these politics in the broader context of policy regimes, ideological and cultural frames of family and gender, and structural changes in post-industrial globalizing economies' (ibid.: 4). This enables us to make sense of the current policy focus upon, and government intensified policing of, fathers' moral management of family life that is exclusively defined in terms of men's failure to sustain the breadwinner role. This US and British ideological selection of the breadwinner role, rather than a more expansive understanding that would include the notion of care operating in other European societies, as the defining characteristic of modern fatherhood has had the effect of pathologizing specific groups of minority ethnic and black men, most visibly African-American men in the United States, alongside sectors of the white working class (Gavanas, 2002). These social groups have been particularly vulnerable to high levels of unemployment and social exclusion as a result of the cumulative effects of a restructuring global economy, as work becomes disconnected from a localized economy and welfare arrangements no longer support male workers, alongside changes in family formations. It should be added that for many minority ethnic and working-class men, there has been a long history of being denied access to the single male breadwinner model, thus denying them the normative ascription of 'normal men' (Mac an Ghaill, 1999). Finally, a major effect of such discursive constructs as the discourse of masculinity crisis is to assume that associated constructs, such as the suggested feminization of the workplace, ensures that women are the social beneficiaries of the new social order. Hence, McRae's (1999b: 1) comment is a useful reminder of the gender ideological work and accompanying distorting effects of such claims. She found that:

> Despite some improvement in recent years in the incomes of the poorest, overall income inequality was greater in mid-1990s Britain than at any other time in the post-war period, and among the persistently poor are lone mothers, single pensioners, and couples with children but without jobs.

Understanding Paternal Masculinities in Late Modernity

Much of the work on fathers and fatherhood, based in the disciplinary departments of psychology and policy studies, in its quantitative search (what Beck and Beck-Gernsheim (1995: 150) refer to as blind empiricism) to establish the truth about men's participation in housework and childcare, has resulted in conceptual closure for understanding contemporary paternal masculinities. These texts tend to operate with degendered male subjects, located outside of wider social relations. Hence, there is little sense of shifts in the social organization of men and masculinities, the emergence of modern male sexed identities or the changing interrelationships between men/women and masculinities/femininities, as cultural categories of meaning, identities and ways of life. Importantly, a major weakness is that this serves to distort our conceptual rethinking of men/women and masculinity/femininity within the context of the fragmenting family as central to the shifting boundaries of an emerging gender order. During the last decade, a range of work, including that of feminist sociology, critical policy theorists and critical men's studies has been produced that enables us to move beyond these limitations. In so doing, they have developed their analysis of rapid changing intimate relationships within the wider context of the defining features of late modernity, such as globalization, risk, de-traditionalism, individualization and reflexivity (Beck and Beck-Gernsheim, 1995; Giddens, 1992; Smart and Neale, 1999).

A major limitation of much writing on paternal masculinities is its failure to place the changing nature of fatherhood and accompanying diverse modes of fathering within the bigger picture of 'plotting the unclear family' (Simpson, 1998), a shifting emotional landscape and the complex transformations of intimate life (Sedgwick, 1994; VanEvery, 1995). For cultural theorists, the context of conditions of late modernity has seen a shift from work as the primary site in which to establish a collective identity to a complex, more open society with multiple sources of potential identification and an accompanying choice of diverse social identities. More specifically, there has been a focus on the pluralization of identities involving processes of fragmentation, fluidity and dislocation. These identities are translated into lifestyles. Currently, various individual men and men's groups invoke the identity of fatherhood, in an attempt to reconnect paternity and social fathering, as a dynamic element of their lifestyle. This shift projects a contemporary version of manhood through a move from cultivating *a public masculinity around work* to the forging of *a private masculinity around fathering*. This may be linked to wider social and cultural change and, more specifically, to implied processes of individualization and transformation in intimacy, explored above (Beck and Beck-Gernsheim, 1995; Giddens, 1992). For example, we have found in our own empirical work evidence of intimate father–son/daughter relationships, resonant of Beck and Beck-Gernsheim's claim about the importance of love, as a visible mode of masculinity appears to be deployed by younger men as a means of distancing themselves from an older male generation's gender order which was translated into distant fathering (Haywood and Mac an Ghaill, 2003). However, work on fathering practices, familialism and care remains remarkably undertheorized.

At the same time, an appreciation of temporality and spatiality as constitutive of paternal identities suggests that there is a potential for the transformation of shifting forms of fathering' (and mothering') practices.

As Ilcan and Phillips (1998: xv) in their introduction to, *Transgressing Boundaries: Critical Perspectives on Gender, Household and Culture*, suggest: 'In studies of gender and household relations, conceptions of space and time have generally appeared peripheral to the more prevalent concerns of familial ideologies and the gendered character of household formation and organization. It has become increasingly clear, however, that the organization, management and meaning of households in geographical settings have significant social, cultural, and political implications'. For us, there emerges a clearer understanding that different material conditions and attendant symbolic signs produce different effects in local geographical spaces. For example, in a British context, regional meanings of fatherhood differ in East Anglia (agricultural), Glasgow (deindustrializing) and London (cosmopolitan). Similarly, a range of diverse social practices and meanings are occurring cross-culturally, in response to equality debates about how to reconcile working and family life (Bergman and Hobson, 2002; Carlsen and Larsen, 1994).

A further analytical move, as indicated above, that desegregates the social institution of fatherhood from notions of the father and fathering, enables us to rethink the contemporary dominant dualistic models of mothering and fathering, tracing the contextual specificity of multiple discourses of patriarchal fatherhoods and new cultural sensibilities of intimacy by desegregating specific origins, causes and effects of familialism in particular periods. We are also able to trace continuities and discontinuities in the relationship between individual lived experience and institutional outcomes in relation to diverse representations and practices of fathering over time (Hobson and Morgan, 2002: 15). This enables us to place the contemporary micro-political realities of male domesticity, paternal intimacy and child nurturing within the bigger picture and on a longer timescale. Such an approach challenges the determinist notion of history without individual actors as active agents, while at the same time rescuing accounts of subordinated paternal social practices, including that of non-cohabiting dads, granddads, disabled fathers, minority ethnic dads and gay dads (Shakespeare *et al.*, 1996; Weeks *et al.*, 2001). This is not simply about adding to a more complex typology of fathers. Rather, the more significant conceptual point is that these categories are constitutive of emerging shifts in the diversity of meaning around paternity, familial masculinity and wider kinship relations. In turn, a focus on the formation of familial masculinities and the accompanying production of paternal subjectivities will help develop sociological knowledge about future families within conditions of late modernity.

Until recently, the traditional patriarchal family has functioned as a main container of the dominant sex/gender order, the central social agency for the making of young femininities and masculinities and a central institution for the affirmation of gender difference. Especially within this site, ' "real" women and "real" men are always heterosexual' (Dunne, 1999: 69). Hence, dominant media images of gay fathers and lesbian mothers are projected as a threat to mainstream society.[2] For example, within the current dominant sex/gender system, gay men are represented in the media and social commentary as having *too little masculinity*. At the same time, gay men are also ascribed a perverse, promiscuous maleness, a myth with a long history of naming 'homosexuals as corrupters of young boys', which currently manifests itself in producing gays as the dangerous men of paedophilia. In contrast, lesbian relationships are conceived as having *too much masculinity*. In turn, this is translated into a major moral panic about the twin social problems of boys being emasculinated within all-women spaces (for example, in primary schools) and the absent father, both of which are seen as a central contribution to what is assumed to be a crisis in the traditional family. However, as recent empirical research finely illustrates, there are alternative understandings (Dunne, 2001; Weeks *et al.*, 2001). First, given the rapidity of current social and cultural change and its impact on heterosexual families, where high divorce rates, absent fathers and stepchildren indicate a rejection of traditional forms of family life, same-sex partnerships may be seen as a cultural resource for the (hetero) sexual majority. In a shifting society, this is an example where that which is socially marginal becomes culturally central. As Stacey (1996: 15) suggests, lesbian and gay families are not marginal or exceptional:

> but rather a paradigmatic illustration of the 'queer' postmodern conditions of kinship that we all now inhabit. Gays and lesbians who self-consciously form families are forced to confront the challenges, opportunities and dilemmas of the postmodern condition with much lower levels of denial, resistance, displacement or bad faith than most others can indulge.

Cross-sex couples' current marital and parenting anxieties may find a resolution within lesbians' and gays' constructions of new ways of mothering and fathering as part of the latter's longer history of having to invent a self, a social identity and a wider community. At the same time, both conceptually and practically, gay fathering makes clear that masculinity is not something that one is born with or an inherent individual possession but rather an active process of achievement, performance and enactment. Gay fathering provides an example of Weeks *et al.*'s (2001) life experiments, in doing gender beyond the confines of heterosexual romance and the traditional nuclear family (Dunne, 2001). Reminiscent of earlier gay stories of 'coming out', the above studies report accounts of gay paternal masculinities as marked by a highly reflexive self, illustrating the creative possibilities of fathering being constituted by egalitarian partnerships, active co-parenting, shared willingness to nurture children, involvement in shared domestic responsibilities and a revisioning of intimacy with and between adults and children. Alongside such academic work, in late modernity, the media is often presented as providing a powerful site in which paternal masculinities are preformed and enacted (Craig, 1992).

Cultural Technologies: Diverse Media Images of Paternal Masculinities

Gillis (1997: 180) traces the historical marginalization of the social positioning of fathers within the symbolic universe. He maintains that: 'For most of our century, the treatment of fathers in film, fiction and television has been satiric, if not dismissive.' Over the last decade, media and cultural studies have joined psychology in providing major disciplinary conceptions of familial masculinity. Within this space as elsewhere, opposing interpretations have emerged of representations of contemporary fathers from the wide range of cultural technologies that constitute the modern media. On the one hand, national newspapers are reported as reproducing a limited debate about family life, with fathers reductively represented in the old oppositional couplet as villains or heroes (Lloyd, 1995, pp. 50–1). In contrast, other readings suggest that the cumulative effect of Reality TV, soap operas, chat shows, men's magazines, young girls' fanzines, photography and advertising has been conceptually to open up discussions of men and family life, with diverse representations of familial masculinity being generated and circulated through the media and changing patterns of cultural production and consumption (Steinman, 1992; Westwood, 1996).

At the same time, the media, as a highly influential space of modern iconography, has made visible the commercialization and commodification of modern (young) men, with projected notions of the *New Man*, the *New Lad* and the *New Father*. Implicit within these cultural representations and the attendant resignification of paternal masculinity is the assumption that men are in crisis and consequently are being coerced into processes of change. This suggests that current restructuring of the home, with a diverse range of fathering styles emerging, is one of the main arenas in which this assumed crisis is located. However, it seems that the preoccupation by cultural theorists and media commentators, as a legacy of the 1980s, with a limiting debate about whether the new man *really exists* has failed to acknowledge that in the early 2000s men are taking on feminine positions as they increasingly occupy the space of consumer rather than producer. In other words, a shift from the 'absent', single breadwinner (producer role) to the two-earner family household, whose life revolves around conspicuous consumption (identity lifestyle) in relation to house purchasing, home improvements, cooking and gardening. Mobilizing such images of the contemporary co-parenting, child-caring, family man suggests that the long pessimistic narrative of the death of the family, divorcing partners and dysfunctional fathers has failed to capture the collective agency of each generation that responds in culturally creative ways to the specific conditions that they inherit of fragmenting families. It is within this context, analytically and politically, that we can begin to explore the remaking of maternal femininities and paternal masculinities, within the emerging gender order of late modernity.

Conclusion

As we have illustrated in this chapter, late modernity theorists have provided fresh frameworks to explore the reconfiguration of elective family lifestyles and changing mothering and fathering practices within the context of wider social and cultural transformations. Most significantly, they have enabled modes of understanding with an emphasis on the constitutive power of parenting practices in actively reshaping notions of intimacy, care and so on, within a context of interrogating the limitations of the private (domestic)–public (outside the home) dualism. Critics of this approach maintain that a serious limitation here is the underplaying of familial social relations of the industrial legacy that so persuasively continues to shape common-sense accounts of the dominant meanings attached to the social positionings and subjectivities of women and men. As McRae (1999b: 24) suggests: 'Both change and continuity characterize British families and households in the 1990s, much of which flows from, or is built upon, profound changes in people's economic opportunities and outcomes, and upon equally profound ideational change – called by some the "second demographic in transition" and by others a changed viewpoint'. At the same time, the new theory is criticised for failing to connect to contemporary lived experiences as exemplified in such politically contentious issues as 'the home/work balance', 'the working mother' and 'divorced/separated fathers' access rights to their children'. For example, currently fathers' rights groups, such as Families Need Fathers and Fathers 4 Justice have been highly successful in their media campaign to gain public recognition of the position of fathers after divorce. However, in relation to legislation as part of the changing settlement between men and women, there is much confusion about the principle of equal parenthood after separation (Walter, 2004). Gender theorists are failing to connect with shifting institutional and cultural imperatives and an accompanying changing sensibility. We suggest that such contemporary practical questions need to be connected to the theoretical and conceptual frames discussed in this chapter.

3

In and Out of Labour: Beyond the Cult of Domesticity and Breadwinners

Introduction

Important infrastructural changes have taken place in the traditional industries of western capitalist countries, such as coal mining, ship building, engineering, car production, fishing and agriculture which have experienced collapse, fragmentation and contraction (Breugel, 2000; Esping- Andersen, 1993). Simultaneously, increased insecurities are pervasive across labour markets, as heightened anxieties emerge within the public services with the introduction of new wave management, work intensification and increased self-surveillance, accompanying the widespread marketization of the public sector (Bradley, 1999; Pahl, 1995; Wood, 1989). In the light of these changes, it is argued that over the past 50 years, patterns of men and women's participation in paid work have undergone major transformation. Indeed, recent accounts have argued that a changing gendered division of labour has blurred traditional understandings of men and women as homemakers and breadwinners (Goodwin, 1999). Within the media, this is associated with the notion of a 'genderquake', suggesting a fundamental shift in social roles, emerging from the breakdown in the established interplay between work and gender.

This chapter explores the suggested changing nature of gender relations, emerging occupational identities and the accompanying production of work-based social subjects, by examining a range of explanatory frameworks, including political economy, organizational theory, structuration theory, and theories of reflexive and aesthetic modernity. We explore recent quantitative data to highlight how the relationship between men, women and work has altered. However, the chapter not only provides a broad overview of large scale patterns of gender and work, but also suggests the need to consider local (spatial) meanings and interpretations of the work place and labour practices; how are men and women making sense of their work?

The chapter picks up one of the themes outlined in the Introduction, by focussing on feminist suggestions that recent changes in the division of labour have not broken with the patriarchal social relations of industrial society. Hence, they are simply new structures of gendered disadvantage or 'old wine in new bottles' (Phizacklea and Wolkowitz, 1995; Pollert, 1981; Walby, 1992; Williams, 1993). These are explored alongside alternative accounts, which claim that emerging patterns of work illustrate the conceptual and analytical inadequacy of using dualistic models of 'gender' to explain men and women's relationship to work (Alvesson and Billing, 1997). Here, the changing nature of late-modern work fused with consumption, particularly in service-based economies, suggests that men and women do not enter the workplace as fixed products in which a gender segregated labour force is simply reproduced. Rather, we need to investigate the specificities of how embodied beings, embedded within specific sites are actively constituted as subjects, marked by notions of contingency, mobility and contradictions (Casey, 1995; McDowell, 1997). Briefly, we see a shift from the conceptual ambiguity of women doing (industrial) work to men performing femininity within contemporary conditions of a new aesthetics of doing work and a suggested cultural revaluing of the feminine.

Making Sense of Labouring in Modernity: Industrial Breadwinners and Homemakers

There has been a wide range of explanations of the erasure of women from the public space resulting in structural inequality and cultural invisibility (Pateman, 1989; Rees, 1999). As explored in chapter one, earlier feminist studies, using patriarchy as an analytical tool, challenged limitations in earlier sociological and political theoretical models, emphasizing the conceptual absence of gender as a core explanatory variable, the undertheorization of gender identity formation, the false dichotomy of the private sphere (home) and the public sphere (work), the demonization of mothering and the social invisibility of women's involvement in paid labour (Phizacklea, 1990; Walby, 1990). A major achievement, conceptually and politically, has been the feminist analytical linking of domestic and public spheres as intimately interconnected through the dynamics of gender relations. In short, we begin to see this couplet as a cultural grid through which modern notions of manhood and womanhood are established and sustained. Working within a political economic theory of social change, feminists traced how historical changes in England from the eighteenth to the twentieth century gave rise to gendered spatial divisions between domestic and public spheres. The gendered nature of small-scale domestic units of production that characterized early industrialisation gave way to a redefinition of men's and women's relationship to the public and the private.

Hollway (1996) suggests that this distinction helped to establish and sustain middle-class ideologies of femininity and masculinity. What is underplayed here is the material and symbolic centrality of the racializing processes in play. For example, as Walter (2001) finely illustrates, historically, Irish female servants were of central significance in constructions of English middle-class masculinity through the cult of domesticity. The interrelationship between middle-class ideologies and industrialisation produced a reordering of the gendered landscape of work. One effect of this reordering was to place work within an oppositional structure of male breadwinner/female homemaker. The dominant Fordist model of production had at its centre the notion of the family wage. This was the shared conceptual and moral position that underpinned capitalism, patriarchy and trade union demands that the family wage earned by the man provided surplus income to enable him to support the home, constructed as a space of caring needs, emotional security, leisure and consumption. Pateman (1989: 187) in her discussion of the establishment of the patriarchal welfare state, in which employment rather than military service is central to citizenship, offers one of the most insightful explanations of the modern industrial worker. She writes that in Britain from the middle of the nineteenth century:

> A 'worker' became a man who has an economically dependent wife to take care of his daily needs and look after his home and children ... What it means to be a 'worker' depends in part on men's status and power as husbands, and on their standing as citizens in the welfare state. The construction of the male worker as 'breadwinner' and his wife as 'dependent' was expressed officially in the Census classifications in Britain and Australia.

At the same time, across the social sciences, feminism challenged the picture of 'men at work' projected by influential studies during the last two centuries that made available frameworks to explain industrial relations (see for example Marx, 1972; Mayo, 1933; Taylor, 1947; Weber, 1958). Feminism identified the workplace as a major site in which representations of men as a generic rather than gendered category lived their lives (Beechey, 1987; Cockburn, 1983, 1991; Pringle, 1989). It was argued that a deeply formative, mutually informing relationship between men and work has been culturally established. On the one hand, men have been understood through the notion of being a worker, with which male identities and subjectivities have been intrinsically invested. On the other hand, the workplace is symbolically ascribed a masculine characteristic in terms of organizational structures, cultures and practices (Collinson and Hearn, 1996).

Mapping Men's and Women's Employment Patterns

Throughout *Gender, Society and Culture*, we return to an organizing theme of contemporary popular thought, that of the discourse of crisis masculinity. Each institutional site deploys its own specific vocabulary to capture the new social conditions. Within the context of the workplace, the key term is that of feminization. Bradley (1999: 1) outlines the repertoire of interconnecting themes in the popular response to the suggested notion of feminization. She notes:

> At times this concern has veered towards becoming a moral panic, over issues such as rising male unemployment and its effects upon young men, the takeover of jobs by well-qualified young women, the challenge to the traditional notion of the male breadwinner as more women enter employment, the crisis of masculinity and the breakdown of family life.

Changing gender participation rates have been projected as one of the most visible and contested indicators of hard evidence of an inversion of the power-based social relations of work in western economies. Here, men are represented as loosing out to women as beneficiaries of the declining manufacturing sector and the ascendancy of the service sector.

Changing Men's Working Lives

Currently, the majority of the world's manufacturing is concentrated in the northern hemisphere, with four-fifths of it being distributed between the United States, Western Europe and Japan. However, processes of the global organization of production and exchange and deindustrialization since the 1970s have resulted in developing countries quadrupling their manufacturing output (Dicken, 1998). In contrast, the northern hemisphere has experienced a slower growth rate, with such countries as the United Kingdom and Germany experiencing a contraction of traditional industries

(World Trade Organization, 2000). The rapid decline of manufacturing industry and the accompanying mass structural unemployment made a major impact upon working-class communities. More specifically, it is argued that the diminishing traditional resources for forging masculinities have produced a 'crisis for men' (Willis, 2000). Interestingly, at a symbolic level these changes are generalized beyond the working class to suggest a major gender crisis for all men.

By using Britain as a local case study we wish to explore this suggested crisis. Our starting point is an examination of men's participation rates. It is important to note that at the beginning of the twenty-first century, over 70 per cent of men compared to under 54 per cent of women are involved in the British labour force (Table 3.1.).

For some, this reads as 'nothing but the same old story' (Walby, 1997). However, this story has an interesting new theme. In real terms, men's participation in the labour force is increasing at a very slow rate, whereas women's participation is increasing at a much faster rate. But the percentage of men involved in the labour force is on a downward trend whereas, for women, the trend is upward (see Table 3.1). These statistics illustrate that over the last 30 years the sex-based constitution of the labour force is changing. As explored below, this 'participation' obscures the fact that many women experience relatively lower pay, and insecure, poor working conditions. However, this story has another interesting twist.

Labour market changes in the United Kingdom are taking place against a context of a restructuring of industrial labour markets. Service sector employment has increased, whereas employment in the manufacturing industry is decreasing. From 1971 to 2000, jobs in the service sector have increased by 36 per cent, from 15.6 million to 21.2 million. In contrast, manufacturing work has fallen from 7.0 million to 4.2 million (see Tables 3.2 and 3.3).

Table 3.1 Labour force by gender of all aged 16 and over (thousands)

Year	Males (%)	Females (%)	All 16+
1971	80.5	43.9	24,900
1976	78.9	46.8	25,700
1981	76.5	47.6	26,200
1986	75.2	50	27,566
1991	73.4	53.1	28,185
1996	72.2	53.7	28,717

Source: Reconstructed From Central Statistical Office (2001).

Table 3.2 All employment by industry sector (thousands-not seasonally adjusted) – Male

Year	Agriculture and fishing	Manufacturing	Banking and finance	Administration
1984	448	3938	1350	1859
1986	396	3955	1510	1891
1988	431	3999	1648	1920
1990	411	4006	1845	1928
1992	404	3656	1774	1966
1994	402	3505	1833	1996
1996	375	3654	1935	2050
1998	354	3656	2182	2042
2000	330	3511	2392	2141

Source: Reconstructed from UK Labour Force Survey Spring Quarters Historical Supplement (1999) and Labour Force Survey, Quarterly Supplement (February, 2001)

Table 3.3 All employment by industry sector (thousands – not seasonally adjusted) – Female

Year	Agriculture and fishing	Manufacturing	Banking and finance	Administration
1984	124	1579	1136	3202
1986	111	1594	1282	3472
1988	130	1617	1456	3595
1990	131	1606	1663	3791
1992	131	1469	1577	4044
1994	133	1370	1635	4224
1996	137	1382	1657	4398
1998	111	1331	1771	4526
2000	96	1228	1880	4788

Source: Reconstructed from UK Labour Force Survey Spring Quarters Historical Supplement (1999) and Labour Force Survey, Quarterly Supplement (February, 2001)

This has implications for cultural representations of men's and women's work. Recent empirical evidence challenges pervasive images of men facing harsh work in creating wealth. British men, alongside increasing numbers of women, in the twenty-first century are more likely to be service sector workers.

These changes have led Goodwin (1999: 44) to argue that the nature and content of men's employment has changed and is continuing to be transformed: 'that men's identification with work in western society, has become a function of (and is maintained by) a social sex-ordered division resulting from both capitalist and patriarchal relationships as developed in Western civilisation'. One of the key features, according to Goodwin has been the fluctuation of men's work, in terms of nature, type and amount. For instance, at the turn of the century, men were concentrated in engineering and heavy manufacturing with the majority working full time. At the end of the century, as suggested above, the decline in heavy industry and the rise of new technology made men main participants in the service sector. Men's full time employment has severely declined at the same time as the number of males eligible to work has increased from 24,900,000 in 1971 to a projected 30,092,000 by 2006 (Central Statistical Office, 2001). In contrast to women's participation in the labour force, men's participation has reduced. This has led some commentators to suggest that work is now becoming feminized. Elsewhere (Haywood and Mac an Ghaill, 2003) we have used the sociological concept of feminization as a device to explain changing employment participation alongside an alternative conceptualization that shifts the focus away from rates of participation, based upon sex, to a consideration of gendered styles. Importantly, the latter notion of feminization suggests a more complex analytical understanding that goes beyond the simpler descriptive framework of male and female employment participation rates (Breugel, 2000; Douglas, 1977; Lee, 2000; Roper, 1994).

Changing Women's Working Lives

Historically, within a US or British context the gendered nature of work and more specifically debates about women's participation in paid employment has had important material and symbolic explanatory significance. Across the political spectrum positions have been taken up. Feminists have argued that paid employment is a major facilitator of the emancipation of women. In contrast, conservative social commentators have maintained that 'working women' are a major cause of social disruption including the breakdown of the traditional family, threatening fixed gender roles and the attendant moral certainty of the natural social order (Dench, 1996; Scott, 1999). At the same time, as indicated above, the workplace has been of central conceptual importance in defining fundamental processes of gendering. Most importantly, men's participation in and women's absence from paid employment has served to promote and sustain a pervasive understanding that dichotomous sexed selves, subjectivities and identities are anchored in this naturalized space in which a gendered doing is translated into being.

Delamont (2001) in her text *Changing Women, Unchanged Men?*, attempts to capture a contemporary take on this issue by locating it within the highly disputed terrain of claims that there has been fundamental changes in the UK Labour market, particularly in relation to the assumption that the cumulative effect of casualization, contract work, out-sourcing and part-time work has ended the notion of a job for life (Cully *et al.*, 1999; Tilly, 1996). Much popular commentary continues to assume that while these changes are impacting upon the general working population, it is particularly men that are under threat. In turn, this popular script assumes that the impact of these changes during the last 20 years is central to the promotion of new styles of being a (working) woman, marked by autonomy, independence, social confidence and a high-flying careerism. This optimistic reading is based upon such academic accounts as that of McRae (1999a: 5), who has written of the shift in the gender composition of the workforce within the context of the 'switch to service' in terms of the statistical growth of women's employment as men's have fallen, with the number of women economically inactive falling by 1 million to 4.6 million, while the number of economically inactive men has doubled from 1.4 million to 2.8 million.

Delamont (2001) outlines the methodological and epistemological disputes about the meaning of the reported findings on women and paid employment (Breugel, 1996; Ginn *et al.*, 1996; Hakim, 1995). For example, as she points out, in the mid-1990s a debate took place in the *British Journal of Sociology* following the publication of Hakim's (1995) article, in which she claimed to identify five feminist myths, or more appropriately fallacies, about women's employment. These were as follows:

1. women's employment has been rising;
2. women's work orientation/commitment is equal to men's;
3. childcare is the main barrier to women's employment;
4. part-timers are exploited in poor quality jobs;
5. women's stability of employment is equal to men's.

Hakim (ibid.: 448) writing from a positivist standpoint, carrying out large-scale survey work, set up a 'dispassionate social scientific assessment of the evidence' against what she saw as the academic orthodoxy among feminist sociologists' representation of women as victims. She polemically argues that they have simply inverted patriarchal myths with feminist myths, which serve ideologically to distort the objective social facts on women and paid employment. For Hakim, a key limitation of this work is the assumed homogeneity of the female workforce. Rather, she suggests that two increasingly polarized trajectories, linked to different life courses, can be identified: 'women who are committed to a career on a continuous basis, and women who have opted for the marriage career but have jobs on an irregular basis' (p. 450). Hence, she maintains that her more grounded approach enables her to provide alternative explanations to those emanating from gender studies, for the continuing sexual division of labour and the changing social function of occupational segregation. In response, Ginn *et al.* (1996), a group of feminist sociologists and economists arguing from a similar methodological position, challenged Hakim's interpretations and the resulting conclusions of her findings, claiming that they were based on misrepresentation of feminist work and the use of selective use of dated surveys. Of particular interest in relation to our concern with men and women's participation in paid employment within the context of rapid social and cultural change, Ginn *et al.* (ibid.: 167) maintain that Hakim's measurement of total hours of female employment, in terms of full-time equivalents, in which there has been little increase, distorts and oversimplifies the overall more complex picture of the increase in women's employment during the post-war period.

The debate is representative of the limitations of theorists working within older static theoretical frameworks based on industrial models of society (Bruegel, 1996). Working within this frame, of particular sociological significance are the continuing gender segregation and inequality in the workplace, and the meanings of the increasing number of married women's and especially mothers' participation in paid employment in relation to their life course history. Scott (1999: 72), writing of the latter, suggests that:

> Whether women choose to work part-time in order to juggle family and work roles, or whether lack of child-care alternatives and a traditional gender-role division of labour within the home leaves them no choice, is something that is far from clear

From a different perspective, as the last chapter illustrated, we are witnessing a fundamental cultural shift from understanding the family in terms of traditional, blood or marriage ties to that in which it has come to signify the subjective meaning of intimate relations. However, within an Anglo-American context, at conceptual, political and policy levels, the ongoing narrative of mothering and fathering – and we might add, the narrative of the economically active and inactive social subject – is being told in an old modernist language – the gendered dualism of *female homemaker/male bread-winner*. It is not able to grasp the generational specificities of emerging embodied femininities and masculinities and an accompanying shifting semantics of gendered relations that is contextually embedded within specific social institutions. Key questions emerge for contemporary gender theorists, within conditions of reflexive modernity as a new form of social order about whether we need to move beyond such modernist conceptions. For example, are men and women's lives and the accompanying masculinities and femininities better understood beyond the cult of female domesticity and male breadwinner? Can or should the suggested demise of the breadwinner be read as the demise of industrial masculinity? With the decentring of work, are other consumer-based cultural arenas now central in the making of postmodern male and female identities as part of broader domesticated lifestyles? How are we to understand the blurring of work and consumption identities and the accompanying emergence of new subject positions? Shifting to a focus on qualitative work, the second section of this chapter addresses such questions.

Changing Work? Changing Gender?

A major theme of *Gender, Culture and Society* is to examine how social change is impacting on men/women and masculinities/femininities and to explore how these changes are being mediated through different sites. Within the context of the workplace, the last two decades has witnessed the descendancy in (male) manufacturing and the ascendancy of the (female) service sector with the accompanying suggested feminization of paid work, mass regional unemployment, and the state recomposition of the working class in deindustrializing societies (Bradley, 1997; Jenson, *et al.*, 1988). The suggested changing picture of working life may be located within contemporary socio-economic, cultural and political transformations (Jameson, 1991; Kumar, 1995). For example, Harvey (1989: 59) operating within a political economic theory of social change, comments upon the new phase that capitalism has entered and argues:

> The tension that has always prevailed within capitalism between monopoly and competition, between centralization and decentralization of economic power, is being worked out in fundamentally new ways … capitalism is becoming more tightly organized through dispersal, geographical mobility, and flexible responses in labour markets, labour processes, and consumer markets, all accompanied by hefty doses of institutional, product and technological innovation.

An alternative explanatory frame of change is offered by late modernity theorists, as outlined in Chapter 1. Here, the emphasis is upon explaining changing gender relations as an effect of a wider restructuring of the global economy, communications networks, networks of power and capital flows, in the shift *From Post-industrial to Post-modern Society* (Brah *et al.*, 1999; Castells, 1996; Kumar, 1995). For example, within the context of employment, changing economic and social processes are seen to be free-ing individuals from the structural constraints of the Fordist labour process within the context of the blurring of worker and consumption identities (see Casey, 2002; du Gay, 1996; Lash and Urry, 1994).

Gender, Class and Power: Gender Segregation and Blurring

Harriet Bradley's (1989; 1996; 1999) writing and research on female paid work, employment and gender relations can be read as a potted history of core concerns around the sexual division of labour in the workplace. Her earlier writing provided a historical analysis of the impact of industrial capitalist development with the drive for accumulation and male social dominance on sex-typing jobs in terms of horizontal and vertical segrega-tion. Her more recent work brings together the anti-foundationalist stance of postmodern and post-structural positions with modernist theoretical frames that have structural inequality as their major analytical focus. This interrogation of classical sociology, that is, the theorists of order, leads her to move beyond systemic theories with a shift of metaphors from that of structures to interacting dynamics, in order to capture the tension between the two faces of social reality: 'continuity within change, order within variability, fixity within fluidity', within the context of interacting forms of inequality (Bradley, 1996: 7). However, throughout her work she has maintained a strong sociological sense of the mutually informing relation-ship between changing social categories of class, race/ethnicity, gender and age as socially constructed and simultaneously as objectively existing lived relationships. So, for example, within the context of the ascendancy of post-structuralist theories, Bradley insists at a conceptual level that alongside the discursive production of categories of difference, there are *real* differences *out there*, most manifest in terms of different access to social resources and power. Operating from a methodological realist position, of particular significance for her is the need to uncover the deeper truths about the sexual division of labour, that is, the common experiences of the impact of organizational processes on gender relations that serve to sys-tematically discriminate against women workers: processes of segregation, sex-typing and exclusion.

Bradley's (1999) text, *Gender and Power in the Workplace*, reports on a research project, carried out during 1992–1993, that was based upon five case studies of work organizations in the North east of England, involving 198 interviews with male and female employees. She stresses the impor-tance of developing a macro theory of social change, emphasizing that while economic relationships do not constitute the totality of social relationships, the economy is increasingly a dominant pervasive force in our lives. She identifies major limitations of earlier macro-explanatory frameworks of female paid employment including dual systems theory and the reserve army of labour, in their failure to accommodate a multidimensional explanation of highly diverse processes of social differentiation. Bradley sets out to chart the changing class and gender dynamics within conditions of global change. Hence, class reconfiguration emerges from the interconnection of a number of elements: polarization and proletarianization; globalization; fragmentation; exclusion and individuation. Changing gender dynamics within the context of employment include segmentation, fragmentation, feminization of employment, polarization and gender homogenization or the blurring of gender boundaries. She argues that in relation to the home – work couplet, women are contesting their gendered positioning which has consequences for a subtle shift in the balance of power. In order to fully explore these changes, she develops a theoretical understanding of gendered power.

As with other gender theorists, including Connell (1987) and Davis *et al.* (1991), Bradley draws upon Giddens' (1984) earlier work, structuration theory and his notion of the construction of power as differential access to control of rules and resources within arenas of interaction. In theorizing change, Bradley proposes a multidimensional model. She adopts an expansive definition of power as the capacity to control patterns of social interaction. Hence, moving beyond the potential closure of patriarchal explanations of gendered power, she defines the latter as the capacity of one sex to control the behaviour of the other. She identifies a range of interconnecting elements of gendered power that are linked to different resources: economic, positional, technical, physical, symbolic, collective, personal, sexual, and domestic. This more open, complex view of power enables her to identify how women deploy elements of power to challenge male dominance, alongside a general argument that empirically there is a tendency for men to monopolize power positions across these elements. Most importantly she illustrates how within specific local contexts contemporary women have increased access to some of these resources. These changes in gendered social relations are occurring at a societal level in response to globalization forces, feminization (increased women's economic participation rates) alongside the impact of equal opportunity interventions. However, this shift in the power balance in the workplace is further complicated, particularly in public sector organizations, that simultaneously are experiencing institutional restructuring, marked by increasing work intensification and risk for all employees.

Giddens (ibid.: xviii) although claiming that his theory is applicable to 'all the concrete processes of social life', does not apply his ideas theoretically or empirically to gender. Bradley, in failing to fully explicate how she is adapting Giddens' structuration theory, leaves implicit the theoretical connection between the latter and her conceptualization of power and gender. More generally, she claims that her approach has enabled her to move beyond the assumed fixed dominant – subordinate gendered positions of patriarchal theory, explaining temporal and spatial variability in the way power is played out between men and women. For example, control of and access to different amounts of each resource at different times and how across different sites, such as the home and the workplace, power operates differently, with the possibility of women controlling more resources in the former. Other feminist analyses make explicit how they are adopting and adapting Giddens' conceptual scheme in explaining gender. For example, Wolffensperger's (1991) study of social hierarchies in higher education suggests two new concepts; *engendered structure* (serving as a lever to make sense of the interconnection of gender, agency and social system) and twofold reproduction (the simultaneous production and reproduction of gender and social system) (see also Davis, 1991 and Whittock, 2000). In so doing, such accounts indicate the explanatory range of the suggested fusion.

Reflexivity and the Re-traditionalization of Gender

In the last chapter we noted that recent feminist theorists, working within the sociology of the family, have generally welcomed the conceptual productiveness of the contribution of late modernity theorists in relation to understanding change. Such theorists as Giddens and Beck are seen as placing family or intimate relations at the centre of a general theory of social change, with women represented as key players in this process. In contrast, Adkins' (2000) analysis, located within the sociology of work, challenges the radical detraditionalism thesis in Giddens' and Beck and Beck-Gersheim's analyses of reflexive modernity, arguing that what is at play here is not a simple process of disembedding of individuals from the normative demands of established social categories, but rather that it involves the retraditionalization of gender, with an accompanying set of new, yet traditional rules, norms and expectations. In so doing, Adkins has raised a number of fundamental questions about the meaning and scope of reflexivity in relation to the social positioning of women. As evidence of such forms of retraditionalism, she cites the work of Lash (1994), who also critically engages with the reflexivity thesis. Referring to what he calls the structural conditions of reflexivity, he has raised the question of why do we find reflexivity in some places but not in others. As he argues, systematic inequalities cannot be addressed within Beck's and Giddens' frameworks which define reflexivity as a freeing of agency from structure; this is seen in

Beck's (1992: 105) suggestion that 'people are being removed from the constraints of gender'. In response, Lash suggests that inequality in late modernity must have 'for condition of existence an interarticulated set of non-social structures' (p. 120). In explaining what these are, Lash makes clear that there is no need to return to structural Marxism or Parsonian structuralism, rather he identifies an articulated web of global and local networks of information and communication structures. So, an agent's life chances, which in industrial capitalism is dependent on access to modes of production, in reflexive modernity depends on access to information and communication structures. Importantly, Lash (1994: 120) addresses the issue of the 'reflexivity losers' alongside the 'reflexivity winners'. He asks:

> just how 'reflexive' is it possible for a single mother in an urban ghetto to be? Ulrich Beck and Anthony Giddens write with insight on the self construction of life narratives. But just how much freedom from the 'necessity' of 'structure' and structural poverty does this ghetto mother have to self-control her own 'life narrative'?

For Adkins, Lash's identification of women's exclusion from information and communication structures (the new reflexive economies) and intensified domestic and welfare servicing in the private sphere provides evidence of a retraditionalization of gender.

Further evidence of the retraditionalization of gender is presented by Adkins' critical exploration of the assumed shift in the organization of workplace socialities from traditional gendered occupational structuring. Exploring a number of studies, Adkins acknowledges the evidence that detraditionalizing tendencies appear to be releasing men and women from modernity's class- and gender-based determining characteristics and furthermore, that 'gender now seems to constitute an object of workplace agency' (p. 262) (Casey, 1995; McDowell, 1997). However, in her study of familial relations in married management teams in the UK tourist industry, she explores who are the beneficiaries of the suggested shifts outlined by theorists of reflexive modernity (Adkins, 1995). In relation to her central concern with the ways in which gender appears to be increasingly constituted as an object of workplace innovation and success, she maintains that 'while for team-husbands, married-team socialities constitute workplace agency, this does not seem to be the case for team-wives' (p. 268). It is important to note that Adkins is not suggesting that retraditionalization is a simple process of rehabilitating traditional gendered social structures but rather involves new positions and new traditionalized socialities. It is the decentralized patriarchal teams operating within post-occupational workplace socialities which enables the manager-husbands to be self-reflexive workers, thus mobilising the rules and resources of gender. In a later paper, exploring late modernity theories that focus on the declining influence of social structure, what she refers to as the 'post-structural social', Adkins (2004: 139) offers a more nuanced approach to the ambivalence of the classical sociological tradition, reemphasizing her stance against the assumed claims of its simple recuperation and the privileging of the male subject. As she innovatively suggests in contrast to classical social theory's exclusion of women from sociality, in contemporary theory woman is '*overdetermined* by the social, indeed cannot escape the social' (p. 150).

Beyond Men and Women of the Corporation[1]

Critical organizational theorists, working across the disciplines, are at the cutting edge in providing innovative analytical frames with which to make sense of institutionally located gender categories (Casey, 1995, 2002; Gherardi, 1995; McDowell, 1997). For Casey (2002), who sets out to revitalize theorizing society, the epistemological collapse of the grand project of modernity has emanated in sociologists avoiding an exploration of the core concerns of modern sociology, including institutions and organizations. For her, the social relationships embedded within organizations are centrally affected by and constitutive of the rapid changes we are currently experiencing in late modernity. A major limitation of current gender theorizing that we identify throughout *Gender, Culture and Society* is the urgent need to search for analytical techniques that will enable us to go beyond the conceptual closure of the overburdened notions of *men* and *women*. Alvesson and Billing (1997) provide such an approach; operating with a gender symbolism framework, they critically discuss the disruption of the assumed relationship between men/masculinity, women/femininity and organizations. They argue that gendered work is 'deeper than sex typing, meaning that not only is a job openly viewed as women's or men's work, but that it refers also to non-explicit meanings, unconscious fantasies and associations' (ibid.: 90). Importantly, this goes beyond overrationalistic accounts and places work within the context of desire, fear and imagination. Morgan (1992) also uses a notion of gender symbolism. He suggests that we should begin to make sense of masculinities and work by identifying a range of 'polarities', 'tendencies' or 'oppositions' that include skilled/unskilled, heavy/light, dangerous/less dangerous, dirty/clean, interesting/boring, mobile/immobile. These oppositions work together in a number of complex ways to establish the gendered nature of work and its symbolic value.

Alvesson and Billing (1997) interrogate femininities and masculinities at work through the use of an empirical example that of women into management, thus, enabling them conceptually to open up the interpenetration of the categories: work and gender. Within an Anglo-US context and from a socio-historical perspective, especially within a US setting, women into management has been a critical issue in the political struggle for gender equality (Kanter, 1997). More recently, the notion of 'breaking through the glass ceiling' is presented in the media as both a major issue of concern and a defining element of the modernization of the world of work. Alvesson and Billing map out the key questions that have engaged organizational theorists over the last two decades. These include the relative absence of women in management positions, women's different styles of leadership, the social and cultural barriers operating against females in managerial posts and the suggested tension between feminine values and exercising institutional authority. They identify and critically explore four positions that have generated these questions, namely, the equal opportunities position, the meritocratic position, the special contribution position and the alternative values position.

The equal opportunities perspective, working from an ethical – political position focuses upon structural conditions, stereotypical cultural ideas and irrational social processes in explaining the discrimination experienced by women seeking managerial jobs. The meritocracy position, operating within a managerial – technocratic logic highlights the potential underutilization of human resources that are available in recruiting personnel for high status posts. So, for example, at a time of the suggested feminization of the labour market, it follows that there is a need to challenge the irrational social forces that act against increasing the recruitment of women to top posts. These two perspectives view men and women as having a common humanity built on shared characteristics, within a system of asymmetrical power relations that operates against women. In contrast to their androgynous urge to downplay differences, the special contribution position emphasizes the political and conceptual meanings of gender differences. On the grounds of sex-specific characteristics, there is a suggestion that alongside the taken – for-granted male dominated managerial technological rationality, there are distinctive female styles of leadership, with their own vocabulary of democracy, teamwork, co-operation, people-orientation, empathy, social skills and participation. Furthermore, it is argued that with the current demand for increased flexibility in rapid changing labour markets built on new production and information technologies, such female traits have displaced an older male hierarchically ordered leadership. An example of the latter has been identified in Lipman-Blumen's (1992: 185) description of a conventional US model of leadership as 'a pastiche based upon a masculine ego-ideal glorifying the competitive, combative, controlling, creative aggressive, self-reliant individualist'. For special contribution advocates the solution to the underrepresentation of women in positions of corporate responsibility is not simply to add more female bodies to the existing institution. Rather, the convergence between business needs and women's distinctive characteristics and skills means that both women and feminine traits/styles are a necessary cultural imperative to a changing workplace. Such a move may serve to prise open the assumed inextricable linkage between managing work, men and masculinity.

An alternative values perspective, underwritten by a feminist standpoint position extends the special contribution position, emphasizing the bipolar culturally normative domains that men and women have been impelled to occupy. For women, this is the private, intuitive communal world of domesticity, while men inhabit the public, logical – instrumental world of the workplace. This perspective provides a critique of earlier positions, arguing for the assimilation or integration of women into contemporary public institutions. In contrast, alternative values advocates stress on a more radical solution, that of reshaping the workplace, challenging the logic of managerialism and constructing social spaces based on alternative feminine values and priorities, as Ferguson (1984), illustrates in her text, *The Feminist Case Against Bureaucracy*.

Alvesson and Billing (1997), citing the argument that women's leadership is more democratic than men's, as illustrative of the limiting frameworks in the field of inquiry, outline a post-structuralist critique of the above positions. They point to the methodological limitations of attempting to fix and essentialize gender, through an assumption that concepts, such as women, men, leadership and democratic represent 'some objective, universal homogenous, robust and easily comparable phenomena out there mirrored in questionnaire responses or observational protocols' (p. 76). In challenging the notion of women managers as a universal fixed essence, that allows a simple casual relationship between sex (women) and leadership (democratic), the post-structuralist emphasizes the discursive instability and cultural constitution of these social phenomena, marked by historical variation, plurality of meaning, and contextual, especially local, contingency, across time and space. It is suggested that such an approach will enable the construction of alternative interpretations, and most saliently, we might add, interpretations that are conceptually repressed by the four positions explored above.

This is the theoretical starting point for Alvesson and Billing in their critical and problematizing search to illuminate organizational cultures and corporate practices in terms of gender. They begin by distancing themselves from the poststructuralist critique, claiming a preference, for empirically based 'modest generalization' and 'local grounding'. They position themselves in relation to gender undersensitivity and oversensitivity. On the one hand, they argue for the mobilization of gender to address its absence in mainstream organizational and management theory. On the other hand, they interrogate a gender reductionist approach in which: 'the metaphors of masculinities and femininities take precedence and repress other metaphors/perspectives as interesting points of departures for interpretations and theories' (pp. 12–13). In challenging gender as the assumed privileged organizational principle of social relations and formation of subjectivities within the workplace, they suggest a number of theoretical and conceptual moves, involving processes of defamiliarization of the social categories, men and women. In order to minimize gender as a totalizing mode of understanding, they suggest widening the interpretive repertoire to fuse gender theory with a range of other intellectual sources, such as Marxism, critical theory and Foucauldian analysis. So, for example, we begin to understand masculinities and femininities as a result of contradictions and syntheses between a range of practices emanating from class-stratified societies, a consumerist – based technocratic consciousness, techniques of power/knowledge regulation and the production of subjectivity.

From their critical – interpretive position, Alvesson and Billing (1997) argue for the need to go beyond body counting, that is, an analytical starting point, shifting beyond a focus on women and men, primarily defined through biological criteria and understood as rigorously exclusive oppositions. As indicated above, they operate with a gender symbolism framework that enables a reading against the grain of established truths within gender theory and everyday life. Here, the suggested focus in exploring the gendered nature of organizational life is to examine the complexity of the processes, practices, interests and values that shape the workplace. Moving beyond a narrow gender lens, they illustrate the productiveness of integrating gender concepts with the multilayered cultural and symbolic world of the organization, with its attendant rituals, vocabularies and artefacts. This intermingling of gender specific and non-specific concepts enables an innovative exploration of the entire cultural subtext of organizational life, focusing upon questions of how it creates and sustains meanings around notions of masculinities, femininities, leadership and so on. They argue:

> An interesting possibility of broadening the impact of gender reflection in the study of leadership would be to go beyond (or beside) the somewhat unproductive comparisons of male and female leadership and the normative position of men and instead study specific examples of leadership processes. Such processes could be investigated in terms of how gendered constructions are accomplished and expressed, rather than through a focus on the biologies of the people involved. The actions and interactions of manager X could then be read sensitively in terms of gendered subtexts, a variety of masculinities and femininities, which hopefully at the time would

add to knowledge about leadership (superior – subordinate interaction) and
add to gender processes in organizations (p. 211).

In our own empirical studies, we have found cultural analysis using a
gender symbolism framework productive in illustrating the limitations,
common in much of the literature on management and organizations, of
simply identifying men's and women's participation rates as constituting a
gendering of work. As we pointed out in the introduction to the book, the
biological characteristics of male and female do not necessarily equate to
masculinities and femininities. For example, in some education sectors the
workforce is predominantly female. At the same time, recent changes in
education policies have directed school organisation towards more masculine working styles in western societies such as 'managerialism' (Haywood
and Mac an Ghaill, 2001). Similarly, in response to the suggested feminization of the workforce, male managers are organizationally constrained to
accommodate themselves to changing cultural configurations, that is, new
values, meanings and cultural (feminine) orientations. As a result, as
Alvesson and Billing's work makes clear, we need to be conceptually open
to accommodate the changing masculine and feminine cultures that
females and males may work within, identify with and sustain. In other
words, we need to track female and male participation in the workforce, as
well as to consider the processes involved in becoming a woman or a man.
This is further explored below in terms of the impact of social change upon
men and women working within the context of the suggested current
reconfiguration of the social division of labour and the reorganization of
work in the service sector.

A New aesthetics of Doing Work and the Cultural Revaluing of the feminine

As argued throughout this chapter, gender relations in the workplace –
processes, practices and politics – have changed rapidly over the last few
decades, often escaping adequate theoretical explanation. In response,
McDowell (1997) advances a challenging synthesis which seeks to preserve
a materialist core from earlier accounts while incorporating insights from
recent interdisciplinary (geography, architecture and urban sociology)
reflection on representation, identity, performance and the self. In so doing,
at a time of the ascendancy of the cultural she illustrates the productivity of
returning the social to critical theory. She presents a fascinating case study
of processes of gender segregation in three merchant banks in the city of
London, exploring the embedded and embodied character of work. Her
study is located within a number of theoretical and conceptual moves that

open up innovative frameworks for a contemporary understanding of workplace performances, the regendering of the labour market and the gender coding of new occupations. She begins by outlining the historical development of a move from a materialist-based division of labour position, in which men and women on entry to the workplace are classified as fixed products that simply reproduce a segregated labour force to that of an emphasis on the negotiation and contestation of ascribed gender attributes in the social construction of both occupations and workers. In short, a move from sexing to re–sexing jobs, that is applicable to the processes of occupational sex-typing, within the context of rapid economic restructuring within a global city, London. McDowell cites Scott's (1988b: 47) suggestion that:

> if we write the history of women's work by gathering data that describe the activities, needs, interests, and culture of 'women workers', we leave in place the naturalised contrast and reify a fixed categorical difference between men and women. We start the story, in other words, too late, by uncritically accepting a gendered category (the 'woman worker') that itself needs investigation because its meaning is relative to its history. McDowell (1997: 25)

In developing her frame of analysis, with an emphasis on the active constitution of multiple organizational subjects (among dealers, traders, analysts and corporate financiers), McDowell makes a move away from earlier studies, in which the site of inquiry is simply a backdrop to gender segregation. Rather, she finely indicates the geographical significance of location and the physical construction of the workplace, highlighting the institutional specificity of the financial services sector within which social action is played out. She illustrates how this enables the constitution of embodied gendered performances – the fathers, the princes – and attendant power relations across a diverse range of spaces.

In several places in *Gender, Society and Culture* we have referred to the way in which the term feminization, as part of a wider discourse of masculinity crisis, has been deployed across social scientific disciplines in exploring the extent and direction of social change. With reference to the historical development of this term, McDowell makes an innovative contribution which she has developed over the last decade (McDowell, 1991). Feminization, which continues to be used in a rather loose way, was used in the 1980s to capture the changing composition of the labour force, with increased participation rates of women in paid employment. Alongside this understanding, McDowell develops an expanding concept of feminization within the context of the mutually constitutive interplay between new ways of work and alternative ways of doing gender, or more specifically, the aligning of a new aesthetics of doing work and a cultural revaluing of the feminine. Her analysis is located within the rapid growth of the service sector, traditionally associated with feminine characteristics of serving and caring, at a time of the emergence of (feminine) styles of management marked by flat hierarchies, democratic leadership, empathy and co-operation (see Kimmel, 1994).

New forms of work and changing organizational structures emerged in the mid-1980s among a new cultural class (or service class) who were seen as making a dynamic economic and cultural contribution to wider socio-economic transformations (Savage *et al.*, 1992; Thrift, 1989). This group exemplifies a move away from understanding production as the primary and exclusive site of identity formation as changing patterns of cultural production and consumption impel a blurring of the boundaries between work and leisure (du Gay, 1996). McDowell presents a specific case study of such a group, professional financial service workers, who illustrate the end of the ideal worker of the industrial era, that of the rational, unemotional, disembodied (male) subject, displaced by a new hybrid subject who is always on display (Urry, 1990). In a shift away from what Baudrillard (1975) refers to as the unbridled romanticism of productivity, this distinct class fraction may be seen as exemplary figures of reflexive modernity, with their celebration of consumarized lifestyles, search for new experiences and the aestheticization of everyday life (Featherstone, 1991b; Giddens, 1991; Lash, 1993).

For McDowell, the feminization of this occupational site is most evident in interactive work practices, in which a pre-occupation with personal appearance and an attendant manipulation of bodily images and emotions, as a defining characteristic of the contemporary selling of products are displayed by men as well as women. Drawing upon Butler's (1990, 1993) theorizing of gender as a bodily performance or masquerade, McDowell explores the potential repositioning of women and men in these new conditions in which femininity is highly valorized within emerging stylized performances. She begins, in exploring feminine parodies and masquerades, by claiming that while masculinized occupational performances by women were doomed, the latter were aware of femininity as a significant cultural resource. For example, focusing upon generational differences among women, she found in her empirical work that older women seemed 'to recognise that a display of overt femininity confers advantages, realising that "feminine" decorativeness may function "subversively" in professional contexts, which are dominated by highly masculinist norms' (p. 197). At the same time, older and younger women, deploying metaphors of performance, disguise and masquerade, recounted strategies of acting more female or less female and adopting diverse images of femininity appropriate to the specific context. Such multiple performances illustrate the fluid and negotiated nature of gender, in which female workers reflexively engaged.

In earlier materialist-based studies of the industrial workplace, masculinity was portrayed as a key resource in the self-production of male identity. More specifically, working-class men were represented as exhibiting compensatory masculinities, with gendered identities standing in opposition to capitalist relations of production (Cockburn, 1983; Tolson, 1977; Willis, 1977). McDowell, within contemporary conditions, captures a fascinating reversal of the cultural reevaluation of gender ascribed attributes with men using femininity as a cultural resource in their self-presentation. She identifies younger men's workplace performances as serving to distance themselves from older men's traditional occupational style of a centred, patriarchal masculine identity. Rather, they portray a gendered style imitative of feminine ways of being and doing. Studies of the formation of class identities have been understood as based upon working *with* the body. Here, for this new cultural class fraction, manhood can be acquired through working *on* the body. Much of the theoretical analysis in this area has focussed on conventional sites of consumption (Falk, 1994; Featherstone, 1991b; Mort, 1996). Adopting a frame that fuses the boundaries of work and consumption, the young male high fliers in McDowell's study make clear how current body regimes are being played out in specific labour markets, marked by decentred forms of complex and multiple subjectivities and the aestheticization of everyday life. A categorical sensibility circulating among these elite workers emphasizes core values around image, appearance and body maintenance in refashioning work identity. Masculinities in this sense could be articulated through an aesthetic/reflexive modernity consumption that could be written on the body.

Politically, this suggested blurring of work practices, in which the visible embodied male joins the conventional female body as corporeal subjects doing gender has the potential to challenge traditional mechanisms of exclusion for women, subordinated within segregated work regimes, in which they have been set up in opposition to an unmarked masculine norm. However, for McDowell, feminization is a complex social phenomenon with unpredictable effects in terms of who has access to the highly valorized femininity, opening up a struggle between 'real' women and masculinized feminine performances or masquerades. She adds that 'It may be that femininity in a self-evidently masculine body will become the most highly valorised workplace performance' (p. 182). McDowell's own empirical study provides evidence that her male respondents as flexible workers, while taking up a highly mobile and reflexive relation to performing femininity, renaturalize women, claiming that in response to new labour market demands women can simply be themselves. Adkins (2002: 79), in a critique of theorists of feminization, including McDowell argues that such responses are central to constructing women as 'reflexivity losers'. Drawing upon the work of Diawara's (1988) discussion of black masculinity and film, McDowell suggests that a reflexive stance in relation to gender is often misrecognized when per-formed by professional women workers as they are positioned as having this immanent relation to femininity. At the same time, the popularized view of feminization as causal of masculine crisis is made evident in men being posi-tioned as sex objects, as women name desired types, 'the natural blond', 'the bright young executive' and so on. As Rutherford (1988: 59), noting a con-temporary culture of sexual diversity, comments: 'The current eroticization of men's bodies, the shifting of gay erotic images into mainstream popular culture, represents a blurring of sexual differences and a loosening of mas-culine rigidity'. However, there are increased anxieties among heterosexual men in these encounters with the naming of men as objects of desire, as reminiscent of contemporary gay men's sexual fantasy typologies.

Jobs for the Girls?[2] *The Future of Gender in the New Economy*

Harris (2004) in *Future Girl* provides a further fascinating account of what is happening to gender within the reconceptualization of the workplace – the workplace as a projected location in which shifting representations have discursively produced the pervasive image of the can do-girl. Harris's work, resonating with the cultural history of women as the flexible subjects of labour markets, cites the work of Walkerdine *et al.* (2001) in identifying a contemporary version in which young women as the neo-liberal subject are imagined as the ideal flexible subject of the new economy. These self-inventing young women impelled to achieve success through making the right decisions, as part of a younger generation who have to make 'choice biographies', are reminiscent of late modernity theorists' positioning of con-temporary women as 'reflexivity winners'. However, Harris critically engages with this concept of the neo-liberal feminine subject, arguing that notions of individual responsibility and inherent risk factors within young women's personal biography are mobilized to obscure the 'social', under-stood as social structures of class and ethnicity that circumscribe the pre-conditions of who succeeds and who fails. At the same time, Harris maintains that the explanatory shift of achieving success from *structure* to *personal responsibility* conceals the investment of global capitalism and the need for stratified labour markets in the maintenance of systemic inequality. Within the context of the dominant representations of overachieving young women in the reconfigured education, training and employment regime, Harris poses the question about which young women are benefiting from the new economy and the different meanings of their experiences. In order to problematize a projected false dichotomy between 'can–do' and 'at–risk' young women, she creates a threefold typology of three broad groupings from economically secure, professional and successful families; those from the lower middle – middle to working classes and those in lower (working) – class or 'underclass' circumstances. This enables her to identify a complex, nuanced picture in which young women are represented at both ends of the continuum of the new work conditions. For Harris, new forms of stratification have been produced by the socio-economic and ideological shifts that characterize the risk society. She concludes:

> This stratification has enormous benefits for the new economy, as it has enabled differently advantaged young women to take up positions that must be filled at opposite ends of the labour market. At the same time the accompanying narratives about choice, self–invention, and opportunities for girls ensure that stratification and disadvantage become reconfigured as merely individual limitations of effort or vision, to be addressed through personal strategies alone (p. 62).

Conclusion

This chapter has traced a shift from the industrial era to a service-based economy in late modernity. The earlier sections noted how in response to the erasure of women from the public sphere early second-wave feminism identified the social reproduction of the gendered division of labour that operated through this spatial segregation of the *public workplace* and the *private home*. More specifically, male breadwinners and female homemakers have been projected as paradigmatic cultural images exemplifying a naturalized social order, functional to the prerequisites of western, industrial capitalism. The latter sections of this chapter may suggest that we are a long way from the spatial containment of the cult of (female) domesticity and (male) breadwinners. However, Williams' (1993) pessimistic picture of the future of gender equality in relation to the workplace is based upon her claim of the continuing cultural overevaluation of men and devaluation of women. Theorists employing late modernity analysis offer a more ambivalent picture suggesting that the workplace is a key site in which processes of detraditionalism, albeit unevenly, are taking place. For example, McDowell (1997) concludes: 'Although notions of gender are tightly bound up with the workplace and with notions of work, it is in the current reconfiguration of the social division of labour and the reorganization of work in the service sector that the possibilities of change perhaps lie' (p. 203). However, conceptual confusions continue to constrain the field of inquiry. For example, the concept of feminization, which has been used to capture these possibilities of change is inconsistently deployed to mean gender inversion and gender hybridity.

4

Interplaying Gender and Age in Late Modernity

Introduction

Children being tagged, an ensuing pension crisis, increasing divorce, teenage pregnancy and the collapse of jobs for life continue to be some of the persistent themes circulating through modern western societies. It is suggested that with the rise of industrialization and technological development, age has been increasingly salient in the reconfiguration of civil society (Hepworth and Featherstone, 1998). Furthermore, it has been argued that age identities that once served to provide structural functionality to modern societies (Erikson, 1968; Fletcher, 1984; Marsland, 1993) are becoming fragmented in a period of late modernity. In other words, key signs of age are being disconnected from traditional meanings. The implication for this chapter is that the resources for the attribution and living out of age identities are no longer secure (Polivka, 2000). This means that the boundaries through which age articulates itself are becoming increasingly contested. At the same time, this chapter suggests that gender is integral to the changing nature of age categories. It is thus argued that the interplay between categories of age and gender are involved in the process of demarcating practices and subjectivities that have been ascribed to particular age categories and gender identities. However, on one hand, it is argued that such changes are reinscribing gender inequalities, through the rearticulation of the centrality of reproductive technologies. On the other, such changes are recreating new social and cultural positions and diverging subjectivities that result in the 'birth of freedom in the economic and cultural transformations associated with post-modern styles of creative, economic and cultural production and consumption that undermine hierarchies of class, gender and ethnicity and create new venues for emancipatory politics' (Polvika, 2000, p. 226).

The chapter begins by examining how age and gender operate within the context of schooling. More specifically, by examining the relationship

96

between childhood and gender, it is possible to critically engage not simply how age and gender work together but also the conceptualized (im) possibilities that are encased within current conceptual frameworks that have been developed by educational researchers. First, this involves considering the importance of meanings of maturity, and second, by exploring the possibility of how existing gendered categories may need to be reshaped in the context of specific age contexts. The second part of this chapter explores the relationship between gender and older age. Rather than be located within a specific context, the second section focuses on broader social and cultural events as means to explore the interplay between gender and older age. Alongside this, the chapter considers how the interplay between age and gender activate particular knowledges and understandings of sexuality.

Schooling, Gendering and Age

To be masculine and be in schools has often been represented as a juxtaposition of cultural resources. Early work by Willis (1977) highlighted how working-class boys viewed schools as a feminized space. Later, feminist educational researchers highlighted how the ideal pupil was projected by teachers as carrying a passive femininity. More recent work on gender in schools has identified the importance of understanding masculinities and femininities as interrelated in the production of pupils' subjectivities. Such theorists have critically engaged with the social organization of schooling by exploring the patterning of gender relations. Connell (1995) draws upon a notion of the 'gender regime'. He uses gender regime to make sense of social relations, suggesting that a 'structural inventory of a particular institution' (p. 99) produces how gender relations operate in local contexts. This structural inventory for Connell involves considering the gendered division of labour, the structure of power hierarchies and the emotional charges of institutions. As Williams (2002: 32) argues: 'Local gender regimes capture meaningful differences in ways communities organize gender relations'; they provide the preferred range of meanings that contribute to the possibilities of experience.

Work in the area of gender and schooling has tended to understand age as an aspect of gender rather than a key constituent. At the level of schooling administration, gender is a central organizing feature of registration, toilets, single files, wearing uniforms and sports changing rooms (Wolpe, 1988). With a different empirical focus, researchers working in the area of childhood studies have contested the simplistic notions of gender and argued that schooling is not simply an institution that arranges and regulates gender relations, schools simultaneously distribute normalizations of adulthood and childhood. In other words, the structuring of the teaching and learning experience is not simply constituted through gendered practices, it simultaneously articulates age-based ascriptions. Thus, the very category boy or girl is *gendered* because it is *aged*. On one hand, Burman (1995) argues that the state of childhood itself is female. This is because childhood is conceived as passive, immature and vulnerable. Thus, social relationships with the child are ones that are based upon care and attention. However, on the other hand, Jones (1999) argues that 'maleness' is the natural gender of childhood. He argues that romantic constructions of childhood are premised upon a natural innocence. Owen argues that this 'naturalness', this non-fettered expression of identity is a masculine attribute. There is a broader issue about how gender and corporeality operate to secure the masculine and feminine, which is further explored in greater depth in Chapter 6. However, in the next section we unpick the conceptual dilemma of the gender of childhood, by examining how gender is articulated through notions of maturity and immaturity.

Making Genders: Regulating Maturity and Immaturity

Conventional approaches in educational research argue that an important institutional resource in the control of pupils has been the ascription of meanings of maturity and immaturity. For example, Chris Skelton (2001) suggests, from her research in two different primary schools, that teachers correlated the ideal pupil with 'girlness', approximating a notion of maturity with a particular gendered style that is carried by children. As outlined above, it could be argued that maturity carried not simply meanings of adult but also feminine codes. More broadly, there has been the claim that femininity is constituted through the meanings that have traditionally been ascribed to childhood: passivity, dependency and vulnerability. However, in the school context, traditional practices that have been designated feminine appear to correspond to an ideal adulthood. Therefore, to be 'immature' is something that is associated with boyness. This is supported by Francis (2000), who found in the primary school that she researched that boys actively 'messed about' more than girls. In this way, gendered identities are closely mapped onto particular practices in the schooling context. Francis suggests that boys who messed around by throwing balls of paper, playing catch with paper, or indulged in verbal abuse 'illustrates the "silly", "immature" or "having a laugh" construction of masculinity' (ibid.: 51). Thus, this conventional view suggests that silly/sensible behaviours are deemed to emerge from the pupils themselves – part of their natural development and indicative of their maturity.

Francis's work on boys and girls in primary schools corresponds to a broader understanding of gender and ageing among educationalists. In earlier work, Francis (1998) suggests that gender is constructed out of two categories: masculine and feminine. As a result, males are ascribed power and agency whilst the female is devalued and subjugated. This occurs through the maintenance of distinct gender boundaries. For Francis, masculine and feminine are set up through a series of oppositions. She argues that in order to capture the nature of schooling relations, it is important to negate the notion of masculinities and femininities. She draws upon McInnes' (1998) work that critiques the concept of masculinities, preferring the idea of notional masculine and notional feminine. Hence, the designation of masculine is a result of how far males and females approximate these gender codes. Importantly for Francis, females can adopt masculine traits but as a consequence such traits become reconstructed as gender appropriate. This means that rather than use the concept of masculinity or femininity, practices become strategies for constructing masculine and feminine. As Francis suggests, all the elements of the ideal list of masculine and feminine categories can never be taken up; only a number can be adopted. Francis' deficit model posits that there are a number of generic qualities that identify masculine and feminine. As a result, the list of attributes operates as a measure of how far someone is masculine or feminine. Male pupils who do not display characteristics that are associated with masculinity are deemed less masculine. Similarly, those females who do not demonstrate attributes of femininity are understood as being less feminine.

Although Francis's work highlights the conventional characteristics that are used to describe male and female pupil practices, they offer limited explanatory purchase on the interplay between age and gender. As Allan (1989: 34) argues:

> in much of the literature on friendship, notions of class, age and gender are treated simply as traits that a person has in some form, rather than being treated as features of a social landscape that facilitates or discourages to differing degrees, in interaction with other aspects of social topography, the emergence of particular social patterns.

The implication of a shift from pre-social universal qualities of gender to one of local accomplishment, brings into play the importance of locally grounded meanings. More specifically, the distinctive institutional context designates what categorical classification systems mean. For example, being a certain kind of boy is not a pre-existing category but is produced through a series of complex interplays between subjectivity, interpersonal relationships and the school institution. Research that we have carried out in the north east of England, explores the interrelationship between gender, sexuality and schooling in a middle school (Walcote West) with pupils aged between 9–13.[1] Interviews and observations were undertaken over a year long period. It was found that teachers perceived that girls' (assumed) quietness and passivity was viewed as evidence of their growing maturity; it was an illustration of girls being able to control their behaviour. David, a music teacher at the school, is indicative of how teachers worked with the nature of maturity and immaturity:

David: I think it is obvious. The boys are somewhat immature ...

Chris: O.K. ... immature ...

David: Well they act silly, do stupid things, there is no difference between year 8 and year 6, they just play about ... mess about.

Chris: And the girls don't?

David: Well, I am not saying that they don't ... they are more quieter though. Yes. More mature. They are certainly developing ... their bodies are developing much faster ... There's a lad in year seven who is probably more physically mature than all of us! No ... they do have their odd 'dramatic', tears and that ... and they can be quite bitchy but they tow the line more.

Chris: So because the girls are less disruptive they are more mature?

David: No, I am not saying that ... you see ... its ... because the girls understand the rules more than the boys, they know how to live by them. The boys haven't got a clue.

Chris: What, all boys?

David: Not all of them. Some are more quieter – they are still children. Yet some like Abdul, he hasn't learnt how to behave properly, he hasn't adjusted.

Interestingly, the notion of quietness was ascribed different meanings according to the gender of the pupil. Therefore the boys' quietness was driven by their child status, whereas when girls demonstrated quietness, this was a sign of their growing maturity, which for the teacher was logically related to their physical development. Interestingly, when girls did disrupt classrooms, they were aligned with boys and their behaviour was often deemed 'unladylike'. As maturity and immaturity became the significant axes of pupil identities and cognitive capacities, good teaching was based on how to deal with these behaviours effectively. As a result, maturity and immaturity were not simply connected to gendered understandings but also imbricated notions of 'good' and 'bad' teaching. According to Baker (1995), schools could not function in their current manner without deploying the specific categories of childhood. This mutually dependent relationship between schooling and childhood frames, organizes and legitimates particular experiences within the school context. Forgetting pencil cases, not being able to answer questions, sitting in friendship groups, playing football and using the internet were among a whole plethora of practices that were explained and interpreted as indicative of their childlike behaviour and as a consequence were labelled as immature.

Of key importance is that teachers had an imagined understanding of what pupils should or should not do. The imaginary thus organized, arranged and distributed pupil practices across good and bad behaviours. Baker also suggests that:

> In the present this means our categorisations of child development, growth and abilities in relation to schooling (signified by labels like 'ready to learn', 'at risk', 'attention deficit disorder', 'emotionally disturbed' etc.) may owe less to 'nature' and more to how we interpret the young in relation to culturally specific ideals (1995: 10).

Similarly, it is argued that at Walcote West the institutional culture was dependent on understanding pupils *as* children, based upon dependence, protection, segregation and delayed responsibility (Aries, 1962). Work in this area by Walkerdine (1990) highlights how the emphasis on civility is also about transforming emotion into rationality. Thus, an indicator of child development is the transformation of childishness into rational think-ing marked by self-discipline and responsibility. She explains:

> The child is created as a sign, to be read and calibrated within pedagogic discourses regulating the classroom. The child is defined and mapped in its relations of similarity and difference with other signs: activity, experience, play rather that passivity, recitation, work and so forth. Through the regula-tion of this pedagogy children become subjected in the classroom (p. 25).

As Walkerdine suggests, the cultivation of childhood insists on the instantiation of a bourgeois individuality. Historically, a key aim of school-ing has been to cultivate a civility that would replace a presumed degener-acy. What Walkerdine is suggesting and what is evident in teachers' understandings of the maturity/immaturity couplet is a notion of the ideal adult. Thus, they judged and measured pupils' behaviours and practices through such an ideal of adulthood. Kunneman (1997) argues that adulthood is constituted by three facets:

1. The modern subject should be rational, acting and speaking logically.
2. The modern subject is marked by autonomy, being able to exercise such things as responsibility and independence.
3. The modern subject is marked by self-control, being able to manage individual desires and bodily impulses and needs.

Breaking down the notion of what constitutes maturity helps us to recon-sider what maturity is. Conventional educational research assumes that maturity and immaturity operate as pre-social qualities. With a whole range of (psychological) studies being conducted on what constitutes maturity (Galambos and Tilton-Weaver, 2000; Scheer and Palkovitz, 1994), it is not self-evident what it means. However, it is useful to situate maturity within the broader formation of modern English schooling. The reframing of education through a moral philosophy to one of a moral psychology resulted in self-governance and discipline as a sign of normality. According to Fendler (1998), the emergence of the modern schooling institution resulted in a transformation of power where individuals are no longer governed by an external force but through their own self-discipline. They argue that: 'The educated subject, then, became endowed with a new sort of power, namely, the power to govern itself' (p. 52). As a result, the individual who is self-disciplined is recognized as educated and civilized. In contrast, Fendler suggests that the inability to control oneself was a sign of the uneducated subject. Maturity thus became the symbolic material that was transferred onto the bodies of pupils to identify 'uneducated' behaviours. In other words, people who displayed a lack of maturity were those who had not learned the correct codes. This returns us to the start of this section that cited the work of Willis (1977). It is argued that gender is constituted through notions of maturity. It is also argued that maturity is closely connected to social class based understandings.

Finally, at Walcote West, categorizations based on the maturity/immaturity dichotomy deriving from the teaching culture also appeared to give shape to the pupil identifications. Unlike the teachers, who deployed the categories to identify good and bad pupils, the boys reconfigured maturity/immaturity to designate more sophisticated understandings of 'boyness'. It is suggested that although the teachers attempt to communicate norms of maturity, the pupils recognizing the institutional grounding of these norms, reconfigure their meaning into their own peer, culturally led understandings. Thus, notions of maturity–immaturity had different counter-cultural resonances. For example, various practices that the boys engaged in were given shape through a reconfiguration of the dominant meaning system. Ian and Danny outline how such social values coded boys' practices:

> *Chris:* You talked about there being different groups of boys, how would you describe those differences?
>
> *Ian:* Well, there is like popular like Gary and Lucas …
>
> *Danny:* … and then there is freaks, geeks and nerds.
>
> *Chris:* Can you give me an example of what the popular boys might do?
>
> *Danny:* Play football, be loud, get into trouble …
>
> *Ian:* … naughty.

Chris: Geeks?

Ian: Well, they go on about Pokemon and WWF wrestling and all that ...

Danny: ... and they follow all the teachers round and do all the little jobs for the teachers and everything.

Ian: Do their library monitoring or something ...

Chris: Freaks?

Danny: They are the way out ones, like monsters ... walk around going mad ...

Ian: Like weirdo's ... you don't know what they are going to do next ...

Danny: ... pretty unpredictable ... start punching you for no reason.

Chris: ... and the nerds ... ?

Ian: ... they are like into their computers, playing games like ... you know Half – Life or Counterstrike ...

Danny: They don't play football ... they try and get in the library on the computers at dinnertime ... they are just sad.

Thus differentiated understandings of 'boyness' were operating across the reinterpretation of codes of maturity. Consequently, those practices that may have been deemed mature, through their correspondence with particular school norms by the teachers, were projected as immature by certain boys. In this analysis, the pupils acknowledge how social value can be reconstructed on their own terms. In doing so, there is a struggle for meaning.

Chris: Would you say that there are differences between year 8 and year 6?

Achiou: No, not wiv' the others ... the popular boys yes ... they are more mature [in an upper class accent].

Chris: What does mature mean?

Achiou: They just want to play wiv ... talk to their friends about computing, wrestling ... they have no respect ...

Chris: Respect – what are you trying to say?

Achiou: For themselves – can't they see that we all laugh at them ...

Chris: But they don't seem to care about what you think ...

Achiou: I know, I know look at Teymour ... I say to him that he is a stinking Indian and he goes 'yes thank you'.

Chris: But why should they care?

Achiou: 'Cos ... they need to grow up ...

Chris: But why?

Achiou: ... 'Cos they are geeks ...

Chris: Yeah, you have said that ... but why ... why should they do what you want them to do ... ?

Achiou: It is not just us is it ... why are they here? They are here ...
here ... They come to school, to learn, learning and they ain't
learning ... they ain't learning how to grow up, they mess around
with their action figures and play football with bottle tops ... they
ain't got none.

One of the themes that emerges from the interviews with Achiou was his
use of ethnicity to simultaneously mark age and gender. Thus he positions
Teymour (Iranian) as Indian, as a means to activate feminized ascriptions.
In turn, this simultaneously operates as a marker of childishness. The
implication here is that Achiou situates teachers' versions of maturity
within codes of 'childlike' and 'feminine'. With the use of accent, he articulates the importance of class as another parameter through which gender
and age interplay. Thus Achiou's meanings not only offer interpretations
about what it is to be mature and immature, but also definitions of being a
good (real) boy.

Boys without Masculinity

Recent theorizing on gender in contemporary social theory has suggested
that the concept of masculinity can be considered as a way of explaining
boys' behaviours in schools. Work by Renold (2000) has sought to examine
how boys behave in the context of primary schools. Drawing upon Mac an
Ghaill's (1994a) explanation of how masculinities in secondary school are
constituted, Renold claims that boys in primary schools constitute their
masculinities through 'misogynistic and homophobic discourses, and heterosexual fantasies' (ibid.: 321). Therefore, in order to achieve their masculinity, boys are involved in symbolic sexual exchanges, public sexual
innuendoes, sexual storytelling and sexual objectification of girls. This corresponds with a broader 'cultural rule' in British/English gender identity
formations, where sexuality operates as an important component in constituting the nature of men's identities. Thus, for Renold, within the English
cultural logic of masculinity, boys continually tried to secure a hegemonic
masculinity that resulted in the 'tenuous' production and projection of
their heterosexuality.

In contrast, fieldwork, interviews and audio diaries from Haywood's
(2006) study examines pupil identities that did not actively appeal to a
(hetero) sexual matrix. In other words, projected and intrajected identifications were not cohered through discourses of (hetero) sexuality (in many
cases they repudiated heterosexuality) (Hollway, 1998). Rather, boyhood
identifications were made through cultural resources that appealed to
childhood rather than adult codes of mature masculinity. For example, a

number of practices enacting fighting, playing on computer games, and collecting play cards drew upon masculine practices but did not identify with or aspire to a mature masculinity. It is argued that gender identities are constituted differently according to age dynamics. It is further argued that masculinity and heterosexuality are lived out differently between other age groups. This is not to suggest that heterosexual styles, ideas, representations and practices do not operate at school; studies suggest that they do. Or that notions and types of masculinity (such as those demonstrated by groups of girls and teachers) are not available. Instead, it is argued that there are possibilities of alternative ways of considering the nature of gendered identities in primary schools that does not resort to adult gender and sexual styles. As indicated in Chapter 1, Butler (1990) maintains that masculinity and femininity are embedded within the heterosexual matrix where the demonstration of coherent masculinities and femininities operate to secure this matrix. However, we suggest that pupils do not necessarily draw upon an adult version of heterosexuality as a key constituent of their gendered identities. Therefore, the interplay between gender and sexuality that secures adult masculinities and femininities may not be appropriate. Furthermore, claims by educationalists that suggest that the alternative possibilities of sexual identities reside in the identification with gay and lesbian sexualities, simply inverts the argument and continues to disengage from the potentially transforming interplay between age, gender and sexuality (Epstein, 1997; Garlick, 2003).

In exploring these issues, this section returns to the research that we have conducted in a middle school in the northeast of England (Haywood, 2006). In this context, it appeared that boys' identifications operated outside an adult-led British/English socially acceptable masculinity. Such a masculinity is supported and constituted through heterosexuality. In contrast, these pupils' identifications with boyness – that of a knowledge of cars, competence at football, ability to use computers and understanding of wrestling – did not include an ordering of 'boyness' through ascribed overt sexual codes. Thus, the demonstration of heterosexuality was not always a conditional access to boyness, and boys' identities were not dependent on the demonstration and projection of heterosexuality. In this way the constitutive nature of boyness at Walcote West suggests that existing notions of masculinity founded on adult notions of heterosexuality may be working with conceptually simplistic, adult-led categories. As Frank *et al.* (2003: 129) suggests:

> Rather than yet another attempt to explain why boys and men do what they do, and a re-determination to 'fix up' the practice of masculinity, with much of our own work (Frank, 1987, 1990, 1991), we want to begin to tease apart some of our contracted ways of knowing which continue to organise and

regulate our thinking and our action as men (Kimmel, 1987b), giving a certainty to boys' and men's lives that is, in fact, not there.

It is argued that Butler's concept of the heterosexual matrix (see ch. 1), does not make sense in this particular social and cultural arena. Such a framework does provide productive explanations in arenas where the possibilities of sexuality and gender identities *are* possibilities. Not only do possibilities have to exist, they warrant through their contextual specificity a claim to stabilization; gender performativity instantiates identities. In this schooling arena, the discourse of childhood stabilized through the gender regime, does not allow the possibility of an authentic (hetero) sexuality. Indeed what appears prominent are a series of sexualizations that do not appear to give coherency to an underlying masculinity premised on a public heterosexuality.

Furthermore, not only did the boys reject heterosexuality they often articulated homoerotic positions. Nayak and Kehily (1997) highlight the extreme dis-identifications with homoeroticism, demonstrating how boys in their study used homophobia as a means to construe the stability and authenticity of their heterosexuality. They linked the position of the homoerotic to pupil metaphors of disease and contagion. Touching and being in contact with that which is deemed homosexual was highly policed by themselves and others. For example they suggest that: 'The complex social make up of masculinities sees many young men using homophobias to conceal uncertainties and attempt to assert a cohesive identity' (p. 17). However, in Walcote West, there was an absence of this publicly defined link between homophobia and heterosexuality; the boys appeared to take up and speak homoerotic positions. Although the talk may have a number of functions that includes institutional resistance, consolidating friendships or humorous performance, this discursive position continues to be deemed 'normal' and popular. The research in Walcote West provided another reading of this situation:

Darren: Sir, I think I am in love with you.
Colin: Yeah, sir, sir, Bret has got a crush on you.

No response

Darren: (in a soft quiet voice) Please don't dump me, not after all we have been through.

No response

Colin: He's a right one isn't he? Build you up knock you down ...
Darren: Yeah ... fucked and chucked ... Who's next? Hey Achiou ...
Teacher: Brett can I help you? (Class laugh) Will you stop messin' around? Have you completed your homework diary?

Fieldnotes

Screams from the back of the library

Thomas: (laughing) … help … help … help   he's   trying   to   wank
     me … arhhg …
Craig: … it is so small … has anyone got any tweezers … giv' it ere!

Fieldnotes

Thomas: Oh Craig – let me suck your toes. I need to suck your toes.
Craig: Please do, please, do oh god you are sooo good.

Audio diary

In her conceptually sensitive research on primary school children's gender and sexuality, Thorne (1993) suggests that: 'A sense of the whole, and the texture and dynamism of interaction, become lost when collapsed into dualisms like large versus small, hierarchical versus intimate, agency versus communion, and competitive versus co - operative' (p.108). It could be argued that masculinity and femininity also fit into the available dualisms, and as a result, studies in this area have tended to lose the subtlety of the social dynamics in schooling arenas. Existing literature that examines boys' identities too easily slides into gendered categories where boys construct their identities as a 'masculinity'. These studies also suggest that central to this organizing frame of masculinity is a notion of the sexual. An analytical move in this chapter has been to counter the insistence of an ascribed understanding of gender by dialectically using age. This is because in most of the above studies, age does not interconnect with gender categories. This means that, regardless of how old pupils are, they can be attributed a masculinity and femininity where sexual forms unproblematically emerge.

This section has considered the interplay between gender and age within the context of schooling. It has suggested that in order grasp the nature of gender relations, it is important to locate them within a local and situational context. This next section thus shifts the focus and argues that the interplay of gender and age should be considered at a broader social and cultural level. It does this by examining femininity and ageing, issues surrounding the menopause and the recent proliferation of lifestyle enhancing techniques.

'Don't You Know You're Not Supposed to ask a Woman Her Age?': Exploring Femininity and Older Age

In the previous section, the interplay between age and gender in the school can be seen as operating through notions of maturity and immaturity.

Furthermore, conventional approaches to the study of gender and childhood appear to attribute adult versions of how gender is constituted in children. In this section, we explore the broader cultural dynamic of older age and femininity. In particular, the cultural etiquette of later modern western society suggests that older women should be treated with a particular social protocol. It appears to be premised on a broader western cultural anxiety concerning older women and their relationship to femininity. It should be added that much work in the area often tends to be from a western perspective. Work such as that carried out on the matrifocal families in the Caribbean highlights how the cultural context is an important shaper and organizer of the meanings of age (Smith, 2003). It is important to reinforce the point. It is argued that there is no causal link between meanings of age and female bodies. Rather it is the meanings ascribed to age that determine the status of women in various social and cultural contents. It is argued in this section that western societies tend to demonstrate a cultural anxiety with older women's lives. It is an anxiety that has a social history of normalization that has regulated and controlled women's lives. Banner (1993) provides an in-depth account of how ageing women have been identified, explained and treated. Early medieval sources talk about older women as 'go betweens'. On one hand, according to Banner, there was the woman who enables the relationship between younger men and women to take place due to her wisdom and knowledge, on the other, was a sexual procurer – a messenger of the devil's work. She argues that rather than being literal types, these characterizations were representative of particular women's lifestyles. They operated to reflect actual sexualized class differences between women, such as the 'guardian older women' and the older 'madame'. The suggested focus on some older women being connected to witchcraft highlights that they may have operated as the cultural other to the rest of society.

One aspect that this research highlights is how folk tales and stories rely upon the exterior body as a bearer of social and cultural status and value. Thus, the exterior became the revelation of the essential nature of the self. Interestingly, the moral essence of a person was revealed by the physical state. It has been argued that historically age has been a cultural resource through which a relationship to morality and spiritual life has operated. More recently, other cultural figures have replaced the witch and the madame. For example, figures such as the 'Mother – in – Law' and 'meddling old women' are caricatures through society which can regulate acceptable and appropriate gender and age practices. Thus, the perception of older age disfigurement has become an indication of moral impropriety. The question posed by Sontag in the late 1970s, *Don't you know you're not supposed to ask a woman her age?* continues to resonate with the notion of social value and perceptions of the body. More recently, chronological age has also become an important indicator of social values. The implication is that chronological age reveals the possibilities of femininities and the attendant designation of what particular women can and cannot do, how they should look and how they should desire. Conventionally, there is less value attached to older than younger women's. Therefore, Sontag's question plays on gendered trauma and the anxiety that emerges from particular aged strata in society. This means that not revealing age is partly based on a need to defend themselves against social ascriptions that age carries. She explains how society is increasingly attributing notions of energy, vitality, appetite and fecundity to younger people. She argues that unlike non-industrial societies, western societies in particular are obsessed by numbers. This is in contrast to men:

> 'Masculinity' is identified with competence, autonomy, self – control – qualities which the disappearance of youth does not threaten. Competence in most of the activities expected from men, physical sports excepted, increases with age. 'Femininity' is identified with incompetence, helplessness, passivity, non-competitiveness, being nice. Age does not improve these qualities. Sontag (1978: 73–4)

Age chronology operates as a social marker that disseminates meanings and understandings about gender. Sontag suggests that this is most clearly seen through romantic relationships, where it is socially unacceptable for older women to have relationships with younger men and women. Yet in contrast, older men having relationships with younger men and women are deemed to embellish their masculinity. Therefore, chronological age pushes women into particular forms of sexual regulation. Thus the candidacy for sexual intimacy is restricted by strong social markers that designate women's 'sexual validity'. Hence, this validity, according to Sontag, is dependent on how well they negotiate the markers of ageing.

It is suggested that one of the reasons for the traumatic experience of growing older is that women's social value is intricately defined by notions of beauty. In western society, beauty is often connected and articulated through notions of youthfulness. The connection between femininity, beauty and youthfulness offers women a precarious status. Given that beauty and youth are perishable values, they will have a detrimental effect on femininity. Whereas 'Male power, embedded in status and wealth tends to increase, not diminish, with age. The impact on identity of these diminished assets of female identity is undeniable' (Powell and Longino, 2002: 223).

The notion of the centrality of women's physical appearance to their femininity is explored further by Fairhurst (1998), who provides empirical data to suggest that growing older for women is a traumatic experience. Fairhurst selected women, 18 of whom were attending a menopause clinic, and 16 who were attending a Well Woman clinic. All her participants were aged over fifty and all were married. At the same time, her research is also supported by interviews with 24 men, who were the women's partners. During the research, it became apparent that women regulated themselves and other women by commenting on how well women managed the ageing process. One of the regulative norms operating with these women was the aim to avoid being, 'mutton dressed as lamb'. According to Fairhurst, the phrase itself has a number of connotations. Culturally, younger sheep are deemed tastier than mutton and points to the value of being younger. At the same time, Fairhurst does not explore the implicit coding of deceit that is also carried through the phrase. The assumption is like the chef in the restaurant trying to dress mutton as lamb, women are also trying unsuccessfully to 'dress' as a means to avoid or contest the 'reality' of their identities. In western societies age has emerged as an objective index of men's and women's 'real' gender identity that is often contained within the claim that men's and women should 'act their age'. Trying to avoid being labelled in this way entails the negotiation of wearing 'teenage' clothes, wearing too much jewellery, heavy make-up, pencil skirts and high heels. Fairhurst uses the practice of dyeing hair as a means to demonstrate the detail through which women's self-presentation takes place. Thus, in this sample, some interpretations were based on hair colour – if the hair was dyed black, then women were perceived to have 'gone too far'.

The most acceptable way through which to manage the ageing process for these women was by 'growing old gracefully'. Coded within this perspective was the need for women to make the most of who they were without 'going' over the top. This self-management and reflexivity became important measures of women's management of the ageing process. In response, Fairhurst found that women often used younger people, such as their children, as judges of whether they had gone too far (see also Beck, 1992). This forms the first of three main themes about the inevitability of ageing. The second theme was the fear that ageing induced in her sample. In comparison to the men that she interviewed, Fairhurst argues that women tended to fear ageing more than men. It is suggested that this fear is generated by women holding pictures in their minds of how old people looked. In contemporary society older people are associated with death, danger, decline and disease. Isaksen (2002) highlights that descriptions of older age focus on bodily failure where the body often becomes a code for the person. Thus, a failing body is also an inadequate person. Furthermore, the privacy that is ascribed to the bodily functions (often through notions of civility, Elias, 1978) is broken down through physical decay: 'The body occupies a territory in which language is problematic, awkwardly polarized between the medical clinical and vulgar demonic'(Isaksen, 2002: 794). Finally, the third aspect of the subjective experience of ageing was the separation of sex and the body. As Paetcher (1998: 50) argues: 'The body is not just constructed by discourse; we experience the world and perform our genders with the bodies that we happen to have'. Importantly, for Fairhurst, older women suggested that they felt that although the body may be ageing, their self-identities were not. This connects with Hepworth and Featherstone's (1998) notion of the 'age mask', referring to the idea that although the body changes, self-perceptions remain the same. Body modification, can in some cases be understood as a process of adjusting the body to meet the subjective experience of age. If, as the perspectives above argue that women's gender identity is connected to old age, then body modification may continue to be taken up by older women.

It is argued however that the interplay of gender and age is also marked by other social categories. Work by Wray (2003) focuses on how existing understandings of ageing are premised on a western ideology. Her comparative work with 170 women aged between 60 and 80 years involved talking to women from a range of ethnic backgrounds including English, African Caribbean and Bangladeshi. Wray argues that conventional gerontological studies posit older women through meanings of decrepitude, poor housing and independence. However, such values are premised on the notion that freedom and individual self-sufficiency are attributes to be valued. Traditional studies on ageing have used these meanings to measure ageing processes. Thus, central to these meanings according to Wray, are middle-class western values and she insists that there is a need for studies on age and gender to move away from economic resources as a measure of ageing, arguing, 'Such an approach is based on Western ideologies of individualism and the responsibility of individuals to care for themselves and exist independently rather than inter-dependant with others' (ibid.: 524). Existing studies of ageing tend to deploy biomedical and welfare meanings to measure ageing, whereas Wray suggests that such indices reinforce western concepts of ageing.

It is also pertinent to consider not only the national/ethnic dynamics of women's ageing but also the class dynamic. The issues surrounding the negotiation of the ageing process are severely marked by class position (Gullette, 1997; Sontag, 1979). It is suggested that higher-class women have relatively sheltered lives, a balanced diet, good medical support with fewer children and have the economic means to negotiate ageing. In response to the retraditionalization of femininity, Andrews (2003) argues that in contemporary society the boundaries that surround age are becoming more fluid. She argues that in contrast to aristocratic and working-class women, middle-class womanhood had a historical location as 'sexless'. The identity of female, it is argued, was based upon a sexual being that was conflated with a family role of wife and mother. More recently, Andrews argues, that the media in particular is representing older women as being independent and adventurous. An example of this has been the phenomena of Calendar Girls. This was where members of the Women's Institute in the United Kingdom stripped naked for a charity-raising calendar. It is argued that older women are beginning to take part in new forms of domesticity, especially in the context where private consumption is becoming publicly conspicuous.

One of the main issues to emerge out of ageing and femininity is their relationship to sexuality. The next section provides a sustained consideration of how the interplay of gender and ageing are reconfiguring the meanings ascribed to femininity. It does this first by focusing on the menopause.

Ageing, Femininity and the Sexualization of the Menopause

One of the key features in western cultures that marks the 'entrance' of women into older age is the onset of the menopause. Much work in this area focuses on the presumed physical effects of stopping menstruation.[2] According to Winterich (2003) studies of the menopause have been based upon a quantitative approach that tries to objectively establish its nature, irrespective of the subjectivities, status and location of women. In contrast, another way of understanding the menopause is to consider it as a 'rite of passage'. What has become important is the menopause has emerged as a significant marker of social identity through its connections to reproduction and conventional understandings of women's sexuality. It is argued that that women's identities have been defined through their relationship to their reproductive roles (Gullette, 1997). Thus, it is suggested that reproduction is a central feature of women's identities in society and that such physiological events have a central part in the establishing of femininities. Importantly, this chapter does not wish to reinforce the connection between femininity and the menopause, rather it focuses on it as an example of how age as a cultural ideology operates to frame a physiological event.

Work on the menopause has highlighted historical and cross-cultural variability of interpretations that are applied to this physiological phenomenon. Historical explanations of the menopause suggested that human bodies were connected to nature and that they were regulated through heat or humours (Martin, 1987). Banner (1993) highlights how early interpretations of the menopause was connected to witchcraft. In Medieval Europe, menstruation was seen as a means of purging the evil that would generate immorality. The comparison that Banner draws is of that between menstruation and bloodletting – a main means of dealing with illness. Although implicating a wide range of social and religious stigma, menstruation was ultimately seen as a necessary condition for women. As a result, the menopause was a sign of potential danger because without cyclical bloodletting, evil would build up in the body. Banner provides a fascinating coverage of how the menopause was referred to throughout English history. In the seventeenth century, she suggests that menopause was called the 'end of flowers'; flowers were deemed as a symbol of beauty. It was also called a 'dodging time'. This, it is suggested, indicates that women concealed the fact that they were no longer productive. In the nineteenth century, menstruation began to be associated with flushing and purging. Such conceptions of the menopause take place, according to Martin (1994), because dominant cultural ways of thinking organized how such physiological phenomena could be understood. Martin argues that with the onset of industrialization, the metaphors of heat began to be replaced by metaphors of commerce. The body became one of saving and expenditure, thus loss and gain became the means through which physiological processes became (de) valued. Thus, Martin maintains that the medical profession dealt with the body through ideas of 'spending'.

Two forms of understanding that were to emerge from this initial approach to the menopause was that it was a pathological condition leading to the descent of the health of the body and that it was also a state of good health. Therefore, medical opinion was divided in the early twentieth century, as the menopause was either a time of illness or a time of release or freedom. The implication of this was that women's bodies began to be conceived through the metaphor of an institution. Through various medical texts, Martin details the various institutions that have been used as metaphors to explain how the body works. One of these institutional metaphors has been that of the factory and the implication that the life course is connected to the body as a production process. From this position, a healthy body is a productive body, with production being the ascendant term. Thus, inability to produce is considered as a state of ill-health. What is central to Martin's analysis is that there is no logical connection between physiological capacity, production and waste. For example, she highlights how during intercourse, millions of spermatozoa are involved in reproduction and as a consequence there are phenomenal levels of wastage. Yet, such a process is often described in terms of a competition or a natural evolutionary process. The notion of waste is rarely mentioned in medical textbooks.

What is significant, are the ways that medical professionals ascribe metaphors that correspond to traditional notions of femininity and masculinity. More recently, communication metaphors have become central to explaining the menopause; the ageing body in this context is seen as a failing signalling system. For example, the system of communication is described in a medical textbook:

From the first menstrual cycle to the menopause, the hypothalamus acts as the conductor of a highly trained orchestra. Once its baton signals the downbeat of the pituitary, the hypothalamus – pituitary – ovarian axis is united in purpose and begins to play its symphonic message, preparing a woman's body for conception and child bearing (Martin, 1994: 41)

Contemporary medical textbooks explain that the onset of the menopause is a failed communication. Poor communication or 'message response' generates confusion for the body. Consequently, the menopause is described as a result of an unresponsive body, whose functions have failed to maintain patterns of communication. Hence, physiology is described through adjectives of decline, atrophy, shrinkage and disturbance. This can be highlighted by the World Health Organisation in 1981 describing menopause as an 'oestrogen – deficiency disorder'. The important point in this section is that such medical explanations are not socially neutral. In other words, these dominant explanations are framing women's lifestyles as highly connected to their reproductive stages. As Gannon (1999: 69) has aptly suggested, such frameworks argue that 'Women don't have problems, women are the problem.'

From a cultural studies approach, Gullette (1997) argues that the menopause has become a major cultural phenomenon. Her research suggests that in the United States there has been traditionally relatively little coverage of the menopause. However, since 1994 there has been a 'menoboom' that has witnessed the proliferation of the dissemination of information, advice, stories and discussion of this phenomenon. According to Gullette, the timing of this 'menoboom' has not only been determined by demography and marketing, but importantly by a male backlash. The male backlash is a result of women reaching middle years and getting more access to positions of power and access to cultural goods. The implication is that older women are gaining equality in areas of life that traditionally have been the sole province of men. As a result: 'midlife women get hit with middle-ageism in the form of widespread public menopause discourse, male science that assumes we've got a "deficiency disease", and male commerce that sells us the supposed remedies' (p. 101). The result is that women's life course history is divided into two halves by this 'magic marker' event. Significantly, women's ageing has become loaded with risk and danger.

According to Gullette, there is currently a war taking place over the discursive representation of menopause. The pharmaceutical industry, biomedical practitioners, beauty product companies and media sponsored experts are emphasizing the risks and physical implications of the menopause. They are presenting the argument that, in order to reduce the loss of beauty, osteoporosis, sexual discomfort, bone fractures and heart disease, women must consume their products. As Gullette argues, it is not clear how menopause generates such conditions and how such conditions can be separated out from broader lifestyle practices. What can be ascertained is that the menopause has generated a series of meanings that not only restricts the experience of the menopause but is emerging as something that is 'demeaning and terrifying':

> no other cohort, male or female, at any age, gets told a future – health-risk story like this. We do not tell girls of eleven, for example, that the childbirth ... [involves] miscarriage, edema, episiotomy and loss of sexual pleasure, caesarean sections, malformed or diseased children; magazine articles don't tell pregnant women all the things that might go wrong in labor (ibid.: 108).

At the same time, the remedy to solve the problems of menopause has come in the form of hormonal replacement therapy (HRT). Yet, according to Gullette, the dangers and the effects of HRT have not been clearly explored in terms of increasing heart disease and breast cancer. However, other research by Roberts (2004) have identified how HRT has been seen as a 'cure' for the unnatural and disabling menopause.

According to Roberts, the menopause has become a 'condition'. In this way, the onset of the menopause is increasingly being understood by medical professionals as unnatural. However, this physiological unnatural event is also understood as a cross-cultural phenomenon. One of the developments in medical research has been to explore the claims that western women are more likely to experience the menopause than non-western women. Moreover, Oudshorn (1994) argues that there is incredible variability between women regarding their chemical cyclicity, as women in non-industrialized communities tend to report less incidence of menopause. Citing evidence drawn from the *British Medical Journal* (BMJ), Roberts identifies research that suggests the reason western women are more likely to experience the menopause is that they have been removed from their natural environment. In short, social modernization and industrialization have created the menopause. Consequently, women, it is argued, will experience increasing amounts of unnatural medical conditions. The menopause, from this perspective, operates as a social or environmental consequence. In order to treat this 'condition', medical practitioners should use hormone replacement as an antidote to this unnatural lifestyle. Conceptually, Roberts argues that this is a chiasmus, a grammatical feature where the order of words in one phrase is inverted in the other. She gives the example of 'He saved others; himself he could not save.' In the context of the menopause, Roberts argues that this physiological process is deemed as naturally occurring through the possibility of sexual difference, whilst at the same time, it is a product of socialization. It is argued that: 'bodies have become transformed into objects that can be manipulated with an ever - growing number of tools and techniques' (ibid.: 5) and thus subject to a social imagination. The implication here, as Roberts usefully points out, is that the necessity of HRT is dependent on definitions of femininity.

From research presented in the BMJ 1992 special edition on HRT, Roberts found that menopause was associated with affluent populations. Reeve (1992), one of the contributors argued that menopause could be deemed to generate bone fractures and heart disease for western women. Therefore, HRT is likely to make women more healthy. The chiasmus is clear – the absence of the impact of menopause on women in less industrialized societies becomes an argument to support the renaturalization of women through HRT. Roberts cites the work of gynaecologist and medical anthropologist Wilbush (1994), who suggests that pre-modern women's reproductive roles were central to their lifestyles. He argues that modern women's relationship to reproduction has significantly changed; reproduction is no longer a central feature of women's lives. Thus, practices such as contraception entail the removal from a natural environment:

> As far as it is possible to conjecture, female Homo erectus, or early sapiens, even women in pre-industrial societies and many today, one basic feature: they were and are, most of their lives, either pregnant or breast feeding. Modern western women are not and do not, instead they menstruate (ibid.: 344, cited in Roberts, 36).

Wilbush argues therefore, in order to avoid the menopause and make women more healthy, women should be given HRT. At the same time, another reason for giving women HRT is the association with youthfulness. It is suggested that giving HRT reduces women's anxiety over loss of beauty, something Wilbush identifies as genetically distinct. As Roberts succinctly points out, there is a juxtaposition with the menopause as socially constructed and beauty as genetic!

Men and Ageing

While the previous section highlights how reproduction impacts upon age and femininity, this section examines how sexuality is implicated in the understandings that circulate through men and ageing. One of the developing themes of this chapter has been the use of metaphor. Earlier, we saw how in Martin's (1994) work metaphors shaped the conceptualization of the body. Metaphors, according to Lakoff and Johnson (1980), shape our understandings of reality. Hockey and James (1993) argue that metaphorical devices are central to how we understand and make sense of different categories of age. They assert:

> Thus, the metaphoric repertoire of a given society is drawn specifically from the range of the familiar, some terms being foregrounded, others discarded. Through such choices, then, particular, culturally specific accounts of that which is unknown or problematic are created. Old age is such an instance, and, crucially, it is within this process of selection that power can be exercised (1993: 40).

Here, age is marked by the use of spatial and motion metaphors. Gullette (1997) in relation to older age has particularly focused on the metaphor of entrance, age categories being something that are entered into. Hepworth (1999), highlighting the importance of such spatial and motion metaphors, suggests that these operate as a means of looking at age through a positivist framework. In this way, age operates as a distinct object that is observable with identifiable points of entrance and exit. The impact of these strategies is that they designate gendered life stages. Consequently, gender identities are transformed by the meanings that age stages carry.

At a popular level, there have been a number of metaphorical connections between chronological age and masculinity. In other words, the size of the abdomen, thinning hair and wrinkled skin indicate certain ways of being a man. It appears that in contrast to women, ageing is considered as enhancing men's social power rather than detracting from it. Hearn's (1995) account of ageing and masculinity suggests that such characteristics were once signs of maturity and wealthiness. He suggests that the meanings ascribed to older age are generational. First, what this means is that the source of men's power has been the patrilineal distribution of material resources through generations. Hearn argues that recent social and economic changes have fractured the idea that the source of men's power is the ownership of material resources. Rather, power now appears to be articulated through the ownership and management of the body. Second, a more complex picture emerges when the body as a central definer of masculinity is being redefined through rationality. Thus, with an increasing valorization of rationality, the potential labour power of the body is no longer a major resource of identity. A further social trend has been the impact of demographic factors. Retirement is creating a sub-class of men that is impacting upon another recent trend concerning men: the modernization of death. According to Hearn, older men are now being considered as 'pre-death' – they have become an invisible social group no longer productive in terms of paid work but also surplus to family responsibility. Further changes involve the redistribution of the law of the father to the law of the state (see ch. 2). This means that the traditional resources of power based upon the rule of the father have been exchanged for one where the state has taken up the exercise of power. Finally, Hearn suggests that consumerism has impacted upon the gendered nature of ageing in the way that is reshaping the categories between older and younger men. However, Hearn is clear that the dynamic of this redistribution of the age resources remains a patriarchal process:

> Indeed it is the very hegemonic power of certain men that undermines older men (and in a different way younger men) through ageism – the power and oppression of age. Accordingly, older men despite and because of their con-tradictory social power may subvert dominant constructions of men and masculinities. (p.113)

In short, as argued by Bauman (1992) men's older identities have been premised upon a 'rightful and secure position in society' (p. 26). According to Hearn, this secure position is being fragmented as age has become a new source of risk to men and their masculinity.

It is suggested that the interplay between gendered identities and age ascriptions in many ways come together to produce a series of discursive possibilities about how age and gender work together. It is argued that this interplay is also articulating itself within the context of the changing nature of the reflexive self. In other words, Markson and Taylor (2000: 137) argue that there has been a turn to visual culture where: 'During the 20th century, the work ethic of early capitalist culture has been transformed into a consumer culture – from "I am what hard work I do" to "I am what I can buy".'

Thus, there may be a particular impact on men and the changing relationship that they are having with their bodies (see, ch. 6). At the same time, Davis (2002: 59) argues that 'The body is something to be ignored, denied or, at least kept firmly out of sight.' It is suggested that for men in western societies, age has been a source of power and respect. Sontag's (1978) highly influential essay made clear that part of the double bind of ageing has been the normalization of femininity and its ascribed value depend upon women's demonstration of natural youthfulness and beauty. The implication of this is that men do not worry about their bodies, given that masculinity is not connected to aesthetics. However, Gullette argues that there has been a cultural change. The traditional pre-occupation and intervention on the ageing body as a means to mediate normal identity is also being taken up by men. However, as Powell and Longino (2002: 224) point out 'men become embodied as they get older.' Therefore, Gullette points out that the cultural traps that women have fallen into are also being laid for men: At the end of the twentieth century, we find ourselves entering a new cultural situation where the body intersects the middle years, traditional norms are being crossed, stereotypes of middle ageing are sliding around with alarming looseness (ibid.: 139).

Gullette maintains that middle age is becoming confusing and problematic for both men and women. The dynamic for this has been a commercialization of men's identities that has men succumbing to the cult of youth and the double standard of ageing is becoming more fragmented. 'Historically, preoccupation with appearance has been gendered feminine, whilst freedom from this bondage has been gendered male' (Haiken, 2000: 394). However, a range of changes have begun to impact on this such as divorce, the rise in visual culture and the increasing number of older men returning to employment.

At the same time, Davis (2002) highlights that men are now the growth market in terms of plastic surgery. In 1998, men made up 10 per cent of those undertaking plastic surgery. According to Miller (2005), this translates as at least 800,000 each year in the United States undergoing cosmetic surgery. As such, it is argued that men are therefore enhancing their masculinities through practices that have previously been associated with women and femininity. It appears that men's participation in cosmetic surgery has been a challenge to the conventional understandings that 'real men' do not care about how they look. Haiken (2000) has mapped out how historically cosmetic surgery was developed in response to integrating men back into society and making them more economically active. In this way, manhood was equated with economic productiveness. War injuries were deemed to remove this by reducing men's market value. However, plastic surgeons continue to view men with suspicion, as plastic surgery is associated with effeminacy and narcissism. The language of plastic surgery contains metaphors of the domestic such as 'stitching', 'draping', 'ironing out' and 'tidying' and has been overwhelmingly associated with women. Davis suggests that because of the focus on the body surgery itself is an affront to a dominant masculine view of the self; plastic surgery puts the body into view. Thus, the feminine values that are ascribed to plastic surgery, in the context of men, is that the reconfiguring of the body is a non-rational admittance of shame.

Another key definer of normal masculinity in western societies has been sexual performance. Sexual performance has been a central aspect with both heterosexual and gay identified men. Historically, men's sexual desire has been located in a number of areas such as their essential spirituality, men's relationship to industrialization and their biological body. Marshall and Katz (2002) identify how the logic of investment metaphors, as indicated above by Martin, have impacted upon male sexual performance. Historically, masculinity is firmly connected with sexual performance, with lack of ability to sexually perform, indicating a failure of masculinity, or the loss of it. Through the notion of saving and spending of semen, men could achieve potency:

> By reasoning that the sex glands contained the essence of masculinity and that old age was a state of depletion of these glands, the rejuvenations promised to restore manhood itself to ageing men who feared that they had lost the ability to function as men within the modern world (ibid.: 293).

However, during the twentieth century, a number of ways of understanding men's sexual performance occurred. First, ageing became characterized by pathological processes; it was an induced process of physical frailty. Second, physical frailty was connected to sexual function, with older men becoming susceptible to sexual incapacity. Alongside this there is the more positive portrayal of older men of wisdom and experience. At the same time, the relationship to men and sexual functioning has taken on a psychological dimension, where sexual incapacity has become reconfigured as an age-related erectile dysfunction. However, what has emerged during the latter half of the twentieth century has been an index of masculinity embedded in the performance of the penis and the ability to gain and maintain erections.

Culturally, older age men have been characterized with greater potential for sexual inadequacy. Such ideas were concretized by the work of the sexologists Masters and Johnston in the 1960s. Their research on sexual response provided a model that has become a standardized method of explaining sexual behaviours. Potts (2004) argues that this work established what constituted normal sexual response: that of arousal, plateau, orgasm and resolution. The impact of this notion of sexual response is that those men who do not correspond to this cycle have to be treated. For example, the strength of an erection has been considered an index of the quality of manhood: 'Masculine sexuality is predominantly portrayed as ever-ready, always willing and desirous, powered by surging hormones and uncontrollable urges' (ibid.: 24). Therefore, male sexuality is unproblematic, there should be no tension between feeling sexual and practicing it. However, older age has been seen as reconfiguring this relationship. One response to this reconfiguration has been the introduction of medication to alter this process, famously through the use of Viagra®.[3] The taking of Viagra® not only reestablishes evidence of masculinity, it provides the possibilities of a particular lifestyle. The emergence of medical discourses to identify and explain the nature of male erections has resulted in traditional pumps, injections and prosthesis being labelled artificial and synthetic. The Viagra® narrative connects with the modernist narrative that insists that in order to be a modern subject a person has to have control over their body and their bodily functions. Viagra® is thus marketed as a means of regaining control over the body.

Pharmaceuticals, such as Viagra®, depend upon the recreation of the 'perfect' and ideal sexual scenario. This ideal scenario consists of heterosexual penetrative sex as a measure of normal functioning. Empirical research carried out in New Zealand by Potts (2004) helps us explore this in greater depth. She interviewed 33 men and 27 women on the social impact of drugs like Viagra®. These men reported that they were experiencing erectile dysfunction. The participants came from a range of backgrounds; the majority were of European descent and heterosexual. She explored the impact of Viagra® on their sexual activities. The striking aspect of the research is that Viagra® works with a particular version of heterosexuality. At the centre of Viagra® is the importance of penetration, with Viagra® providing repeated or multiple erections. The impact on men's and women's sexual relationships was that in some cases men were achieving more satisfying relationships with women by not taking Viagra®. This was due to men and women developing more intimate and erotic relations that were not dependent upon penetrative sex.

Mamo and Fishman (2001) explore the impact of Viagra® further by suggesting that Viagra® is part of the medicalization of men's lives. They highlight that pharmaceutical companies are not simply developing drugs to deal with life threatening situations, they are developing drugs to deal with physical and social situations that are deemed *life limiting*. Thus medicalization operates to provide lifestyles that makes lives more enjoyable. It is argued that central to the success of Viagra® has been its marketing. Thus, in Pfizer's (the company that manufactures Viagra®) advertising material, two forms of promotional literature that are drawn upon are the medical pamphlet and the mass media advert. Embedded in this literature is the notion that Viagra® is something that is natural. This is established because it supports a normalized view of bodily function. In doing so the characteristics of sexual control that have been seen to constitute masculinity are contained within Viagra®. But the marketing of the drug does not play on the absence of desire but rather the facilitation of it. In this way, the desire that men feel is innate and essential to the truth of their being. Consequently, Viagra® is a natural means of enabling this desire to be expressed by emphasizing impotence as a physical quality. Therefore, in the context of age and gender, ageing does not affect masculinity; ageing simply disrupts the possibilities of its expression with the genitals simply as a conduit for real desire. As Mamo and Fishman (2001: 21) point out: 'Viagra® transforms a bodily (re) action to sexual stimulation into a techno-assisted erection and brings with it a litany of scripts about the linkages between nature and technology, disciplined sexuality and the logics of binary gender.' This model depends on an omnipresent notion of desire. Desire is not the problem; desire is not the implant facilitates the expression of desire. Chemicals enable the connection of desire to physiology.

Conclusion: Postmodernity, Age and Gender

This chapter has focused on two life stages: childhood and older age. It has suggested that the interplay between age and gender is generating specific meanings about masculinity and femininity. One of the explanations for this fragmentation is provided by Zygmaunt Bauman's (1992) analysis of the forces that constitute identity. For Bauman, the post-Second World War was an era where the cultural context is becoming increasingly marked by social uncertainty. He identifies four areas where this uncertainty is taking place. First, at a political level, both nationally and internationally, politics is marked by a more fragmented set of social interest groups vying for a more diverse set of interests. Thus, it could be argued that there is an increasing pluralism and/or political appeal to age collectivities such as young people, pensioners, mid-lifers and so on. Second, social uncertainty is being produced by a universal deregulation of capital and finance that in effect are breaking up traditional roles and responsibilities. Evidence for this might be in the civil disenfranchisement of the young people of access to housing, full-time work and social security (Jones and Wallace, 1992; Payne, 1995). The collapse of the 'job for life' scenario is another example of this. Third, alongside these and constituted by the first two aspects, traditional social safety nets are collapsing or are being weakened. This entails the loss of traditional social bonds. Winn (1983) has highlighted the move towards children becoming the emotional anchors for parents undergoing major relationship change (see also Beck, 1992). Finally, Bauman argues, that uncertainty is generated by the cultural sensibility through social technologies such as the media has changed the nature of social relations. Consequently, as Beck (1992: 277) points out:

> We now see greater variability and complexity in the life course with a weakening of universal age related transitions and status passages within institutional structures such as work and the family. In effect there has been a deinstitutionalization of the life course. Hence, there is greater insecurity and a sense within consumer culture that the life course, like one's lifestyle, should be regarded as less a question of fate and more a matter of individual responsibility and construction.

Beck is thus suggesting that social relations no longer carry the same meanings or more importantly the authority to legitimize, that they may have done. In other words, identities based upon secure notions of gender and age are becoming increasingly fragmented and under threat.

5

Shifting Gender Connections: Sexuality, Late Modernity and Lifestyle Sex

Introduction: The Instability of Sex/Gender Categories and Boundaries

Across contemporary western societies, gender and sexuality have appeared as a stable conceptual couple, a natural union grounded in biology, or, simply a reflection of the natural order of things. Throughout this book, we emphasize the transformations in late modernity that are taking place in and through gendered lives. In this chapter, we address the intimate relationship between gender and sexuality and more specifically focus on rethinking this couplet within the context of transformations in social practices. Presently, emerging representations circulating across British popular cultural technologies suggest a shifting intersection between gender and sexuality. For example, lifestyle magazines, advertising and Reality TV tell of the imperative for young men to disavow traditional forms of dysfunctional heterosexual masculinity. Such a move may indicate an inversion of a dominant popular cultural practice of maximizing the differences while underplaying the similarities between the sexes and sexualities (Weeks 1986). It may also suggest that with straight men 'acting gay' – exemplified in this reading as displaying their *feminine side* – in order to attain their object of choice – a girlfriend – the conventional bonds forged between gender and sexuality that ensured the conventional, modernist gender hierarchy is being inverted.

This chapter explores the changing relationship between gender and sexuality. It does this first by exploring how feminist and queer theorists are resolving this analytical relationship and second, exploring how the modern understanding of confessional sexualities and the compression of time and space is impacting upon sexuality and gender. More specifically, the chapter ends with an exploration of these two areas in the context of communication technologies, sex tourism and media representations. This inquiry accords with de Lauretis' (1987: x) claim that contemporary representations of gender are produced by a number of distinct technologies of gender, such as cinema or advertising, and that we, as gendered subjects, can be seen to be 'constructed across a multiplicity of discourses, positions and meanings, which are often in conflict with one another and inherently (historically) contradictory'. For some, these discursive contradictions, as part of wider processes of detraditionalism, are providing a contemporary cultural space in which refashioned gendered and sexual identities, marked by dislocation, fragmentation and pluralism are reflexively being performed (Giddens, 1991; Laclau, 1990). Hence, such representations may suggest that there is a potential freeing of 'sexuality from the phallus, from the overweening importance of male sexual experience' (Giddens, 1992: 2), which in turn suggests that the mainstream deployment of the feminine as 'lack', 'abject', 'aberrant' and 'repulsive' has fundamentally shifted. An alternative reading recalls that there is a long cultural history of (heterosexual) men appropriating the feminine, supporting Battersby's (1989) argument that in western culture it is *femaleness* not *femininity* that is devalued.

A further reading suggests a more complex picture of social continuity and cultural change with ongoing sexual subordination, as feminist and gay research continue to report on the structural exclusion of women and gay men situated in (ef)feminized positions in relation to patriarchal power, alongside the emergence of hybridized sexed subjects' performances as manifest in the appearance of metrosexuals (see Merck *et al.*, 1998). These different positions suggest that this field of inquiry is highly contested in terms of how we understand the mutually informing impact of gender and sexuality in relation to contemporary social and cultural changes. A key aim of this chapter, in searching for a renewal of social and cultural analysis of gender, is to map out some of its more intricate and intimate positions as they articulate the shifting boundaries of gender and sexuality in the context of late modernity. It is important to note that the relationship of gendered identity formations with wider social relations remains unresolved, as is highlighted in postmodern accounts of gender domination that abstract practices from institutional contexts (Seidman, 1993).

Alongside this, there is an urgent need to move beyond earlier sexological and psychoanalytic classifications of sexual identities in order to capture the articulation of new ways of thinking about the formation of gender and the organization of sexuality in a dynamic, historically and socially specific relationship that involves a complex play of power relations (Bristow, 1997; Richardson, 2000). In so doing, we emphasize that in the dominant binaries, such as man/woman, masculinity/femininity and heterosexual/homosexual, identities are defined and lived out in an internal relation to each other as fluid, ambivalent and shifting. At a time when it is recognized that sex is the truth of our being, the chapter also focuses on the potency of sexuality as a contemporary resource for demonstrating *who and what we are*, and *who and what we wish to be* (Foucault, 1981).

Forgetting Social Constructionism: Moving Towards a Radical Theory of Sexuality

During the 1990s, early feminist and gay/lesbian studies associated with an identity politics position were projected as being theoretically left behind by a cultural politics of difference position, as exemplified in queer theory. In contrast to the limiting critical vocabularies of the former, queer theory, emphasizing the interpenetration of sexual spaces and gendered signs, claimed to resonate with a postmodernist sensibility of cultural hybridity and reflexive subjectivities (Johnson, 2003; Lash and Urry, 1994). Merck *et al.* (1998: 3), in their collection *Coming Out of Feminism?*, critique the range of geneologies that have addressed the relationship between feminism, gay studies and queer theory. They outline the way in which:

> Often, the presumption of feminism's seniority constructs it as the matrix, womb or closet from which lesbian/gay and then queer consciousness is said to have emerged: older, but not necessarily wiser in a political moment which prizes 'post'eriority. If this is so, have contemporary sexual politics (including what is often called 'post-feminism') not just 'come out' but also 'grown out' (in both senses) of their presumed predecessor? Does this explain the widespread rumours of the decline of women's studies in the academy, replaced by a more contemporary consideration of sexuality? Should feminism accept that it has done its work and productively led, like all good ideas, to ways of thinking that supersede it? Or is the relation less one of precedence and supersession than one of continuing confrontation, positive and negative, between two bodies of thought more similar than different? In the present – continuous tense of our title ... is there the suggestion of a motion - from or a motion with?

The American anthropologist Gayle Rubin (Rubin and Butler, 1998) has written of the tendency of contemporary writers on sexuality to erase its theoretical origins. Within an Anglo – US context, there is a long history of struggles around the sex/gender order. For example, late nineteenth century/early twentieth century sexologists and radical movements, created many of the sexual ideologies of today, especially the idea that sexuality is not so much an act, more an "identity" with a bodily or medico-constitutional base

(Epstein and Johnson, 1998: 37) More recently, the relationship among gender identity, sexual/erotic desire and power, both conceptually and politically, has been explored extensively in a wide range of feminist and gay/lesbian studies (Jeffreys, 1994; Segal, 1990). Edwards (1994: 37), in a critical review of the 1980s, highlights the tensions between positions developed during this period. He cites MacKinnon (1982) as representative of a radical feminist position with an emphasis on gender as the prime mechanism through which women's sexuality is oppressed.

> Sexuality, then is a form of power. Gender, as socially constructed, embodies it, not the reverse. Woman and men are divided by gender, made into sexes as we know them, by the social requirements of heterosexuality, which institutionalizes male sexual dominance and female sexual submission. If this is true, sexuality is the lynchpin of gender inequality. (Ibid.: 29)

Edwards contrasts this approach with those arguing that sexuality is itself a system of oppression. Rubin (1984: 293) has provided one of the most important formulations of this argument, stressing that:

> Sex is a vector of oppression. The system of sexual oppression cuts across other modes of sexual inequality, sorting out individuals and groups according to its own intrinsic dynamics. It is not reducible to, or understandable in terms of, class, race, ethnicity, or gender.

Within a British context, the classic texts, McIntosh's (1981) 'The Homosexual Role', Weeks' (1977) *Coming Out: Homosexual Politics in Britain from the Nineteenth Century to the Present* and Plummer's *The Sexual Stigma* (1975), alongside the US-based Gagnon and Simon's (1974) *Sexual Conduct* and Altman's (1983) *The Homosexualisation of America* were central in establishing the foundations of the new intellectual inquiry into sex and sexuality. However, the above writings have tended to be occluded in changing academic fashions or subsumed under queer theory's popularizing of Foucault's *The History of Sexuality* as the defining text in contemporary theorizing about sexuality.[1] In what Weeks (1986) refers to as the invention of sexuality, he argues that Foucault's work gave a focus for questions already being formed, with the latter going further in querying the category of *sexuality* itself: its historical and social construction.

More specifically, the cross-disciplinary amnesia tends to erase the contribution of social construction theory thus underplaying its links with queer theory. A defining conceptual move by social constructionism, in questioning earlier essentialist understandings of sexuality as a pre-social category was to focus upon the deep cultural mediation of sexuality within social spheres (Fuss, 1991; Richardson, 1996). In so doing, it challenged ahistorical, biologically based approaches and their deployment of 'nature' as a key explanatory category of (hetero) sexual and gendered lives. Scientific discourses, particularly spoken through psychological conceptions, have the effect of naturalizing sexual and gender relations, suggesting that they are determined by an underlying 'natural' force. For example, Freudian and Darwinian hydraulic models assert that sexuality is an innate and overwhelming drive that is necessarily controlled/repressed in society (Edwards, 1994). This work, which can be linked to historical constructions of nature deriving from Enlightenment understandings, continues to be highly influential with considerable rhetorical and persuasive explanatory power. In contrast, as Vance (1995: 42) acknowledges: 'Social construction work has been valuable in exploring human agency and creativity in sexuality, moving away from unidirectional models of social change to describe complex and dynamic relationships among the state, professional experts and sexual subcultures' (see Gergen, 1999).

Late Modernity: The Promise of Disconnecting Gender Identity and Sexual Desire

Among a diverse range of theoretical commentators, Rubin's work is regarded as an influential articulation of significant conceptual moves in contemporary cultural inquiries into gender, sexuality and kinship, including, according to Butler, setting the methodology for feminist theory *and* for lesbian and gay studies (Bristow, 1997; Rubin with Butler, 1998). The specific theoretical context of Rubin's essay, 'The Traffic in Women: Notes on the "Political Economy" of Sex' (1975) was a critical engagement with the limitations of Marxism to address the specificity of the non-economic structures of gender, including core issues of gender difference, gender oppression and sexuality. The essay was inspired by anthropological literature on kin-based systems of social organization, with the regulation of sexuality viewed as integral to kinship practices trading on women's bodies. She developed the concept of a sex/gender system, which was defined as a set of arrangements by which a society transforms biological sexuality into products of human activity.

In a later essay, 'Thinking Sex: Notes for a Radical Theory of the Politics of Sexuality' Rubin (1993) reformulates her earlier theoretical position that both gender identity and sexual desire derive from the organization of kinship systems. She elaborates upon the relative autonomy of the social organization of sexuality, which she claims cannot and should not be understood as simply derivative from gender binaries. Critically exploring the discontinuities between kinship-based systems which fused gender and modern forms of sexuality, she argues for the uncoupling of gender and sexuality, and in so doing reconfiguring their relationship in a more complex and contingent way (Weeks *et al.*, 2003). She sees this analytical separation as essential, in order to reflect more accurately their separate social existence. Drawing upon Foucault's *History of Sexuality*, she points to his claim that a system of sexuality acquired significant autonomy in emerging out of earlier kinship forms.

> Particularly from the eighteenth century onward, Western societies created and deployed a new apparatus which was superimposed on the previous one, and which, without completely supplanting the latter, helped to reduce its importance. I am speaking of the deployment of *sexuality* ... For the first (kinship), what is pertinent is the link between partners and definite statutes; the second (sexuality) is concerned with the sensations of the body, the quality of pleasures, and the nature of impressions (Foucault, 1978:106).

A major breakthrough for Rubin was that Foucault enabled her 'to think about the outlines of another system that had different dynamics, a different typography, and different lines of force' (Rubin with Butler, 1998: 58). Her position, in search of explanatory pluralism, was developed against specific versions of feminism, such as the antipornography movement, which she accused of theoretical totalization. Such an approach was particularly inappropriate and insensitive to the ascendancy of the New Right cultural politics in the United States and the accompanying moral panic against diverse sexual practices, including the use of AIDS to incite virulent homophobia. As a sex radical, Rubin (1993: 33) claimed:

> Gender affects the operation of the sexual system, and the sexual system has gender – specific manifestations. But although sex and gender are related, they are not the same thing, and they form the basis of two distinct arenas of social practice.

The implication of this work is the potential conceptual space through which to collapse the relationship between gender and the object of desire.

Late modernity's promise of disconnecting gender identity and sexual desire has also been driven by queer theory. For Sedgwick (1994: 8) 'Queer can refer to: the open mesh of possibilities, gaps, overlaps, dissonances and resonances, lapses and excesses of meaning when the constituent elements of anyone's gender, of anyone's sexuality aren't made (or can't be made) to signify monolithically.' As a deconstructive project, it seeks to destabilize socially given identities, categories and subjectivities, around the common-sense distinctions between homosexuality and heterosexuality, men and women, and sex and gender. It does this by establishing the social and historical specificity of sexual categories, linking them to processes of state and institutional control. Queer theorists also seek to collapse the boundaries that separate sexual normality and abnormality, suggesting that separate discrete oppositions are mutually constitutive rather than exclusive. Furthermore, they contest the adequacy of matching existing sexual categories to the complexity of people's lived experiences. Queer theorists develop the possibilities of sexual being and doing outside of the conventional identities and subjectivities (including gay, lesbian and bisexual identities). However, as the literature makes clear, the relationship between the categories sexuality and gender remains highly contested and increasingly confused. For some, queer theory's suggestion of a disconnecting of the categories is seen to be privileging sexuality or the erotic over gender, with some critics locating a gender-blindness in its roots in Foucauldian theory (Wilton, 1996). However, as Sedgwick (1991: 30) makes clear, though gender and sexuality are inextricably locked together in mutual dependence in expressing each concept

> in twentieth-century Western culture gender and sexuality represent two analytic axes that may productively be imagined as being distinct from one another, as say, gender and class, or class and race. Distinct, that is to say, no more than minimally, but nonetheless usefully.

In our own work on forging 'proper' forms of young masculinity through a (hetero) sexual identity, we identified some of the ways in which inhabiting particular forms of heterosexual masculinity enables young males to negotiate wider gender relations within specific institutional gender regimes (Epstein and Johnson, 1998; Haywood and Mac an Ghaill, 1996). However, it does not immediately explain why these 'proper' forms of masculinity are heterosexual. A question arises: what is it about occupying 'proper' forms of masculinity that almost inevitably implies a heterosexual identity? The answer to this seems to lie in the fact that, in mainstream contemporary Anglo-American cultures at least, heterosexuality and gender are profoundly imbricated (overlapping). For example, Butler (1993) argues that gender is routinely spoken through a 'heterosexual matrix' in which heterosexuality is presupposed in the expression 'real' forms of masculinity or femininity. Thus, she (ibid.: 238) writes:

> Although forms of sexuality do not unilaterally determine gender, a non-causal and non-reductive connection between sexuality and gender is nevertheless crucial to maintain. Precisely because homophobia often operates through the attribution of a damaged, failed, or otherwise abject gender to homosexuals, that is, calling gay men 'feminine' or calling lesbians 'masculine', and because the homophobic terror over performing homosexual acts, where it exists, is often also a terror over losing proper

gender ('no longer being a real or proper man' or 'no longer being a real or proper woman'), it seems crucial to retain a theoretical apparatus that will account for how sexuality is regulated through the policing and the shaming of gender.

In a later preface to *Gender Trouble*, Butler (1999: xii–xiv), in response to some queer theorists, who make an analytical distinction between gender and sexuality, arguing that there is no causal or structural link between them, maintains that in one sense she supports the idea that heterosexual normativity ought not to order gender. However, she feels that the implied notion that there is no sexual regulation of gender, involves an important, though not exclusive dimension of how homophobia works going unrecognized.

Sedgwick's (1991) work on changes in Anglo-American male-male relations has begun to fill in some of the historical background to our current experience of the imbrication of gender and sexuality, suggesting that the ever-troubled homosexual–heterosexual oppositional couplet is of central significance to the construction of modernity. She (1991: 1) opens her book *Epistemology of the Closet*, proposing that

> many of the major nodes of thought and knowledge in twentieth-century Western culture as a whole are structured – indeed, fractured – by a chronic, now endemic crisis of homo/heterosexual definition, indicatively male, dating from the end of the nineteenth century. The book will argue that an understanding of virtually any aspect of modern Western culture must be, not merely incomplete, but damaged in its central substance to the degree that it does not incorporate a critical analysis of modern homo/heterosexual definition; and it will assume that the appropriate place for that critical analysis to begin is from the relatively decentred perspective of modern gay and antihomophobic theory.

For Sedgwick, the current exclusion of male-male erotic contact from 'proper' forms of masculinity has its origins in an eighteenth-century shift from the religious to the secular discursive construction of sexuality. An important consequence of this 'endemic and ineradicable state of homo-sexual panic' (ibid.: 185) has been the fact that homophobia is used to police the boundaries of acceptable heterosexual male behaviour and identity as well as more overtly (and often violently) being used to police homosexual behaviour and identity.

However, in suggesting that masculinities are 'spoken through a hetero-sexual matrix', it is not argued that laddishness, for example, is inevitably coded as heterosexual. Nor is it suggested that everyone who inhabits hegemonic forms of masculinity experiences themselves as heterosexual and that everyone who inhabits subordinated forms of masculinity experiences themselves as homosexual. As the gay men's 'clone' style of the 1970s and 1980s demonstrated, highly physical and macho forms of masculinity can be successfully rearticulated so that they signify homosexuality. Equally, as we have found with a younger generation of English males, groups of friends organized themselves around a version of high camp that flaunted characteristics identified as quintessentially 'feminine' and 'poofy' by the forms of masculinity hegemonic in school life (Redman, 2001; Redman and Mac an Ghaill, 1996). Despite this, not all such groups identified as gay. The existence of gay machismo and heterosexual camp should alert us to the fact that the subject positions made available by discourses of masculinity do not determine subjectivity. Within particular constraints, they can be read against the grain. In the examples given, both hegemonic and subordinate forms of masculinity are deployed as cultural resources and their meanings are rearticulated: gay is macho; 'poofy' is superior, more refined. However, while the subject positions of hegemonic masculinities can be clearly subverted or lived in contradictory ways, they more commonly act as resources through which heterosexual subjectivities are produced, lived out, and policed in local circumstances: they provide the social vocabulary through which heterosexual men are both 'spoken' and come to 'speak themselves' as heterosexual.

Lifestyle Sex: Confessional Sexualities

The complex relationship between sexuality and gender as outlined above is not occurring in a social and historical vacuum, rather it is taking place through particular intelligibilities or ways of knowing. One style of knowing outlined by Foucault (1981) and contiguous with modernity is the notion of the *confession*. The religious notion of confession and the discursive declaration of truth has become a key feature of contemporary identities premised on sexuality and gender. It has been argued that one of the features of late modernity is the intensified pursuit of sexual truth and an amplification of what McNair (2002) has termed 'striptease culture'. This system of knowing has become a pervasive technology that is operating to instantiate sexuality. Through confession, subjectivity is materialized into a discursive form and as a result, desire and its relationship to the object becomes subject to control and regulation. This connects with the tradition of how confession could establish truth. As Foucault suggests (1978: 59):

> Western man has become a confessing animal. Whence a metamorphosis in literature: we have passed from a pleasure to be recounted and heard, centring on the heroic or marvellous narration of 'trials' of bravery or

sainthood, to a literature ordered according to the infinite task of extracting from the depths of oneself, in between the words, a truth which the very form of the confession holds out like a shimmering mirage ... the confession is a ritual of discourse in which the speaking subject is also the subject of the statement.

After the Enlightenment, the original religious concern for the management of sin became reworked into a technique that would enable the governmentality of populations. As such, a range of public regimens such as census collection, medical examination, educational achievement or psychotherapy began to operate in a confessional manner. Closer engagement with this idea highlights that through discourse, the individual instantiates themselves and that sexual truth is articulated through discourses. This suggests a broader connection; that sexuality is not simply made available through talk and language; rather talk and language are part of a broader system of knowing.

An example of how this system of knowing has influenced our understanding of the gendered connection of desire to an object can be found in Butler's (2004) discussion of David Reimer. She highlights how both social constructionist and endocrinologists sought to shape this person's gender identity through the reconstruction of his/her social and physical life. At the age of 8, this person accidentally had his/her penis burnt off. Subsequently, the boy was subject to invasive therapies that attempted to establish the 'reality' of his/her gender. From being coached in femininity to the reconstruction of the phallus, at various moments this person's life became dependent on establishing a truth of being. According to Butler, dependent on establishing the intelligibility of the person, was the reliance on what the person said. Thus, from being constructed as Brenda and then constructed[2] as David, talk became the evidence for how to shape the body. Thus, central to establishing the nature of gender was the centrality of self-observation and self-reflection. In short, confessional style was an epistemology of truth.

As a result, various social and cultural institutions such as schooling, the media, medicine, social welfare agencies have emerged as key institutions that operate and depend upon establishing, identifying and revealing sexual truths. It is this ritual of instantiation that marks a modern form of inquisition focusing and magnifying the sexual/gendered cultural fault lines. It is suggested here that contemporary gender and sexual identities are not simply being reflected by practices of confession and revelation; rather, sexual and gendered identities are being refracted and shaped by those very practices. As McWhorter (1999: 28) argues: 'the sexual subject is constituted, in its very essence, as a confessing subject ... where sexual subjectivity is, essentially, an epistemological phenomenon'. Importantly, as Foucault (1994) suggests, the confession in early Christian times operated as a means not only to disclose the self but as a means of renunciation. Modern confessions, however, have dropped the implicit renunciation and have become positive expressions of self. If contemporary culture is confessional, then the processes involved in the demonstration of sexual and gender identities may be changing.

Technologies of Intimacy: New Forms of Inter-face

The implication of a growing style of sexuality as confessional has manifested itself through a series of new practices connected with the rise of Information and Communication Technologies. With a confessional style of sexuality, there is a growing emphasis on normalized connections between desire and acceptable objects, alongside a simultaneous declaration of that connection. Therefore, in the context of technological development, the communication of sex and sexuality and its attendant relationship to gender is being articulated through a range of technological interfaces. Sexuality and gender are being transformed by the development of technologies such as digital (video) cameras, webcams, MUDs/ MOOs, DVDs, mobile phones and 3G phones that are being used across a range of different forums that include chat rooms, photo swaps, internet dating agencies and fetishist communities. This detailed and useful work connects changing technologies to existing erotic templates. One of the impacts of technology upon sexuality is that the boundaries that have traditionally held between the public and the private are breaking down; social change is collapsing conventions that have designated what sexual privacy means. Sexual communication is now taking place across local and global spaces and it is becoming increasingly difficult to track how sexuality and gender are being mediated.

Accounts of new forms of communication often point to the transformation of existing norms and values. For example, in a recent editorial in *Sex and Relationship Therapy*, Delmonico (2003: n.p) argues:

> On the internet, relationships are virtual – that is, not based in the same reality on which we have created relationships for thousands of years. Our five senses are often lost or distorted during these interactions. I cannot see, hear, touch, smell, or 'taste' the individual with whom I am trying to form a relationship. There are attempts to approximate these senses; however, efforts at videoconferencing and voice chatting are far from replacing the real world.

In response, it is argued that relationships have always been mediated through a range of communicative contexts, such as language, art, writing, and that communication itself is a mediation constituted by social, cultural and historical specificities (Thompson, 1995). Therefore, the emerging centrality of more recent technologies must also be considered as being part of a broader historical transformation of gender, sexuality and technology. One aspect of this is the impact that technological development is having upon the relationship between gender and the object of desire. One popular response to this relationship has been the notion of individuals being dislocated from the norms and values surrounding erotic intimacy. It has been suggested that the propensity for more disinhibited behaviours is likely to occur through communication technologies that allow a relative anonymity (Joinson, 1998). This means that as the traditional forms of communication such as face-to-face interaction become substituted for other forms of communication, the strategies that are involved in confessing the gender/object relationship become less clear. The result, often termed deindividuation, means that individuals because of their relatively anonymous communicative practices suspend their conventional norms and values. For example, research by Thurlow and Brown (2003) involved collecting the last five text messages from 135 first year undergraduate students on their phones. Alongside social arrangements and friendship maintenance, messages also included sexual and romantic messaging. What they identified was that text messages generated an unusual mix of intimacy and distance that was also characterized by 'relative licentiousness'. They argue that one of the reasons for this is a relative anonymity.

It has been argued by Flannaghan and Sullivan (2003) that there is nothing to suggest that the introduction of communicative practices have led to a dislocation from norms. Instead, they cite research which suggests that people might reinscribe existing social norms and values in ambiguous situations. This they suggest, would be due to a lack of apparentness of the rules of social engagement in certain communicative contexts. An example of the rise of new technologies and its impact on gender/object of desire relationship has been that of mobile phone text messaging. On 14 February 2005, Valentines Day, 92 million text messages were sent across the United Kingdom in comparison to 12 million cards (Text.it.com 29 March 2005). Overall, between 1999 and 2005, the amount of text messages had risen from 1.1 billion to 26.2 billion. In the context of Norway, research by Ling (2004) has indicated that teenagers and young women are more likely to send text messages whereas teenage boys and men are more likely to use voice. From this position, new technological processes appear to fit into existing gendered and sexual practice.

Doring (2000) suggests that from a feminist perspective, it could be argued that new technological advances may be enabling the removal of patriarchal pressure. As the internet works outside conventional norms and values, the gendered moral baggage that circulates through sexuality can be negated. The anonymity afforded by the internet lends itself to the possibility of engaging in more sexual liaisons without the sexual stigma. Furthermore, Doring argues that because of the nature of the medium women can achieve qualitatively better sexual experiences via cyberspace. This, it is argued, is because women can afford to be more discerning in their search for partners. A key implication of this is that conventional notions of sex (heterosexual and genitally focused penetration) are problematized in cyberspace with a plethora of sexual possibilities emerging that can liberate women's sexual experience and emotional investment. The possibility of different sex is also named by Doring (2000: 19) for example:

> Cybersexual scenarios which deviate from otherwise practiced sexual scripts but are not a part of the coming out process can be seen as an enjoyable sharing and symbolic living out of fantasies which cannot be lived out, or can only be limitedly lived out, in the material world. These include sex in various virtual embodiments (e.g. as a person of a different gender and/or another sexual orientation, as an animal or a mythical being), unusual sex practices or atypical social constellations (e.g. sex in public places, sex with several people at the same time).

However, Doring (2000) also argues that the internet can be understood within a victimization perspective. This perspective suggests that gender in cyberspace is marked by violence, aggression and sexual exploitation. According to Lewis (2004) one of the most prevalent questions in chat rooms is 'A/S/L?'. This translates as 'please tell me your age, sex and location.' Females' experience of chat rooms suggests that they tend to be harassed more than men. This means that the hierarchies that are present in other domains of society are present in the virtual domain; thus cyberspace results in a series of relationships between men and women that result in online harassment, cyber rape and cyber prostitution.

An often cited article that gives evidence to the claim that conventional gendered relationships are reconstructed in cyberspace, is Julian Dibbell's (1993) '*A Rape in Cyberspace*'. This took place in a Multiuser Dimensional website which is defined as: 'a kind of database especially designed to give users the vivid impression of moving through a physical space that in reality exists as descriptive data filed away on hard drive'. (n/p). This is a place on the internet where individuals can log on, create their own characters and then interact/interface with other characters in rooms that can be created. Individual users control their characters and the interfaces that take place. However, one aspect of the website was that there was access to a 'Voodoo doll' – a piece of digital coding that could attribute 'actions to other characters that their users did not actually write'. The Voodoo doll became central as Mr Bungle logged into the chat room and forced against their will, characters to engage in a series of sexual actions that involved:

> forcing her [Starsinger] into unwanted liaisons with other individuals present in the room, among them Legba, Bakunin (the well-known radical) and Juniper (the squirrel). That his actions grew progressively violent. That he made Legba eat his/her own pubic hair. That he caused Starsinger to violate herself with a piece of kitchen cutlery. (Ibid.: n.p)

It was only after 'Mr Bungle's' actions were frozen by another user that the series of actions stop. In this example, cyber space did not liberate women from oppressive social values, technological developments provided the means through which the impact of patriarchy was increased. Indeed, the popular press have been quick to celebrate/malign this dislocation. For example, *The Sun* newspaper recently ran a discussion on sex and the internet entitled 'So is this YOUR husband?' quoting one man's participation in a new website:

> There are certain women who I had never slept with who I wanted to try out – black, Indian and Japanese girls particularly. The last two I am still waiting for. I allow women to live out their fantasies when they are with me. One woman likes me to spank her, another likes us to wear an earphone of an iPod each and have sex in time with the music – it is amazing.

Such 'newsworthy' reports combine distaste with fascination and importantly do not generate sympathy or compassion for those involved. At the same time, popular approaches celebrate the fantasy of deindividuation, where people transgress conventional sexual norms and values (marriage) and opt for carnivalesque sexual relations. Doring attempts to resolve the tension between victimization and liberationalist approaches. She does this by arguing that cyber space can be seen as an empowering process, where the internet provides the possibility of creating a more reflexive and critical approach to gendered hierarchies and the possibilities of pleasures.

Rather than simply understand cyber space as reinforcing or rejecting the relationship between gender and the object of desire, other research has suggested a more complex relationship. As argued above, given the centrality of gender to sexuality in substantiating normalized objects of desire, the release of time – space compression, has the potential for men and women to disconnect their bodies from their gender identities. A sophisticated understanding by Haraway (1990) provided a highly productive critical conceptual schema through which to make sense of the interface between technology, gender and sexuality. Central to this work was the idea that technology was generating a new ontology – the very possibilities of being. As Haraway (ibid.: 150–1) points out, 'The cyborg is a creature in a post-gender world: it has no truck with bisexuality, pre-oedipal symbiosis, unalientated, or other seductions to organic wholeness through a final appropriation of all the powers of the parts into a higher unity'.

Thus, the conventional boundaries that augment gender and sexual relations are no longer steadfast. This entails the breakdown of three oppositions. First, the oppositional distinction between human and animal is fractured. The identified connections between animal and human, it is argued, has questioned the uniqueness of the human state. The second opposition is between animal/human and machine, where that which is deemed mechanical and organic is no longer self-evident. Finally, the last opposition is that of the division between the physical and the non-physical. Haraway argues that it is communication technologies and biotechnologies that are reshaping the relationship between nature and culture. Consequently, the parameters that designate the body as finite, fixed and marked by limitations are breaking down; new communication and biotechnologies are redefining what the body means.

The result of the changing boundaries between technologies and bodies is that relationships may be taking place where the social cues of gender and sexuality are not apparent. This can be understood through the notion of 'gender bending'. Turkle's (1995) ethnographic work with men, women and children who use the internet, highlights the differential experiences women and men experience in online interrelationships. The internet provides the possibilities of women being men who are playing women and the alternative position of men being women who play at being men. The implication of this 'net/work' is that men and women across Computer Mediated Communication have differential experiences. In her study, notions of freedom, self-enhancement and increasing experience (not precluding pain and confusion) were themes through which men and women cultivated romantic relationships in a gender-bending context. Furthermore, interesting work by Suler (1999) suggests that it is usually men who change their online identity from their real life identity. In criticism of Turkle's approach, schraefel (1999), writing in the context of the United States, suggests that disconnecting the body from gender identity is more acceptable than that of disconnecting the body from racial identities. Politically, taking up the subjectivity of different genders appears to limit the possibilities of gender identities, as women continue to be ascribed gendered characteristics. The impact is therefore to silence women's voices. However, work by Van Zoonen (2002) provides a different approach to understanding the femininity or masculinity of cyberspace. She suggests that future research needs to offer more systematic consideration of how gender is being defined and what gender means. Van Zoonen argues that it is the analytical frame of gender that requires greater consideration. One of the implications of this work is that gender should be considered within the social context through which technology is used and made sense of. This suggests that cyberspace and other forms of technologically mediated communication needs to be grounded in how such technologies are gendered by their use.

This section has concentrated on the impact of communication technologies upon the relationship between gender and the object of desire. One of the features of work in this area has been research that tends to operate through discrete categories. In contrast, it has been argued throughout this book that in order to understand sex/gender identities, researchers need to examine the simultaneous articulations of a dispersed, localised and shifting nexus of social power. In short, we need to understand how gendered identities as simultaneously classed, ethnicized and sexualized are realized through communication technologies. Therefore, we need to think about, not the ways social categories accumulate, but the ways that they inflect. The next section addresses this question.

Travelling Desires

If the confessional is about the representation of the relationship between gender and the object of desire, then the development of other particular social and cultural practices may also offer the potential for a more 'liquid modernity' (Bauman, 2000). Although many of the debates surrounding time–space and gender and sexuality have been productive in virtual travel, other forms of travel are also magnifying issues around sexuality and gender. In light of the proliferation of what Urry (2004: 7) understands as the 'Tourist Gaze', it is possible to understand how the locals in tourist places reconstruct their appearance in order to convey a 'spectacular corporeality':

> There has been a massive shift from a more or less single tourist gaze in the nineteenth century to the proliferation of countless discourses, forms and embodiments of tourist gazes now. In a simple sense we can talk of the globalising of the tourist gaze, as multiple gazes have become core to global culture sweeping up almost everywhere in their awesome wake. There are countless mobilities, physical, imaginative and virtual, voluntary and coerced.

The impact of globalizing forces on gender and sexuality can be explored through the notion that changing understandings and meanings attached to 'the holiday' is reconfiguring the relationships between sexuality and gender. With its historical roots in economic privilege, travel in western societies has emerged a popular practice. It is argued that changing patterns of consumption have resulted in a shift from the search for cultural authenticity, to a range of functions such as cultural learning or enrichment (Mowforth and Munt, 1998). Alongside the changing importance attached to tourism and travel, the meanings of tourism have also undergone significant change. Melas (2005: 148) suggests that: 'Tourism can resembles imperialism in many respects, particularly in the Caribbean where it wears uncannily similar faces, with relatively wealthy white visitors (although there is also an increase in black middle class heritage tourism) served by black natives.' The nature of this imperialism has come through the tourist gaze 'whereby local people are depicted (and sold) as being exotic/erotic objects of the tourist gaze. The Western obsession with the cult of beauty is fed through marketing campaigns containing explicit images of young, beautiful, exotic natives' (Smith, 2003: 50).

In the context of changing meanings and consumption, it is argued that the 'holiday' itself is a sexual practice. Thus, the emergence of the notion of the sex tourist can be seen as a new configuration of the relationship between gender, sexuality and globalization. Opperman (1999) interprets this emerging relationship between sexuality, gender and tourism through two interrelated processes: production and consumption. He suggests that sex tourism can be understood, from one perspective as being mediated through a form of economic and cultural exploitation.

In the context of the production aspect of sex tourism, Pettman (1997) identifies a political economy of sex where Third World countries with their developmental policies, local economic restructuring, wars and state violence are producing poverty. In some cases, responses to this poverty often mean participation in migration and/or sex work. Bodies, according to Pettman, operate as tradable commodities operating through local, national and transnational configurations of power. The implication is that the compression of space and time has intensified sex work as a form of production and increased the possibility of vulnerable groups being involved in such relations. Consequently, men from developed nations and women from developing nations, exist in unequal economically led sexualized relations. From this perspective colonization, imperialism and exploitation become the key descriptors of how the compression of time and space is generating ways through which the relationship between sex, desire and object is taking place. Such a compression not only simply involves relationships between developed and developing nations, it also involves the migration of women in more local underdeveloped areas and nations. The impact of social change is that it is reinforcing conventional links between gender and sexuality by promoting increased patriarchal control and regulation. In terms of production, the sex industry is of major financial importance given the immense profit that is being generated through diverse revenue streams: prostitution, child prostitution, pornography, trafficking and sexual slavery.

(Jeffreys, 1999; 2003) addresses such sexual inequalities through her work in this area. The increasing prevalence of sex work production is forcing women, children and young men into particular sexual practices. For example, in post-socialist, post-colonial and Third World countries, the changing political landscape at a global level is expanding the prevalence of prostitution. One impact of this has been the rise in organized groups managing, regulating and controlling sex work cartels that are involved in some highly disturbing figures:

- Almost 200,000 Nepali girls, many under the age of 14, are sexual slaves in India.
- Experts estimate that 10,000 children between 6 and 14 are virtually enslaved in brothels in Sri Lanka.
- 15,000 children were sold into sexual slavery in Cambodia between 1991 and 1997.
- The Thai government reports that 60,000 Thai children are sold into prostitution. NGO experts estimate there are 800,000 every year.
- An estimated 10,000 women from the former Soviet Union have been forced into prostitution in Israel.
- Asian women are sold to North American brothels for $16,000 each.
- 20,000 women and girls from Burma have been forced into prostitution in Thailand.

Salvation Army International (2005).

Jeffreys suggests that one of the overwhelming patterns in figures such as these is the integral links between sex work and men's violence. As sex work often involves 'unwanted sexual intercourse' there is little emotional vocabulary for sex workers to explain and describe the violation that they experience. Jeffreys also draws attention to the increasing prevalence of sexual harassment, such as visual and verbal harassment. The sexual exploitation is further exacerbated by military presence providing a sex tourist infrastructure in certain geographical locales. As a result, and in spite of national legislation and military legislation, sex industries have prospered in areas such as the Philippines, Vietnam and Thailand.

Making further connections between gender and sexual practices, O'Connell Davidson and Sanchez Taylor (1994) argue that a key dynamic within sex tourism is the nature of men's identities. The cultural worlds of men who use prostitution highlight the range of meanings that are ascribed by men to make sense of their sexual practices. They found that in Thailand, there were three 'varieties' of sex tourists: the Macho Lads, Mr Average and the Cosmopolitan Man. The Macho Lads tended to be British manual workers, many of whom tend to play pool, ride motorbikes, drink beer and sunbathe. Another masculinity that used sex tourism was the 'Mr Average'. The latter are older men interested in cultivating romantic or emotional attachments. Finally, the 'Cosmopolitan Man' does not identify with the notion of sex tourism and tends to holiday in remote areas, viewing themselves as 'worldly'. They also pay for sex but they argue, will only do so in Thailand. The commonality between these men is that their sexual relationships with local women is enabled because men have access to sexual practices by virtue of their greater economic power. This ability to pay for sexual intimacy transforms the nature of their sexualized identities that they would have in Britain. At the same time, O'Connell Davidson and Sanchez Taylor (1994: 11) point to the antipathy towards certain femininities:

> In short, sex tourists express a kind of misogynous rage against women who have the power to demand anything at all – whether it is the right to have a say over who they have sex with and when or the right to maintenance payments for their children. Psychodynamic theories which view all eroticism as an expression of infantile rage, revenge and hostility (see, for example, Stoller 1979) might explain these men's particular passion for women who are perceived as powerless and sexually available through reference to childhood experiences of rejection and humiliation.

Alongside these patterns of emotional investment in women, the men also identified with particular forms of heterosexuality that was based on traditional genitally focused penetration. According to O'Connell Davidson and Sanchez Taylor, this heterosexuality appears to be inflected by racializations. Prideaux's *et al.* (2004) work on the relationship between the erotic and the exotic explores how representations circulate through various holiday locations and often operate to secure sexualized fantasies. Such representations were operating in Thailand as men tended to connect sexual morality with ethnic/racial heritage. Thus men from the Middle East – 'Arabs' – were seen as sexually dirty, overdemanding and morally degrading to women. The sexual immorality of 'Arabs' was in contrast to the ascribed demure Thai femininity of women. Interestingly, rather than focus on the identity of the men, O'Connell Davidson and Sanchez Taylor identify that there are specific dynamics to the sexual transaction in Thailand. First, the low cost of sex workers and the 'diversity' of sex workers' style. Second, the different process of monetary exchange (the less contractual nature). And finally that these men operate through sexualized masculine styles that are deemed radical from the everyday sexual norms of 'home'.

It should be emphasized that it is predominantly men who use prostitution and are involved in broader processes of sexual exploitation. There is though an emerging literature that provides an interesting inflection to the issue. If the time–space compression is influencing sexual identities, then tourism appears also to be transforming women's identities. Sanchez Taylor (2001), in direct criticism of explanations that rely on patriarchy, argues that the definition of prostitute user identified as male obscures broader social changes that are taking place among women and sexuality. Female tourists participating in sexual relations have been defined by Pruitt and Lafont (1995) as engaging in 'romance tourism'. Sanchez Taylor (2001) explores how women tourists also engaged in sexual relations whilst on holiday. Methodologically, Sanchez Taylor administered questionnaires to 240 women tourists in resorts in Jamaica and the Dominican Republic. Single women who spoke English were approached on beaches at different times and asked to complete the questionnaire. She found that 75 had engaged in sexual relations with local men. However, the meanings attached to the sexual relationships were in terms of a holiday romance. At the same time, the women admitted that they provided an economic element to the romance buying drinks and dinner, somewhere to sleep and clothes. However, the women did not view these erotic/material transactions as prostitution; they simply saw it as a romantic liaison.

A similar approach is adopted by Phillips (1999), who undertook an ethnography of local young men or 'beach boys' in Barbados. One of the features of women having relationships with Caribbean men was the emphasis on the search for the 'quintessential hypersexual black male'. Women whom she researched often viewed black men as sexually virile and able to perform sexually for long periods of time. At the same time, the beach boys suggested that European women were sexually more adventurous. What Phillips found was that the local men took up personas as hustlers and viewed women tourists as a source of economic revenue. For example, the men would introduce their 'girlfriends' to particular shops where their friends worked. The women would buy consumer goods at their friends' shop and afterwards the two men would share the profits. Even though other indigenous men who lived in Barbados did not see dreadlocks as part of their local dress, the 'Beach Boys' adopted the dreadlocks to emphasize their 'black' ethnicity and connect with European women's notions of the black body. As with sex tourists in Thailand, women holidaymakers who visited Barbados were of particular styles. Taylor identifies women who are understood as the *situationer*. These women do not intend to get involved in romantic liaisons but participate when the opportunity arises. They also see that the relationships are not based on any economic transaction. However, when meeting with local people, they spend time in the hotel together, buy food and drink. Another form of sex tourism tended to involve older women. These women return three of four times a year, they are wealthier and may have had 2–3 local boyfriends. They often buy clothes and send money when they are not in the country. They may also invite their boyfriends over to the United Kingdom. Finally, there are those participating in 'One Night Stands' and these simply have sexual relations with other men for pleasure.

The implications of much of this work suggests that the 'Tourist Gaze' generates a particular relationship between gender and sexuality. As with anonymity, afforded with technological communications, research indicates that whilst on holiday some women articulate sexual identifications that would not necessarily be taken up whilst at home. This is something that Thomas (2000), undertaking five focus groups with women tourists also suggests. In these focus groups, women expressed less worry about their reputations when abroad and this was a defining feature of the styles of relationships in which they participated whilst on holiday. However, the assumption that time – space compression produces certain forms of exploratory sexualities in the context of tourism might also be naïve. Khan *et al.*'s (2000) work with young people who followed Rave music highlights that the contextual factors might be crucial to how sexual processes are generated. For example, they did interviews with 47 ravers, both before they went on holiday and after they had returned to the United Kingdom. Interestingly, with this group of young people, one of the key findings was that people were more likely to have sex whilst at home rather than abroad. They also highlighted that they were more likely to have fewer sexual partners whilst on holiday. In the context of the rave, the holiday operated simply as an extension of the weekend, where conventional forms of leisure activities were simply extended and enhanced.

The growing significance of tourism as a social and cultural practice is generating new sensibilities about who, what and where we are. In the context of the confessional mode of sexuality and its cultural conspicuousness, travel and tourism can be seen as a new form of confessional ritual. Therefore, part of the move towards confession as an adjunct to contemporary sexualities is that it provides the possibility of a different emotional vocabulary; new forms, modes and styles of sexual expression: We belong to a society which has 'ordered sex's difficult knowledge, not according to the transmission of secrets, but around the slow surfacing of confidential statements' (Foucault, 1981: 63.) Thus, shame and redemption, traditional repertoires of early Christian confession, are being articulated through erotic signatures of liberation and vilification. At the same time, one of the continuities from older forms of confessional practices to more contemporary forms has been the importance of the audience; those who are able to hear the confession may operate as a centrifugal force in contemporary sexual and gendered identities. In this way, the confession simultaneously operates as surveillance. Rather than repression, the confession may also act as a means of instantiating the possibilities of the relationship between sexuality and gender, which is explored in the next section.

The Proliferation of Sexual Possibilities: Monstrous Masculinity and Feminine Fatales

> School Sir raped and abused pupils for 20 years. He even married three of them. How did he get away with it? For over 20 years evil paedophile teacher Geoffrey Johnson preyed on his innocent pupils – raping and molesting a string of young girls while posing as the perfect schoolmaster. (*The Sun*, 17 October 1999)

This section suggests that the media, and the press in particular, is intensifying its pursuit for the truth of sexual identity. This pursuit is constituted through the idea that gender harbours fundamental sexual secrets that can be identified. In this way, the reporting of events and episodes draws it out, enables it to speak, situates it and materializes the relationship between gender and sexuality. More specifically, this section focuses on the 'sexual others'; men and women who have been subject to media attention because of their sex crimes. The importance of this is to highlight how 'the shock and horror' of the reports on sexuality is not the closure, the repression of the subject, rather it is the proliferation of the possibilities of its existence. Media accounts are not simply stating the truth, they are making the truth, insisting on it and representing it. Rather, truth is discursively constituted by juxtaposing representations of truth and reality. More specifically as Baudrillard (1981: 174) points out:

> There is a proliferation of myths of origin and signs of reality; of second hand truth, objectivity and authenticity. There is an escalation of the true lived experience; a resurrection of the figurative where the object and the substance have disappeared. And there is a panic-stricken production of the real and the referential above and parallel to the panic of material production.

The proliferation of the myths and the panic-stricken production of the real has invited the media to take over the functions of the church in producing social cohesion and moral conscience.

One of the most obvious characteristics of the media's coverage of sexuality and gender has been the rise of the sexual abuser. The discourses surrounding the paedophile, the child molester and the child abuser have now become a key part of English cultural imagination. The emphasis on the public domain and the underreporting of sexual abuse in families (Collier, 2001) helps reconsider the changing nature of the paedophile. The paedophile has initially been characterized as the psychological invert through representations of an inadequate masculinity such as the 'the dirty old man' or the 'the flasher'. Such representations have coexisted alongside a medicalized degendered version of the sex offender. Cowburn and

Dominelli (2001) highlight how paedophilia is currently represented in the media through physiologically and psychologically orientated classification systems. The result is a individualizing and pathologizing of the practices. Such a medicalization of the paedophile in their view obscures the gendered nature of the crime and puts distance between 'sick' individuals and ordinary men. Cowburn and Dominelli suggest that the medical discourse provides the paedophile with a rationality of calculated and cunningness where: 'The paedophile, usually but not always, operates within the spaces and protection offered by public agencies and is construed as cunning because he manages to fool his so-called professional co-workers and employers' (pp. 404–5). However, the discursive construction of the paedophile is changing. At one time, the medicalized discourses were the main form of representations within the broadsheet and tabloid media.

More recently, although a pathologization of the paedophile has taken place, there is a greater emphasis, especially in the tabloids, towards a set of 'mythological' or non-human discourses. It is argued that the medical discourses are now being supplemented with a phantasmology of the child abuser. This means that the paedophile has begun to operate phantasmatically. The phantasy is an imagined scene where rather than refer to a desirable identification (a fantasy), the phantasy is an imagined scene of dis–identification. As Butler (1993: 22) argues: 'Identities operate ... through the discursive construction of a constitutive outside ... of abjected and marginalized subjects ... which return to trouble and unsettle the foreclosures which we prematurely call identities'. Thus, in this way the foreclosures that constitute identities 'are phantasmatic efforts at alignment' (ibid.: 22). This is part of the general formation of sexual and educational identities in this arena. As Hall (1996: 33) suggests, identities 'are ... always based on excluding something and establishing a violent hierarchy between the two resultant poles'. Central to the possibilities of identities is a mutually informing impossible presentness. As that which is needed is forcefully rejected in order to establish itself (Derrida, 1978; Cf. Dollimore, 1991), where identity is not 'a point of origin and stability but ... is ... constantly destabilized by what it leaves out' (ibid.: 33). That which is excluded is subject to a positing of extreme violence. It is argued that media accounts are staging the paedophile through this phantasmatic constitution of identities. The force of such language not only depicts the level of sensationalism of paedophilia and its consonant entertainment (Keating 2002) but it provides a 'vocabulary of evil' that generates feelings of despair and helplessness among the public (see, Collier, 1998, 2001). Furthermore, one of the impacts of this is to disqualify paedophiles from civil liberties.

Whereas fantasies recover that which is lost through fairytale characteristics, the phantasy is an imaginary repudiation that, in the context of the media, tends to work through contemporary representations of horror. The usefulness of the phantasy is that it is etymologically bound into the notion of the phantasm and its supernatural powers. As phantasm, the paedophile is considered as possibly anywhere and anyone. This can be understood as the paedophile is the phantasm, a ghostly spectre that haunts cultural consciousness. Importantly, like ghosts they are virtually undetectable only knowable through various traces. Thus, the paedophile is located as a different being, something outside of normal everyday society. Importantly, there are no characteristics that identify this sexual offender; their dangerousness is constituted by a lack of identifiable criteria. It is a truth of the sexual that cannot be known. Ohi (2000: 204) points out:

> To sustain a stable picture of the paedophile, it is thus paradoxically necessary to assert that paedophilia cannot be detected, that a paedophile cannot be pictured at all. The same gesture that renders him locatable and quarantined, makes him unlocatable, omnipresent, and dangerously at large: just the way we like him.

In the reshaping of sexuality and gender there is an important element that has been overlooked. The paedophile has become a force that is exciting emotions. The unknowability and dangerousness of the paedophile has been reconstructed out of medicalized discourses into a sensational mythology. Thus, media accounts can be seen as operating to activate the fascination of the reader, or more disturbingly, to seduce the reader. As Hartley (1998: 61) argues:

> Children are 'powerless' over their image, presumed incapable of self-representation, not imagined to have a collective interest which needs to be defended in the news, and represented in ways which are comparable to a colonized people; perhaps the West's last colony in discursive terms.

One of the reasons for being seen and not being heard is the possible unambiguous juxtaposition of victim and predator. The narrative can only rely on uninterrupted textual sequences to activate an erotic semiology. The power and voracious proclivity of the paedophile is often set against the child victim. For example, in this extract Geoffrey Davidson is ascribed power through his insatiability:

> He treated his large comprehensive school near Leeds Yorkshire – we are forbidden to name it – as a personal meat market, feeding his odious appetite for sex slaves with a constant supply of wide – eyed virgins. (*The Sun*, 17 October 1999).

Greer (2003) argues that sexual stories in the media tend not to use explicit language to describe the nature of the crime. In Greer's perspective the most important aspects are the selection of the story and how it is told. The notion of the 'forbidden' helps contextualize how the story should be read. In this story, the pupils as children are metaphorically described as meat who are 'fed', having no agency and no subjectivity. Furthermore, the notion of the sex slaves invokes the invisibility of the person and interestingly the child. The removal of the meanings of childhood, and a focus on the sex slave is continued with their description of 'wide-eyed virgins'. Deriving from the Qu'ran the term refers to the rewards that martyrs will receive in heaven. The fascination with the virginal, along with the wide-eyed ('meaning curious'?) girls, tends to represent an abuse case in mythological terms. The paedophile is reconstructed as subhuman, a beast, monster, a fiend existing in the shadows or the fringes of the social order (Greer, 2003). Most importantly, this report does not generate sympathy or compassion for the victims in the case. Rather, the account appears to make the teacher fascinating, exciting and enjoyable. In contrast, the account reconstructs the victims as sexual objects. This means that the victims themselves are eroticized within the framework of the paedophile desire. It could be argued therefore, that the paper actually metonymically reenacts the sexual scene. It is a sexual scene that proves to be economically productive, with readership figures improving in light of such scandals (Greer, 2003).

Finally, we cite the case study of Amy Ghering as a means to explore how the media is generating understandings about the sexual possibilities of femininity. This incident is based upon allegations by three pupils that they were indecently assaulted by their teacher, Amy Gehring. Working as a supply teacher in November 2000, Amy befriended a number of pupils at a comprehensive school in Surrey. She met the pupils both inside and outside the school. During her time there, it was alleged that she had sexual intercourse a number of times with one of the boys and that at other times had sex with his brother and another boy at a New Year's party. The prosecution's grounds for a conviction was based on the claim that: 'In essence she became too close, behaving like one of the pupils and ignoring the boundaries of the teacher–pupil relationship' (*Daily Mail*, 22 January 2002). This closeness was conveyed through the sharing of youthful practices. Instances of drinking, smoking and stories about drug taking were combined in the context of shopping, sleepovers and parties. The pinnacle of these youthful practices resulted in her on one shopping trip, having her belly button pierced. The prosecution alleged that such practices demonstrated that there was parity – too much parity – between Amy and her students. The prosecution claimed that Amy conceived of no social barriers and no professional boundaries that would disrupt the forming of intimate relationships with the pupils. Thus, sexual intercourse with these pupils was not so much a gendered transgression but demonstrative of a particular youthful femininity.

Such reports did not reject the possibilities of a femininity that could form intimacies across age groups, and it should be added that the prosecution did not present Amy Gehring as a pathological child abuser. The sexual nature of the intimacies became the dynamic for gendered ambivalence. For example, the case for the defence argued that the teacher was working in difficult conditions with *'unwanted sexual gestures and touching in class'* (*Daily Mail* 4 February 2002). More specifically:

> Everyday there was inappropriate sexual conduct towards me, with comments and suggestions. There would be grabbing, touching and gestures to the point it was out of control. There was no respect towards myself in the classroom. It was basically out of control. I wasn't really teaching, more of a glorified babysitter for lots of classes (*The Sun* 31/01/02).

A main feature of sexual scandals is the susceptibility of those involved (Lull and Hinerman, 1997). It is argued that in this case, young female teachers carry such susceptibility (as do men, Collier, 1998) but this is operationalized through the cultural projections of teachers as sexually repressed (Grumet, 1988). The media reports thus project an imagined account of femininity: 'A young biology mistress seduced three teenage boys within weeks of her appointment as a supply teacher, a jury heard' (*Daily Mail* 22 January 2002).

In contrast to masculinity, sex crimes by women are often marked by notions of fantasy. Butler (1993) suggests that the use of fantasy describes how psychically, individuals recover loss through an imagined scene that reunites them with the lost (never to be attained) object. So the fantasy allows the reunification with those objects that are inaccessible. It is argued that the media through the reporting of women's sex crimes focus on a voracious female sexuality. The media accounts generated a version of the female teacher as possessing a powerful insatiability of desire that disregarded moral, professional and legal codes of conduct. She stands outside the normal, simply by making female sexuality visible. In a post-1945 period, it appears that female sexuality could only exist positively as procreative in a motherly sense (Grumet, 1988). Therefore, in English society, sexuality and femininity are elided, with socially marginal femininities often recoded as a cause of deviant sexualities (Lees, 1994; Hey, 1997). The media, by disentangling the sexual from the feminine, makes female sexuality both a fascinating and repulsive sexual spectacular, something that tends to be constituted by a pathological instability. Thus, this cultural extremity was almost a mythical voracious sexual femininity; the teacher almost becomes the object of attention in the Victorian 'freak show'. This representation of the sexual 'freak' is often reinforced by news reports that explore the accounts of teenage boys. The mood of the papers was captured by the judge's claim that the jury should not be misled that this is a 'School boy fantasy' and that the gender of the defendant should be irrelevant. Such a comment taps into English cultural imagination of the suspiciously sexual nature of female teachers. As Miller (1996: 6) reports the 'school mistress' has a 'gartered and saucy ring'. In this context 'mistress' connects both with an older traditional form of teaching that can be associated with discipline. However, a notion of discipline carries a sexualized cultural image of the dominatrix. (The mistress *as* teacher is a main theme of contemporary pornography.) Alongside this, the mistress is also a cultural figure who is on the margins of sexual relationships, who is not in control carrying both a sexualised relationship and one where access to relationship legitimacy may be questioned. Even in a sexual sense, Amy Gehring appeared on the margins.

One aspect of the media connections between gender and sexuality is that the reshaping of how sexuality is instantiated may generate alternative forms of sexual subjectivity; subjectivities that may question the conventional understanding of sexuality itself. Lyotard (1988) argues that the linkages between speech events are uniquely heterogeneous and determine the possibilities that may exist between two phrases. He argues in the context of injustice that there are two distinct types of the differend. One is the possibility of alternative forms of experience that are not recognized. For example, in order to claim justice, victims can revalue actions and have it recognized as injustice. This secures their status as victims. In the context of sexuality, there may be sexual experiences such as gay–lesbian that are politically important to claim legitimacy. However, Lyotard argues that there are also the possibilities of knowing that there is no idiom through which experiences of knowledges are available. In the context of this chapter, we suggest that moving beyond the structuring processes of the linkages between gender and sexuality enables us to think outside of the conventional categories. In other words, there are different ways of looking at gender and sexuality that do not fall within existing languages and the semantically violent linkages that they demand.

Conclusion

This chapter explores the interplay between gender and sexuality and in the process critically engages with the privileged binaries through which differences circulate through man/woman, masculinity/femininity and heterosexual/homosexual. At the same time, it is involved in conceptually opening up categories of analysis in order to explore their interplay. The claims that a postmodernization of sex provides a moral circuit of sexual choice and unharnessed desire has implications for gendered lifestyles and self projects. Self-reflexivity has become a key feature of the growing sexual economy, with a burgeoning selection of self-help guides that offer to reveal our secret natures, alongside the emergence in popular scientific magazines of an evolutionary psychological argument that genetics is the basis of social behaviour. This is seen most clearly in the celebration of the discovery of the 'gay gene'. At the same time, popular television programmes provide 'sex tips' to a national audience, whilst email spam interrupts daily routines with revelations of how to optimize our sexual performances. Popular culture commends that we should all become experts in sexual knowledge and fluent in sex talk. Texts such as *Men are From Mars, Women are from Venus, Sexual Power: What Is It?-Who's Got It-and How to Use It to Succeed in Love and Life* and *How to Give Her Absolute Pleasure: Totally Explicit Techniques Every Woman Wants Her Man to Know* not only establish that there *is* a truth of a gendered sexuality but offer methodologies of how to access it. Commercially, the economic return and cultural prevalence of conspicuous sexual consumption has been phenomenal (Stranack, 2002).

6

Representing Engendered Bodies: Producing the Cultural Categories 'Men' and 'Women'

Introduction: Engendered Bodies

Across western cultures, the human body has occupied a central position within common-sense understandings of the naturalness of differences between men and women. In turn, this chapter explores the diversity of work arguing for the central location of the corporeal (the body) in the making of gender relations, sexed subjects and sexual desire. However, in contrast to the former, in which bodies are seen as determining patterns of masculinity and femininity, with an attendant cultural attachment to a two-gender classification, the latter suggests that bodies are arenas for the complex production of gendered subjectivities. While the common-sense position is informed by biological essentialism, popular psychology and current developments in genetics, recent gender theorists invoke notions of culture, representation and history. For example, in socio-historical studies of masculinity, we can identify a major cultural shift from working *with* the body (*focus on the industrial employee*) to working *on* a culturally inscribed, aspirational and narcissistic body (*focus on the aesthetically stylized body image*) of reflexive modernity (Lash, 1994; Mac an Ghaill and Haywood, 2003; Mort, 1996). This cultural shift can be read as an effect of a broader movement of the merging of the social relations of production and consumption and the emergence of hybrid subjects, as a key dynamic of contemporary social conditions and how we live our lives (du Gay, 1996; Falk, 1994; Lash and Urry, 1994). We begin with an exploration of the sociology of the body in the 1990s, in which human body projects emerge as a defining feature of identity formation and power relations in conditions of late modernity (Bauman, 1992, 1995; Featherstone *et al.*, 1991; Giddens, 1991). Following this, in exploring the representation of engendered bodies, we argue for the continuing significance of materialist accounts of patriarchal domination, grounded in women's experience of the disembodiment of feminine sexuality that serves to reproduce phallocentric-based images of gender relations. At the same time, we address more recent work, exploring how bodies become marked as male and female subjects. This work has developed a range of productive and controversial concepts: sexed embodiment, performativity, heteronormativity, gender transgression and the third sex (Butler, 1993; Diprose, 1994; Gatens, 1992; Grosz, 1999; Herdt, 1994; Jackson and Jones, 1998). In response, concern is expressed that the materiality of the 'biological' body is disappearing, with accounts of gender performativity and the social imaginary projecting bodies as simply sexual signifiers of difference (Connell, 2002). The latter refers to the ascendancy of cultural theories of embodiment among gender theorists. This is illustrated through a focus on marketing men, refashioning masculinities and desiring male bodies in late modern visual culture. As a result, the chapter is located within the main current conceptual tensions – and, we might add, confusions – in this field of inquiry.

Human Body Projects: A Changing 'Body Order' in Late Modernity

The last two decades have witnessed a remarkable shift in the changing status of the body across the humanities and social sciences in western societies (Frank, 1990; Featherstone, *et al.*, 1991). Building on earlier work, most notably that of Turner (1984, 1992), Shilling's (2003) *The Body and Social Theory* is now established as a sociological classic. He makes a number of theoretical and conceptual moves that open up innovative frameworks for understanding the contemporary body. Shilling maintains that classical sociological texts, rather than being simply viewed as operating with a disembodied approach, reflecting the traditional Cartesian mind/body dichotomy in which the former is privileged over the latter, should be seen as displaying a dual approach, that of the body as an absent presence in the discipline. He addresses a central theoretical concern in sociology, that of the intellectual incoherency of the failure to synthesize the limiting dualism of biological and social explanations, evident in naturalistic and social constructionist positions. Moving beyond an additive to a relational perspective that enables a shift beyond the mind/body and nature/culture divisions, he insists that a more adequate conceptualization is achieved through viewing the body 'as an unfinished biological and social phenomenon, which is transformed, within certain limits, as a result of its entry into, and participation in, society' (ibid.: 11).

As Shilling maintains, in order to understand the current increased interest in the body, we need to investigate the conditions which have formed the context for this trend. Human embodiment has come to be identified as a key site upon which epistemological disputes, the redundancy of established social categories/classifications, emerging economies of signs and space, and the fragmentation of political positions are played out (Bourdieu, 1984; Frank, 1991; Lash and Urry, 1994). From a contemporary perspective with the development of the 'somatic society', the emergence of imagined cyborgs, transgendered identities and posthuman bodies may appear as a defining element of the late twentieth century (Halberstam and Livingston, 1995; Haraway, 1990; Turner, 1992; Wolmark, 1999). However, historical and anthropological work finely illustrate across time and space, the diverse range of classifications of male and female bodies and the accompanying cultural expressions of masculinities and femininities (Cornwall and Lindisfarne, 1994; Laqueur, 1990). Historians of the human body make clear the changing cultural investments in the shifting meanings of the corporeal within different periods. For example, Laqueur (1990) investigating medical and philosophical literatures, examines the move from the one-sex to the two-sex model of the body. This move, signalling a changing understanding of the boundaries between male and female from one of degree to that of kind, demonstrates the mutability of modernist foundational claims about the naturalness of the diamorphic body. As Laqueur (ibid.: 5–6) argues, thus:

> the old model, in which men and women were arrayed according to their degree of metaphysical perfection, their vital heat, along an axis whose telos was male, gave way by the late eighteenth century to a new model of radical diamorphism, of biological divergence. An anatomy and a physiology of incommensurability replaced a metaphysics of hierarchy in the representation of women in relation to men.

Anthropology, as a discipline, has been particularly productive in placing the corporeal at the centre of its work. For example, Mary Douglas' (1966) highly influential account of the body as a cultural text has enabled theorists across a range of disciplines to identify the cultural specificity of codes of masculinity and femininity that a western vocabulary of insular concepts and reified types is unable to capture.

Theorists of late modernity suggest that modern subjects in detraditionalizing western cultures are intrinsically linked to social and cultural transformations, involving processes of fragmentation, dislocation, risk and mobility (Beck, 1992; Giddens, 1991; Laclau, 1990; Urry, 2000). Within this socio-cultural context, what appears to be specific to the conditions of late modernity is a heightened anxiety as a new body regime emerges, marked by individualization, discipline and self-regulation (Bourdieu, 1990; Lash and Urry, 1994; Pile and Thrift, 1995). Politically, this may be read as the production and regulation of the neo-liberal subject (Callinicos, 1999; Hennessy, 2000). This intensified self-management of body image is underpinned by an explosion of technologies of control, resulting in the blurring of body (inside)/non-body (outside), which is accompanied by a moral economy of shifting and unstable meanings of what bodies are for. This very instability makes it a much valued cultural resource, as diverse body techniques and technologies of the self are drawn upon, in an ever-changing impulse to refashion identity and rein-vent the self. However, Nixon (1996: 117) warns against overgeneralizing this account, and argues:

> Whilst it is true to say that the boundaries between gay and straight, or even between male and female, are becoming more blurred in terms of media representations, the marketing of upmarket fashion and the consumption patterns of some affluent and professional groups, this barely marks a sea change in the entire population where categories of male and female, straight and gay, black and white, remain remarkably stable.

At the same time, there is a tendency for the body as a primary site of desire and cultural consumption to become increasingly central to a sense of self-identity (Featherstone, 1991a; Nixon, 1996). As Grosz (1989: 10) suggests, the body is 'an externality that presents itself to others and to culture as a writing or inscriptive surface'. So, for example, diverse masculinities and femininities are currently articulated through con-sumerism that is written onto the body. Alongside the impact of consumerism, recent studies suggest the need to understand bodies within a broader social and cultural framework that includes issues of globalization and transnationalism (Sweetman, 1997). In this book, we suggest that global processes are gendered and that we find it useful to understand global processes beyond corporeality (Featherstone *et al.*, 1991). The theoretically challenging aspect of this latter understanding of globalization is that naturalized gender, racial/ethnic and sexual categories become detached from the epistemological anchor of the body. This means that modernist, essentialized oppositions such as male and female, black and white or heterosexual and homosexual collapse (see ch. 8).

Engendered Bodies: Embodied Femininities and Disembodied Masculinities

Troubling Engendered Bodies: Male Sexual Violence and the Politics of the Body

A main argument of *Gender, Culture and Society* is the need to hold onto the productive tension between the different sociological/cultural studies explanations in order to generate more comprehensive accounts of gender relations (Haywood and Mac an Ghaill, 1997a). There is a tendency in recent sociological and feminist work on the body to erase the contribution of earlier materialist accounts produced by feminists in the 1970s. We refer to this erasure in a number of places in this book. However, within this specific context it is remarkable. Early second-wave feminism as a social movement reinstated women's corporeal or bodily specificity into history (Scott, 2000; Smith, 1987). From within this framework, the organization of gendered identities was perceived as deriving from a fixed base of social power with the male body identified (named as male violence, male sexuality or the penis) as the source of women's oppression. During this period, within western societies, there was an explosion of writing grounded in activism, which redefined the classical concept of the *body politic* into struggles over the control of the *politics of the body* (Bordo,1993a). Political activism was manifest in a wide range of activities including setting up childcare facilities, women's refuges and rape crisis centres. Feminists created an audience for their interventionist theorizing. Alongside their own consciousness-raising about the causes of their social subjugation, they were highly successful politically in communicating the story of a phallocentric-centred patriarchy to a wider public. In constructing a new explanatory vocabulary, they named men's social practices across a number of sites as integral to the patriarchal society women inhabited. These wide-ranging embodied male practices included domestic violence in deconstructing ideas of the benign 'family man' and the 'good father' (Hanmer and Maynard, 1987), pornography as gendered speech (Dworkin, 1981, MacKinnon, 1987), the sexual politics of reproductive technologies and medical control (Stanworth, 1987) and the pervasiveness of child abuse. Most significantly, the scale of men's violence within the home, on the street, within sporting arenas, inside public institutions and imperial military activities, called into question conventional understandings of normal (heterosexual) masculinity (Burstyn, 1999). It is important therefore, while acknowledging the political achievement of second-wave feminism as a historical success, to recognize the social impact of its legacy on the cultural landscape in the early 2000s.

Beyond Sexual Equality/Sexual Difference

The recent history of feminist conceptualizations of women's corporeality or the embodiness of social encounters has been projected as operating along a major fault line. The main classification of these various positions was narrowly cast in terms of the sexual equality–sexual difference couplet. Grosz (1994b: 15–19) attempts to capture this history in terms of a threefold typology: egalitarianism, social constructionism and sexual difference. Egalitarian feminists, working within a political logic of inclusion, adopted a strategic response to the specificities of the female body. Identifying biological (reproductive) difference – 'menstruation, pregnancy, maternity, lactation etc.' – as central to women's exclusion from the public domain, they argued for the need to go beyond the constraints of the body; thus, campaigning for body modification and transformation (Mary Wollstonecraft, Simone de Beauvoir and Shulamith Firestone). From their modernist stance, new technological developments were advocated as a major instrument in furthering women's liberation. In contrast, social constructionists bringing society into the body emphasized its social significance (Juliet Mitchell, Julia Kristeva and Nancy Chodorow). Working within a logic of cultural reconfiguration, they claimed that there is no simple reading of biology, rather that historically, the western (masculine) social order has ascribed negative values to the biological body, with which women are intimately connected. In response, social constructionists suggested the need to minimize biological differences, while generating alternative meanings and values to them. The third category, sexual difference, is defined against egalitarian and social constructionist positions, in emphasizing that the body should not be understood as an ahistorical, biologically given, acultural object (Luce Irigaray, Gayatri Spivak and Jane Gallop). Rather, the focus should be on the lived body, that is, as it is represented and used in specific cultures. Whereas social constructionists highlight the epistemological advantages of denaturalizing common-sense assumptions about embodied being made possible by the (biological) sex and (social) gender distinction, sexual difference theorists seek to undermine this distinction and the associated mind/body dualism. Hence, there is less interest in the question of the social construction of (feminine) subjectivity than in the materials out of which such a construction is forged.

By the early 1990s, a central question emerged, whether the sexual equality–sexual difference debate exhausted explanatory frameworks, within which to make conceptual and political sense of women's corporeal specificity. For example, Gatens (1992: 129) pointed to the shared assumptions that informed the debate, with both strands conceiving of the body as a fixed biological object, which either has or does not have certain ahistorical characteristics and capacities. In other words, the debate was seen to be caught within a narrow framework which assumes a body/mind, nature/culture dualism, in attempting to answer the question of which should be given priority: the mind or the body, nature or culture. A way forward, as argued by Scott (1988b) was to move beyond the existing political discourse by rejecting the notion that equality versus difference constitutes an opposition, thus reconceptualizing both terms to claim that equality is grounded in differences. In order to make a shift beyond the limits of the duality, it was necessary to make a break with the dominant conceptions of the body in philosophical, social and political theory.

Bio-power, Discourse and the Docile Body

A multidisciplinary stance has been of central importance to feminist theorizing of the body, including Merleau-Ponty's (1962) lived experience of the body, Goffman's (1963) management of the body, Garfinkel's (1967) managed achievement of sex status in an 'intersexed' person (Agnes) and Bourdieu's (1984) transmission of class habitus. However, probably, Foucault's analysis has had the most pervasive influence (Sawicki, 1991). Diamond and Quinby (1988: x) speaking from a feminist position, identify four convergences between feminism and Foucault that are particularly pertinent:

> Both identify the body as a site of power, that is, as the locus of domination through which docility is accomplished and subjectively constituted. Both point to the local and intimate operations of power rather than focusing exclusively on the supreme power of the state. Both bring to the fore the crucial role of discourse in its capacity to produce and sustain hegemonic power and emphasize the challenges contained within marginalized and/or unrecognized discourses. And both criticize the ways in which Western humanism has privileged the experience of the Western masculine elite as it proclaims universals about truth, freedom and human nature.

As Bordo (1993a: 193) indicates, initially, feminists adopted such concepts as 'discipline', 'docility', 'normalization' and 'bio-power', while in critical response postmodern feminists, arguing for the ubiquity of resistance, emphasized 'intervention', 'contestation' and 'subversion'. More specifically, in relation to work on the body, Foucault provided a range of theoretical and conceptual frames with which to deconstruct the modernist notion of the body–mind split and associated western philosophical dualisms, including nature/culture, emotion/reason, private/public and most saliently its inflection in the (biological) sex–(cultural) gender split. Here, the biological, often invoked as the central naturalizing mechanism of differentiating between the sexes – authoritatively establishing *what is really female* and *what is really male* – is itself conceived as socially and historically constructed. For feminists, Foucault's (1980: 139) notion of modern power, which he sees as evolving in two forms, a regulation of the body and a surveillance of populations is particularly productive in relation to the question of sexual difference:

> One of these poles ... centered on the body as a machine: its disciplining, the optimization of capabilities, the extortion of its forces, the parallel increase of its usefulness and its docility, its integration into systems of efficient and economic controls, all this was ensured by the procedures of power that characterized the disciplines: an anatomo-politics of the human body. The second focused on the species body. Their supervision was effected through an entire series of interventions and regulatory controls: a biopolitics of the population.

No longer vested in a central point from above, power is conceptualized as decentralized and productive of social relations in everyday encounters and exchanges (Turner, 1991). This diffusion of power throughout society produces the docile bodies within social space of western cultures. For Alsop *et al.* (2002: 167), the early work of Foucault enables a view of the regulated body, in which dominant discourses prescribe gender norms that work through female and male subjects. Citing the work of Bordo (1993b: 91), they suggest that the subjects' attempt to regulate their bodies to conform to them is a central mechanism of becoming constituted as masculine or feminine: 'through the organization and regulation of the time, space and movements of our daily lives, our bodies are trained, shaped and impressed with the prevailing historical forms of selfhood, desire, masculinity and femininity'.

With a shift away from the natural to the discursive body, it is suggested that gendered forms of embodiment are produced through the play of power relations invested in and exercised through unstable, fractured and shifting bodies with multiple potentialities over time. Interestingly, Nixon (1997: 323), drawing upon the later work of Foucault, has written of the range of techniques of the self, such as that of care, consumption and leisure, involving practices of grooming, dressing and shopping, with reference to the more recent focus upon men's pleasures in shaping and decorating their bodies, which is further explored below. Similarly, in our own work (Haywood and Mac an Ghaill, 1997b) linking techniques of the body and corporeal performance, we found among young unemployed men from the West Midlands, in England, who were experiencing dramatic and condensed disenfranchisement from the local labour market, forms of masculine validation centred around body 'makeovers'.[1] They offered explanations of where the best makeovers could be obtained, which in this context meant the more convincing transformation of self. They engaged in a range of cultural practices that they insisted could validate and display their masculinities. For them, a real, authentic masculinity could be achieved by working on the body, thus, transforming their identity.

There are a wide range of feminist criticisms of the limitations of Foucault in relation to the gendering of bodies and more specifically to sexual difference. For example, Bartky (1990: 65) asserts that Foucault operates with a unitary notion of the body:

> as if the bodily experiences of men and women did not differ and as if men and women bore the same relationship to the characteristic institutions of modern life. Where is the account of the disciplinary practices that engender the 'docile bodies' of women, more docile than the bodies of men? Women, like men are subject to many of the disciplinary practices that Foucault describes. But he is blind to those disciplines which produce a modality of embodiment which is peculiarly feminine … Hence even though a liberatory note is sounded in Foucault's critiques of power, his analysis as a whole reproduces that sexism which is endemic throughout Western political theory.

Other feminist work, operating within a Foucauldian framework, emphasize that while the production of gendered subjectivities are subject to these normalizing techniques, power is always accompanied by resistance (cf., Butler (1993).

Men, Materialism and Social Embodiment

Although the last two decades have witnessed an explosion of writing across the social sciences and the humanities on masculinity, until recently, with the exception of critical studies on sport and the body, there has been little interest in the embodied subjectivity of men (Hall, 1996; Messner, 1992)[2]. Within this context, Bob Connell's (1983, 1987, 1995, 2002) work has been highly influential. A central concern throughout his writing has been a critical engagement with the notion of *natural difference* in relation to an understanding of the gendered body. More specifically, his focus is the western cultural assumption of the 'reproductive dichotomy/dimorphic body' as the primary determinant of gender and sexuality. In the early 1980s, he established major limitations of scientific explanations, such as sociobiological ideas about innate difference (later developed by evolutionary psychologists and geneticists) with their claims to provide hard evidence of the truth about gender patterns of behaviour, which, in turn, serve as a major ideological validation of the existing gender order. He begins, with a conceptual stance that remains throughout his work, taking seriously both biological and social forces; he acknowledges the significance of evolutionary processes in enabling us to produce and sustain human life. However, a defining characteristic of the human species in comparison to other species is that with few exceptions, such as those who are assigned as chromosomally male cannot give birth, humans have remarkable shared capacities and common abilities across the sexes.

For Connell, who suggests that the evidence might indicate renaming the literature sex similarity research, these theorists of sex difference are involved in a double move of suppressing body similarities and exaggerating body differences, as exemplified in different stages of the life cycle, such as in children and in old age, which are marked by relative body similarity. He refers to Rubin's (1975: 179–80) commentary on the cultural emphasis on difference between the sexes:

> Men and women are, of course, different. But they are not as different as day and night, earth and sky, yin and yang, life and death. In fact, from the standpoint of nature, men and women are closer to each other than either is to anything else – for instance, mountains, Kangaroos, or coconut palms. Far from being an expression of natural differences, exclusive gender identity is the suppression of natural similarities.

As Connell (1987: 81) argues, contemporary western societies' paradoxical preoccupation with maintaining 'natural differences', for example, through the cultural adornment of the body, in an attempt to sustain a dominant social definition of gender, is premised on the fact that the *'biological logic,* and the inert practice that responds to it, *cannot sustain the gender categories'* (original italics). He (ibid.: 69) concludes that sociobiology is pseudobiological as it is not based on serious biological investigation of human social life, being unable 'to produce for inspection the mechanisms of biological causation on which theories rest'. A major flaw of such explanations is that they disconnect the biological body from the social. So, for example, discussions of the prevalence for violence among men rather than women takes place outside any reference to institutional gender arrangements, such as men's traditional engagement in the military or dominant cultural conceptions of manhood. This disavowal of social processes produces reductionist claims that men's behaviour simply emerges naturally out of male bodies. As Connell stresses, they also precede bodies in terms of the lived conditions in which bodies develop.

More recently, Connell (1995), in reviewing the literature, has spoken in metaphorical terms of two opposing conceptions of the body: the body as machine (explored above) and in social constructionist approaches, the body as a canvas, a surface or a landscape. He emphasizes the productiveness of the latter, as exemplified in feminist developments of Foucault's work, suggesting that gendered bodies are the products of disciplinary practices. However, the tension Connell wishes to maintain between the materiality of the biological body and social constructionist accounts collapses; with the overemphasis on the signifier, the signified is written out. He cites Carole Vance's (1989: 21) warning against the emergence of a disembodied sex. She suggests that 'to the extent that social construction theory grants that sexual acts, identities and even desire are mediated by cultural and historical factors, the object of the study – sexuality – becomes evanescent and threatens to disappear'. Similarly, Connell argues that work on the semiotics of gender, the performativity of bodily styles and the inscription of cultural meanings onto blank surfaces provide a partial view. In short, biological determinism is culturally exchanged for social/cultural determinism. Humans as mere objects, as exemplified in images of the docile and disciplinary body is not sufficient. There is a need to assert the agency of diverse material bodies, historically and spatially located within social processes, without anchoring masculine identity to the demands of a biological foundation.

In addressing this dilemma, which at conceptual and political level, has been of central concern to gender theorists, Connell (2002: 47) suggests the need to move to a different framework, that he refers to as social embodiment, in which he builds on earlier work which conceptualizes the body as body-reflexive practice, that is, human conduct in which bodies can be seen to be located within a complex circuit as simultaneously both objects and agents of social practice. He describes the process of social embodiment in the following terms:

> The practices in which bodies are involved from social structures and personal trajectories which in turn provide the conditions of new practices in which bodies are addressed and involved. There is a loop, a circuit, linking bodily processes and social structures. In fact, there is a tremendous number of such circuits. They occur in historical time, and change over time. They add up to the historical process in which society is embodied, and bodies are drawn into history.

Furthermore, another major theme in Connell's work emerges here – the need to assert the agency of bodies in *social processes* in order to understand gender politics as an embodied social politics. Connell's work continues to find a wide resonance among gender theorists, at a time of the ascendancy of cultural theories of embodiment, to which we now turn.

Marketing Men: Refashioning Masculinities – Desiring Male Bodies in Late Modern Visual Culture

Recent sociological accounts of late modernity across western societies have placed the ascendant position of cultural industries as central to explanations of social and cultural change. For example, as Lash and Urry (1994: 111) make clear, contemporary notions of reflexivity involve not simply a freeing of individuals from social structures but a replacement of the latter by information structures. They suggest that: 'Without the presence of information and communication structures, enabling a certain flow of information and accumulation of information-processing capacities, reflexive individualization (and modernization) is impossible.' More specifically, theorists of late modernity have highlighted the increasing centrality of consumption and the consumer economy to the ordering of economic and cultural life (Baudrillard, 1988; Bauman, 2000; Cronin, 2000; Jameson, 1983). Most significantly, within an analytical model of postmodernity, consumption (desires) as a set of social, cultural and economic practices is seen as a key dynamic move away from production (needs) as shaping contemporary identities, meanings and self-expression – in short, how we enact contemporary lifestyles (Baudrillard, 1988; Bocock, 1993). At the same time, processes of regendering are central to this move, with media-led projections of aspirational and narcissistic young men refashioning masculinities, while desiring male bodies within the context of the traditionally defined female space and the accompanying feminine codings of the consumer (Bowbly, 1985; Mulvey, 1989).

From a contemporary perspective, Christianity's traditional aesthetics of the soul can be read as displaying a critical stance in relation to consumption. This is exemplified in the rhetorical warning: what does it profit a man (*sic*) if he gains the whole world and loses his soul? Until recently, Anglo-Saxon Puritanism has played a specific cultural role in interpreting this scriptural message for a modern British generation, helping to shape ascetic values and patterns of consumption (Bocock, 1993). It has been argued that the separation and elevation of the spirit over the body, culturally reinforced by the Cartesian binary logic and its attendant argument of the primacy of logocentrism has left a historical legacy among western men of distrust and uncomfortableness with their bodies and sexuality (Featherstone, 1991a; Rutherford, 1988). Recent cultural commentators have debated whether an inversion of this cultural legacy has taken place within contemporary consumer societies, and most significantly through technologies of visual culture, with expanding significations of embodied masculinity exemplifying the postmodern condition (Edwards, 1997).

Hall (1997a) in *Representation: Cultural Representations and Signifying Practices* indicates the theoretical appeal of examining a notion of shifting identities and subjectivities through what he refers to as the circuit of culture, with its focus on the interconnecting concepts of representation, identity, production, consumption and regulation. Addressing the question of the complexity and ambivalent meanings of representational practices, he explores how signifying practices structure the way we 'look' and 'how different modes of "looking" are being inscribed by these representational practices' (Hall, 1997b: 8). There has been an unprecedented rise and con- solidation of theoretical analyses relating to consumer and visual culture, reflecting a symbiotic interest with media projections of the 'to – be – looked – at' consumer male as a cutting-edge descriptive category, which it is claimed is illustrative of wider-changing representations and relations of gender (Mulvey, 1989). At the same time, in a rapidly shifting site, a dis- cursively produced or performative embodied masculinity, marked by pluralism, instability and contingency is made manifest in the recent his- tory of these texts, which are littered with discarded iconographries, including those of the 'new man', as nurturer and narcissist, the 'new lad', the yuppie and old industrial man (Beynon, 2002; Butler, 1990).

The cultural historian, Mort (1988), in his empirical work carried out in London in the mid-1980s, anticipated the current theoretical foregrounding of body surfaces as a primary arena for the display and enactment of con- temporary masculinities. He reported on the emergence of an individuality, articulated, for example, through body-grooming, hair-styling and ways of moving that were on offer to metropolitan young men, incited through commodities and consumer display. Arguing against a notion of simple manipulation of young people by advertising/marketing, Mort presents young heterosexual men as actively stimulated 'to look at themselves – and other men – as objects of consumer desire' (ibid.: 193). He claims that this self-pleasuring and sexualization of the male body challenges earlier heterosexual masculine representations that, as indicated above, were excluded from this female domain. For Mort, of particular importance here are the visual messages transmitted, for example, by advertisements, through which the new man imagery fractures traditional codes of masculinity. He stresses that male sexuality is conjured up through the commodity, with the 'sexy body' produced through the product. Hence:

> the sexual meanings in play are less to do with macho images of strength and virility (though these are certainly still present) than with the fetishised and narcissistic display – visual erotica. These are bodies to be looked at (by oneself and other men?) through the fashion codes and the culture of style'. (Ibid.: 201)

Beynon (2002) maintains, as exemplified in Mort's argument, that during the 1980s a major shift in the politics of looking permitted a male – on-male gaze among young style-conscious metropolitan men. This suggested move is part of a wider discussion about the resignification of mobile and reflexive masculinities and the search for their meaning in the wider context of a detraditionalizing sexual politics (see Halberstam, 1998; Hennessy, 2000). Nixon's (1996) work, *Hard Looks: Masculinities, Spectatorship and Contemporary Consumption*, both captures and contributes to the emergence of the phenomenon, the stylistically self-conscious male, condensed into the iconic figure of the *new man* and an attendant non-phallic masculinity (Chapman and Rutherford, 1988). A particular strength of Nixon's sophisticated analytical framing is to avoid the divisive choice of privileging either 'texts' or 'institutions' that continue to pervade cultural and social analyses. In so doing, he brings together a wide range of theoretical positions and conceptual arguments, weaving together a psychoanalytically inflected cultural analysis of representation and subjectivity with a critical discussion of the restructuring of consumer markets within conditions of an expanding globalization of production made manifest in the expansion of new forms of flexible specialization (post-Fordism). In response to what he sees as the proliferation of accounts with an exclusive concern with the cultural moment in the circuit of culture, Nixon makes a critical engagement with the institutional practices of the production and circulation of the new man imagery. He focuses upon three sets of institutional practices, that of developments in the design and selling of menswear, advertising and market research and magazine publishing industries. The interconnection of these practices, he argues, helped to constitute a new regime of representation. A major focus of Nixon's work is a detailed exploration of how flexible specialization underpinned the discursive emergence of the new man as spectacular performance that was produced within consumer industries. For him, this is most clearly illustrated through the developments of visual culture. For example, the new codings of masculinity produced by magazine fashion photography opened up new subject positions for men, through practices of fashion, style and individual consumption and the accompanying modes of spectatorship which induced self-pleasuring among men. In turn, this shifting terrain of masculinity is reflected in a move away from dominant images of assertive power displayed in the muscular masculine physique to a media-led gaze on male bodily practices – technologies of looking – as spectacular performance invoking images of passive sexualization.

Throughout *Gender, Culture and Society*, we continue to return to the issue of the need for a social and cultural theory of change. More specifically, within the context of sexual politics, in response to the demands of feminism, the question is raised: are men changing? Edwards (1997) in his

Men in the Mirror: Mens' Fashion, Masculinity and the Consumer Society, illustrates the difficulty for many commentators in answering what appears as a simple question. In his account of exploring the marketing of men's fashion as the marketing of masculinities, Edwards critically addresses the work of Mort (1988) and Nixon (1992) as part of a broader theoretical and empirical critique of contemporary cultural analyses of the concept and practice of men's fashion. Acknowledging that masculinity is increasingly premised on consumption rather than production, he begins his critique claiming that the above cultural approaches are sociologically underdeveloped, in providing explanatory frameworks that give primacy to the impact of sexual politics with the injunctions of feminism for men to look at themselves and other men *as men* or more specifically the suggested crisis of masculinity (see Ch. 9). In contrast, Edwards stresses wider developments in consumer society, such as marketing and advertising, with the opening up of a wide range of markets for masculinity in response to demographic changes, including an increase in men living alone, part of a childless partnership, divorced or seeking earlier independence. In short, he suggests that the increasing pervasiveness of images of masculinity and the accompanying significance of fashion, dress and appearance, is not simply a cultural phenomenon but rather is dynamically driven by economic change. He notes:

> If men's style magazines respond to anything in sexual politics then it is to the undermining of definitions of masculinity in terms of production or traditional work roles, and a deep-seated set of anxieties concerning the lack of future focus for young men, which has almost nothing to do with reactions to second-wave feminism and almost everything to do with the fear of unemployment. (Ibid.: 182)

A central focus of Edwards' argument is to question cultural theorists' assertion of the reconstruction of masculinity through the practices of representation and consumption and more specifically in terms of the processes of *looking*. For example, Craik (1994: 203) maintains:

> Changing conventions of men's fashion have entailed re-worked attributes of masculinity that have transformed male bodies into objects of the gaze, of display and decoration. This radically undercuts the Victorian and post-Victorian idea of masculinity as a display of restraint in a disciplined body.

This is not simply a contentious empirical question resulting in different conclusions. Edwards specifically addresses Mort's and Nixon's theses of the emergence of diverse representations of masculinity as emanating in changing social practices. For example, Mort (1988: 194) has referred to the development in the 1980s of: 'a new bricolage of masculinity is the noise coming from the fashion house, the market and the street'. Edwards is questioning the apparent autonomy that cultural theorists assign to the 'cultural' with reference to relations of power in the transition to an era of reflexive modernity. For Mort and Nixon, the signifying practices of the diverse representations of masculinity within contemporary popular forms, such as advertising, men's style magazines, fashion photography and menswear retailing, structure the way we look. Thus, for Nixon (1997: 328):

> the new man imagery was distinctive in sanctioning the display of masculine sensuality and, from this, opening up the possibility of an ambivalent masculine sexual identity: one that blurred fixed distinctions between gay – and straight – identified men. In this sense, much of the significance of this imagery related to the way it redrew relations between groups of men through the codes of style and consumer spectatorship.

In contrast to this suggested opening up of an expansive embodied masculinity, Edwards posits the reproduction of an old hierarchal division of social bodies, with advertisers' valorization of the young, white, muscular, virile, healthy, successful, sexy young man. In stressing the sexualization of traditional values of virility and success in advertising and marketing campaigns, Edwards persuasively points to the conservatism and phallocentricism of the much celebrated advertisements for Levi's 501 jeans, 'as the model's cock is constantly hinted at and yet only momentarily glimpsed through the product' (ibid.: 51). Most importantly, drawing upon Dyer, he suggests the self-contradictory nature of the assumed progressive representations of the *new passive man*.

> On the one hand, this is a visual medium, these men are there to be looked at by women. On the other hand, this does violence to the codes of who looks and who is looked at (and how), and some attempt is instinctively made to counteract this violation. (Dyer, 1989: 199)

Edwards raises a number of limitations of the assumed breakthrough of the new embodied man of the 1980s: including that the suggested plurality of masculinities identified in men's style magazines have had little impact on men in the wider society, the need for a more complex understanding of the complex process of the interpretation of the viewer–viewee relationship, the understating of the exploitation and fetishization of male gay sexuality and the arrival of the *new lad* in the 1990s. For him, there is much irony in the fact that the new embodied man is bearing 'many old views and values' (ibid.: 43). There is a resonance in Edwards' argument with that of Connell, grounded in a shared sceptical politics that contemporary gender relations at the level of both institution and subjectivity have been significantly troubled by the arrival of the new man. In short, they do not see men behaving well in a post-patriarchal society!

Inseparable Categories of Embodied Difference: Beyond a Simple Binary Colour-coded System

Carby's *Race Men* (1998) opens with the contrasting cultural visibility of the international iconic images of the bodies of Michael Jordan and Tiger Woods with that of the social invisibility of hundreds of thousands of black male bodies in North American prisons. With the ascendancy of the cultural turn within the academy, and difference as the new orthodoxy, this is an important reminder as Dollimore (1997: 18) suggests: 'No consideration of cultural/or racial difference should ever neglect the sheer negativity, evil, and inferiority with which the "other" of such differences has been associated throughout history.' In other words, there has been a long history when displaying the 'wrong body' served to position subordinated social groups as 'monstrous others', resulting in their annihilation. Various writers have provided fascinating materialist accounts of how representations of major divisions of bodily classifications and moral evaluation, including those of women, the working-class, national and minority ethnic groups, such as the Irish, Asians, Africans and African-Caribbeans, the disabled, gypsies and gays, have been positioned against the normative image of white European, middle-class, heterosexual, able-bodied men (Paterson, 1998).

A major limitation of this latter work is that ethnicity is often understood as a simple binary social system. At the same time, there is a tendency in much social science to conflate ethnicity with colour that is composed of a juxtaposed white superiority and a black inferiority. So, for example, early research on young black male bodies has projected them, in response to institutionalized racist systems, as simply enacting masculine expressions of political resistance. In our own work, we have sought to examine the formation of young masculinities through the dynamics of ethnicity as not simply about exploring the intersubjective dimensions of 'blackness' and 'whiteness' but as also contained within lived and imagined ethnic (national) histories. Across institutional spaces, it is possible to identify different masculinities as constitutive of racialized/ethnic identities. As a result, embodied masculinity may become the dynamic through which race/ethnicity is circumscribed (Mac an Ghaill, 1999). We particularly found such notions as techniques of the self and corporeal performance useful in exploring how contemporary ethnic subject positions are inhabited within the context of England.

As argued above, Foucault's earlier work on the production of identity as an effect of discourse has been influential in rethinking contemporary gender and sexual identity formations. However, at times this approach reads like a displacement of political economic determinism by discursive determinism, with its accompanying emphasis on the regulation and disciplining of the subject. In his later work, Foucault has suggested exploring identity as a technology of the self, where subjectivity is a socio-historical formation of dispersed institutional arenas of power (see Foucault, 1988a and in Rainbow 1984). This work develops the notion of agency, enabling us to explore more sensitively the specific historical dynamics of the production of complex and diverse racialized/ethnic subjectivities. One of the main concepts adopted by recent theorists is the notion of the techniques of the self, that is, modern forms of managing/producing the self. Foucault speaks of four types of techniques 'that he says agents practise on themselves to make themselves into the persons they want to be' (in Martin *et al.*, 1988: 18). They are technologies of production, which permit us to produce, transform or manipulate things; technologies of power, which determine the conduct of individuals; technologies of sign systems, which permit us to use symbols of signification; 'technologies of the self, which permit individuals to effect by their own means a number of operations on their own bodies and souls, thoughts, conduct, and way of being so as to transform themselves in order to attain a certain state of happiness, purity, wisdom, perfection or immortality'. As Nixon (1997: 323) maintains, in his work on masculinity, of particular significance here is that:

> Foucault's comments on "practices of the self" open up the possibility of conceptualising the articulation of concrete individuals to particular representations as performance based upon the citing and reiteration of discursive norms; a performance in which the formal positions of subjectivity are inhabited through specific practices or techniques.

An exploration of these techniques begins to address the absence of a conceptualization of the body in earlier literature on racism and ethnicity.

The move from a materialist to a post-structuralist position can be seen as signalling a shift from a concern with *labouring with* the racialized body, for example, in work on black slavery, labour migrants and the overrepresentation of minority ethnic communities in low skilled employment, to that of *labouring on* a culturally inscribed body within conditions of reflexive/aesthetic modernity, for example, in the work on the complex investments of a younger generation of white working-class men inhabiting black youth styles (Mac an Ghaill, 1999). One way of moving forward here is to link questions of the body to an exploration of the function of binaries within the formation of ethnic, racialized and national identities. For example, this process might involve deconstructing how Anglo-ethnicity gains an ascendant position in relation to minority ethnic groups through these binaries. In doing this, ethnic identity formation can be read as performative. Performative from a post-structuralist position suggests that ethnic, racialized and national identities are a continual establishment and articulation of binaries (Abbinnett, 2003). Linking techniques of the self and corporeal performance opens up an exploration of the concrete ways in which context mediates how racialized subjects deal with the lived realities of specific institutional locations. In response, materialists have criticized post-structuralists for assuming that identities are available to everyone, with the opportunity to take up, reposition themselves and become powerful. In the area of sexual politics, Butler (1993) has challenged this interpretation. She argues that the very conditions of identity formation are the interrelated cultural matrices of institutional and psychic gendered/sexual practices. As lived-out and state-regulated cultural representations, these practices in themselves become ontological evidence of an essential identity, even though, according to Bulter, such evidence is illusory.

In our own empirical work, we have explored how ethnicity is used as a cultural resource to live out young heterosexual male subjectivities. Fanon (1970), in *Black Skins, White Masks*, lucidly captures how the racialized black 'other' operates as a central dynamic in white identity formations. For Haywood (1993) in his ethnographic study of a sixth form college (post-compulsory), race created a number of complexities for white English males in their articulation of particular masculine heterosexualities. These male students conflated notions of Englishness and whiteness that became key components in circuits of desire. Those males who were part of a heterosexual culture that was premised on sexual athleticism experienced a range of psychic and microcultural contradictions because of their racist and homophobic dis-identifications with embodied black men and women. Englishness from their perspective was about being 'not black and not gay'. Through the demonstration of their masculinities, these young men were simultaneously articulating a racialized politics. At the same time, such dis-identifications limited, restricted and thus contested their claims to a sexual desire that was 'uncontrollable': a mainstay of their heterosexual masculinities. The relations between them also involved a psychic structure, including such elements as desire, attraction, repression, transference and projection in relation to a racialized 'sexual other' (Pajaczkowska and Young, 1992). There is much work to be done in this area in order to understand the ambivalent structure of feeling and desire embedded across institutional spaces (Bingham, 2001; Fanon, 1970).

At the same time, among the (Anglo) majority ethnic and minority ethnic young men living in England there has developed much emotional investment and cultural attachment to US black popular cultural forms, such as music and sport. These embodied cultural forms act as significant resources in their creative explorations of the shifting contours of cultural and political identities. It is particularly important to consider subjectivity not as a product, not as something possessed but rather as a complex and multifaceted process – the focus shifts from an emphasis on *being* (Anglo) ethnic to an emphasis on *becoming* ethnic. For young people living in multicultural urban settings, we have moved beyond the era of post-war colonial migration to that of English born minority ethnic communities. This marks a shift from the old corporeal certainties of skin colour as the primary signifier of social exclusion to more complex processes of regionally and institutionally based inclusions and exclusions. However, at conceptual, political and policy levels, the ongoing narrative of the post-war immigration of Asians and African Caribbeans is still being told in an older language of race and empire that is not able to grasp the generational specificities of emerging interethnic social relationships and their engagement with a different racial semantics. In short, within the context of a shifting visual sensibility, we are suggesting that we cannot simply read off social relations from fixed oppositional categories of black and white young men, which fail to capture embodied formations of identity, subjectivity and cultural belonging. Rather, we have found productive work that has deployed an inclusive notion of power and the complex self, recognizing how the intersection of inseparable categories of identity serve to constitute each other (Gilman, 1985). Earlier hierarchies of embodied difference, which privileged a unitary concept of race or gender as the determining category of regulation, are displaced by complex configurations of dynamic lived experience, shaped by national and cultural specificities, marked by globalization, cultural belonging and desire (Stecopoulos and Uebel, 1997).

Conclusion

We have illustrated in this chapter that the notion of engendered bodies continues to be highly contested. Early feminist work was highly successful in constructing a new explanatory vocabulary that named men's embodied social practices across a number of sites: the state, medicine, family life and cultural technologies, as instituting and reproducing control and exploitation of women's bodies as the locus of relations of ruling and the accompanying masculinist power. While holding onto the continuing significance of these accounts of materialist patriarchal domination, the chapter also addressed current third-wave feminism and queer theory that is attempting to go beyond the limiting effects of the polarity between the biological and the cultural in relation to sexed identities, alongside theorists of posthuman bodies questioning how cultural meaning is constructed in relation to bodies and selves (Halberstam and Livingston, 1995). Simultaneously, masculinity theorists in exploring a media-led gaze on male bodily practices – technologies of looking – as spectacular performance, in response to the global fragmentation of social relations, read this new cultural trend alternatively as evidence of the discursive emergence of the new (heterosexual) man or the stabilization of an existing hegemonic sex/gender order (Edwards, 1997; Nixon, 1996).

7
Media Masculinities and Femininities: Sporting Genders

Introduction

The rise of contemporary communication technologies has had a profound impact on everyday lives. Everyday practices and processes are being transformed by the emergence of new technology platforms, the compression of space and time and the generation of new products of consumption, resulting in what Urry (2003: 3) has called a 'kind of enforced proximity'. Historically, the transfiguration of communicative events has generated much anxiety around gender. For example, the development of the print media and the making of literature more accessible generated much fear in the seventeenth century that women reading literature would produce 'dangerous emotions' (Briggs and Burke, 2002). Similarly, the introduction of cinema, according to Fetveit (1999), was marked by moral guardians' apprehension that watching 'moving pictures' would 'damage' women's potential to give birth. Hargreaves (2001, np) argues that this is part of a historical trend where 'Biological arguments have been applied systematically to women's body ... in order to control cultural practices.' However, more recently researchers in men's studies also suggest that the media is generating a number of masculine roles that result in underdeveloped emotional growth and psychological damage (Garbarino, 1999; Pollack, 1996). For example, current public concern in the United Kingdom and the United States focuses on the impact of inappropriate music genres and violent computer games on boys' behaviour (Katz, 1999; McFarland, 2002). It is suggested that a major element of the anxiety surrounding the interface of technology with gender is a result of the media operating outside traditional institutions such as the church, family, schooling and education (Gorman and Mclean, 2003; Lasswell, 1948). As McLuhan (2001: 6–10) suggests:

> The medium, or process, of our time-electric technology is reshaping and
> restructuring patterns of social interdependence and every aspect of our

personal life. It is forcing us to reconsider and re-evaluate practically every thought, every action, and every institution formerly taken for granted. Your education, your government, your family, your neighbourhood, your job, your relation to 'the others'. And they're changing dramatically.

The implication of this is that the media is a developing authority on gender relations, designating and ordering legitimate and authentic masculinities and femininities. An authority, that unlike other institutions, is connecting the public and the private in new ways.

The impact of this new authority is that it is seen to be central in stabilizing and destabilizing traditional genders. In this way, media institutions engage gender through strong moral positions, often appointing themselves as speaking on behalf of nation or reflecting society's norms and values (Croteau and Hoynes, 2000). As a result, the media is a site for the projection of a cultural imagination with the 'media as an agency of collective fantasy' (Watney, 1987: 42). Cultural imagination is defined here to designate representations of history, tradition, heritage, and memory that tend to be mediated through language (cf. Kramsch 1998: 8). More specifically:

> Imagination is the selecting out and re-arrangement of "facts" in order to provide coherence, framework and unity between ideas and action or more precisely to provide a basis for the direction of social relationships and the social creation of categories. (O'Callaghan, 1995: 22)

Thus, particular social practices become a staging ground for the negotiated representation of gender (Huhndorf, 2001; Smyth, 2001). Embedded in this imagination is a moral economy, a machinery for incitement that authorizes, elevates and positions gendered being and doing. In order to explore this further, this chapter examines how the media represents the relationship between gender and sport. First, we examine how sport is understood to stabilize versions of femininity and masculinity. Second, we offer a number of caveats through which this stabilization can be read. Finally, the chapter argues that the media might also be seen as authoring other gendered possibilities as it is actively involved in the deconstruction of conventional categories of male and female.

Sport, Media and Gender

Concentrating on the notion that the media operates as a cultural imagination involved in the production of gendered identities, this chapter focuses on the media coverage of sporting events. Historically, such events were highly localized with the audience in close physical proximity. The mediation of the event across time and space was limited to the existing communication technologies such as oral, written or pictorial accounts. In this way, the mediation of sport to a larger audience was marked by a time – space delay as the technologies of distribution of the event were temporally and spatially staggered (Rowe,1999). As Tomlinson (2002: 275–6) writes:

> The story of sport has been increasingly interwoven with the story of the growth and spread of innovative … communication technologies and influenced by cultural entrepreneurs who seized with messianic zeal the opportunity to remake sport hand in hand with the broadcasting executives and corporate sponsors.

However, a rise of communication media has led to a reconfiguration of the time – space relationship and the ensuing selections and definitions of what constitutes sport and the events that are be mediated. 'Mass media', defined as: 'communication from one person or group of persons through a transmitting device (a channel) to a larger audience or market' (Biagi, 1996: 546), reflects the proliferation of the circulation of messages to 'mass' or large scale audiences. Furthermore, the interface between sport and media began to shape how sport gained exposure. Televisual sports began reshaping the format in which we watch sport as evidenced by the increasing use of close ups of athletes, multiple angles, player cams, slow motions, freeze frames and textual graphics. Furthermore, Real (1998) highlights how technical production is able to shape the nature of sport through narratives such as treating sporting events through the lens of soap operas with ensuing plots, characters, climax and resolution. The World heavyweight title fight between Muhammad Ali and Joe Frazier and subsequently their daughters, is an example of this. In other words, the mediation of the event is generating a different spectacle, an event with a particular sensibility in how we understand it. Thus, as Horne *et al.* (1999) suggest, with the introduction of cheap printing, cinema and television, technology has been reshaping the meanings of sport. As a result, the media: 'does far more than simply relay an event. It selects, frames, juxtaposes, personalizes, dramatizes and narrates. In the process, space and time are recomposed in order to enhance the education value' (ibid.: 169). Therefore, the mediation of sport carries and expresses the norms and values of society where transmitting 'structured play' is not simply about transparent communication but is involved in a complex amalgam of social, cultural and economic forces (Rowe, 1999).

Central to historical development has been the continual negotiation of the criteria that designates what constitutes authentic/'real' sport. It is argued that the technological processes involved in the communication of sporting events are simultaneously involved in a process of gendering

(Horne *et al.*, 1999). In other words, according to Creedon (1994), gendered categories are integral to the criteria of 'real sport' and she argues: 'Contemporary mass media, like play, epic poems, fairy tales, fables, parables and myths before them, preserve, transmit and create cultural information' (ibid.: 6). For example, sporting practices are overwhelmingly associated with tough, aggressive, competitive often violent and some-times dangerous practices combined with the rejection of that which is associated with femininity (Wright and Clarke, 1999: 229). As a result, sport itself implicitly expels norms and values of femininity and implicitly and often invisibly locates sport as a masculine practice. As Sabo and Jansen (1998) point out, the male athletic body is a body that defies its normal limits – a cultural archetype – one that many men may aspire to but few will ever reach. Embodying a disciplined and muscular body, the media becomes the theatre for sacrifice; a place where the hero can emerge. As a result, the media provides a valorizing space for athletes to exhibit violence and aggression whilst at the same time disparages those who display emotional or physical weakness.

The structuring of this gendered inequality has been identified by a number of perspectives that include liberal feminism, socialist feminism and more radical approaches (see introduction), alongside men's studies (especially in the United States). These perspectives share the position that the media is a socialization agent that not only involves teaching females to be inferior to males but is also involved in limiting the social roles and responsibilities that men are able to take up. One key explanation of this socialization is the concept of patriarchy. In this context, the unequal relationship between men and women is secured through the mediation of sport. In short, this mediation operates to secure a system of patriarchy, a set of patterns that according to Hartmann, (1994: 570) refer to 'a set of social relations between men, which have a material base, and which ... establish or create interdependence and solidarity among men that enable them to dominate women'. For instance, early research on the media's gendering of sport considered how representations cultivated sexism and reproduced stereotypes (Tuchman, 1978). This approach has its origins in the media effects research that was predominant in the United States in the mid-twentieth century. Such research was particularly concerned with how the media has negative effects on human behaviour, where what we do is caused by media messages (Giles, 2003). As such mediations service patri-archal interests, not only by reflecting the organization of society, they reproduce it, spreading it to other social and cultural spheres:

> The continued under-representation of women in sport and the denigration and trivialisation of their sport experience provides strong support for the myth of female passivity and frailty. This myth is manifested in barriers to

women's participation in traditionally male activities, perhaps most crucially, in traditionally male occupations. (Therberge and Cronk, 1994: 290)

Bryson (1994) argues that this structuring of inequality produces a number of effects; it creates a fraternity that legitimizes men's superiority over women, creates the situation where women accept that men are better at sport and patterns of oppression that become common sense. 'Sport is a powerful institution through which male hegemony is constructed and reconstructed and it is through understanding and confronting these processes that we can hope to break this domination' (ibid.: 47). The media is seen as a central aspect of this hegemony through its linking of masculinity with highly valuable and visible skills. The next section further develops *how* this structured gendered inequality manifests itself through the mediation of sport.

Gendering Sports News

Globally, there is an interesting pattern developing, in terms of women's participation in sport as increasing numbers of women are taking it up. For example, the International Olympic Committee (IOC) has recorded a growing number of women Olympiads, alongside an increasing number of sports in which they participate. In 1908, there were around 2000 female participants. In 2000, that had risen to over 4000 (men's participation was over 10,000). Likewise, in 1908 there were three women's events out of a total of 107 events. In the year 2000, women's events had grown to 132 out of 300 events. In sports, in England, women's participation in sport between 1987 and 1996 has risen to 38 per cent, whilst men's participation has fallen from 57 to 54 per cent. In terms of sports, women have increased their participation in keep fit/yoga (from 11 to 15 per cent) and swimming (from 12 to 17 per cent) (Sport England, 1999). The increasing parity between men and women's sport, may also be seen as generating parity in the coverage that it receives. For example, Buysse and Embser-Herbert (2004) conducted comparative research over a number of years. They examined the cover photos for the National Collegiate Athletic Association (NCCA) division I media guides that included United States female and male sports teams in basketball, golf, gymnastics, tennis and softball/baseball. They found that in 1990 out of the 307 covers analysed 47 per cent portrayed women's sport, whilst 53 per cent portrayed men's sport. In 1997, the proportions had altered, with 51 per cent showing women's sport and 49 per cent showing men's sport. As the authors suggest, on the face of the statistics it would seem that in terms of the pictorial representations, there appeared some kind of parity.

At one level, this supports the claims that journalists operate with values of objectivity, accuracy and fairness. In line with Kant's inconsequential-ism, where adherence to the rule is more important than the potential effects of that adherence, the principle of objectivity operates as a means to report events without bias. Central to reporting is the notion that events can be relayed or represented in a mirror like fashion. Journalists therefore operate as detached outsiders simply relaying the real world that exists out there. The emphasis on a mirror representation of news is increasingly assumed, given the shift in technology that provides 'live' coverage of the event. The emergence of digital technologies have increased the possibility of on the spot coverage and have reshaped how news is watched. In this way communication channels appear to operate as empty vessels, a neutral carrier of information where facts are separated from values. Thus, the media make appeals to truth by operating an objective stance. By advocat-ing values of objectivity, an active gendering of the news cannot take place because it simply reports the event. However, research has highlighted how news is 'put together' and produced, detailing how journalists, organizations and institutions operate in the production of the news (Clayman and Heritage, 2002; Schlesinger, 1978; Tuchman, 1978). From this perspective, journalists' everyday 'news routines' (Fishman, 1980), underlying social norms (Mermin, 1999) and ascribed values of the speakers (Graber, 2002) infiltrate and form the basis of objectivity. Such a position suggests that news organisations do not simplistically capture events and relay them through objectivity, rather they are important shapers and creators of news content (Croteau and Hughes, 2000). With this in mind, news does not simply report events, through its gendering, it creates them (Tuchman, 1978).

One of the ways that the mass media gender sport is through its practice of naming and non-naming of sporting events. It is suggested that most sport coverage is implicitly marked as male without stating it. An example of this would be the 100 metres in athletics. Unless it is prefaced by the 'women's' 100 metres, the event is implicitly coded as male. The media through 'simple' reporting, implicitly designate gendered assumptions about sporting events. As Sabo and Jansen (1998: 204) suggest:

> In Gestalt-like fashion, men have been naturalized and back-grounded by their historical omnipresence in sport. This has served both to expand and deepen the and rocentricity of representations of athleticism in western cultures while at the same time, camouflaging them.

The implication of this, is that female sport is often deemed inferior and less important. The definitional parameters of women's sport are implicitly and immediately problematized, as men's sport becomes an index of what constitutes proper, true and real sport. At this point, Irigaray's (1985) deconstruction of Freudian conceptions of female sexuality offers a useful conceptual purchase on the notion of this invisibility. Irigaray argues that the feminine is only known through the masculine. As a result, the female in the masculine schema is an inferior mimesis, purely constituted through the possibilities enabled by what is contained by the masculine. As a result, masculine norms and values depict and recreate the possibilities of women's sport as something less than the male version, a version that is judged and measured against the authenticity of masculine sport. As Kennedy (2000: 61) suggests: 'Gender appears then not as a discrete element in the televisualisation of sport, but as central to the disparate ideological themes around which sports narrative is constructed.' Thus, women have much difficulty in occupying the position of sporting 'hero' or 'saviour'. As a result, women may become athletes but their sex mediates an interrelationship between their athletic possibilities and the femininities that are held.

Using conventional communication research methods, further work has been conducted that measures across a wide range of communication media, the level of coverage that women's sport receives. This work demonstrates that a structured relation of inequality is evident. In a review of the coverage of sport in five European countries, Von Der Lippe (2002) highlights how they disproportionately cover women and men. More specifically, Capranica and Aversa (2002) explored Italian television coverage of the 2000 Olympic Games. They found that over 218 hours of Olympic events were broadcast. The coverage of women's events amounted to no more than 64 hours and resulted in only 29 per cent of the overall Olympic broadcast covering women's activities. Harris and Clayton (2002) argue that the inequality of coverage is contributing to the structuring of hierarchical power relations between men and women. They investigated 1348 sports related reports in two of the best selling UK tabloids in the summer of 2000. Key events at the time included Wimbledon, the beginning of European Football championship and the impending 2000 Sydney Olympics. Looking at the prose of the news reports rather than advertising, photography or cartoons, they found that 1157 reports were male-only focused. In contrast, women's sports received 80 reports. The remainder were non-specific or mixed gender. Other research in the United States, such as that of Duncan and Messner (1998) highlight that in 1994 men received 93.8 per cent of television coverage (see also Eastman and Billings, 1999; Tuggle and Owen, 1999). Although this appears as a very visible inequality, it is rarely contested or questioned and supports MacKinnon's (2003) claim that:

> when events brought to us by the media can seem so transparent and real, then the values that come with them appear not to be values at all, but part of the

natural world. This is exactly how masculinity becomes hegemonic – when ideology appears to be nothing of the sort but sheer, obvious common – sense'. (p. 102)

In earlier work on the mediation of sport, men have been seen to be actively involved in the 'symbolic annihilation' of women (Tuchman, 1978). As a result, meanings, choices and decisions about sports coverage shape women's participation and constructions of femininity. More recently, as Bernstein (2002) argues, it is not simply the amount of coverage but what that coverage contains. She emphasizes that the reporting of sport generates and reinforces social superiority through representations of male physicality and muscularity (Kane and Greendorfer, 1994). In this way, sports reports fuse gender expectations into physical dimensions and, as a consequence, position femininities as antithetical to sport. Moreover, not only does female physicality 'trouble' the legitimacy of male sporting participation, it activates a series of narratives that produce ways of reading female sporting activities. Choi (2000) argues that the media deal with this troubling by repackaging female athletes through sexuality, by making them sex objects for the masculine gaze that the positioning of them as married or mothers. Similarly, Harris and Clayton (2002) argue female sports stars are not simply represented as athletes, they are understood as *heterosexual* athletes. Indeed, their analysis of women's sport identified that coverage of tennis was often premised on a sexualization of the women involved rather than simply on their sporting achievements. Their examination of visual production, language, terminology and commentary marked them out as fundamentally heterosexual, thus positioning them as desirable to men as sex objects. For example, their focus on the tennis player Anna Kournikova illustrates that although relatively unsuccessful on the tennis circuits as a singles player, the media provide the player a high level of coverage. Yet this coverage was connected to a mode of reporting that juxtaposed traditional masculine and feminine traits. Therefore, in newspaper reports that examined male performances, the emphasis was on control/skill, strength/power and aggression/violence. In contrast, sportswomen tended to be understood on appearance as eligible heterosexual women. In this way, Kournikova was continually understood both through newspaper texts and photography as a sex icon, extolling her virtues of beauty, sex appeal and glamour. At the same time, Bernstein makes a telling point in suggesting that Kournikova is actively involved in her own sexual projection.

The projection of women in sport through conventional femininities is illustrated in Wright and Clarke's (1999) discussion of the reporting of a female rugby union team. They argue that media reports are responding to an increase in women playing men's sport. During 1996 and 1997, Wright and Clarke collected articles about women's rugby and considered how each of the reports drew upon particular notions of femininity and sexuality. They suggest that male journalists used traditional feminine stereotypes such as passivity, vulnerability and emotional dependency to emphasize the inappropriateness of females playing rugby. They maintain that women who play 'men's' sport appear to problematize what it means to be male. In response, newspapers reconfigure female sporting practices by adopting a discursive strategy that emphasizes the 'real' femininity of women playing rugby. In Wright and Clarke's (1999) assessment, athletes who display traditionally female characteristics are non-threatening to the essential masculinity of the sport. Therefore, in order to recuperate the threat, the media disparage the authenticity of their sporting activities employing misogyny, ridicule and belittlement. For example, in one news report, women's participation in the sport is defined through appearance. Wright and Clarke highlight that one of the devices used in the demarcation of femininities is a juxtaposition of the 'active sports woman' and the 'off the field woman'. Such a juxtaposition emphasizes how underneath the sports person women are really women. 'In other words, when you wash the mud off these hard hitting rugby players, a truly feminine and heterosexual woman will be revealed' (ibid.: 235). They also noted another interesting feature which was that sports reports were more likely to focus on those women who corresponded with a traditional heterosexual feminine stereotype. Thus, the use of the women's families to further normalize their participation was often used through an emphasis on the rugby players' motherly behaviours. As a result, Wright and Clarke argue that the media by working through discourses of the male gaze and heterosexual femininities exclude the possibility of lesbianism. Therefore, through a series of neutralization practices, sports reports can maintain traditional gendered categories.

If women are configured through traditional representations of femininity, it is argued that men are also bounded by specific masculine cultural forms. Furthermore, feminists argue that the messages being conveyed in the media aim to promote particular masculine subjectivities. According to Kennedy (2000), this subjectivity is constituted through a 'hero narrative'. She bases her analysis on Mulvey's (1975) notion that televisual sports media, in order to secure the gaze as masculine, have to exclude the possibility of the feminine and project a masculine narrative of the sports hero. Kennedy argues that in order to place the hero in sport, the media have to constitute that hero through the designation of a masculine subjectivity. Adopting Easthope (1992) notion of masculine style, based upon clarity, banter and obscenity, a 'hero' can emerge in the media when these characteristics are activated. Kennedy uses two televised sports to illustrate this. First, she argues that motor sport productions emphasize the technical and scientific aspects of racing and as a consequence generate a masculine character. Furthermore, the banter between the sports commentators and the drivers refer to a familiarity, a fraternity and finally the obscenity of the event is apparent through the dirt and the filth of the occasion. These elements combine, according to Kennedy, to make the winner of the race a hero of a masculine narrative. In the second sport, snooker, Kennedy also argues that masculine subjectivity can be constituted in similar ways. For example, the quality of clarity is generated by the personal skills of the snooker player. At the same time, the ability to control emotion is a central masculine attribute that appears to resonate with the British sensibility of 'gentlemanness' that surrounds snooker. The banter between the commentators and the snooker professionals generates an intimacy. Overall, the production of male-orientated sports and the corresponding narratives limits the potential positions that women can take up and occupy. At the same, Kennedy highlights how class codes can operate through these sports and how such class codes secure masculinities. Furthermore, those masculinities that occupied the spaces outside the official versions of masculinity were feminized.

Resonating with this gendering of sport, it is also argued that as a result of women's liberation and the visibility of gay rights, male hegemony has responded by cultivating a particular masculinity through televised news reports and commercial advertising. Jansen and Sabo (1994) suggest that: 'sport/war tropes are crucial rhetorical resources for mobilising the hierarchical values that construct, mediate, and maintain when necessary, reform or repair hegemonic forms of masculinity and femininity' (p. 186). For example, Messner *et al.* (2000) explore how the mediation of sport through patriarchal values is impacting upon boys. They identify the *televised sports manhood formula* that is constituted through ten themes that cultivate how boys should view gender and sport. It is a formula that socializes boys into a particular form of manhood. They provide a coherent and consistent message about what it means to be a man. For example, sports news by it's overconcentration on men tells boys that it is natural for them to participate in sport. When engaged in sport, it also tells them that in order for them to win, they must be tough and aggressive. Furthermore, the use of violence is not only accepted but expected if boys want to be competitive. Other aspects of the manhood formula involve thinking of sport as war, showing 'guts' and giving up their body for the team. Reinforced by masculine-orientated advertising, sports on US television operates as a pedagogy to young men. Playing on their insecurities, it shows them how to avoid shame and overcome embarrassment by imitating the values that sports programmes and their associated advertising projects.

Another technique that is used to displace women's claims to be accepted in sport has been through the practice of infantilizing women.

This is a process where the media represent women's femininities as closely connected to childhood. Sports coverage symbolically connects women's activities with cultural codes of childhood. One of the ways to produce this is explicitly to designate women as girls. Duncan *et al.*'s (1994) exploration of the televisual coverage of women's basketball highlights how these women's achievements were contextualized by references to the connections between their childhood and adult status. This was further reinforced by interviews with the women's mothers. According to Duncan *et al.*, in this sport, women tended to be referred in more adult terms unlike other sports. For example, they considered sports such as tennis, where women tend to be referred by their first names, unlike men who are referred to in a much more formal address. This infantilization corresponds with a trivialization of women's sport and in effect gives men adult status. It is further argued that this trivialization questions the sporting legitimacy of women's participation in such activities. Messner *et al.* (2003) analysed televised sport over a six-week period that included 251 sports news broadcasts across three television networks. They found that where reports focused on sport in more depth, these tended to be 'pseudo sports'. For example, the longest news report on women's sport was a focus on a WWF (World Wrestling Federation) woman wrestler renowned for her strong sexual dominatrix style. The report covered her during a photo-shoot and discussed her appearance in Playboy. According to Messner *et al.*, this focus on wrestling porn resonated with the unofficial policy of the channel to take up a position of sexual voyeurism. Across the three channels there was a differentiation in the style of the media reports, however, overall there was a tendency for all programmes to prioritize discussion of women who offered a means for sexual titillation.

The reproduction of women's roles can also be found in the visual organization of televisual reports. Screen theory which developed in the 1970s analysed films through a psychoanalytical perspective, exploring how the text fixed the spectator (Mulvey, 1975). A similar perspective is adopted by contemporary feminists. MacNeill (1994) identifies a number of characteristics of the mediation of sport and gender on television. She suggests that the camera angle is significant for audiences and explains how they make sense of the images. In her comparison between women's weightlifting and aerobics, she found that an overwhelming amount of shots in the televising of the aerobics routine were aerial and an effect of this was that it accentuated women's cleavage. A similar practice has been identified by Duncan's (1990) analysis of ice skating. When looking at the female figure skater the camera looks down, when viewing the male skater, the camera looks up. This presentation of figure skating according to Duncan adopts the camera views of soft pornography. This was identified by McNeil (1994), who also found that in the aerobics programme, the generation of sexual imagery was emphasised by shots of the women bending over with close ups of thighs, hips and buttocks. In contrast, the camera in the body-building competition concentrated on long shots where the camera was not tilted. As a result, the long shots enabled viewers a fuller evaluation of the bodies in the event. Furthermore, although the aerobics programme was aimed at encouraging women's participation in the activities, the exclusivity of shots on women's bodies limited the directions of the aerobics instructor. It should also be added that the camera shots of the aerobics class operated in a similar fashion to the camera angles that are used in pornography. The implication is that such representations limit the possibilities of women's subjectivity. In other words the possibilities for an active female sporting subjectivity is circumscribed by these processes of mediation.

Reframing Gendered Representations

The above work has been crucial in identifying the gendered absences and exclusions that circulate through the mediation of sport. However, such accounts tend to suggest one dimensional notions of masculinity and femininity. In other words, these critical analyses of gender in the media tend only to view representations as gendered or non-gendered. As a result, other social categories such as class or sexuality simply operate conceptually as constitutive of gender. For example, accounts of heterosexuality or sexualization are deemed to be consolidating unequal gendered relations. There is little use of sexuality itself as a distinct category that is not underpinned by gendered representations. Thus, what appears absent from accounts is how social categories work together to produce gendered representations that are inflected by other social categories. Identifying this limitation, Wensig and Bruce (2003) acknowledge that media applies 'rules' to women's sport (such as gender marking, compulsory heterosexuality, appropriate femininity, infantilization and trivialization). They, however, suggest that a new rule should be added. This is a rule of ambivalence, a refusal to analyse media representations simply based upon juxtapositions between men and women.

In looking at the 2000 Sydney Olympic Games, Wensig and Bruce (2003) provide a case where the traditional rules of sports journalism and gender appear to be breaking down. Over a period of one month they looked at 700 articles about Cathy Freeman, an Australian athlete, who was tipped to win the women's 400-metre running race. They argue that rather than support the conventional rules about women in sport journalism, news reports in this period contested and challenged them. For example, Wensig and Bruce argue that media accounts did not gender mark the 400-metre race.

Furthermore, they suggest that the Australian media tended to identify the 400 metres as the most important track and field event and became a central part of a national imaginary. This was reinforced by the media prioritizing the women's 400 metres race before that of the men's 400 metres race, with the implication that the main race 'just happened to be the women's 400 m'. A similar process occurred after the 2004 Olympics in Greece, as Kelly Holmes won the 800 metres and the 1500 metres running events. Her success eclipsed the men's race, and subsequently, the media has tended not to prefix the race with a specific gender. In Australia, Wensig and Bruce go on to argue that the construction of Cathy Freeman's identity did not operate through either traditional female or aboriginal stereotypical characteristics. Such characteristics tend to presuppose emotional weakness and an inability to cope under pressure. Rather, media accounts projected the athlete in absolute control of her emotions. This was also emphasized by representing the athlete as 'strong, powerful and physically capable'. Furthermore, the eye-catching clothing that Freeman wore tended not to be referred to as a fashion statement that enhanced her traditional femininity by emphasizing her heterosexuality but rather was understood as a technological innovation.

As highlighted in the previous section, media reports in Anglophone regions tend to insist on making visible and understanding female sports stars through notions of heterosexuality. Yet the research by Wensig and Bruce suggests that although passing references were made to Cathy Freeman's heterosexuality – this was already common cultural knowledge before the games – it was not covered in depth. In short, Cathy Freeman did not depend on sexual attractiveness to frame the possibility of her achievement. Although there were instances where Freeman was described as childlike, corresponding with her own disbelief that 'this is happening to a girl like me'; the designation of girlness was not simply a gendered category. According to Wensig and Bruce, this is intricately linked to Australia's racial/ethnic politics. For example, the infantilizing of Freeman as the girl was also connected to how she had become the daughter of the nation. Cathy Freeman was not simply female, she was also Aborigine and it is suggested that her participation and success in the Olympic Games functioned allegorically with Australia's racial/ethnic sensibility. Rather than gendered, Freeman's sporting success became a space where a national imaginary could be worked through. She was not only the symbol of a successful Australian nation, she also came to represent a nation's racial/ethnic reconciliation. Therefore, Wensig and Bruce argue that Cathy Freeman became reconstructed as the daughter of a divided nation, ethnically and racially unifying the country through her sporting success. Underlying this analysis is the notion that social and cultural categories do not operate in isolation, rather they work together to constitute representations. As a result, this is not to suggest that national concerns replaced gendered concerns, but rather that gendered representations were reworked within the context of a national imaginary.

The interconnection between gender, sport and nation have been highlighted by a number of studies. Archetti's (1999) study of sport and masculinity in Argentina provides a fascinating insight into how gender and nationality in the context of football are intertwined. Due to British immigrants, football became one of the most pervasive sport in Argentina in the nineteenth Century. At this time, football styles appeared to embody national identities, thus, football teams emphasized strength, organization and courage. However, in 1913, Racing Club, a football club that had both Spanish and Italian ethnicities, won the football league. Of importance was that they adopted a different football style that was based upon dribbling and technical skill or *viveza criolla* (cunning play). This creolization of Argentinean football enabled a new sense of masculinity to be developed, that of a masculinity based upon small 'boy' looking agile and a technically gifted player. Rodriguez (2005) provides an intriguing insight into the contemporary gendered practices of football fans and media representation. These include how female football fans are both excluded from media reports but also become symbolic of the Argentinean nation. The importance of national history to gender and sport is also highlighted by Von Der Lippe's (2002) study (mentioned above), which demonstrates how women's handball in Denmark, Germany, Hungary, Norway and Romania has been highly contextualized by its national identity. Thus media reporting of handball used metaphors of war in order to describe competitive matches. The interplay between war and sport has been aptly captured by Jansen and Sabo (1994: 1) who argue that 'sport/war tropes are crucial rhetorical resources for mobilising the patriarchal values that construct, mediate, maintain, and, when necessary, reform or repair hegemonic forms of masculinity and femininity.' Furthermore, the elision of metaphors of sport and war with romance may implicitly provide a nationalized structuring of the gendered intimacy.

A second limitation of the above studies is that they assume that there is an unproblematic relationship between media messages and the effect of the message. In other words, a concept of patriarchy is used as a methodological tool through which to uncover how the message is formulated and then simultaneously used to explain why that message is being communicated. This means that the studies in the previous section suggest that the mediation of sport is part of patriarchal organization of society and perpetuates a masculine hegemony. It assumes that media organizations are run by men and actively function to sustain and maintain men's interests. At the point of encoding messages, media industries are involved in the process of negotiating gender at a number of levels. In their multilevel analysis of gender and media, that included content, production and audience, Knoppers and Elling (2004) found unequal amounts of space given to male and female sport. From national newspapers and television stations in Holland, they collected reports over a period of 16 regular days. They found that women's sports received 6 per cent of space in newspapers and 4 per cent in television. As mentioned above, such a disproportion of coverage indicates a highly unbalanced reporting of male and female sports. In order to explain this, Knoppers and Elling held 15 interviews with (10 male/5 female) journalists/editors who were employed in national newspapers and television. By asking the journalists to describe their news routines, they were able to consider how journalists promoted gendered understandings.

According to Knoppers and Elling, the main criterion for the selection of a sporting event is not through gender discrimination but through the notion of 'top performance'. It emerged that journalists used an informal categorization of what counted as 'top' sport. This categorization was constituted by international events, professional sports and performances by popular Dutch athletes. As a result, the journalists through their notion of 'top performance' implicitly marginalized women's sport. Another dynamic involved in the journalists' organizing the space in the newspaper was a notion of what the public wanted to read. Journalists and editors considered that 'public interest' was a key factor in defining what was a 'top performance'. This was also qualified as a commercial concern, as the success of the paper was premised on its ability to connect with its readership. The journalists maintain that they are disinterested, suspending their interests for that of their readership. As a result, 'men's sport' was covered because their audience wanted it. Finally, the deployment of resources based on tradition determined which events were being covered. Traditional sports events tended to be men's sport that had been commercially successful.

Creating Mediations/Creating Genders

It is argued that the studies above tend to presuppose that the media exist as a homogenous entity. However, it may be productive to deconstruct what we understand as the media; recognizing that the 'media' is a product of relationships that occur within the institutional making of media. By deconstructing the media, this approach opens a critique that focuses on the undertheorization of the communicative event. Stuart Hall's (1980) classic theorizing of the communication process gives analytical purchase on how context may be built into the coding of gender. Hall's theory breaks down the communication process into three stages: the sender, the message and the receiver. These correspond to the production, circulation, distribution and consumption of communication. In each of these stages, a particular moment central to these practices is the instantiation and configuring of meaning. The sender, for example, in the first stage, is in a process of encoding the message. This involves 'the institutional practices and organizational conditions and practices of production' (Corner, 1983: 266).

The above study by Knoppers and Elling provides an interesting line of enquiry when considering the organizations and practices of production. If objectivity is considered as a masculine practice, then how does this position female journalists? Advocating ideals of objectivity would therefore result in a masculine practice that would on the evidence of the above study continue to marginalize women's involvement in sport. This would open up traditional feminist accounts that simplistically identify patriarchy as something to do with men. It appears that women are engaged in – from this perspective – their own subjection. As a result, patriarchy is an overall ideology that envelops men and women. This is explored in Milkie's (2002) case study of magazines aimed at teenage girls in the United States, who highlights the complex relationship between institutional negotiation of content and perceptions of the audience. A key aspect of this work is to identify how stereotypes that distort women's role in society are perpetuated in women's magazines. She argues that research on girls' responses to images in female magazines often criticize the magazines for their narrow and distorted view of female beauty. From around the United States, girls were voicing concerns that magazines never show images of 'real' women, that is, those who do not correspond to images of femininity based on thin, 'barely there' bodies. As a result, magazines through their narrow versions of beauty are participating in cultural oppression. This 'symbolic annihilation' presents a narrow distorted version of feminine beauty; the media creates a gap between the lived and the ideal. However, she argues that in order to grasp the complexity of the issue, representations of femininity have to be considered as an institutional negotiation.

To explore this further, Milkie conducted interviews with staff at a teen magazine to ascertain how institutions produce such images. Through face-to-face interviews with ten editorial staff (nine out of ten were women) and a marketing representative she found how editors legitimated their inaction towards girls' concerns. Although some agreed that girls' claims about the unreal presentation of bodies is oppressive, the editors maintained that they could not change what images were included in the magazine. For example, these editors suggest that they are unable to control photographers and the art department and the production of the images. According to Milkie, the editors did try to incorporate more real life images into the magazines but these were met by resistance from photographers who wanted to create the most aesthetically appealing images. Another claim was that advertisers preferred to have non-real images in their magazine. Advertising is what makes the magazine function – the revenue enables the survival of the magazine, therefore the editors have to respond to the interests of the advertisers. Advertisers required particular female bodies to sell the product that often promoted normative notions of beauty and attractiveness. Finally, other editors suggested that they had limited choice over the inclusion of body images because the organization was part of a broader cultural oppression.

A second set of responses from the editors was that girls' responses to the body images were misguided. The editors suggested that the images are supposed to be fantasy, where images are merely there for enjoyment and leisure, not lifestyle guides. Furthermore, editors also suggested that such body images should be understood in the context of the magazine's broader ethos of self-indulgence, individuality and self-expression. Hence, girls were misreading the magazines by not receiving the full message that incorporated and empowered young women. As a result, the magazine continued to represent femininity through these images. Thus Milkie suggests that 'Editors are operating within and are a key part of both organizational, market, and institutional constraints and symbolic constraints as they negotiate multiple voices and demands about the portrayal of femininity' (ibid.: 855). In this account, the production of the representation of femininity is a complex situation that oscillates between personal integrity and market forces. Fundamentally, Milkie's study highlights that the generation of traditional feminine stereotypes cannot be reducible to men's interests.

If Milkie's study of the production of gendered images considers the first stage of Ang and Hermes, (1991) process of mediation. The second stage concerns the 'text' itself. This refers to the subject positions that are encoded within the text. Ang and Hermes (1991: 321) argue that this is the point where the symbolic material of gender positioning can be found. In other words, media consumption can be understood as a complex gendered practice where 'its modularity and effectivity can only be understood by close examination of the meanings that "male" and "female" and their interrelationships acquire within a particular context'. The third stage of the communication pattern focuses on how 'message content' is read. At this moment, the message becomes symbiotically connected to those who take up the message. Ang and Hermes (1991) develop this third stage. They argue that feminist media accounts implicitly suggest that the messages that are circulated are transparent and unambiguously project meanings. As such, according to Ang and Hermes, the semiologies embedded in the media texts and the audience they target are conflated. In response, Ang and Hermes suggest that it is important that work in the media focuses on how texts are actually engaged: 'Textual generalizations about the "the female spectator" turns out to foreclose prematurely the possibility of empirical variation and heterogeneity within actual women's responses (p. 311). This is in contrast to many of the studies in the previous section which argue that messages are encoded with gender-related meanings and understandings. Furthermore, they maintain that when audiences are confronted with these messages, the content flows unproblematically. The political implications can involve the stabilization or disruption of social norms and values. A good example of this would be pornographic magazines and violent videos. Legislation surrounds these areas because it is assumed that audiences absorb such messages and act on them. Thus State concerns over the circulation of media have been premised on the assumed power of the media as generating consciousness, shaping minds and 'effecting audiences'. Early communication theory framed the media as a 'magic bullet' or a 'hypodermic needle', where messages are injected into audiences. From this position it appears that many analyses of gender also adopt a hypodermic model of the media. In contrast, Ang and Hermes suggest that men and women read texts differently according to their prior experience. Thus, the impact of gender positionings need to take into account the relationship of both the rational and emotional with 'concrete' subjects (see Fiske, 1987).

Transformations in Sports Media

At the beginning of this chapter it was suggested that the media had transformed localized sports events into mass media phenomena and as a result were involved in the construction of gendered boundaries. However, it has also been argued that the technologies around the mediation of sport is creating the conditions whereby sport, rather than simply consolidating traditional gendered boundaries, is becoming an important cultural site in contributing to their fragmentation. This can be related to Davis' (1994) notion of the postmodern paradox. Drawing upon Lyotard (1984), Davis argues that the current social and cultural condition is not about the consensus of meaning, rather it is about the stabilizing of uncertainty. In her case study of cheerleading in the United States, Davis explores how cheerleading has shifted from an exclusively male practice to one that has, since the 1940s, been naturalized as something feminine. Furthermore, conventional understandings place cheerleading as a feminine practice that services men's sport and operates in the interests of the heterosexual male gaze. For Davis, however, cheerleading is experiencing a number of tensions. The increasing visibility of female cheerleaders at women's events is beginning to problematize the nature of gendered relationships within sport. The generation of this paradox, according to Rail (1998) is a result of the media beginning to loosen the relationship between the signified and the signifier. This cultural studies approach argues that it is no longer predictable what sporting representations mean. The media it is argued is producing an implosion of meaning. For example, contemporary audience subjectivities that sport is generating are being transformed through increasing technological advances that involves the amplification of noise, collage, graphics, cuts and simulations. Rail suggests that sport is no longer fixed as a spectacle in a traditional sense. Rather, sport is being transformed into something that is dissected, examined, appraised and consumed. In other words, the current mediation of sport is a fetishized spectacle.

In a gendered sense, it could be argued that integral to the loosening of the signifiers is a fragmentation, a loosening of the boundaries that demarcate 'real sport' and the gendering that has traditionally held that 'realness' in place. This fragmentation could be observed as more women take up sports that are culturally coded as exclusively male. Such codings presuppose that women are unable or unwilling to participate, as the inherent characteristics of sport symbiotically connects it to male psychology and physiology. One such sport is boxing with women's participation increasing dramatically. For example, in the United Kingdom, there are over 50 amateur women's boxing clubs, while in Sweden this has reached over 300. However, although the spectacle of women's boxing dates back to the seventeenth century, it has only once, in 1908 been considered as an Olympic sport. It may regain its exhibition status in the Olympic Games in China in 2008 but the earliest it could have parity with men's sport is 2012. Women's participation in boxing is paradoxical because, as Hargreaves (1997) argues, women's participation deconstructs the symbolic boundaries through which masculine and feminine operate. Given that boxing cultivates aggression, violence and danger, Hargreaves maintains that boxing is a sport that is at odds with traditional notions of essential femininity. Thus the media coverage of women's participation in the sport is fracturing the traditional categories of gender. The area is further complicated as Hargreaves argues that women from middle-class backgrounds are becoming involved in a sport that tends to be coded as working class. Therefore, the fracturing of gendered sports should not be read simply as male–female oppositions but are also marked by other social categories, such as class, age or race/ethnicity.

If the relationship between sign and signifier is breaking down, then one issue that is gaining much media attention is the participation in sport by transsexuals. Discussions of transsexuality are often accompanied by issues of drug testing as transsexualism also antagonizes notions of equality of participation. More specifically, gender reassignment, from male to female, is deemed to give women an unequal and unfair advantage because of previous muscular development. Thus, the Women's Sport Foundation (WSF) argues that current legal rulings on transsexual cases are determined by a number of physiological tests that identify male–female performance parameters. According to the WSF, such equality has an appeal to a biological frame which in turn resonates with previous modernist assumptions:

- that anyone exposed to testosterone at puberty will be a good athlete;
- that all males make better athletes than all females;
- that males will change gender in order to reap rewards in women's sport which they are unable to obtain by competing in men's sport.

(Women's Sport Foundation, 2003, p. 4)

A number of mediated events have taken place that have begun to question the modernist constructions of gender and sport. One of the first to gain media visibility was the tennis player Renee Richards. She was a male to female transsexual who was playing on the US tennis circuit in the mid-1970's. What came to light was that when she applied to play in the US tennis Open, the official bodies involved in the sport excluded her. After winning a case in the Supreme Court – that designated her legally female – Renee Richards took part in the 1977 US Open and lost in the first round. Birrell and Cole (1994) suggest that media reporting of the event rearticulated bipolar oppositions of men and women. Other sports that continue to ban transgendered participants include European and United States golf tours. However, in 2004, Mianne Bagger, a male to female transsexual, became the first to play in the Australian Women's Open. In contrast, women's golf organizations in Europe and the United States do not allow transsexuals to participate unless they are born female. Similar reluctance to transsexuals can be found in other sports. For example, in Canada, leading members of the women's downhill mountain-bike team have publicly distanced themselves from Michelle Dumaresque. Dumaresque was chosen to represent Canada at the World Championships where none of the other women riders bar one talked to her. Although suspending her licence, the Canadian Cycling Association and the Union Cycliste Internationale (UCI), the authorities which regulate both the Tour de France and World Cup mountain-bike racing, reissued it because her birth certificate was amended to read female. It appears that in the above cases the appeal for nostalgia is increasingly made to definitions of physiological sex. As Joyrich (1996) argues: 'such gender implications take on new meaning in the post-modern age as the threat of fluctuating signs, unstable distinctions and fractured identities provokes a retreat towards nostalgia for firm stakes of meaning' (p. 405). As Chapter 7 suggests, this appeal to the natural and retreat to nostalgia is itself part of a contemporary social and cultural condition (Gatens, 1996)

The mediation of sport also confuses the boundaries around masculinity. Rowe *et al.* (2000) argue that traditional notions of masculinities that circulate through sport are becoming increasingly destabilized. They argue that the mediation of sport is actively involved in making bodies visible. However, the bodies that are being made visible are no longer the disciplined, honed bodies of sports men and women but are carrying other forms of symbolic and material rewards. The reconfiguration of the sports person as an object of cultural desirability and consumption is problematizing what have been traditionally heavily masculinized bodies. For example, Sabo and Jansen (1998) in their discussion of the construction of masculinity suggest that western media have connected male athleticism with strength, power, virility and potency. Resonating with war, politics and science, it is argued that athletic perfection has become a major cultural benchmark for the measuring of masculinity. However, other work has argued that events outside of the sports arena are now contributing to a fissuring of the masculinities that are central to constituting that sport. For example, Rowe *et al.* (2000) suggest that the media has become one of the technologies that have been actively involved in the dissolution of racialized athletic masculinities. They highlight how key sporting personalities Ben Johnson, Michael Jordan and Mike Tyson have functioned to problematize the 'naturalness' of sporting masculinities. These stars have been involved in major reconfiguration of their cultural status through drug taking, contracting HIV and rape. The implication of the controversy that has surrounded these stars has been through the existence of 'sporting' excess. The underlying natural aspects of the male athlete – desire to win, aggression and hypermasculinity have generated an excess that has in turn problematized those very attributes. Furthermore, as Dunbar (2000) in her discussion of Dennis Rodman, a National Basketball Association player who cross-dresses suggests, the excess itself works itself back into the sporting performance. The impact is the conflation between the erotic body and the athletic body and that Rodman's emphasised sexual ambivalence through the carrying of traditional feminine signifiers is opening up these traditional gendered boundaries. Such ambivalence is emphasized by Rodman's emphasis on a hypersexual 'black' masculinity where the phallus has a central organizing dynamic.

Another example of the notion of excess is explored by Whannel (2000) in his discussion of David Beckham. Media reporting of the England football captain has generated a number of narratives that have focused on his masculinity. Alongside being the epitome of an English football masculinity that circulates through meanings of courage, bravery, hard work and patriotism, the cultural framing of David Beckham positions him, as Miller (1998: 349) suggests, on the 'edge of conventional masculinity'. The class politics of English football has operated mimetically with other traditional masculinities that are constituted through work with the body, the (industrial) body was the adjunct, the interface between labour process and material rewards (see ch. 3). There are important limitations of linking masculinities with class identities. Hearn (1992) suggests that it is important not to simply reduce kinds of occupations to simple masculinities. For example, Carrington (1998) identifies how black footballers can occupy different class-based masculinities. However, the emergence of football as a global industry has repositioned footballers as global spectacles that involve footballers not simply working with their bodies but working on their bodies. Central to the work of the sports star is a paradox, the repositioning of the football icon not through labour with the body but that which is on the body.

In England, there has been an increasing media-led fascination with sports stars and their lifestyles off the pitch. More recently a series of high profile sexual incidents by footballers has reframed the excess of their sports performance back inside masculine class codes. Therefore the masculinity of sports stars has moved beyond body function to body style, the parameters for the evaluation of that style are constantly being reframed within and through traditional class codes of the footballer. A productive analysis of this process has been provided by Cashmore and Parker (2003), who connect conventional sports stars with the concept of conspicuous consumption. However, unlike previous accounts of conspicuous consumption that is premised on the accumulation of wealth, contemporary conspicuous consumption is connected to the demonstration of a particular lifestyle. As Cashmore and Parker suggest, Beckham carries a range of representational capital that marks his masculinity with ambivalence. For example, alongside the cover shoots for gay men's magazines, his wearing of a Sarong and painted nails and the continual restyling of his hair, marks an emphasis on troubling the masculinity/femininity boundaries. At the same time, this emphasis on 'body masculinity', where the key cultural codes appear to be premised on lifestyle rather than sporting prowess is reinforced by his display and projection of his familial masculinity with his sons in football kits and the tattooing of his family on his body. The implication is that the media reporting of David Beckham is not simply on the football pitch, rather it is highly focused on his lifestyle away from the pitch. In short, this lifestyle, this conspicuous consumption operates as a code to depict his success as a footballer.

Conclusion

This chapter has considered the relationship between the mediation of sport and practices of gendering. The first section highlighted the multiple ways in which the media upheld and consolidated traditional gendered binaries. In response, the next section held this approach in tension, critically considering some of the assumptions that lay behind the media as a producer of gendered binaries. The final section considers how the media is generating the possibility of the fracturing of these binaries. Overall, there appears a need to review the representations of masculinities and femininities that are being made available by popular cultural technologies such as television, films, the internet and music. It is suggested that the emergence of other technological platforms are continuing to reconfigure gendered relationships in alternative ways. As explored in Chapter 6, the impact of various platforms (digital, satellite and cable) have reshaped how we meet sexual partners – telephone dating, internet chat rooms, mobile phone meeting groups and blue 'toothing'. The increasing scope of the channels has impacted upon the nature of the message they convey. The use of technology is enabling the configuration and shaping of gendered relations. In other words, ways of communicating are becoming orientated whereby the process of interpretation, production and distribution of gendered messages is being transformed. Consensus about the nature of that transformation has yet to be reached.

8

Men and Women of the World: Emerging Representations of Global Gender Relations

Introduction

It is argued that we live in a global community with transformations across space and place generating new forms of social and cultural practices. It is further argued that we are part of a global community that is subject to the possibilities of being and becoming through the emergence of contemporaneous gendering processes. A key aspect of this argument is to explore how the dispersal of cultural forms across regional and national boundaries are shaping gendered subjectivity and forms of belonging. In short, globalization can be understood as the unparalleled transfer of social, cultural, economic and political processes, procedures and technologies across national borders. Such movements are produced through a compression of time and space and the generation of a sense of immediacy and simultaneity about the world (Brah *et al.*, 1999).

A wide range of theorists have made an important contribution to how globalization, imperialism and post-colonialism are constituting gender identities (Bhabha, 1990; Gilroy, 1993; Kearney, 1988; Spivak, 1988b). As Chow (2003: 244) suggests the constitution of subjectivity is being impacted upon by new social and cultural forms that include: 'processes of worldwide economic, social, cultural and political expansion and integration which have enabled capital, production, finance, trade, ideas, images, people and organisations to flow instantaneously across boundaries of regions, nation states and cultures'. Central to this chapter is the notion that such global processes are not simply neutral disembodied processes, but operate to configure possibilities of fantasy, fear and desire that are impacting upon what it means to be a woman or man at local or global levels.

Feminist theory and Men's Studies have provided important insights into these interstices of gender and globalization. As we shall indicate

195

below, these fields of enquiry are varied in their theoretical analyses. One of the shared grounds of these diverse approaches has been to establish the gendered nature of global processes (Eschle, 2004). Much mainstream work on global processes tends to see them as gender neutral. This means that at a common sense level, global practices such as capital transactions, trade and aid organizations operate beyond the sphere of gender relations. As Connell (1998: 58) points out: 'Neo-liberal politics has little to say, explicitly about gender. It speaks a gender neutral language of "markets", "individuals" and "choice".' This means that at a philosophical level – the level of ontology (the foundations of reality) – global practices operate without gender distinction or variation. Thus, one of the central aims of much work on gender and globalization has been to illustrate ways within which gender is ontologically connected to global processes. The methodological implication of this 'realist' position is that gender is important only if it is something specifically to do with men and women's lives. Therefore from a conventional economic position some practices are inherently gendered whilst others are not.

This framework is highly dependent on the conceptual separation of object and the meanings attached to that object. In doing so, the realist immediately participates in an exclusionary political action. It can be argued that at that point of separation a gendering – by default – has already taken place (Harding, 1991). Much work by feminist theory and Men's Studies has suggested that global processes cannot be separated from gender relations. Rather, gender is constitutive of global processes. Drawing upon a range of feminist theoretical positions, Eschle (2004) maps out and provides a comprehensive discussion of the different ways that gender and globalization have been brought together. She outlines two distinctive approaches to which this conceptual engagement has taken place. First, she argues that feminist theory (and we would add some Men's Studies texts), have focused on the *economic political* perspective that considers how global forces influence national and regional economies and institutions. The *economic political* approach is aptly illustrated by work by Pearson (2000) who argues that one of the ways of bringing gender back into the analysis of globalization is to understand the differential effects of globalization on men and women. More specifically, she argues that across the world, the expansion of economics, trade, technology and the migration of people is resulting in increasing participation of women in the labour force. The impact of such transformations, she argues, might be seen as reorganizing traditional patriarchal hierarchies and the troubling of male breadwinning roles. Furthermore, Pearson argues that the opposite effect of women moving into the labour market is not drawing men into the sphere of domestic labour. This is resulting in a double burden for women who continue to occupy temporary low-waged work, while taking responsibility for the domestic sphere. This is also being exacerbated by men becoming the main migrants across deregulated trade borders resulting in changes in public and private responsibilities for men and women. This understanding of globalization is considered in Chapter 9.

The usefulness of this argument is that it assists in identifying the particular patterns and structures of gendered relationships that are being generated by global processes. As Aguila (2004: 6) argues:

> From the Maqualadora in Mexico ... to assembly plants and export process zones in Central America, the Caribbean and Pacific Rim, to subcontractors and garment sweatshops in global cities and nations of the periphery, it is women's labour that allows and guarantees maximum profitability for the corporate elite, a tiny minority of the world's inhabitants.

In terms of the political, Sylvia Walby's (2002) work provides a detailed examination of how the diffusion of political ideas, such as democracy, are impacting upon the economic and political position of women across the world. Looking at the broader patterns that connect women's democracy and global change, Walby highlights the importance of capturing the inter-relationships between local practices with global processes. Her work considers the rise of women's representation in parliaments across the world and links it to a number of processes. She finds that women's increased participation in democracy is not simply due to economic factors but also the impact of international feminist movements. Walby's work helps to situate not only how global processes impact upon women's lives but suggests that we need to look at the local and global organization and patterning of gender relations. Thus, an important means of making sense of the gendering of globalization has been to consider how globalization itself contains gendered values. Furthermore, such work is valuable in situating within a historical context who wins and who loses on a global scale. Within this frame, pro-feminist Men's Studies on masculinity and globalization have emphasized the importance of looking at men's practices within a global context as a means to understand how power relations are distributed (Morrell, 2002; Pease and Pringle, 2001). These accounts demonstrate how men's practices exploit and oppress women and other men. Such accounts connect with theories of patriarchy that not only operate within local specific relationships but extend across nations and world regions, something that is considered in greater detail below.

The second area that Eschle identifies is that of *cultural social perspectives*, an approach that considers the particular meanings and understandings that are being generated by global processes. Haywood and Mac an Ghaill (2003) consider this area in great detail in relation to the cross-cultural significance of different male practices. They argue that globalization not only impacts upon political and economic relations, but it also does this through the constitution of identity, subjectivity and desire. This is not to displace more materially orientated accounts but to consider that such accounts need to be contextualized by how global experiences are gendered through experience, understanding and the attribution of meaning. For example, Peterson and Runyan (1993) highlight that political actions may be considered masculine and feminine based upon the interpretation of those activities. They argue that males are expected to conform to masculinity and females to femininity and that those ascriptions operate cross-culturally. However, in a global context such meanings require much negotiation and are closely linked to how work, power and pleasure are organized. In this way, gender is not simply affected by globalization in a one-dimensional causative relation; rather it is privileging particular gendered ways of being.

Global Gender Regimes

Dunch (2002: 3) argues

> the transformations of the world in the modern era has involved the global extension not only of political relations, industrial production, and trade, but also cultural forms, nation states, rationalism and science, secularism in politics, constitutional government, and mass education (in certain forms and emphasizing certain subjects), and these changes have been intimately related to structures of power and dominance, and to colonialism in particular.

Globalization in this context establishes the supremacy of certain gendered forms and their attendant subjectivities and desires over others. From this account, culturally specific artefacts with their regulative normativity are transported and imposed onto other regions, nations and people. Schiller (1976) argues that globalization should not be understood as a heterogeneous process, rather global processes need to be linked to the political and economic dominance of particular nation states and regions. In earlier work, Schiller argued that global forces manifest themselves across hierarchical relationships between three economic sectors of the First, Second and Third World. The result was that First World countries were shaping Second and Third World countries' political and economic infrastructures, in order to sustain and increase their dominance. However, his more recent work moves beyond his initial account of such definitive sectors and acknowledges the emergence of more geographical and political diversity that include post-socialist countries such as North Korea, Vietnam and Cuba. This is alongside emerging economic regions such as Eastern Europe, Africa and East Asia. However, cross-cutting these regions is the pervasiveness of cultural products from the United States. More recently, rather than simply operate through older forms of economics or militarism, the dynamic of global force now includes cultural industries and new communication technologies. Thus, with more capacity to cross borders and travel across regions, the United States sets the standard for worldwide export and imitation. In the current context, the immediate frame of the cultural imperialist refers to the 'national (largely American) media-cultural power has been largely (though not fully) subordinated to transnational corporate authority. A total cultural package – film, TV, music, sports, theme parks, shopping malls and so on – is delivered worldwide by a small number of multi-billion-dollar media companies' (Schiller, 1991: 14).

Conceptually, in this chapter, we use Schiller's notion of cultural imperialism to engage with the interrelationship between globalization and gender. Thus, from a cultural imperialist approach, the privileging of one set of values over another takes place not only as part of economic or colonial militaristic relations but also through the transference of culture. Culture from this position is expansive, incorporating not only US television, but rather may take place through a range of practices that include shopping centres, theme parks, music, news agencies and fast food. Another form through which cultural values are conveyed, as we shall consider later, is children's toys. In relation to gender relations, cultural imperialism is a process of homogenizing men and women's lifestyles, collapsing local distinctions and imposing hierarchies of difference. Thus, it can be argued that cultural commodities operate across boundaries and impose norms and values from dominant cultures. The cultural trajectories of dominant cultures involves the reconfiguration of local subjectivity, fantasies and desires.

Capital and Terror: Emerging Gender Regimes

One of the ways through which to make sense of global processes, is that they are configured to benefit one group of people over another group. This hierarchical patterning of norms and values through the transmission of cultural products has been taken up by those explaining the impact of globalization on gender relations. The implication is that the circulation of norms and values has resulted in the patterning of gendered lifestyles. It is argued that the designation of norms and values that global forces are creating forms the basis of unequal relationships between men and women. The circulation of dominant gendered forms in global formations has been taken up and developed by Connell (1998). In his analysis, Connell argues that across history a range of hegemonic masculinities of the world have emerged. For example, starting with imperialism in the fifteenth century, nations' quest to colonize other nations resulted in the disruption of indigenous gender hierarchies. A second era of world masculinity came about as colonial powers attempted to secure their regional boundaries through the establishment of empires. Thus, a masculinity founded on racial difference and cultural superiority began to emerge. The third form of historical masculinity that Connell considers is that which is currently hegemonic: transnational business masculinity.

This hegemonic masculinity in the context of contemporary social change, Connell argues, has resulted in the centrality of those men who control the dominant institutions. These include business and political executives who are involved in global economic and political management. These are men who are egocentric, have less sense of loyalty and responsibility for others, have no permanent commitments, have a libertarian sexuality and tend to commodify women. Connell argues that this new form of masculinity has a number of variants which he identifies as Confucian and Christian. However, the general pattern of this transnational business masculinity is that it operates within a world gender order, operating through progress, action and achievement exercises in business relations. Such relations build upon the dependency of poor men and women and such exploitation is continued into a transnational business masculinity participation in the sex tourist industry. Ling (1999) suggests that companies often structure their business relations through the gendering of local and global markets. Thus, the local is interpreted as feminine whilst the global takes on a masculine character. As a result, an emerging hypermasculinity that involves the rejection of all that which is deemed feminine can be identified. Thus, global masculinities are not simply connected to structures of economic production but are constituted and constitute cultural forms.

Although Connell considers global masculinities, it is not self-evident how femininities in this framework operate. Furthermore, there is a tension surrounding the predominance and valorization of femininities for global capitalist projects. It could be suggested that in terms of the generation of surplus value, there is a pervasive and predominant gender form that excludes traditional (dominant) masculinities but also femininities that are based on domesticity. Salzinger (2003) provides an extremely insightful understanding of how femininity becomes the sought-after gender form in Mexican capital relations. In Mexico, in the 1960's, Mexican men crossed the border into the United States to take up work. However, the United States closed the border and as a result, Mexico faced the prospect of over 200,000 unemployed men. This prompted the formation of tax-free processing plants in Mexico on the US border. Thus, these foreign-owned plants or 'Maquilas' were designed to accommodate this labour surplus. However, rather than employ men, the dominant ideology of many of the firms was to employ women. The rationale for this was the notion that women carried a 'productive femininity'. Through Salzinger's sensitive ethnographies of three Maquila factories, she highlights how the recruitment strategy was to encourage more women than men into the labour force. She argues that this preoccupation with female workers has resulted in the disconnection of meanings of femininity from the family and the recreation of a new 'productive femininity constituted by "cheapness", natural docility, dexterity and tolerance of boredom (p. 37)'. The impact of the recruitment of women's labour as opposed to men's created anxiety about the collapse of traditional family structures. According to Salzinger, this generated much gendered anxiety as the popular media discussed the emergence of the new breadwinner. Combined with the growing scarcity of female workers, the downturn in the 1980s US economy began to produce a more militant response to Maquilas managers. As a result, men were being employed but even then companies, in order to generate female labour, would often bus women workers into the factories for journeys over two hours. Salzinger's account enables an understanding that it is not self-evident how gender articulates when the global and the local meet.

Salzinger's three ethnographies were carried out in different Mexican factories that she names as Panoptimex, Andromex and Particimex. In the factory that was mass-producing televisions, Panoptimex, a highly structured visible surveillance hierarchy clearly demarcated different sets of workers. One of the techniques of this was through the use of clothing, where women wore light blue and men wore dark blue smocks. This signalled a visual gender differentiation. Recruitment was also based upon physical attractiveness and how far they would correspond to the productive femininity model of being passive, dextrous and controllable. The impact of this was that shop floor men did not occupy a legitimate masculinity and Salzinger argues that men had difficulty obtaining a legitimate gendered subjectivity. In contrast, in Particimex (an automobile factory) women's identities appeared to be in opposition to the ideology of the productive femininity. Although the company recruited women on the basis of their productive femininity, the women in the factory operated through a culture of independence, assertiveness and decision making. As a result, they stood outside of the local familial patriarchal structures but also outside of the transnational prerequisite ideal worker.

This notion of gendering is exemplified in Salzinger's final factory, Andromex, a factory that produces sterile disposable hospital garments. Here, it was difficult to differentiate between men and women as undifferentiated uniforms made gender difficult to mark. Work practices, such as sewing, were not gender specific. Indeed sewing, which was deemed hard work with high turnover, was taken on by men and women. As such, the shop floor operated with a notion of worker. Salzinger argues that women's subjectivities were corresponding to this masculine-led notion of the worker and the conflation of worker with masculine. This meant that all workers were deemed to be breadwinners. The implicit assumption of the worker as male and the privilege that this entails is thus taken up and articulated by the women on the shop floor. Salzinger's argument considers how global capital articulates itself through gender relations. Thus, central to Salzinger's analytical frame is the notion that gender is not an embodied characteristic or attribute, it emerges out of the meaning structures that are generated in particular social contexts 'where femininity is a trope – a structure of meaning through which workers, potential and actual, are addressed and understood, and around which production itself is designed' (p. 15). It is an interrelation between masculinities and femininities that are being cited and interpellated between workers and managers. From Salzinger's account, we can usefully acknowledge that gender is not dependent on the body; gender is not a quality of the individual, it is contingent on the local and global practices through which it is encoded.

Although Connell highlights global masculinities through international capital, it might also be useful to consider other global masculinities through the representation of the 'terrorist'. Since the attack on the World Trade Centre in the United States, terrorism has gained intense global visibility and has become an increasingly important register through which gendered identities are being coded. From a similar perspective as Connell, Kimmel (2003) argues that at a national level and at a global level men are privileged through a series of inequalities such as wages, labour participation, ownership and control of property, unequal control over the body and cultural sexual resources. In the context of globalization, Kimmel argues that there is a hegemonic masculinity emerging that is also producing inequalities between men. The main force of Kimmel's argument is that these global masculinities are serving to 'flatten' or 'eliminate' local or regional gender specificities. The result is that new groups of men are collectively resisting forms of globalization, such as those in terrorist groups. Examining two particular politically organized groups of men, Aryan groups and Al Quaeda, he argues that these two groups both deploy masculinity as symbolic capital and ideological resource to resist global social and economic restructuring. They do this in three ways:

1. as a means to understand and explain their weakening power and influence;
2. as a strategic response in order to differentiate between themselves and those whom they identify as 'Others';
3. as a means of recruiting and generating collectivities.

Part of the dynamic for their terrorist activities is that they engage in forms of nostalgia, longing for a time when men took up places in society to which they were deemed entitled. Kimmel thus argues that groups of men that participate in terrorist cultures are part of a political mobilization of restorational rather than revolutionary politics. Therefore their activities are designed to stop the erosion of public and domestic patriarchy. Kimmel provides three case studies. However, in the next section we focus on only one – Al Quaeda.

Kimmel explores the profiles of those who were involved in the bombing of the United State World Trade Centre on 11 September 2001 that killed 2986 people. They were under 25, well educated, lower middle class and apparently downwardly mobile. Kimmel argues that these young men were opposed to the spread of western values and globalization. Central to their agenda is that they were trying to recover a manhood that had been emasculated through the distribution of western cultural products. He argues that the collapse of public patriarchy entitlement led to the fatal reassertion of that power. Thus, the terrorists operating through the remasculinizing of men and refeminizing of women can be seen as a form of addressing a crisis of masculinity through processes of masculine protest. This is explored by Weaver-Hightower (2003). The author argues that 'Terrorists' tend to consist of those groups that are defined by nation-states as dangerous. However, 'terrorists' only exist because of the values held by the nation-state and the meanings that are ascribed to those who are deemed to contest them. In other words, the terrorist becomes the site through which national identities are fashioned. Weaver-Hightower (2002) provides a useful consideration of how the United States responded to the 11 September Trade Centre attacks. This involved a valorization of masculinities concerned with national and international security, as the State projected itself through a tough masculinism. Weaver-Hightower claims that the response to terrorism should be seen in the context of the United States as a masculine state that has been symbolically injured:

> The President has thoroughly established a cowboy persona for himself through his twang, his western dress while on vacations, his oft-stated love for his ranch, and his frequent use of western idioms. His responses to the tragedies have included more of the same. Gunslinger catch phrases like 'dead or alive' and refusals to conduct diplomacy with a sovereign state under threat of war are examples of particularly masculine posturing. Violence before discussion (whether right or wrong in this particular case) certainly fits the pattern of hegemonic masculinity in the Western world, typified by the rugged men of the John Wayne western – the epitome ... of U. S. masculinity (N/P).

Thus, the response has been to position the terrorist through a masculine lens of the gangster and outlaw – those who stand outside the contours of a just and righteous civil society. Central to the representation of terrorists' gendered identities is a notion of civility. Given that those who are subject to terrorism tend to redefine the masculinities of those involved outside normal gendered parameters. Such men evince monstrous masculinities that are extreme in that they have either too much masculinity in an extremist sense or that such men have a lack of masculinity.

Moving away from the specificities of the United States, other countries around the globe, such as, Japan, Iceland, Russia, China, United Kingdom and Israel, are inciting an emergent terrorist masculinity. Media responses to the attacks in Madrid and London are highlighting how the gender of terrorism is also highly marked by ethnicity. For example, London bombings in 2005 by young men, some of whom had been born in Britain, prompted questions about integration and assimilation of young males into the dominant culture and notions of citizenship. The mobilization of policing strategies to combat terrorism such as detention without charging, has recreated contestations of legal citizenship that at one time were primarily used against the Irish, but are now intricately connected to legitimate 'Muslim' masculinities.

Interestingly, accounts of terrorist activity clearly shows that to posit terrorism in terms of masculinity often erases women's participation in terrorist struggles. As Cunningham (2003) highlights, the invisibility of women within terrorist discussion is often premised on the notion that women are victims of attacks. The successful discursive production of the terrorist as gangster and outlaw depends upon them operating within masculine parameters. The logic of this, as Talbot (2001) has highlighted, is that when women cross over the threshold into terrorism, they lose or forfeit their femininity. Talbot argues that:

> This masculinization of women terrorists occurs in different ways; first, through descriptions of women having more body hair and displaying male personality traits (competitiveness, aggression) as defined by men; second, through a systematic denial of maternal instincts in the representations of them; finally, the equation of feminism with armed subversion appears in the subtle insinuation that women who terrorize are not feminine, not real women. (p. 6)

At the same time, conventional versions of terrorism prioritize a representation of a terrorism that is constituted by a public militarism. However, not only are there many examples of women taking part in terrorist activities but also terrorist activity has been defined specifically in masculine terms. The notion that women participated in terrorist attacks through, and close to, the domestic sphere (as was the case in the Northern Ireland) disrupts conventional accounts of global terrorists who cross borders and regions to destroy their targets. Furthermore, much conventional discussion of terrorism operates by insisting on a particular version of femininity. More specifically, much of the western political discourse on the terrorist is often accompanied by the representation of female Muslims as oppressed. However, Cunnigham (2003) notes how women across the world including Muslim women, such as those in the Al-Aqsa Martyrs Brigade in Palestine, take an active stand against those deemed as occupiers:

> Women have been operational (e.g. regulars) in virtually every region and there are clear trends toward women becoming more fully incorporated into numerous terrorist organizations. Cases from Colombia, Italy, Sri Lanka, Pakistan, Turkey, Iran, Norway, and the United States suggest that women have not only functioned in support capacities, but have also been leaders in organization, recruitment, and fund-raising, as well as tasked with carrying out the most deadly missions undertaken by terrorist organizations – suicide bombings. (p. 175)

Because security is operationalized through versions of femininity and masculinity, State responses to terrorist activity may be highly susceptible. Thus, recognizing that terrorists may be female challenges conventional analyses of gender and terrorism that suggests that women's invisibility is equivalent to women's (innate) pacifism. To posit masculinity as a singular explanation of terrorist activity reinstates gender relations across biological divisions.

Fashioning Femininities

What the above highlights is that global representations are providing the parameters for the possibilities of femininity and masculinity. According to Varney (1998) one of the most influential representations of femininity can be found in dolls. In particular, one of the most successful brands has been the Barbie doll. The manufacturing and distribution of this cultural product has operated as a powerful representation and iconic femininity being simultaneously coded by gender, race and nation. As a product, Varney argues that somewhere in the world, a Barbie doll is sold; it is the leading toy in 100 of 140 countries. However, central to Varney's analysis is that the global distribution of a femininity is contesting the legitimacy of local femininities. She suggests that this highly complex and multifaceted symbolic coding of the doll can be traced back to the homogenization of United States society in the 1950s. It is argued that the twentieth century Cold War between the United States and Soviet Union generated a range of normative modes of masculinity and femininity. Embedded in Barbie's character are notions of freedom based upon values of individualism and consumerism that appeared counter to the Soviet Union's emphasis on communal goods and shared ownership. Varney argues that the company is selling an American dream of individualism and consumerism. In this account, the suggestion is that the buying of Barbie is a process of buying into real life and the corresponding names, professions and accessories that are sold with Barbie. Items that can be bought with the doll include a Chevrolet, a Ferrari and a horse. Furthermore, she is often represented through American names such as Malibu Barbie or Californian Barbie and has embodied a series of professions that includes a presidential candidate, marine corp. sergeant, and a waitress at MacDonalds. Consequently, Varney argues that through the gendering of Barbie, the ideal of the 'American Dream' is circulated to a broader audience beyond the borders of the United States.

Varney's analysis highlights that the distribution of cultural products does not simply convey American femininity but a particular form of American femininity. Of key interest is that Barbie is a doll that conveys United States' cultural values, and, as a result, imposes these values through the representation of cultural difference. This means that although Barbie is the export of a US-based femininity, it also conveys the US understanding of other cultures. Therefore, Barbie is not simply transmitting a US femininity but also American representations of other cultures. For example, the Australian Barbie doll is imaged in a way that does not necessarily reflect the intrinsic nature of the culture itself. This means that there may be little connection with the host cultures in which it is marketed. In other words, the product is an attempt to cultivate an imagined subjectivity. Thus, Barbie embodies a particular femininity associated with a particular economic class but also aspects of cultural norms that valorize hygiene, tidiness and specific versions of physical beauty. A similar process of distributing femininity can be identified in Donald and Lee's (2001) study of the Disney film *Mulan*. They explain how Disney transformed a traditional fifth century Chinese poem which explored the courage of a girl who went to join the army and repackaged it into a romanticized love story based on individual ambition. In the process of making the film the underlying values of filial piety, preservation of family honour, devotion to one's country and major personal sacrifice were lost within what could be called the disneyfication of the story.

It appears that cultural products provide representations of dominant and desirable ways of being men and women. However, it should be added that cultural products are part of a broader relationship in the reshaping of gender. We argue that the reshaping of masculinity will implicitly have an impact on the constitution of femininity. One example of this might be how global products establish the dominance of men over women. Thus, the promotion of one form of masculinity is dependent upon and intrinsic to a different femininity. Embedded within cultural products can be the global transference of patriarchal relations. As such, the processes of globalization are deemed to manifest themselves through the circulation of particular kinds of being a man or more specifically hegemonic types of masculinity, privileging certain ways of being men or 'hegemonic masculinity' and 'emphasized femininity' (Connell, 1995: 10–11). The impact of this is that men take on transnational identities, while serving to maintain local traditional gender lifestyles of women. Derne's (2002) work on Indian men provides an example of this. He looks at the ways that the impact of transnational flows of culture has resulted in the reorganization of men and women's social and cultural identities. Of key importance is that the circulation of authoritative masculinities are worked through women's identities. The argument supporting this is that because of men's centrality in the public sphere in Indian society, they are exposed to global flows more easily than women who tend to occupy the private sphere of the home.

Derne argues that at various points in India's history the resolution of masculinities has occurred as a result of the organization and regulation of women's identities. In order to support his claims, Derne conducts research with filmgoers in contemporary India. He suggests that Indian cinemas are increasingly showing Hollywood films and, as a result, men are exposed to particular masculinities. At the same time, the Hollywood format – low emotional content, low symbolic content with a dependence on narrative, violence and aggression – is influencing the nature of films that are being made in India. Thus in Derne's interviews with 22 male filmgoers, none of whom spoke English, attraction to violence was one of the main reasons why the men watched the films. He suggests that this contributes to patriarchal masculinities 'Trans-national cultural forms may extend and exacerbate men's attachment to violent forms of male dominance' (p. 150). However, he argues that this was not a simple trans-mission and replacement of one set of values for another. Rather, there was an emerging tension felt by the men of how such values that are associated with western values could exist alongside their own traditional Indian values.

On one hand, they understood the importance of the centrality of Hindu spirituality, whilst on the other hand, desiring what they viewed as 'modern' western identities. One of the areas where this ambivalence was being worked out was in the context of their home life: 'film going men handle their ambivalence about western ways through their commitment to marrying obedient (and therefore Indian) women' (p. 157). Central to the adoption and acceptance of western lifestyles is a concern about women also taking on Western subjectivities. They argue that women when confronted with western values might be tempted to negate their home values; traditional 'Indian' family responsibilities. As a result, Derne argues that, in his sample, men would secure their identifications with western cultural products through a valorization of traditional Indian femininity. Therefore, as long as women maintained their traditional femininity, men's ambivalence about their own participation in western culture could be resolved. Derne identifies a similar process in Indian men's history in the context of British colonialism. During this era, western economic rationality was deemed to be replacing traditional Indian values of spirituality. According to Derne, men's anxiety about the displacement of their spirituality was carried by the domestic responsibilities of women. Therefore, the identification with rationality was relationally constituted through urging women to reclaim their ethnic origins through Indian national practices such as religious practice. At the same time, the reclamation of traditional Indian spirituality simultaneously became a means of displaying a particular gendered nationality that supported and sustained patriarchal dominance. The implication of Derne's work is that processes of globalization can create and strengthen traditional national identifications. For example, Hodson's (1999) work on masculinities in Kenya, highlights how strategies to increase tourism resulted in the reinforcement, if not recreation, of traditional masculinities.

The men in Derne's study imagine that globalization may result in gendered identities that disrupt existing gender hierarchies. In order to consider this claim further, we focus on the work by Chari (2004), who suggests that even though gender relations may be transformed, those transformations do not necessitate a change in the distribution of power. In a detailed consideration of the impact of globalization, Chari (2004) explored the transformation of the hosiery industry in a southern Indian province within the twentieth century. He considers the rise of the Gounder peasant caste in the hosiery industry and explores how forms of masculinity and femininity operated to secure social relations of production. These relations were secured through the designation of gendered 'natures' that in themselves justified gendered hierarchies in the hosiery community.

In terms of values, men of the lower Gounder caste were designated as enterprising men who had migrated from rural lands to urban centres in order to make profits, where 'Gounder toil was a specific resource that Gounder men could recall, through their shared agrarian and colonial history' (p. 238). Thus, based on this enterprise, Indian society witnessed a replacement of a religious and ethnic heterogeneous aristocracy, with a more homogeneous group of men. However, such natural characteristics of this agrarian class were secured through a range of fraternal ties that were often consolidated through marriage. Therefore, the cultural values of resilience and determination were commonly and secretly supported by finance from close family members or friends. Alongside this, women through their dowries (both the men's mothers and their wives) were the source of finance or they owned the land to support the business ventures. At the same time, family ties also became central to the recruitment of new members to the business.

However, during the 1980s a number of changes, prompted by globalization, transformed the gendered nature of the working environment. With export centres located in various cities around India, hosiery production in Tiruppur was a small-scale local industry where garments had been traditionally sold onto these cities for export. However, with the rise in transport and accommodation, foreign buyers were able to come directly to the hosiery centre and, as a consequence, they could undercut the price regimes of other cities. The relocation of major export companies to the region meant the generation of new forms of work connected with the export process. In order to fill these new positions, the export companies began to recruit women and migrant men. Thus, with the impact of global industries in the region, a discourse of feminization began to emerge where new ways of working became occupied by women. This increase of migrant workers into the labour production process fractured the hegemony of the work process that required masculinities deriving from agrarian toil. The unionized formation of the Gounder caste was being contested by other workers who were often excluded from the unions. Therefore, as a means to avoid the unionized Gounder workforce, women's labour was bought in. However, importantly, this was not the substitution of men for women's work. It was the use of women into entirely new forms of work such as developing processes of checking and finishing. In this way, women's entrance into the workforce although facilitated by globalization, continued to value women's productivity with wages below that of men.

The above account highlights how the global transmission of cultural products impacts upon gendered identities and, as a result, supports and sustains patriarchal dominance. Thus, the cultural artefacts that are transmitted across societies operate in a negative fashion – replacing and reconstituting the generic cultural values of the place where they are articulated. In contrast, the next section, suggests that the availability of certain cultural products does not necessarily result in the reproduction of dominant masculinities and subordinated femininities. Rather, it draws upon Appadurai's (1996) notion of the intersection of local and global cultures where local people self-reflexively reconsider, restate and inaugurate those cultural aspects of that which is deemed Other. Importantly, those who are understood as Other in a particular cultural context are not simply unproblematically issued those identities. Rather, they are constituted at a local level. As Karam (1997) highlights, in her exploration of gender and Islam in Egypt, religious leaders operate to incorporate particular norms and values into religious ideology and practice. In doing so, a number of discriminatory values are ascribed religious authenticity and thus cannot be challenged.

The next section explores this issue in greater depth. However, it does not appeal to overarching principles of the inflection of global cultural processes in local terms. Rather, it considers how that inflection manifests itself subject to a range of localized dynamics.

Inflecting Genders: The Importance of the Local

One way of considering the importance of local processes is to consider Hardt and Negri's (2000) discussion of globalization. They suggest that globalization is not simply a tension between the global and the local. Rather, they suggest that the local is part of the global and the global is part of the local. In doing so, they collapse the notion that global is simplistically applied and inserted into people's subjectivities. They suggest that processes of subjectification are part of contesting and competing regimes of regulation that are enmeshed and mutually constitutive. For example, they argue that 'Globalisation, like localisation, should be understood as a "regime" of the production of identity and difference, or really of homogenization and heterogenization' (p. 45). They use Foucault as a means of explaining how globalization articulates itself as a power relation regulating and distributing the possibilities of identity. In doing so, they borrow two key concepts. First, that there has been a move from a disciplinary society to society of control. According to Foucault, disciplinary society has been about juridical forms of power that are articulated through the rule of law. Thus, different institutions would assemble a range of specific and detailed laws about what those within institutions could and could not do. However, with a shift to a society of control, power relations are dispersed and not accountable at some generic source. The shift to a society of control has meant that rather than the force of discipline being applied externally, people control themselves. This means that: 'discipline has become something that is increasingly interiorized, with subjects themselves reconstructing the meanings of cultural products' (Hardt and Negri (2000: 23).

The second concept that Hardt and Negri adopt from Foucault to make sense of globalization is 'bio-power'. Rather than society simply designating rules through which individuals increasingly apply to themselves, the notion of bio-power situates the sources of the designation of norms and values not as something applied but as generated from within: 'Bio-power is a form of power that regulates social life from its interior, following it, interpreting it, absorbing it, and re-articulating it' (ibid.: 23–4). This means that power – situated within broader global forces – becomes enmeshed within individuals. The importance of this perspective is that it is suggested that transmission of cultural goods as a means of imperialism or colonialism is not simply a one-dimensional process. Hardt and Negri argue that in order to make sense of the broader social and economic organization of globalization, it is important not to break down social relations into binary forms, but rather to see globalization, in Foucaultian terms, as a means of producing ways of understanding and knowing in the world. One way to use this perspective is to consider how global processes makes available social categories that do not simply control and regulate gendered bodies in oppressive patterns, they simultaneously provide the possibilities through which to transgress. In their study of Filipina workers in Hong Kong, Chang and Ling (2000) explore the nexus of these two global processes, where regimes of labour intimacy involves the servicing of those participating in techno-muscular capitalism. Filipina women experienced high levels of discrimination that included restrictions surrounding changing employers, their type of employment and having the right to terminate contracts. However, they were likely to earn a wage six times more than those who had stayed at home. However, Filipinas in Hong Kong society are characterized as being untrustworthy as there is ascribed a desire to obtain financial security with Hong Kong men. The sexualized profile of the Filipina pervades public discourses with scare stories of Filipina women exploiting Hong Kong businessmen. This is exacerbated by a moral censure of Filipina women who are characterized as leaving their families and their children behind in the pursuit of economic wealth.

One of the strategies that Filipina women use to deflect this discursive position is a public demonstration of their allegiance to God, family and country. One of the social and cultural conduits in which to achieve this is through the Filipina communities that have come together in Hong Kong, such communities often hold Catholicism as central to the rules and norms of social relations. Chang and Ling suggest that Filipina women in their sample not only identify with Catholicism, they often mythologize a traditional Filipina culture that bears little reflection to everyday life, norms and values in the Philippines themselves. As part of their redefinition of their life in Hong Kong, these women reconfigured their 'service work' as God's work. In doing so, the sexual codes that are associated with servicing men are neutralized. Similarly, the women invoke a familial role of wife, mother and daughter to counteract sexualizations by the Hong Kong media. However, there remains a tension as the cultural and religious values that offer a means to deflect the sexualizations simultaneously operate as oppressive and restrictive in terms of these women's autonomy and independence. Thus, an alternative to the restriction and control in these migrant communities is the identification with a same-sex desire identity that is identified as 'Tomboyism'. This is where the Filipina women wear men's clothes, have short hair and take up masculine behaviours. They are also seen as having liaisons and affairs with other Filipina women. In this way, the women cross the sexualizations that exist within the context of heterosexuality of Hong Kong society. They are thus positioned as strong and faithful women outside of the heterosexual moral economy that deems them as morally cheap and sexually available. In this way, this same-sex identification operates as a means of displaying romance and intimacy without being sexually deviant within the contours of a valorized hetero-sexual femininity.

In considering how the global and local inflect one another, it is important to identify the continuities between them. One way of understanding this is to see the local and the global articulating themselves through the specificities of the social and historical context through which gender is produced. One of the limitations of the cultural imperialist approach is that the global product appears to be overly deterministic in terms of patterning existing gender relations. As a consequence of this approach, gendered forms do not exist outside of globally distributed representations. Therefore, global representations are simply reconstituting pre-existing gendered forms and reshaping local masculine and feminine values. Work by Chang and Ling (2000) suggest a more complex picture. They argue that the global process can be conceptualized in two ways. First, they suggest that globalization often takes the form of a 'techno-muscular capitalism' that circulates through global finance, production, trade and telecommunications. From this position, global processes valorize the social and cultural norms that are associated with western capitalist masculinity. Thus, similar to Connell's version of hegemonic transnational masculinity, privatization, deregulation and consolidation operate as themes through which hegemonic versions of gender-masculinity are circulated. At the same time, they argue that there is an alternative means of making sense of the impact of global processes and this is called a regime of labour market intimacy. This involves women participating in usually low paid, low skilled service work that often involves leaving the family home and enduring poor working conditions that involve harassment and abuse.

A Local Gender Politics

It is possible to argue that political regimes are operating as global forces implicitly creating the possibilities for the emergence of new femininities and masculinities. True (2003) explores this idea in the context of Czechoslovakia's political history. She considers how gender relations have been forged through the social and economic organization of society. On one hand, communism that served to deny or eradicate gender difference, implicitly cultivated a gender regime that was embedded with multiple inequalities between men and women. On the other, western – globalizing – forms of neo-liberal political economy generated forms of gender relations through consumer choice that has tended to cultivate and depend upon gender differences. Since the democratically elected socialist state in 1948, the official party ideology was that the move to a socialist state has liberated women. As a result, True argues that the visibility of political groups that sought to promote women's interests in the socialist state diminished. However, in the late 1960s, public debate increasingly became popular, as Czechoslovakia began to reflect on the nature of communism. At this point, gender relations began to gain ground as a public issue. Cut short by the Velvet revolution – the invasion by the Soviet Union and the installation of a Soviet chosen leader – women's inequality post-1968 became hidden in a society whose wealth generation and collective identity became founded on ideals of industrial productivity.

It is argued that women's domestic contribution was eclipsed by a classless ideology. As a result, women's gender identifications were simultaneously dis-identifications with Czech communism. With the revolution of 1989 and the subsequent annexation of Slovakia from the Czech Republic, processes of globalization become increasingly visible. True argues that the move to capitalism has resulted in greater freedom of expression of gender identities that has resulted in major economic and emotional investment in consumer goods. Since this period, imports of consumer goods increased from 5 billion in 1988 to 36 billion in 2001 despite a decline in national income and economic productivity. True also suggests that there has been a phenomenal rise of global commercial companies. For example, she highlights how of the top 20 advertising companies in the Czech Republic, only two of the top ten were indigenous. Although consumer goods during the communist regime symbolized subversion and resistance to state collective identity, in a capitalist regime, they appear to have generated alternative femininities. Logically, it could be assumed that this transformation would mean that there would be a swathe of western led notions of gendered identities. However, True argues that the lack of censorship in advertising is not simply free market economic exploitation but in itself a means of a gender/sexual subversion both in relation to socialist roles and also conventional western roles.

In particular, True explores how *Cosmopolitan*, the world's best-selling women's magazine, is refracted through the local relations of Czech society. The magazine, although looking towards western conspicuous consumption, nevertheless devotes much of its contents to women's welfare issues and has become key, according to True, in furthering a feminist agenda. This suggests that:

> The emergence of a market orientated consumer economy is manufacturing new gender-specific needs and desires and engendering new identities. Marketing stresses masculinity and femininity to sell goods and services in this region. However, in the aftermath of communism, these new identities are as much a source of liberation as domination (pp. 129–130).

This provides an insight into the limitation of the cultural imperialism thesis as cultural forms do not have intrinsic meanings but are actively produced within the context through which they are articulated. In this case *Cosmopolitan*, a global product, provided a means through which alternative forms of femininity were being given visibility. True goes on to suggest that at the same time, gender inequalities in the home and at work, between men and women have not only persisted under capitalism but have deepened with more unequal pay, employment discrimination, sexual harassment, domestic violence, rape and sexual abuse, state welfare and protection and the increasing fragmentation of women as a class experiencing acute forms of poverty. These trends are therefore held in tension with a complex interplay of the meaning that men and women make of the developing social and economic context.

The relationship of global cultural products, political change and gender relations is explored further by Johansson (2001) who discusses the reintroduction of advertising into Chinese society. In socialist China, women's femininity has carried norms and values associated with China's national identity. With post-Mao reformation, the gendering of the Chinese female could also be linked to this national identity and its growing concern with modernization. She argues that initially, the introduction and valorization of western values through advertising did appear to be taking place, but that such advertising became contextualized by particular social and cultural conventions that involved the recreation of authentic Chinese femininities. With the Chinese State advocating communism, class roles tended to displace gender as the salient political category. In official documents, representations offered 'strong' masculinized versions of women in a whole range of non-western gendered occupations. Of importance was the displacement of one form of gender identities over another – Chinese non-gendered women as opposed to the westernized hedonistic individualized women concerned with and consumed by their own preoccupation with beauty.

Johansson examines in depth how, with the reintroduction of advertising in China, representation of women began to change. She explores the nature of advertising in two popular women's magazines from the 1980s to the 1990s: these are *Chinese Women* and *Marriage and Family* with 550,000 and 300,000 readers respectively. One of the features of the advertising in pre-1990s China was the notion that the content of the magazine usually involved black and white drawings with pages of text. The content of the adverts often consisted of ordinary young women who were casually dressed. Johansson suggests the advertising in these magazines was tentative and cautious. Also, the magazine front covers often displayed political messages. Initially, with the use of advertising, Chinese magazines took on western notions of femininity with photos that emphasized glamour, individualism and hedonism. Tentatively, women began to be represented with increasing nudity. This began a trend as advertisements began to be characterized by daring, often through nudity. According to Johansson this was represented by Caucasian women in swimsuits and underwear. Another interesting aspect of the advertising style was that the women in the advertisements would be positioned as looking at the camera. However, magazines became transformed as they became glossy and the content shifted. For example, Johansson looks at the marketing of the Yue Si Cosmetic company and suggests that the company was educating women how to dress and use make-up. In other words, they positioned themselves as a company with a moral responsibility to teach women how to become authentically Chinese. As a result, the emphasis of this company was to beautify rather than exoticize. Consequently, advertisements began to redefine sexuality as something sensual and in the process reconfigured western ideals of females' sexuality. As a result, this consumerist practice did not simply export western identities, it enabled the consolidation of imagined indigenous identities. An example of this was the shift in advertising that focused on naked women's bodies to that of women's invisibility and the codes of invisibility. As a consequence:

> Consumer culture as global phenomenon incorporating and spreading ideas and images of a 'modern', 'western', hedonistic, and individualistic lifestyle is evidently capable of resolving, at least, symbolically the seemingly contradictory relationship between 'traditional' and 'modern' lifestyles. In this case it seems that the idea of consumer culture leading to homogenisation does not hold true. On the contrary, the consumerist discourse of advertising partakes in the construction of indigenous identities (ibid.: 120).

The recreation of national identity through a social imaginary is also considered in section three of this chapter with the focus on migration, nationality and gender. However, it is important to point out here, that the notion of indigenous identity may itself be a social and cultural imaginary that is intricately connected with global interpretations of national gender identity.

Gendering of Migration: Irish Masculinities and Sexualities

If the above studies focus on some of the broader themes that have characterized analysis of gender and globalization, this section specifically considers the importance of migration in terms of local specificities. This work, located in our own research on young Irish men in Britain is undertaken in a post-colonial framework. This suggests that within the changing morphology of urban sites, new identities are being manufactured, marked by diaspora (movement of people-dispersal), hybridity (mixing of cultures) and syncretism (pluralistic forms of cultural belonging) (Bhabha, 1990; Gilroy, 1993; Spivak, 1988a, b). Here, we have attempted to rethink the dominant cultural imperialist theoretical perspective that has focused on homogeneity and heterogeneity to develop a response to the emerging vocabulary of the new politics of cultural difference in the context of a post-colonial British nation-state located within a new European citizenship (Favell, 2001). This enables a number of conceptual moves within a gender analysis that include acknowledging a more inclusive notion of multiple, decentred nationalisms, racisms and ethnicities, including those of the Anglo-ethnic majority, marked by a logic of relationality and contradiction, exploring the different subject positions that are inhabited within these various categories and in analysing the interconnections between migration, class, gender and sexuality, taking account of the *positionality* of subjects' different national belongings with respect to one another (Brah, 1996). Most importantly, understanding post-colonial ethnicities as gendered exhibits a complex interweaving of sameness and identification alongside that of difference and dis-identification (see Baldwin, in Troupe, 1989).

From a post-colonial position, migration can be seen to be represented in mainstream academic literatures exclusively as a political–economic phenomenon. As we have highlighted above, feminist accounts have made a significant contribution in challenging this position, explicating the interconnecting co-construction of discourses of gender and neo-economic approaches (Yuval-Davis, 1997). For example, Walter (1995: 35) has argued:

> It is often assumed that ethnicity, racism and nationalism are monolithic structures which have the same meaning for, and impact on whole collectivities. However, not only are representations of Irishness and Britishness highly gendered constructions, but the material experiences of being a woman or a man within the Irish community and an Irish woman or Irish man within British society are very different.

Consequently, in earlier texts the gendering of migration has tended to be erased. This has resulted in a number of effects in relation to the Irish diaspora in Britain. On one hand, for example, women and their specific experiences have been excluded from studies of migration, which ironically includes the fact that Irish-born women outnumber Irish-born men in Britain since the 1920s (Hickman and Walter, 1995). On the other hand, immigration has been represented in terms of a generalized other, resulting in the gender dynamics of men's experiences been undertheorized. In other words, gender is not seen as constitutive of the processes of migration, which in turn helps reconstitute the meaning of Irish womanhood and manhood in Britain. Contemporary accounts of Irish experience of Britain that are beginning to emerge in Centres of Irish Studies are continuing a labour history tradition that privileges the political–economic dimension of migration. This work is important as part of an unfinished political project that is contesting the conceptual invisibility of the Irish diaspora as a racialized minority ethnic community. Nevertheless, it tends to share with mainstream migration studies an erasure of other social and cultural categories, which are subsumed within an all-encompassing and totalizing Irishness (Garrett, 1998).

In contrast, literary and cultural studies have explored Irishness during the nineteenth and twentieth centuries which was projected as an essentially feminine race (see Cairns and Richards, 1988; Nash, 1993; O'Brien Johnson and Cairns, 1991; Renan, 1990). As Walter (1999: 80) argues:

> In the nineteenth century ... the Irish were racialized in two distinct ways, each strongly gendered. Masculine images were of uncontrolled subhumans incapable of self-government. Feminine images were of weakness requiring protection. Both representations justified continued British rule whilst bolstering images of the ruling centre as the antithesis of these negative characteristics.

The more recent degendering and desexualization of migration serves to underplay the complex historical and contemporary interplay between Britishness and Irishness in relation to the question of nation, nationalism, masculinity and desire (Nandy, 1983; Walshe, 1997). The acting out of these complex interconnecting categories was illustrated in our recent work with young Irish gay men, in terms of the policing of sexual boundaries among themselves through appeals to external threats to a subjective sense of their national identity (Mac an Ghaill and Haywood, 2003). These young men discussed the implications of white Irish gay migrants being able 'to switch' between ethnic and sexual minority/majority gendered positions. In so doing, they served to highlight, from the different perspectives of majority/minority cultural positions, the political investments in the maintenance of fixed collective identity boundaries within specific contexts. Homophobia was spoken through nationalism which was taken up as a cultural resource to make claims for an authentic Irishness through which homophobic practices operated. From an Irish heterosexual position, to be gay as an Irish man in England was to become like 'them', to become English. Such a strategy was highly effective in policing possible gender and (hetero) sexual boundaries.

The links between nation-making and these young men's gendered subjectivity has its own specific history of cultural exclusion. For example, at a time of projected threats to the nation-state from global forces in the early 2000s, it is instructive to revisit a key moment in the making of the Irish state after Independence. Walshe (1997: 5) in his article, 'Sex, Nation and Dissent', describes the exclusion of a progressive sexual politics from the dominant nationalist politics during this period. He argues:

> The post-colonial struggle to escape the influence of the colonising power became a struggle to escape the gendered relation of male coloniser to female colonised. Therefore the post-colonial culture could not permit any public, ideological acknowledgement of the actuality of the sexually "other".

The two major representations in British academic, political and popular accounts of Irish masculinity in the last 30 years have been that of low-status manual workers living in segregated ethnic occupational enclaves *and* the criminalization of Irish masculinity, with pervasive images of Irish men as of low intelligence, feckless, drunkards and bombers (Mac an Ghaill, 1999). The legacy of Irish masculinity as a highly contradictory formation as it is a subordinated masculinity, having been denied the patriarchal privileges ascribed to the masculine role of power, control and authority. Historically, this derives from the British ascription of a pre-modern state of being in which Irish men's masculinity was claimed to pre-date the modernity project with its emphasis on rationality, reason and scientific progress. For the Irish diaspora in Britain, versions of masculinity were institutionally secured – shaped and lived out – within male workplaces, community pubs and clubs and at Gaelic games. A specific ethnic gendered regime was constructed, underpinned by an infrastructure of a male dominated hierarchical Catholic Church and an Irish nationalist politics that displayed a wide range of cultural signifiers of masculinity. This included the pervasive playing of the national anthem at public gatherings (translated in English as *The Soldier's Song*) and the obligatory response in terms of a military-style stance, the high visibility of the Irish flag, the tricolour, at social events, the consumption of traditional Irish music, recalling the blood sacrifices of male Irish heroes and the celebration of Irish literary figures. Women and femininity were written out of this hypermasculine fantasy narrative. This response carries traces of an earlier nationalist inversion of the British imperial positioning of the Irish as a feminine race, referred to above (Renan, 1990). There are diverse class-cultural affiliations among young Irish men, but many of them recall childhoods accompanying their fathers to these all-male community spaces, identifying with their protest form of masculinity and the gendered dynamics of living out an authentic Irishness, that was dislocated from the island of Ireland. At the same time, they contrast their fathers' cultural outsider status with their own confidence in public spaces, as part of a broader youth cultural transnational trajectory, in which emerging new male ethnicities are ascribed different meanings (Appaduri, 1991; Glick Schiller *et al.*, 1992).

By the late 1990s, the British ambivalent desire to be Irish reemerged. In shifting from a colonial-based race to post-colonial ethnicity, Irishness is represented as a highly seductive culture–a key 'signifier for hedonism with soul' (O'Sullivan, 1996). Within British popular consumerism, contemporary Irish cultural forms are projected as high status cultural icons, with Irish masculinity translated into a notion of cool, as indigenous British parents name their children Callum, Sean, Conor and so on. At the same time, Irish masculinity has served a long apprenticeship here within Britain's economy of signs. The Irish, or more specifically Irish masculinity, can be read as providing a diverse range of cultural archetypes within changing social formations in early and late modernity – the age of global migration (Lash, 1994). Irish men have been ontologically positioned as the 'significant other' for centuries, the longest standing representation of what British masculinity is not and cannot be. Historically, the main cultural shift has been from a racialized masculinity with a focus on working *with* the body (for example, the navvy) to an ethnicized masculinity of working *on* the body (for example, the dancer) (Sherlock, 1999). This cultural shift can be read as an effect of a broader movement from production to consumption, as a key dynamic of contemporary social conditions and how we live our lives (Lash and Urry, 1994). And so an archaeology of the recent past might culturally reveal Paddy the exile, Paddy the lumpen proletariat, Paddy the socially excluded, Paddy the urban terrorist and Paddy the iconoclast of popular (cool) culture. However, these latest national/ethnic images do not simply replace earlier racialized and sexualized images of the Irish. Rather, they co-exist, adding to the latest version of the complex relationship of how the two countries are viewing each other. A traditional caricature of Irish sexuality, marked by both its fecundity and the uncivil (alongside anti-Catholic references), is being displaced by cultural representations of youthful adventure, bodily pleasure and vitality. This has been consolidated by recent celebrations of Celticism.

Conclusion

Understanding the impact of globalization on gender relations involves a number of limitations from a cultural imperialist approach. In relation to the context of religion, Dunch (2002) provides a thorough critique of the cultural imperialist approach that has much relevance for this chapter. Central to his critique is the idea of effect and process where, it is assumed that global processes simplistically impose gender values. Furthermore, that imposition is directed by an unproblematic desire for global products. In turn, there is the assumption that local meaning systems have implicit connections with the meaning systems that are carried by global processes. As such the distribution of power remains undifferentiated. Not simply is it undifferentiated in terms of the global reach but also in relation to the gender relations within local context. In short, it is assumed that gender relations in local contexts are unchanging. Implicitly, the assumption that globalization is the *only* motor of social change appears to contextualize some of the studies mentioned earlier. Finally, it remains unclear, in cultural imperialist perspectives, where the impact of globalization begins and where it ends. In other words, globalization has almost become part of a sensibility in which transnational impacts can be measured. In many ways, there is a tension between identifying a qualitative shift in the reconfiguration of gender relations, whilst at the same time, mapping the emerging patterns through concepts such as regularity and uniformity.

9

Gender on the Move: The Search for a New Sex/Gender Order in Late Modernity

Introduction: Shifting Representations of Sexual Politics in Late Modernity

Over the last two decades critical theorists established that central categories in the field of gender studies, such as woman/femininity and man/masculinity, did not simply have their own individual histories based on a linear model. Rather, these unstable constructions have been constantly contested with new meanings emerging in relation to social, cultural and political transformations (Meyers, 1997; Riley, 1988; Westwood, 1990). Feminist, gay and lesbian fragmentary literatures have suggested an intensely complex conceptualization of (post) modern femininities, masculinities and sexual politics[1]. These texts argue that contemporary issues around gender inequalities and sexual difference can be seen to be *constitutive of* as well as being *constituted by* wider socio- economic, political and cultural changes. In other words, notions of decentred forms of performing genders and hybrid sexualities are being constituted within a wider arena of 'the cultural logic of late capitalism', which in turn they are helping to shape (Jameson, 1991). A main message conveyed by these texts is the need for more sophisticated theoretical work, in a field of inquiry that belies easy political categorization.

The representation of gender identity and difference, which may be seen as the starting point of any political project, is one of the most contested arenas of contemporary cultural life (Phillips, 1998b). Brunt (1989: 152) maintains that there are two questions which need to be addressed in relation to the issue of representation. The first is 'how our identities are represented in and through the culture and assigned particular categories'; the second is 'who or what politically represents us, speaks and acts on our behalf'. She suggests that, in answering these two questions, we get a sense of how we both 'make sense' of the world and get a sense of our 'place' in the increasing range of identities made available to us. Drawing upon Spivak's (1988a, b) critique of political radicals' self representation in their construction of the 'Third World' subject, provides a productive rereading of sexual politics in Britain at the start of the twenty-first century. There are two ways, she suggests, we may understand the act of cultural representation. On the one hand, there is representation as representation, as interpretation. On the other, there is representation as 'speaking for' the needs and desires of somebody or something else. Spivak's analysis forms part of a broader methodological reflexive shift, most clearly articulated by Third World feminist scholars and played out in the discipline of anthropology, around the crisis of representation and an accompanying understanding of multiple interpretations and techniques of data collection as technologies of truth production (Alvesson and Skoldberg, 2000; Denzin, 1994; Mohanty, 1988; Ong, 1988; Scheurich, 1995).

By the early 2000s, with an intensified sensibility of how we live with difference, various interconnecting forms of sexual politics can be identified marked by fusions, hybridity and body crossings. From a contemporary perspective of talk about post-feminism, masculine backlash and new men's movements in western societies, the history of sexual politics includes the new social movements of second-wave feminism and its discontents, gay and lesbian mobilizations, men's groups' protests, gendered ethnic and national visibility, transgendered voices and the more recent cultural projects such as HIV/AIDS activism and queer interventions (Bryson, 1999). These more recent culturally based political projects remind us that a political understanding of this field of inquiry is not simply an empirical question. As we argue throughout this book, specific conceptual and methodological limitations emanate from the undertheorization of social and cultural change. In short, there is little political consensus about what constitutes change in a society, marked by diverse understandings of patriarchy, compulsory heterosexuality and homophobia, alongside more recent conceptualizations of living with difference. In turn, as outlined in the introductory chapter, there is a difficulty in exploring the question of sexual politics at local and global levels. For Mohanty (1992), writing of the shift from the politics of transcendence to a politics of engagement, deploying nonwestern cross-cultural studies serves to illustrate other potential ways of making sense of shifting gender structures, identities and practices.

Feminist Politics: The Future is Female – Reclaiming the Feminine

During the 1990s, there emerged a diverse range of internal political engagements with the legacy of second-wave feminism. As Segal (1999: 231–2) indicates: 'Given the diversity of reformist, identitarian, deconstructive, activist, therapeutic and power feminisms, it is true that we can indeed take many different routes as feminists leaving the twentieth century'. The academy and the media are two of the main sites within which these debates have taken place, which as Phillips (1998a) argues have served to transform the meaning of politics, and its associated oppositional dichotomies of public/private, rational/emotional, active/passive that have traditionally been ascribed to embodied male and female subjects.

Beyond the Equality–Difference Dualism: Beyond Gender Neutrality Gender Visibility

Antioppressive politics, around ethnicity, sexuality and gender, has inherited an enduring tension between the struggle for equality and the right to (cultural) difference. For example, this has been vocally manifest in the politics of race and culture in a variety of dichotomous forms: assimilation or differentiation; integration or separatism; social inegalitarianism or cultural differentialism; multiculturalism or antiracism (Mac an Ghaill, 1999). Earlier classifications of these terms highlighted a central dilemma for social minorities: whether it is possible to attain social justice by transcending or going beyond the categorical visibility of the collective self, that is being black, gay, a woman, in a society that continues materially and symbolically to be grounded in particular normative frames of the social majority. Similarly, during the last two decades, the key debate that informed major feminist political agitation and mobilization has been that of a projected double play around (in)equality and difference. These concepts are understood not as simple descriptive categories but as complex political processes, with their own highly developed positions on the constitution of gender and the meaning of feminism as an advocacy project in the wider culture.[2] Hence, although, presently some of the most exciting and productive work in feminist theorizing is addressing conceptual and strategic attempts to go beyond this dualism, there remains a residue in the literature making strong counterclaims for each strand.

One effect of bipolar oppositional thinking has been that theorists of difference have underplayed the radical social imaginary of early feminist campaigning around equality, that offered a new political language and accompanying new moral vision. As Phillips (1992) maintains, located within enlightenment values, early feminism made claims for a shift beyond (male) particularity to the universal extension of civic rules, rights and equalities that were assumed to be men's birthright, in order to complete the promises of modern democracy. She continues that:

The belief in an essential human equality despite all secondary differences; a scepticism towards prejudice and tradition; the confidence in external standards of rationality and justice against which to measure the world; all theses formed an important context for feminist principles and debate. (p. 10)

Second-wave feminism as the inheritor of this ethical lineage, seeks to challenge the pervasiveness of social inequalities both manifest in and legitimated by the logic of gender difference that imbues traditional gender positions, across multiple sites, including reproductive capacities, equal pay, and exclusions from public institutional life. In direct contrast, as explored below, difference feminists reclaim femininity, in seeking to challenge the centrality of androcenticism (male-centredness) across cultures in the social devaluation of women.

Among a diverse range of feminist classifications, attempting to capture an understanding of gender in political theory, Squires (1999) has produced one of the most comprehensive and intellectually engaging analytical frames. She presents a threefold typology of inclusion (seeking gender neutrality), reversal (seeking recognition for a specifically female identity) and displacement (seeking to deconstruct the discursive regimes that engender the subject). Within the context of mapping the equality and difference debates, she suggests that the strategies of inclusion, reversal and displacement take the form of endorsing equality, difference and diversity respectively (p. 116). She has a particular interest in delineating the strategies necessary to make the move beyond dichotomous thinking. She identifies two main approaches: synthesis and deconstructive diversity. Given the suggested settlement of drawing upon the best insights of both the equality and difference perspectives, the synthetic approach tends to lack theoretical distinctiveness and innovation. Squires contrasts this with the theoretical distinctive contribution of the diversity perspective, which deploying deconstructive strategies, seeks to 'go beyond' the equality/difference binary itself. She illustrates the specificity of the diversity approach by setting it up against difference theory. As transformative projects, they both have a shared history of interrogating the foundations of political theory with reference to gender, thus defining themselves against the integrative approach of equality's aim to 'add women' to the existing social order. However, drawing upon the work of Scott (1997), Grosz (1994a) and Ferguson (1993), Squires maintains that currently gender theorists are primarily focused upon the dissimilarity between the difference and diversity forms of these political projects, which are imagining alternative futures. For example, Ferguson (1993), argues that in the former, 'men – male power, male identities, masculinity as a set of practices – are problematized'; in the latter, 'the gendered world itself becomes a problem' (p. 3). She highlights the complexity of the relation between those who attempt politically to recentre female experience within the context of phallocentric discourse or patriarchal society and those who wish to deconstruct the notion of margins and centres. Rather than overemphasizing their contrasting themes, she suggests that in practice each position draws upon the other and might usefully be deployed as creating 'different, albeit related, possibilities for knowledge and politics' (p. 6).

As outlined above, throughout *Gender, Culture and Society*, working within a New Social Movement framework, we have explored these contemporary political tensions in terms of identity politics (feminism/gay liberation) and the new politics of cultural difference (postmodernism/post-structuralist/queer theory) positions. Early feminist theorizing, in developing explanatory frameworks of gender relations, tended to erase other social categories. As Mohanty (1992: 83) argues: invoking a notion of universal sisterhood which is defined as the transcendence of the 'male' world, 'ends up being a middle-class, psychologized notion which effectively erases material and ideological power differences within and among groups of women, especially between first and third world'. Similarly, early pro-feminist men's groups, in responding to the much vaunted masculinity crisis, have been criticized in the sociological literature for their profile as white, middle-class males, thus, excluding working-class, gay and black men. These exclusions are read through an identity politics position that serves to challenge the underrepresentation of minority groups. Throughout this book, we examine the limitations of this position, building on what we identified and developed as innovative frameworks for making sense of sexual politics, namely the dynamics of sexuality, age/generation, social class and ethnicity. We suggest that political and cultural questions of representation were always implicit in the older conception of the women's liberation movement. They now need to be reassessed in a context where earlier antipatriarchal and class-based certainties no longer hold.

The politics of race and culture has been a highly productive arena in which these political tensions have been worked through. For example, Knowles and Mercer (1992), operating from within a politics of cultural difference framework, explore the possibilities of developing an antiessentialist and pragmatic feminist and antiracist politics of mobilization against the vagueness of the enemy of state racism and white power. They provide a very interesting discussion of the limits of materialist accounts in which oppression is simply read off from 'experience'. They are critical of the latter position with its emphasis on the inscription of racism and gender inequality within processes of capitalism, colonialism and patriarchal social systems, which Knowles and Mercer see as producing overly functionalist arguments. They maintain that racism and sexism should be viewed as a series of effects which do not have a single cause. Brah (1992) has responded to this critique, in which she wishes to hold onto the productiveness of both materialist and politics of cultural difference positions. She accepts the limits of the former position, that the level of abstraction of

categories such as capitalism and patriarchal relations do not lend themselves to clear guidelines for political organization and that racism and sexism are not monocausal phenomena. However, she argues that she cannot
see how conceptualizing racism and sexism as a series of effects produces
a more useful strategic political action. Brah suggests:

> The main issue is not whether we should jettison macro-level analysis of
> gender or racism in relation to capitalism, colonialism or state socialism in
> favour of empirically grounded analysis of the concrete manifestations of
> racism in a given local situation, but how each is overdetermined by, and
> also helps to determine, the others. (p. 138)

Young (1993: 123–4), writing within a US context, has provided a productive
way forward that moves beyond the limits of an identity politics problematic, while suggesting the complex interrelation between social positioning
and subjective identity formation. In her paper that explores how political
actors conceive group difference and how they might best conceive it, she
writes:

> Historically, in group based oppression and conflict difference is conceived
> as otherness and exclusion, especially, but not only by hegemonic groups.
> This conception of otherness relies on a logic of identity that essentialises
> and substantialises group natures. Attempts to overcome the exclusion
> which such a conception generates usually move in one of two directions:
> assimilation or separation. Each of these political strategies itself exhibits a
> logic of identity; but this makes each strategy contradict the social realities
> of group interfusion. A third ideal of a single polity with differentiated
> groups recognising one another's specificity and experience requires a con-
> ception of difference expressing a relational rather than substantial logic.
> Groups should be understood not as entirely other, but as overlapping, as
> constituted in relation to one another and thus shifting their attributes
> and needs in accordance with what relations are salient. In my view this
> relational conception of difference as contextual helps make more apparent
> the necessity and possibility of political togetherness in difference.

A key issue for theorists is whether we can identify differentiated forms
of social power without relinquishing forms of structured oppression. In
other words, holding onto the tension between a politics of redistribution
and a politics of recognition/difference (Fraser, 1989, 1998). The development of policies aimed at reducing inequality require a more sophisticated
conceptual framework accompanied by a more empirically grounded
critique, which we illustrate throughout the book through use of ethnographic studies. Berman (1983: 24) makes an interesting contrast between

nineteenth-century thinkers, 'who were simultaneously enthusiasts and enemies of modern life, wrestling inexhaustibly with its ambiguities and contradictions' and those in the twentieth century who 'have lurched far more towards rigid polarities and flat totalizations'. He concludes that 'open views of modern life have been supplanted by closed ones, Both/And by Either/Or'. Throughout our book, we attempt to recapture a 'both/and' view. Hence, producing more coherent analyses within the sociology of gender and sexuality demands an understanding of the tension between identity politics and a more recent post-identity politics position. We agree with Gamson (1995: 400) when he argues that: 'The problem, of course, is that both the boundary strippers and the boundary defenders are right.' He suggests that a distinction between the two approaches can be understood as one of identity building and identity blurring.

Media Mobilization: Consuming New Feminism – post-feminism

A major change since early second-wave feminism, with the suggested shift from production to consumption as central to embodied identity-making has been the development of the global-based media as a critical site for the constitution of the meaning of feminism (Brunsdon, 1997; Modeleski, 1991). This highly influential space of modern iconography has projected a range of overlapping notions, variously branded as new feminism, power feminism and post-feminism. However, there is little consensus about what is being claimed for these concepts that mark changing times in the late modern period. For example, some argue that the project of feminism is completed, having attained equality between the sexes, others emphasize that feminism has lost it's way, while others argue for moving beyond 'victim feminism' (Brooks, 1997; Coppock *et al.*, 1995; Denfeld, 1995; Paglia, 1992, 1993; Roiphe, 1994). Dunphy (2000: 131) in his review of some of the key debates within feminism during this period has identified common and recurrent themes:

> The extent to which second wave feminism has achieved most of its goals; whether feminism has gone too far or not far enough in its battle to change gendered power relations; whether feminism as an ideology is still relevant in the so-called postmodern world; whether society is still patriarchal; whether profound social contradictions still characterize our type of society; and whether feminist strategies for change should emphasise sexual difference or sameness.

From an identity politics position, he adds that: 'the intensity of these debates and the prominence they have received in some sections of the press is a measure of both the impact feminism has had since the 1960s and the backlash it has endured since the 1980s'. What is understated here is the mobilization of a diverse range of representations of women and femininities. Implicit within the circulation of cultural images and attendant resignification of femininity is the assumption that a younger generation of women are dynamically leading the way in the processes of change, with both 'old-style' feminism and 'old-style' men being left behind.

New Feminism

New feminism, with its optimistic portrayal of a world of 'girl power', citing contemporary female icons, such as the Spice Girls, Madonna and Britney Spears tends to have an empirical rather than an analytic purpose. It provides an eclectic range of descriptions of gender relations in recent years for a new generation, whose political and cultural lives are presumed to exhibit increasing dissonance with that of their mothers and grandmothers (Walter, 1999). In attempting this, one of the main concerns has been to capture how younger women are experiencing contemporary gender relations. As Richardson (2000: 5) notes: 'This is a feminism that has been characterised as more popularist, more inclusive, more willing to embrace power, more tolerant in crossing political boundaries, a feminism that belongs to men as well as women, conservatives as well as socialists'. For example, Wilkinson (1999) in declaring that we are all power feminists now presents a revisionist reading of the former British prime minister, Margaret Thatcher, as a free market feminist, redefining the dominant relationship between women and power. A central text is Walter's (1998) *The New Feminism*, which provides a useful survey of contemporary women's lives, presenting a paradoxical picture, that of unprecedented female freedom and independence (that serves to question the old certainties of feminism), alongside continuing blatant inequalities. This paradox is especially explored in what the media has projected as the defining problem of the new century, that of the balance between home and work in conditions of post-industrialization.

In relation to social change, Walter's main argument is that following major successes in the 1970s, feminism narrowly shifted to an exclusive concern with sexual politics and culture. She contends that the latter's focus on attacking cultural manifestations of inequality has distracted women from materially achieving full social, economic and political equality with men. She writes:

> We lack equality and everything that comes with it. We lack the commitments to parental leave and flexible working that would make men and

women equal players in the workforce. We lack support for women facing grinding poverty, for women bringing up their children alone in miserable conditions. We lack training and education for women in dead-end jobs. We lack support and refuge for women fleeing violence. We lack women's voices in the highest courts and debating chambers of the country. (ibid.: 8–9)

Walter suggests a potted history of feminism in a series of moves from its outsider status in the nineteenth century, with women forced to campaign from the edges of society, through establishing a separate space for women in the 1970s and 1980s to claiming an insider status at the beginning of the twenty-first century. She demonstrates that a key move of new feminism is a break with a defining ideological slogan of second-wave feminism: 'the personal is political'. She claims that the decoupling of the personal from the political enables a cutting edge to social and political demands, while freeing up the personal realm. These material demands are outlined in terms of the need to implement five goals. They are revolutionizing the organization of work; creating a new national network of childcare; encouraging men to take on domestic responsibilities; supporting women and their families who are caught in poverty; and legislation and welfare support for women facing sexual and domestic violence (ibid.: 222–3). These demands appear as a substitute for both explanations of women's current social position and a theoretical framework that might help politically to answer the question posed in her final chapter: Where do we go from here? As Segal (1999: 228) points out:

But quite how (new) feminism will manage to deliver, once it remedies its ways and adopts 'a new, less embattled ideal', remains mysterious. Walter's analysis promotes no particular collective political formations or affiliations. We are simply told: 'We must understand that feminism can give us these things now, if we really want them'. Fingers crossed! Although pleasantly symptomatic of many women's goodwill towards a 'feminism' they feel free to fashion, it lacks the very thing it hopes to promote: political seriousness.

In terms of social and cultural politics, new feminism appears as rather limited. New feminist texts, as exemplified by Walter, read like reformist political programmes, which are much indebted to New Labour Government's Third Way and its exchange of ideological critique for pragmatic policies. Given Walter's claims to provide an authentic political voice for a younger generation, it strangely reads like a rather dated, 1950s British parochial manifesto, with its normative assumptions about privatized nuclear heterosexual families operating without extended family networks, for example, currently common among minority ethnic and white working-class communities; underplaying the diversity of current households, thus, for example, making invisible lesbian and gay families and a specific socially imagined western version of heterosexual young women, who take for granted contraceptive and abortion rights, thus returning to an earlier moment in feminist politics that erases 'non-western' women's experiences. In other words, Walter in distancing herself from the perceived reductionist strategies of the 1980s focus on sexuality returns feminism to a narrow project that writes out difference.

Post-feminism

The concept post-feminism appears as a highly confused term due to the diverse ways in which it is deployed, including a popular descriptive account of post-feminism as signalling a generational shift in understanding and perhaps a remaking of social relations between men and women. For example, Bolotin (1982) in an article in the *New York Times*, based on interviews with 18–25 year women, reported that they actively dissociated with traditional feminist politics that was seen as a threat to contemporary heterosexual relationships. An alternative understanding of post-feminism that returns us to the academy has been developed by feminists working within a cultural politics of difference position (Brooks, 1997; Yeatman, 1994). They locate post-feminism within a wide range of antifoundationalist movements, including postmodernism, post-structuralism and post-colonialism. In contrast to identity politics theorists, who interpret the concept of 'post' as a temporal term signalling what follows the completion of the feminist political project, here 'post' is understood as part of a long process of ongoing cultural and social transformations.

From an identity politics position, the concept is often projected as antifeminist in its reading of recent social and cultural changes. More specifically, the media is seen as of central significance in leading a backlash against feminism in which the use of post-feminism is primarily a polemical tool with limited analytical value (Coppock *et al.*, 1995). Two key texts provide evidence of an attempt to recuperate a lost masculinity in response to feminist political gains: French's (1992) *The War Against Women* charting the global history of patriarchal oppression and social change and Faludi's (1992) *Backlash*, exploring contemporary gender relations in the United States. Identity politics theorists identify the US cultural theorist Paglia (1992) as an influential media post-feminist guru, who has been highly successful in articulating a pervasive view of second-wave feminism as a victim feminism. Nostalgically combining an (earlier Freudian) biologically based essentialist understanding of gender with a libertine notion of sexuality that celebrates the naturalness of male energy, strength and sexuality, she maintains that we need to recall the inspiring progressive principles and global consciousness of the sixties. This would enable a new mode of feminism that 'stresses personal responsibility and is open to art and sex in all their dark, unconscious mysteries' (p. vii). She adds that: 'the feminist of the *fin de siecle* will be bawdy, streetwise, and on – the-spot confrontational, in the prankish sixties way' (p. vii). Controversially, she argues against what she sees as the academy's illegitimate involvement in policing sexual relationships, including the issue of date rape. Her internal critique of feminist politics has led to her being aligned by identity politics theorists with men's rights groups in interpreting recent changes as institutionalizing role reversal, a gender switch, with men being oppressed in the feminized new social order.

The above has identified the academy and the media as two main sites within which feminist debates are taking place within a broader political arena in which it is popularly claimed that the future is female. It is within this wider context, that we need to locate the suggested increased visibility of men as a gendered category and the associated emergence of masculinity politics. There is a need to challenge the assumed easy symmetry between Women's Studies and Men's Studies. The remarkable success of feminism (albeit uncompleted) as a political project is explicitly acknowledged by men's political mobilization. Reading through the literature, one is struck by the conceptual and methodological sophistication of feminist theorizing over the decades. In contrast, Men's Studies lacks rigour and consistency. A range of questions arise. Are men coming out as a gendered social collectivity? Do men consider themselves to constitute a specific gender? Is a modernist notion of patriarchy sufficient as an explanation of contemporary gender relations? What has generated the discourse of male crisis? Do we need to desegregate different levels of meaning: examining men and masculinities within broader sociological problems, including essentialism/social constructionism, structured action/subjectivity and categoricalism/deconstructionism?

Men as a Gendered and Political Category

Across the academy there remains little analytical interrogation of contemporary male political subject positions and masculinity politics. Within this discursive space, over the years, different versions of feminism implicitly or explicitly have provided a range of responses to the question of men's political relationship to women. For example, in the 1970s, while radical feminists emphasized that men rather than masculinity was the problem for women, sex-role reformers argued that men also suffered from hegemonic masculinity. Working from within a pro-feminist position, Hearn's (1987) early text *Gender and Oppression* provides a conceptual frame within which to understand the asymmetrical political relations operating between men and women as sexual classes, structurally located within the dual relationships of patriarchy and capitalism (see McDonald, 1981). Sexual classes are defined in terms of structures and superstructures, where masculinity is a structured ideology of males' biological relationship to reproduction. He maintains that: 'While men persist in the base of reproduction, masculinities persist in the "ideology" of production' (ibid.: 98). Hence, masculinity can be connected to an individual male's relationship to the economy, and collective masculinities result from men's shared structural location.

More recently, Whitehead (2002) has addressed the notion of men as a political category, locating his argument within the discourse of crisis, which he sees as primarily a struggle over dominant representations of masculinity and their relationship to femininity. In distancing himself from the materialist-based pro-feminist work of Hearn (1987) and Stoltenberg (1989), he overstates their limitations. For example, Hearn's research has led the way in arguing for a move beyond categorical theories, such as the deployment of the overinflated concept of patriarchy, suggesting that gender/sexual relations are shaped by a single overarching factor. Adopting a Foucauldian position, Whitehead identifies the limitations of materialist models of class power, 'as inadequate in terms of understanding the (micro) processes of resistance, differentiations and networks of collusion across and within the gendered categories of woman and man' (ibid.: 60). He prefers the term gender political categories, which he suggests combines the possibility of identifying power differentials without inferring a reductionist position of being able simply to read off the notion of women and men as uniform classes of being. Having established the need to see men as a political category, Whitehead makes the important point that it is equally important to examine how the category is sustained. He suggests that alongside men's instrumental desire for power over women, we need to address the more profound conditions of what he refers to as discursive association. In other words, we need to understand the processes involved in the way dominant knowledges serve to reify the contingent category of men, as an effect of the authoritative construction of norms that privilege attributes associated with masculinity.

Men and Masculinity Politics: Multiple Discourses of Masculinity Crisis

It is important to locate the specific narrative moment when the concept of masculinity politics emerged, with its potential to destabilize men's unmarked generic position in the social order. Connell (1995: 205) offers a useful definition of masculinity politics as 'mobilizations and struggles where the meaning of masculine power is at issue, and with it, men's position in gender relations. In such politics, masculinity is made a principal theme, not taken for granted as background'. As indicated in the introductory chapter, we suggest that these mobilizations and struggles are a key constituting element of the notion of sex/gender as a cultural flashpoint. Across western post-industrial societies, in response to major social and cultural transformations, highly anxious discussions are taking place about the social role of men and the constitution of masculinity. Lingard and Douglas (1999: 32) write:

> this reassessment has been most visible through the work of academics, political activists, men's groups, therapists and writers, and spans a range of positions from what might be termed the recuperative (attempting to recapture men's traditional social roles) to the progressive (looking forward to the constitution of a new diversity of masculine expressions and more equal gender relations).

Most significantly, the narrative moment is grounded in multiple discourses of crisis which are circulating through the media around images of *masculinity in crisis, male emotional illiteracy* and *men as the victims of feminism.* Hence, men's movements as a political project, compared to feminism and gay/lesbian mobilizations, often appears as a reactionary force, with little sense of a collective purpose. These confused and undertheorized notions of crisis are tautologically claimed to be both cause and effect of the feminization of social life (Coward, 1999). However, they carry high interpretive and seductive power in framing popular debates about changing gender relations, with projected images of the ascendancy of women and of imploding men as a defining feature of late-consumer societies. In turn, as suggested above, some feminists have sought to explain this shift primarily in terms of a 'war against women' – a misogynistic backlash against the political gains of second-wave feminism, attempting to recuperate a regressive heterosexual masculinity (Faludi, 1992; French, 1992).

During the 1970s, men's movements tended to have little political resonance among men, who as a group did not identify as a specific gendered collectivity. A key argument of this book is that we are experiencing a shift from the establishment of the social constitution of gender, associated with modernity politics, to the gendering of society that has an intensified resonance among (heterosexual) men and women. For example, across the popular media the sex wars is a constant reference point in making sense of current events. However, by the early 2000s, this has not manifested itself in terms of widespread mobilization of men into political groupings. Rather, we are witnessing highly fragmented responses, in which it is difficult to make sense of the structure and meaning of men's sexual politics (Pease, 2000).[3]

Male Liberationists: Reforming Male Roles

Male liberationists, working within a sex-role approach, mobilized liberal feminist discourses of equal rights and fairness to argue that both women and men suffered from the sexism generated from negative gender stereo-typical socialization (Farrell, 1974; Nichols, 1975). They spoke of the burden and emotional damage of being men, thus focusing upon the negative attributes of the male role as *oppressed* rather than that of *oppressor*. As Pease (2000: 124) points out:

> They saw consciousness-raising groups as vehicles by which men could get in touch with their feelings, free themselves from sex-role stereotyping, learn to be more caring for other men and struggle together against the imposition of the socially oppressive male role.

A particular strength of this approach is to challenge biologically based determinist explanations of gender interactions. It points out that if young boys are socialized into acting out society's expectations of the male role – 'a boys will be boys' approach – dominant masculine characteristics, such as aggression, competitiveness and fear of intimacy, can be relearned. Hence, it is argued that women and men can (and should) form political alliances that address their shared needs. In so doing, this will enable them to eradicate the sexism inherent in traditional sex roles. There is evidence of the achievement of this reformist approach in local and national European political spaces, that tends to be under reported by academic commentators. These include implementing equal opportunities initiatives within public institutions, developing antisexist educational material, co-parenting, and developing antidiscrimination laws at a local state level (European Commission Network on Childcare, 1993). It may also be credited, as part of the wider movement of liberal feminism, in establishing antisexism as a legitimate policy goal for the modern era.

Pro-feminism: A Radical Heterosexual Position

Pro-feminist men creatively developed a political strategic approach that opposed a tendency by some men of a radical rejection of their masculinity, which was seen as essentially tied up with a relationship of power. This is illustrated in Stoltenberg's (1989) *Refusing to be a Man*. At the same time, they focused on the political limitations of the men's Liberationist approach that emphasizes a voluntarism, thus, underplaying the social structures and cultural ideologies within which individual men and women are embedded. Pro-feminist groups have produced detailed accounts of their political activism in relation to gender (Jardine and Smith, 1992; Kimmel and Mosmiller, 1992; Metcalf and Humphries, 1985; Snodgrass, 1977; Tolson, 1977). Seidler's (1992) British collection of writings, written during the period 1978 to 1984, that were published in *Achilles Heel*, the journal of men's sexual politics, makes clear the innovativeness of this position (See also *Changing Men* (United States) and *XY* (Australia). The index to the collection indicates the critical self-exploration and reflexivity of a group of men, who made their sex and sexuality the key object of political inquiry. Aligning themselves with socialist and radical feminist positions, pro-feminist men named themselves as complicit with patriarchal power relations and the accompanying institutional oppression of women. Remembering their sexual and domestic biographies, they focused upon diverse sexist practices around issues of the self, sexuality, violence and pornography. The techniques and processes of the women's liberation movement were adopted and practised, as they collectively imagined non-oppressive, life-affirming ways of being men, in their relationships with women, gay men and other heterosexual men.

A number of limitations have been identified with this position. Most importantly, progressive men's groups continued conceptually to conflate notions of men and masculinities that are conventionally elided in the social science literature. Hence, in living out the contradictions of embodied heterosexual masculinities, it was not clear if the object of their political organizing was to change themselves, as a gendered social majority, or to change the wider structures, ideologies and discourses that shaped the sex/gender order and the accompanying dominant political regime. At the same time, while progressive heterosexual men's groups responded to feminism, they failed to engage with the gay liberation movement. Dunphy (2000: 64–5) has described the difficulty that social theorists have in answering questions concerning the meaning of heterosexuality. More specifically, with reference to male writers on masculinity, he notes that they claim *masculinity* rather than *sexuality* as their sexual identity. Hence, they have failed to make strategic alliances with gay activism around the issue of redefining social ways of being men, as part of the latter's longer history of having to invent a self, a social identity and a wider community, which might be adopted as alternative cultural resources by heterosexual men. In so doing, they might begin to operate beyond the institutional ideologies and discourses of gender regulation and self-surveillance that maintains the fixed boundaries of modern manhood. This is particularly salient at a time when it is claimed that heterosexual men are in crisis. For example, Faludi (1999) in her study found a generation of American men whom she sympathetically portrays as unable, personally and collectively, to find a progressive resolution to the effects of contemporary social transformations that they interpret as challenging their sense of manhood. She suggests that they are asking the wrong questions and that instead of relentlessly seeking the meaning of masculinity, they should concentrate on what it means to be human. What becomes clear from such texts is that the heterosexual male crisis is premised on a cultural shift from a social identity that was assumed to be fixed, coherent and stable, being displaced by a sense of doubt, uncertainty and anxiety (Mercer, 1990). This is experienced at individual, social and psychic levels that are circumscribed by the local – global nexus of cultural transformations, which the new men's movement has addressed. In so doing, they adopt a conservative political position in their attempt to recuperate an assumed lost masculinity.

The New Men's Movement

At one level, male liberationists and pro-feminist men tend to define political positions and more specifically their political alliance to feminism against each other, producing debates that have little resonance outside their own membership. At another level, these progressive groups define themselves against men who take up a conservative position in relation to feminism. Again, this results in debates with limited political effects. Conservatively orientated men's groups are often represented by the former as a homogenous movement. In fact, we can identify a number of strands, involving variants of pro – male, antifeminism and antiwomen stances, which illustrate both the changing historical development and cultural specificity of conservative men's sexual politics within different nation-states (Bertoia and Drakich, 1995; Reynaud, 1983). For example, a number of articles in *The Guardian* newspaper, including Baker (1994) and Millar (1997) have usefully mapped out the development of the UK Men's Movement during the last decade, with its challenging the legitimacy of the Equal Opportunities Commission, its arguments for repealing equal rights legislation and direct attacks on rape crisis centres. Alongside, and sometimes overlapping, with this embryonic movement, a range of grassroots action groups have emerged in Britain around men's issues.

Writing from a different location, Connell (1995) names the gun lobby as a specific form of masculinity politics, that he sees as central to defending hegemonic masculinity in the United States. He also identifies the changing politics surrounding masculinity therapy over the last 20 years, which he sees as presently the most talked about in the United States. He traces its shift from the early 1970s association with countercultural therapy and its pro-liberal feminist stance of breaking out of the traditional male role, to a 1980s emphasis on a separation from the feminine in search of the deep masculine. Bly's (1990) *Iron John* is one of the most celebrated books about men, among academics, professionals and journalists. Invoking 'mytho – poetic' concepts, he argues for the restoration of a lost, traditional masculinity – for the urgent need to encounter *the hairy man*. From a British perspective, there is much scepticism about 'meeting the god-woman in the garden', 'bringing interior warriors back to life', and 'the wild man in ancient religion, literature and folk life', which are chapter headings in Bly's book. However, there is much resonance with emotional self-exploration, male bonding and recovering damaged relationships with fathers. Placed within a structure of a traditional masculinity, this enables individual men to be actively involved in affective relations, underpinned by the security of images that do not threaten their participation in the traditionally feminine world of emotional work. In short, gendered and sexual power relations are reinforced rather than subverted – you can discover your authentic masculinity, becoming a 'hard warrior' rather than a 'soft wimp'. Bly claims a pro-male rather than an antifeminist stance. However, feminism is cited as one of the key sources of the feminization of contemporary men. Hence, he maintains there is a need for men to renegotiate their relationship to feminism. Others, working within masculinity therapy, have developed a more stringent antifeminist stance in reworking this relationship. In contrast, the British therapist, Rowan (1987), who like Bly is working within a Jungian tradition, describes the productive engagement of men with strong women produced in feminism, arguing for the need to get in touch with a female goddess tradition (See also Rowan, 1997).

The men's rights lobby is the form of masculinity politics that currently has widest resonance across different societies, including Britain, Australia and America. It has been central to a cultural shift in which the idea of the men's movement, which from the early 1970s was associated with a progressive identification with feminist politics is now popularly understood as an organized defence of men as the victims of contemporary gender arrangements. In contrast, failing to develop a language to explain the changing meanings of what it is to be a heterosexual man, progressive men's groups have made little impact on challenging a popular media image of men being forced to make adjustments to structural changes within the workplace and family life under increasing pressure from feminist and gay activists. Key texts on men's rights include Lyndon (1992), Thomas (1993) and Farrell (1994). Farrell moved from an earlier pro-feminist position as a member of the influential National Organization of Women (NOW) in America, to an attempt to provide a theoretically coherent framework for a men's rights politics.

The above pro-male position might implicitly indicate the need for a class and ethnic-based analysis to make sense of these complex sets of contemporary material changes in late modernity. However, for Farrell these complex questions are answered in terms of a simple explanation that men are now the gender victims as a result of feminism having gone too far, with men having increased responsibilities but few rights around issues of marriage, divorce, child custody and access to children. Modern legislation is seen to be over protective of women's interests, resulting in discrimination against men at a time when they are under increasing threat within a rapidly changing society. For example, the feminization of institutional life is experienced within the context of the decline of traditional male work and its accompanying implications for the male 'breadwinner' role, alongside the increase of women in the feminine-friendly service sector (See ch. 3).

For all the differences between different strands of men's groups, a number of underlying themes can be identified. First, arguments for a more inclusive approach to gender relations – that is, to include men as central participants – can be read as politically important in highlighting the interdependence of men and women, masculinities and femininities. This might suggest the need to modernize our understanding of relations between men and women. For example, Connell (1995: 211) is undoubtedly right that:

> although such texts like Bly's are nostalgic and the mythopoetic imagery can be strikingly reactionary, the tendency of therapeutic practice is towards accommodation between men and women, adjustment at the level of personal relations. The larger consequence of the popular forms of masculinity therapy is an adaptation of patriarchal structures through the modernization of masculinity.

Second, the historical development of men's groups has marked a theoretical shift of interest from men's patriarchal presence in the public world and an accompanying politics of social justice for women and men to that of a preoccupation with men's emotionally damaged inner world. For conservatives, this is translated into challenging their projected disempowerment. For progressive men's groups, this has resulted in a movement into therapy (Digby, 1998).

Refusing the Cultural Injunction to Become Heterosexual: Forging Dissident Femininities and Masculinities

A major aim of this book is to denaturalize sex, gender and desire, emphasizing the active cultural production of contemporary femininities and masculinities within the wider context of the social organization of the sex/gender order. One productive arena in which to accomplish this is to explore those who have not taken up the cultural injunction to become heterosexual women or men that includes a wide range of sexual minorities: lesbians, gay men, bisexuals, transsexuals and transgendered groups. There is a long history within medical and popular discourses of linking sexual choice and gender with an assumed association of homosexuality with femininity and lesbianism with masculinity. This association serves to deny the validity of same sex desire, while producing heterosexuality as conceptually inescapable (Pringle, 1992). As Richardson (1996: 4) suggests: 'Historically, lesbians have been portrayed as virtual men trapped in the space of women's bodies: "mannish" in appearance and masculine in their thoughts, feelings and desires, rendering their existence compatible with the logic of gender and heteronormativity.' She adds: 'Although she is necessary to this logic, the complementary femme "type" of lesbian is mentioned much less frequently in representations of lesbians in scientific discourses and popular culture – perhaps not surprisingly as she is more problematic' (ibid.: 4).

Gay and lesbian scholars and activists have been one of the most dynamic contributors to recent sexual theorizing in destabilizing sociological and common-sense meanings of men/women and masculinity/femininity within the broader structure of gender relations (Bristow and Wilson, 1993; Kirsch, 2000). For example, Marshall (1981: 134) identifies 'five basic components to sexual identity' that are assumed to give 'rise to both "normal" and "deviant" identities'. These include biological sex, gender identity, gender role, sexual behaviour and sexual meaning. It has been an important contribution of gay and lesbian movements to deconstruct these connections. At the same time, we emphasize the analytical purchase of gay and lesbian narratives and concepts in helping to reshape mainstream sociology leading to the extension and development of our theoretical understanding of the processes and patterns or conflicts that produce the gender order within specific historical and geographical spaces (Stein and Plummer, 1994). For example, as Pronger (1990: 2), writing of the political paradox of contemporary meanings of gay masculinity argues:

> In our culture male homosexuality is a violation of masculinity, a denigration of the mythic power of men, an ironic subversion that significant numbers of men pursue with great enthusiasm. Because it gnaws at masculinity it weakens the gender order. But because masculinity is at the heart of homoerotic desire, homosexuality is essentially a paradox in the myth of gender.

In turn, the changing processes of being and becoming men and women lived out by gays and lesbians, respectively, resonate with the wider picture of changing institutions, fluid and changeable relationships, a shifting emotional landscape and the complex transformations of intimate life in a global age of uncertainty (Giddens, 1992; Jamieson, 1998; Rubin, 1993; Sedgwick, 1994; Weeks, 1995).

The early autobiographical sexual stories of inventing dissident femininities and masculinities, written in the 1970s and early 1980s, which provide fascinating insights into lesbian and gay disinvestment in traditional modes of (heterosexual) femininity and masculinity are marked by a highly reflexive self. As Weeks (1990: 134) maintains:

> lesbians and gays have a sense of their own creativity because they are, day by day, involved in self-making, constructing their own meanings, networks, rituals, traditions, calling on inherited traces of the past, but responding all the time to the challenges and possibilities of the present.

Emerging decentred female and male gay subjectivities provide concrete evidence that femininity and masculinity is not something one is born with or an inherent possession, but rather an active process of achievement, performance and enactment (Plummer, 1981; Weeks, 1977). Furthermore, the development of a wide range of lesbian and gay male styles makes clear the meaning of the living out of fractured femininities and masculinities, involving a diverse range of women's and men's investments, anxieties, fantasy identifications and contradictory emotions, in modes of femininity and masculinity that they were actively manufacturing within safe social spaces. These texts, which were informed by the radical intention of liberating all genders, illustrate the internal cultural technologies involved in sex/gender identity work, reordering meanings, rescripting roles and reinventing values, that has emerged into the development of a new moral economy and sexual citizenship (Altman. 1983; Evans, 1993; Weeks, 1995).

More recently, queer activists have argued that the established gay community, in campaigning for community identity recognition and validation by straight society, has adopted an assimilationist position (Simpson, 1996). The perceived limitations of this political strategy are resonant of those voiced by black radicals in the 1970s concerning the State setting the agenda on which racialized minority ethnic groups were to be included within white society, on terms of liberal acceptance rather than human rights. A major concern for queer activists, operating from an antiessentialist position, is that mainstream inclusion involves the state regulation and surveillance of a sexual minority identity that implicitly produces the homosexual – heterosexual boundary of a fixed sub – cultural type. Furthermore, for queer activists, the gay movement in targeting its political energies towards straight society has not addressed a wide range of internal sexual exclusions, including bisexuals, transsexuals and transgendered groups, alongside social closures, around age, ethnicity and disability, arising from the narrow conception of gay identity itself. In contrast, queer politics, adopting a utopian stance, is open to all dissident eroticized minorities, while simultaneously claiming that the effect of transcending the homo/hetero divide is to challenge the sexual regulation and repression of the sexual majority – heterosexual desire. This political position makes clear that 'queer is also a way of cutting against mandatory gender divisions' (Warner, 1993: xxvii). Though, Warner adds, gender continues to be a dividing line. In other words, working against traditional sexual and gender hierarchies, in which sexuality and gender as social categories of analysis act as containers that operate normatively to fix the boundaries of how we should live our lives, queer activists emphasize the openness, fragmentation and diversity that infuse contemporary ways of being.

Two key elements in the development of queer theory/activism have been, first, the scholarship of literary and cultural theorists working in gay and lesbian studies. They have provided a philosophically rich range of concepts that have been explored throughout this book, including deconstructing the hetero/homo boundary, the heterosexual matrix and gender performativity (Butler, 1990; Dollimore, 1991; Sedgwick, 1991) (see Ch. 6). The second element, has been emerging political responses to the AIDS crisis in the 1980s/early 1990s. For example, the radical activist group Queer Nation deployed forms of political activism promoted by ACT UP (the AIDS coalition to Unleash Power). Within a British context, we can note two critical developments: the changing age profile of non – heterosexuals, and the gay community's creative response to the AIDS epidemic, mediated through safe sex practices, new reproductive technological advances and repressive state legislation. The latter involved the British government's introduction of Section 28 of the Local Government Act 1988, which banned local authorities from supporting the 'promotion of homosexuality' or the validation of 'pretended family' (homosexual) relationships (Aggleton, *et al.*, 1999; Stacey, 1991).

There are a range of criticisms of queer theory/politics, including that it is a development of a social constructionist tradition rather than a radical break with established social theory, that it privileges significatory systems, discourse and discursive power, it colludes with postmodernism in underplaying the importance of socio – economic structural differences; its elitist concern with abstract theorizing and accompanying disinterest in the 'ordinary', and most significantly its downplaying of gender in discussion of heteronormativity (Dunphy, 2000; Hennessy, 2000; Kirsch, 2000; McIntosh, 1993; Morton, 1995). Queer theory remains highly abstract, disconnected from the way people are living their lives within the institutional constraints of economics, the state and cultural traditions (Edwards,

1998; Kirsch, 2000; McIntosh, 1993). The histories of gay and lesbian politics illustrate the need to reconnect contemporary material conditions to questions of representation, culture and the self in order to grasp what is at stake in troubling the dominant sex/gender system and the accompanying production of masculinities and femininities (Dunne, 2001; Weeks *et al.*, 2001). However, as a postmodern politics, queer activists celebrate the transgressive potential, both discursive and social, of the implosion of existing gender and sexuality categories, enabling us to reimagine inhabiting a range of masculinities and femininities and the full diversity of sexual desire.

Under Western Eyes: Global Mobilizations, Culture and Difference[4]

Historically, diverse sources, including the discipline of anthropology, the substantive field of international relations and gay/lesbian global mobilizations have provided productive comparative data, raising questions of how well western concepts travel from the North to the South in terms of making sense of everyday cultural practices. By the early 2000s, these sources suggest that multiple representations and performances of femininity and masculinity are being politically forged within the context of the growth of western capitalism, with cultural imperialism, articulated in and through hegemonic sex/gender orders, traversing international boundaries (Mirande, 1997; Shire, 1994). For example, Altman (2001: 148) in his book *Global Sex*, provides fascinating evidence of sex/gender identities on the move. He writes of 'the interplay between gender orders within global capitalism producing a range of novel identities and patterns of relationship, sexual communities and political processes. They belong neither to local or metropolitan cultures, but in a sense to both – and more exactly, to the new global society that is emerging'. This serves to destabilize the assumed universal claims of what it means to be a man or to be a woman in relation to the western gendering of being and doing.

More specifically, feminist analyses within these global sites have interrogated the conceptual and methodological adequacy of western sex/gender categories with reference to local contexts and meanings across transnational spaces. These debates intensified with the deployment of the discourse of globalization in the 1980s, which may be read as a way of understanding socio-economic and cultural changes taking place in advanced capitalist societies in the post-war period (Bauman, 1998). Within the context of this global restructuring, social theorists in and of the South set out to rethink limiting categories and frameworks in response to the rapid development of new information technologies, the rapid expansion of global networks of communication, and the emergence of complex global systems of production and exchange (Castells, 1996). International feminist networks were well placed to lead this theoretical and political work. Stienstra (1994) reminds us that historically, although women have been active organizing internationally for over 150 years, it is only recently that there has been a recognizable field of feminist international relations theory. In a later text, Stienstra (2000) traces a specific response to global restructuring, that of women's transnational organization. This is explored as a particular site of resistance in relation to the five United Nations conferences between 1992 and 1996. Most importantly, the women's caucuses at these conferences served to bring 'together women active in community-based, national, regional and international networks and organizations' to develop political strategies that challenged the impact of restructuring at local and global levels (p. 209).

In a rapidly expanding literature, the different interpretations of globalization, which are inextricably linked with the movement of capital, labour, commodities, and cultural practices, can be located within a framework of materialist and post-structuralist positions. Materialist accounts, emphasizing new circuits of imperialism have pointed out that there is a long history to the increasingly global extent of the international division of labour, new communications networks, technologies and financial flows that continue to be dominated by western multinationals and post-colonial powers, as new circuits of capitalism are imposed (Sivanandan, 1989). Materialist feminism, revealing the partial understandings produced by male-dominated narratives on the Third World, identifies the contradictions of the shifting social relations of gender, accompanying global economic restructuring. For example, the notion of the feminization of work often carries with it a politically progressive assumption that the future is female. However, within a Southern context, while increasing numbers of women have entered paid employment, they are disproportionately located within the low paid service sector rather than hi-tech jobs, experiencing increased unemployment in specific regions and women are particularly exploited in the non-unionized 'free trade zones'. At the same time, structural adjustment programmes, instituted by the International Monetary Fund and the World Bank, have resulted in an increase in women's unpaid domestic labour, resulting from public spending cutbacks on welfare services (Desai, 2002; Smith, 2000). Materialist feminism continues to be important in providing critical commentaries on the absence of women as non-state actors in politics, the need for national governments and international aid development to recognize the specific needs of women, the importance of the informal economy of domestic work, the impact of militarism on women and children, the global redistribution of power, prostitution and sexual violence (Morgan, 1984; Spike Peterson and Sisson Runyan, 1993).

During the 1970s, the language of 'difference' and 'culture', which became increasingly mobilized in the discussion of social, economic and national questions, as well as questions of identity, was taken up by gender theorists (Silverman, 1992: 89). A post-structuralist position, focusing upon emerging forms of cultural hybridity among transcultural communities and the proliferation of identities and difference, has problematized that which social sciences have taken as given, bounded, national social formations. Currently, cultural theorists are preoccupied with fundamental shifts that have taken place in the direction of a global economy, with its associated, internationally prevalent effects on patterns of lifestyles, consumption and communication (Appadurai, 1996; Hall, 1991). Ong (1999: 5) exploring the cultural logics of transnationality with reference to the flexible citizenship of Asian immigrants, argues for a synthesis of the political, economic and cultural positions. She maintains:

> When an approach to cultural globalization seeks merely to sketch out universalizing trends rather than deal with actually existing structures of power and situated cultural processes, the analysis cries out for a sense of political economy and situated ethnography. What are the mechanisms of power that enable the mobility, as well as the localization and disciplining, of diverse populations within these transnational systems? How are cultural flows and human imagination conditioned and shaped within these new relations of global inequalities?

Enloe (1989: 9) in her classic text, *Bananas, Beaches and Bases: Making Sense of International Politics*, writes of how by the late 1980s, new understandings emerged 'of the ways in which international feminist feminizing and organizing (had) to be rooted in clear explanations of how women from different, often unequal societies, are used to sustain the world patterns that feminists seek to change'. Here, she is identifying a central conceptual and political weakness of the materialist position, that of, its failure to incorporate the dynamic complexity of the interrelationship between different categories of experience, such as gender, class and ethnicity. While in the North, a strategic response has been to recognize a plurality of feminisms, an unresolved tension remains, that of the concept of feminism, or indeed gender relations itself being doubly marked as a sign of the future (modernization) and the past (cultural imperialism). This tension has had a specific resonance within the South, in which the collective historical memory associates the latest wave of globalization with earlier global domination anchored in imperialism and colonialism.

The late 1980s witnessed a new generation of theoretical work produced by Third World feminist scholarship on the cultural politics of representation, difference and subjectivity (Grewal and Kaplan, 1994; Lazreg, 1988;

Mohanty,1988; Ong, 1988; Sassen, 1998). Focusing upon transnationalism, diaspora and the formation of identities, they make clear the limitations of established male-centred writing on global politics. At the same time, they interrogate how feminist analysis from the North is conceptually flawed, marked by its own modernist forms of essentialist and universalizing interpretative frames. Mohanty's (1988) 'Under western eyes: Feminist scholarship and colonial discourses', and Ong's (1988) 'Colonialism and modernity: Representations of women of non-western societies' explore the neo-colonialist discursive positioning of Third World women. Ong (ibid.: 80) captures the prescribed hierarchical relationship between Northern and Southern women, claiming that: 'For feminists looking over-seas, the non-feminist other is not so much patriarchy as the non-Western women.' Working with western epistemological premises, a range of asso-ciated binary oppositions are operated – western/Third World, modern/ traditional and (sexually) liberated/repressed – that reductively serve to produce a geo-political distinct, monolithic image of Southern women, denying the multiple realities of their lives (Chowdhry, 1995). Of central importance for Mohanty (1988) is the way in which Northern accounts, in addressing Third World women's experience of marginalization and dis-empowerment, revert to a conventional understanding of power. Here, experience is compressed within a powerful/powerless couplet. In other words, there is no empirical, analytical or theoretical space beyond the domination and subordination of these asymmetrical positions. An alter-native reading is to see that social relations are in a continual constitutive process. As Foucault (1981: 99) suggests: 'Relations of power-knowledge are not static forms of distribution, they are "matrices of transformations".' In this way, we have to move towards understanding structures and hier-archies as not completely stable and not completely forceful as well as engaging in a process where outcomes are not entirely secured.

Alongside these feminist internal critiques of the North, are the complex histories of resistance among Third World feminists. As Smith (2000: 7) argues: 'Non-westerners were understandably distressed because many of the early feminists in India, Egypt, and elsewhere had been middle and upper class with ties to such western ideologies as democracy, the free mar-ket and individualism. They searched for a way to be "authentic" in their feminism as opposed to mimicking the values of the imperialist powers.' In response to these complex histories, patriarchal – based, post-colonial regimes have adopted reactionary positions against women's interests, while aligning with the 'ruling relations' of male-centred global inequali-ties as manifest in transnational corporations and global markets (Connell, 2002; Smith, 1987). A further element of the complexity of global sexual politics as a strategic movement is that both materialist and culturalist analyses tend to share a privileging of political movements which organize at the international (North American and European) level, which, in turn, serves to marginalize indigenous or national women's movements across, for example, Latin America, Asia and Africa (Stienstra, 1994). In the late eighties, Bulbeck, (1988: 8–9) made clear that western feminism's universalistic assumptions about the meaning of patriarchal oppression posed particular problems for non-western women. She argued:

> These two strands of contemporary feminist analysis – its focus upon women to the exclusion of men, and its recent reorientation away from economic welfare to physical and psychic welfare – troubles women of colour and the third world. These women often claim that the most pressing concern for them – and their menfolk – is economic security, freedom from starvation or poverty. In contrast, issues concerning the representation of women in advertisements or films, or even in terms of access to contraception or freedom from infibulation, seem remote concerns.

Bulbeck in a finely argued analysis illustrates this complexity of operationalizing a global sexual politics, maintaining that western feminism should not be dismissed as mere lifestyle politics, which would be to reinscribe male-dominated discourses that morally value the public over the private sphere. In other words, integral to the public events of nation-making and economic modernization are the private concerns that shape everyday life: the personal continues to be a necessary site for political struggle, making visible its intimate relationship to that which continues to be redefined as its opposite, the public. Nevertheless, by the early 2000s, for the estimated 1.2 billion of the world's poorest people, that is, those living on less than a dollar a day, with the intensification of North American neo-liberal, socio-economic politics, famines, AIDS and ethnic cleansing, BulBeck's main argument continues to have salience, in relation to political mobilization to meet the urgency of their immediate needs.

Conclusion

This chapter explicitly addresses one of the main aims of *Gender, Culture and Society*, namely, to engage with the main academic accounts of the struggle for gender and sexual equality at a time of rapid global change, in which there is criticism from the political Right and Left of the limits of feminist politics and the emergence of men's movements in the West, alongside alternative responses from developing countries that show the limits of western accounts. In response, we suggest holding onto the tension between theoretical frameworks made available by New Social Movements: *identity politics* and *the new politics of cultural difference*, which are two of the most dynamic contributions to contemporary debates. Most importantly, working within this framework highlights the need to connect an understanding of sexual politics, recent mobilizations and a sense of intimate belonging *with* wider social and cultural transformations as mutually constitutive. In turn, this enables an exploration of the extent and direction of change in relation to the social relations of gender, sex/gender identity formations and subjectivities. This serves to highlight the lack of political consensus about what constitutes change in a society, marked by diverse understandings of patriarchy, compulsory heterosexuality and homophobia, alongside more recent conceptualizations of living with difference. The chapter tracks the shift from early feminist political agitation and mobilization involving the double play around (in) equality and difference to that of the future of sexual politics and the Queer search for post-identity position, that opens up questions of sexual politics at local and global levels.

Conclusion

The Introduction set out to provide a commentary on the context in which existing studies of gender and social change is being undertaken. This commentary has imbricated itself throughout our engagement with various texts in the field. A principal purpose of this Conclusion is to revisit the main aims that were outlined in the Introduction. In our first aim, we suggested that contemporary gender relations can be understood as an important cultural flashpoint. We argued that such a flashpoint has emerged in conjunction with changing social structures, emerging cultural forms and the reconfiguration of subjectivities. Across each of the chapters, we have considered how such a flashpoint is impacting upon gender relations. We have been keen to point out and acknowledge that one of the impacts of the flashpoint has been to produce a cultural consolidation. Something that Gullette (1997: 98) defines as:

> a discursive phenomenon in which for a space of time – which can last for decades – a set of beliefs and issues and verbal formulas and tropes and binaries become fixed as the only terms in which talk on a particular subject makes sense to speakers.

In short, knowledges and understandings that we have available to make sense of gender have become part of the fabric that binds the current moment of social change. Briefly, the interplay of gender and social change can appear as the stabilization of what we already know about gender. Patterns of gendered inequalities, such as those witnessed around sex (prostitution) tourism, demonstrate that gender as a cultural flashpoint identifies how such parameters are not only being consolidated, but also how they are vicarious. New contexts of gendering are emerging where older forms of inequality are not only being lived out, they are becoming more intensified. The implication is that a popular gender intelligibility that links biological categories of sex to traditional gendered social roles are being reinforced and strengthened. As such, continuities exist between early and more recent social configurations of gender relations.

At the same time, *Gender, Culture and Society* has considered existing work in the field not simply as stabilizing what intelligibilities are articulated through gender relations, but can operate to *obscure* what we are able to know. As a result, the conceptual and empirical spaces through which gender is maintained, thought about and given existence are the very spaces that disable and disrupt the possibilities of knowing gender in other ways. Thus, approaches to gender operate to assemble the logic, the rationale and the conceptualizing through which the possibilities of knowing gender become available. The cultural flashpoint therefore, appears not simply to reinforce existing ways of knowing about gender, it operates to fracture, dislodge and question what we know and how we know. Identifying the discontents of gender creates new ways of examining gender relations both at the level of the context – how it is being lived out – and at the level of the conceptual, how gender theorists are being able to make sense and explain gender outside of existing theoretical parameters. We have suggested at various moments across all of the chapters that the existing narratives surrounding gender relations and social practices do not appear to be corresponding to the old cultural gender stories.

Given the importance attached to gender and its discontents, we argue that the search for a new gender settlement continues. The parameters of such a search remain highly contentious as there is much speculation over the 'winners and losers' of later modernity. For example, the psychiatrist, Anthony Clare (2000: 68), writing of the serious trouble that afflict men at the beginning of the twenty-first century, explains that there has been a cultural inversion of the moral economy of male and female characteristics. He claims:

> Being logical, disciplined, rational and competitive are now seen as the stigmata of deviance ... (whereas) the traits which once marked out women as weak and inferior – emotional, spontaneous, intuitive, expressive, compassionate, empathetic – are increasingly seen as markers of maturity and health.

However, such texts, are low on empirical evidence to justify the selection of the category gender rather than, for example, class or ethnicity, (or a fusion of these categories) as a universal explanatory frame within which to explore contemporary men's experiences of rapid social and cultural transformations. For example, there is a long history of national/ethnic minority men's mobilization against colonial subordination and structural racism as the major cause of their social positioning as 'non-proper' men, thus challenging the assumption of a unitary crisis of masculinity (Hooper, 2001; Mac an Ghaill, 1999; Messner, 1997). Thus in gendered cultural flashpoints, the strategies that are often used to resolve them, tend to simply reproduce the normative assumptions on which they are based. Therefore in the process of 'levelling' gender practices, they implicitly rely on the mobilization of categories of masculine and feminine/male and female to create a gender settlement.

Our second aim has centred on epistemological formations. In many of the chapters, we have constantly reflected on how various approaches operate to secure ways of knowing. As with our understanding of gender as a cultural flashpoint, the conceptual processes embedded in the explanations that are drawn upon secure and exclude the possibilities of knowing. Gender is a product of the emergence of modern industrial societies that have witnessed the proliferation of declarative categories of being. Declarative, in this sense means that categories do not simply order social relations, they carry and speak about how those relations should be organized. Thus, the emergence of categories that serve to designate who and what we are appear to have shifted from institutionalized positions connected to social class and status, to that of representation of and through the body. Consequently, accounts of gender and social change are being produced within the context of much epistemological confusion as the focus of inquiry is contested. What remains constant is an appeal to an empirical source – social practices and cultural processes. What becomes contested is the aspect that is designated with epistemological status.

In other work we have highlighted how studies of masculinity tend to apply existing methodological approaches to the field of study. In the context of gender relations similar issues are apparent. The main methodological processes involved in discussions of gender and social change operate through an empirical framework – empirical, in that social and cultural phenomena are observable. Gender research is marked by what counts as valid evidence. Thus, at an individual level, work around standpoint epistemologies identifies that knowledge about gender emerges from women's and men's experiences. Central to this approach is the claim that the experiential operates hermeneutically, with knowledge, understandings and feelings being the source of knowledge. In contrast, a quantitative approach relies on collecting data in a numerical sense. Thus, it is not simply experience that matters but the preponderance of practices alongside experience. From this position, social change is not accessed through individual experience; rather it can be obtained at the level of collectivities. For example, men and women's participation in particular labour processes can be measured and compared spatially and temporally. The results can be used as evidence to measure how far social change has or has not taken place. It has been argued that such research practices secure the relationship between gender and social change.

By suggesting that gender and social change is also enmeshed in a politics of representation, *Gender, Culture and Society* argues for an epistemological base that pulls away from traditional understandings of empirical evidence. In doing so, it recognizes that studies of gender relations are imbricated in designating what counts as evidence. Hence, there is a need for a methodological shift away from establishing the *evidence of identity* towards approaches that question the *identity of evidence*. Across various social space and cultural sites, studies that we have drawn upon attempt to utilize a number of strategies that are used to substantiate (persuade) the validity of the accounts. It appears that there is much focus on the evidence – whether statistical or ethnographic – that provides the interpretive force. On closer examination, some of the more post-structurally inflected approaches to methodology appear not to be having much impact. For example, an awareness of the crisis surrounding representation, the possibilities of multiple subjectivities alongside a recognition of relativity of truth claims are not inflecting methodologically in studies of gender. In short, the conceptual and theoretical sophistication of much post-structural work is not evident in their methodological approach. It is not that there is a need for methodological purism, but given the emphasis on the interrogation of gender relations as rhetorical, the methodologies that are used to attain this position appear to remain 'off limits' to the same analytical procedures.

Finally, our aim was to consider the notion of the collective political subject and the notion of the pluralization of identity. This division has been a source of tension within and between, feminisms, Men's Studies and post-structural approaches to gender. Holding onto the tension between identity politics and the politics of cultural difference positions, we explore this both in terms of the absence of social minorities and the constitution of multidimensional heterosexual male and female subjectivities. *Gender, Culture and Society* critically explores materialist accounts of a feminist problematic. We are particularly concerned with the limitations of an antioppressive position as a conceptual framework and its failure to capture the dynamics of local, that is, nationally based, institutional spaces that are experiencing and producing major social, economic and cultural change. In this way, we locate an anti-oppressive analytical position, promoted by earlier versions of socialism, feminism, antiracism, and gay and lesbian liberation, as theoretically incomplete. In testing the limits of the new social movements, we are suggesting that a post-identity politics position provides a wider vocabulary to capture the complexity of our gendered/sexual lives. However, in exploring contemporary social and cultural transformations, the new politics of cultural difference does not have to be seen as displacing an earlier feminist politics. Rather, the politics of difference as part of 'new times' provides an opportunity to reread earlier antipatriarchal texts in a way that strategically enables us to rethink their limitations. More specifically, it is suggested that the new politics of cultural difference, in making problematic the grand narratives of political–economic analyses of patriarchal domination, do not have to result in questions of representation, culture and difference, erasing the 'big questions' around social reproduction, state regulation and institutionally-based exclusions.

Political and cultural questions of representation were always implicit in the earlier conceptions of the women's liberation movement. They now need to be reassessed in a context where earlier antipatriarchal and class-based certainties no longer hold. Squires (1999: 5), in her highly reflexive account, reminds the reader that an effect of the imposition of a typology of men and women, in a complex field of inquiry, is the production of a specific frame of analysis. As she acknowledges, her own critical engagement with sexual politics, as part of the current ascendancy of difference/diversity debates in gender theory, unintendedly results in the exclusion of other positions. More particularly, the cultural shift within these debates often with their focus upon subjectivity tends to downplay the continuing importance of other materialist theoretical positions such as socialist and Marxist feminist theorists (Hennessy, 2000). Writing from a socialist feminist position, Segal (1999: 231–2) provides a recent account of ways of securing effective vehicles for change that open up spaces for women. For example, she suggests that women should collectively cherish the left:

> whether in alliance with social democratic forces (fighting to preserve their redistributive egalitarian instincts, which will never be smoothly compatible with commercial entrepreneurialism, while opposing their traditional paternalism); with trade unions (continuing to overturn their erstwhile, straight, white male hegemony); with whatever manifestations of local or international struggles emerge to defend those at the sharpest end of the market forces or regressive nationalisms, persisting racisms and xenophobia.

An overview of the argument of representation identifies a rhetoric that places representation within specific metaphorical parameters. This means that the vocabulary that we use to talk about representational politics immediately configures how we are able to talk about it. Discussions around this issue often draw upon spatial and numerical metaphors such as in/out and collective/individualized. Through such metaphors, the fundamental legitimacy of representation is established. In other words, distance and numerical value become an index of truth, and conceptual arguments operate as a 'treatise' or a 'framework' on how to establish a politics of sexual difference. In suggesting this, there is a recognition that there needs to be a sustained attempt, analytically (and in effect, politically), to disrupt the conventional logocentric relationship between gender and notions of representation. At the same time, there is the need for the reconnection of the political to everyday worlds. However, such reconnections should not take place in a traditional sociological format, rather there is a growing awareness of the need for a creative and imaginative uses of epistemology that addresses: 'the ways in which people with different perceptions and experiences conceive of being in the world and how globalism and localism are configured in contemporary conditions (Shurmer-Smith and Hannan, 1994: 80).

We began *Gender, Culture and Society* with the claim that something is happening to gender relations. We suggested that we are at a particular cultural moment where gender no longer carries the understandings and feelings that have prevailed in modern societies. This book, at one level, is a means of documenting this moment. At another level, it is arguing that conversations about gender are becoming increasingly important. Yet, at this juncture, when imaginative and creative intellectual action is most needed to generate a new conceptual and theoretical vocabulary, some scholars in the field of gender have responded by closing interpretive spaces. In many ways, our methodologies for speaking about gender have been marked by a modernist frame that is constituted by a quest for certainty, validity and vindication. There is an urgent need to acknowledge uncertainty of interpretation and resist the need to immediately use existing theory and concepts to explain emerging social processes and cultural practices. The immense body of knowledge that enabled decades of investigation of gender relations is providing the opportunity to research the possibilities of knowledge. In many ways, the story that this book wishes to tell, is the need for passionate pursuit of a reflexivity that may enable other forms of knowledges and the possibilities of other ways of thinking and being in the world to be generated.

Notes

Introduction: Gender Relations in Context

1. Post-structuralism suggests that meanings cannot be read off in a simplistic manner from an identifiable source. For example, in terms of exploring men and women and masculinities and femininities, this means that the living of sex/gender categories and divisions is more contradictory, fragmented, shifting and ambivalent then the dominant public definitions of these categories suggest.

   Queer theory seeks to destabilize socially given identities, categories and subjectivities. At the heart of this destabilization, the established gay and lesbian community is being provoked into exchanging the (partial) security of their social identity for a range of political identifications/alliances that are in the process of being assembled (see Mercer, 1991).

2. In an earlier period, Hall, S., Critcher, C., Jefferson, T., Clarke, J. and Roberts, B. (1978) suggested that as the post-war social democratic settlement imploded in the 1970s, racialized minorities became a lens to make sense of wider social transformations in relation to Anglo-ethnic internal discontents. At the start of the 2000s, recent migrants, including refugees and asylum seekers have joined established minority ethnic social groups in having the internal discontents of the (Anglo) majority displaced onto them (see Mac an Ghaill, 1999; Lawrence, 2005).

3. Spike Peterson and Sisson Runyan (1993: 190) provide a definition of a gender-sensitive lens as:

   a way of looking at the world that enables us to see the extent and structure of gender hierarchy. It permits us to examine both how social constructions of masculinity and femininity shape our ways of thinking and knowing and how women's and men's lives are patterned differently as a consequence of gendered practices.

4. Post-colonialism indicates a period where subjectivities are generated by and marked by a previous imperial ruler.

5. A social theorist of sexual modernity.

1. Approaching Gender: Feminism, Men's Studies and the Cultural Turn

1. The term queer has an interesting history. In the United Kingdom, such colloquial phrases as, 'there's now't as queer as folk', make clear that the term has been defined in terms of strangeness. It is also used as a pejorative label against people participating in non-heterosexual relationships, including gays, lesbians and bisexuals.

2.   Fragmenting Family Life: Beyond Maternal Femininities and Paternal Masculinities

1. See Chapter 3 for discussion of the continuities in young women's lives across this period, as argued by Harris (2004).
2. Social and political discussion of sexual minorities' domestic, sexual and emotional arrangements has gained an international media profile (Ali, 1996; Velu, 1999). Much theoretical and empirical work on gay fathers and lesbian mothers is carried out in America (Goss and Strongheart, 1997; Sullivan, 1997). However, an increasing number of European countries, at national or local government level, are instituting some form of gay partnership recognition, including Holland, Germany, France, Denmark, Iceland, Norway, Sweden and England (Fox, 2000). In September 2001, the new London Partnership Register was launched, providing official civil recognition of lesbian and gay unions. In the United States, official recognition of lesbian and gay civil unions varies from state to state with a major backlash against them by the early 2000s.

3.   In and Out of Labour: Beyond the Cult of Domesticity and Breadwinners

1. This refers to Kanter's (1997) text, *Men and Women of the Corporation*.
2. This is the title of Harris's (2004) chapter on gender relations and work in the new economy.

4.   Interplaying Gender and Age in Late Modernity

1. Walcote West is a pseudonym that is used to protect the identities of the school, the teachers and the pupils.
2. Menopause is often known as a stage of the human female reproductive cycle that takes place as the ovaries stop producing oestrogen. This, it is argued, causes the reproductive system to gradually shut down.
3. Viagra® is a substance called sildenafil citrate. Viagra is its retail name and is marketed as a product to treat male erectile dysfunction (impotence). It is developed and marketed by the company Pfizer.

5.   Shifting Gender Connections: Sexuality, Late Modernity and Lifestyle Sex

1. The ascendancy of queer theory in the academy is also marked by broader theoretical shift and accompanying new modes of analysis. More specifically, this has included a shift away from empiricism, historicism and sociological methods to other theoretical approaches such as literary criticism, linguistic-based semiotics and psychoanalysis. As Spargo (1999: 40–1) notes 'Queer

theory employs a number of ideas from poststructuralist theory, including Jacques Lacan's psychoanalytic models of decentred, unstable identity, Jacques Derrida's deconstruction of binary conceptual and linguistic structures, and, of course Foucault's model of discourse, knowledge and power.

2. We use constructed again here rather than reconstructed – to emphasize that there is no original gender to reconstruct.

6. Representing Engendered Bodies: Producing the Cultural Categories 'Men' and 'Women'

1. A makeover in England has become a popular phenomenon, especially on daytime television, with which these young men were well acquainted. At the beginning of these programmes, individuals (usually women) appear in their normal attire and by the end, they are transformed with new hairstyles, new clothes and a new outlook on life-thus, becoming new people. Usually, the end effect is a more glamorous or chic presentation. What is important is that by simply working on the body, young unemployed men (in our own study) had the potential to gain social status without working in the labour market.

2. See Easthope, 1990; Kimmel, 1987a, b; Morgan, 1992; Mosse, 1996; Patersen, 1998; Whitehead, 2002.

9. Gender on the Move: The Search for a New Sex/Gender Order in Late Modernity

1. See Edwards (1994), who distinguishes between sexual politics and the politics of sexuality.

2. Squires (1999: 115) usefully describes the ideological and geographical frames of analysis to make sense of the history of sexual politics. 'Those interested in delineating ideological positions have mapped the pursuit of "equality" onto liberal or socialist forms of feminism and the pursuit of "difference" onto radical or cultural feminism. Those more interested in geographical diversity have mapped equality and difference perspectives onto Anglo-American and French or Italian feminisms respectively'.

3. This is an updated version of an earlier typology (see Haywood and Mac an Ghaill, 2003).

4. This is a reference to Chandra Mohanty's (1988) paper 'Under western eyes: Feminist scholarship and colonial discourses'.

References

Abbinnett, R. (2003) *Culture and Identity: Critical Theories*. London: Sage.

Acker, J. (1989) 'The problem with patriarchy', *Sociology*, 23, 2, pp. 235–40.

Adkins, S. (1995) *Gendered Work: Sexuality, Family and the Labour Market*. Buckingham: Open University Press.

Adkins, S. (2000) 'Objects of innovation: Post-occupational reflexivity and re-traditionalisations of gender', in S. Ahmed, J. Kilby, C. Luria, M. McNeil and B. Skeggs (eds) *Transformations: Thinking Through Feminism*. London: Routledge, pp. 259–72.

Adkins, S. (2002) *Revisions: Gender and Sexuality in Late Modernity*. Buckingham: Open University Press.

Adkins, S. (2004) 'Gender and the post-structural social', in B. L. Marshall and A. Witz (eds) *Engendering the Social. Feminist Encounters with Sociological Theory*. Buckingham: Open University Press.

Aggleton, P., Hurry, J. and Warwick, I. (1999) *Young People and Mental Health*. New York: John Wiley.

Aguila, D. (2004) 'Introduction', in D. D. Aguilar and A. E. Lacsamana (eds) *Women and Globalization*. Amherst, NY: Humanity Books.

Ali, T. (1996) *We Are Family: Testimonies of Lesbian and Gay Parents*. London: Cassell.

Allan, G. (1989) *Friendship: Developing a Sociological Perspective*. London: Harvester Wheatsheaf.

Allen, G. (ed.) (2000) *The Sociology of the Family. A Reader*. Oxford: Blackwell.

Alsop, R., Fitzsimons, A. and Lennon, K. (2002) *Theorizing Gender*. Cambridge: Polity.

Altman, D. (1983) *The Homosexualisation of America*. Boston, MA: Beacon Press.

Altman, D. (2001) *Global Sex*. Chicago, IL: Chicago University Press.

Alvesson, M. and Billing, Y. D. (1997) *Understanding Gender and Organizations*. London: Sage.

Alvesson, M. and Skoldberg, K. (2000) *Reflexive Methodology: New Vistas for Qualitative Research*. London: Sage.

Andrews, M. (2003) 'Calendar ladies: Popular culture, sexuality and the middle-class, middle-aged domestic woman', *Sexualities*, 6, pp. 385–403.

Ang, I. and Hermes, J. (1991) 'Gender and/in Media Consumption', in J. Curran and M. Gurevitch (eds) *Mass Media and Society*. London: Edward Arnold, pp. 307–28.

Appadurai, A. (1996) *Modernity at Large: Cultural Dimensions of Globalization*. Minneapolis, MN: University of Minnesota Press.

Appaduri, A. (1991) 'Global ethnoscapes: Notes and queries for a transnational anthropology', in R. G. Fox (ed.) *Recapturing Anthropology: Working in the Present*. Santa Fe, NM: School of American Research Press.

Archetti, E. P. (1999) *Masculinities: Football, Polo and the Tango in Argentina*. Oxford: Berg.

Aries, P. (1962) *Centuries of Childhood*. New York: Vintage Books.

Baker, P. (1994) 'Who's afraid of the big bad woman?', *The Guardian*, 24 January.

Baker, B. (1995) 'Defining the "Child" in Educational Discourse: a history of the present', Paper prepared for the *Australian Association for Research in Education*, Hobart, Tasmania, November 26–30, 1995.

Banner, L. W. (1993) *In full flower: Ageing women, power and sexuality: A history*. New York: Vintage Books.

Barrett, M. (1992) 'Words and things: Materialism and method in contemporary feminist analysis', in M. Barrett and A. Phillips (eds) *Destabilizing Theory: Contemporary Feminist Debates*. Cambridge: Polity Press, pp. 201–19.

Barrett, M. and McIntosh, M. (1982) *The Anti- social Family*. London: Verso.

Barrett, M. and Phillips, A. (eds) (1992) *Destabilizing Theory: Contemporary Feminist Debates.* Cambridge: Polity Press.

Bartky, S. L. (1990) *Feminism and Domination: Studies in the Phenomenology of Oppression.* London: Routledge.

Battersby, C. (1989) *Gender and Genius: Towards a Feminist Aesthetics.* London: Women's Press.

Baudrillard, J. (1975) *The Mirror of Production.* St. Louis, MO: Telos Press.

Baudrillard, J. (1981) *For a Critique of the Political Economy of the Sign.* St. Louis, MO: Telos Press.

Baudrillard, J. (1988) 'Consumer society', in M. Poster (ed.) *Selected Writings.* Cambridge: Polity, pp. 29–57.

Bauman, Z. (1990) *Thinking Sociologically.* Oxford: Blackwell.

Bauman, Z. (1992) *Intimations of Modernity.* London: Routledge.

Bauman, Z. (1995) *Life in Fragments: Essays in Postmodern Morality.* Oxford: Blackwell.

Bauman, Z. (1998) *Globalization: The Human Consequences.* Cambridge: Polity.

Bauman, Z (2000) *Liquid Modernity.* Cambridge: Polity.

Bauman, Z. (2001) *The Individuated Society.* Cambridge: Polity.

Bauman, Z. (2002) *Society Under Siege.* Cambridge: Polity.

Bauman, Z. (2003) *Liquid Love: The Fragility of Human Bonds.* Cambridge: Polity Press.

Beck, U. (1992) *Risk Society: Towards a New Modernity.* London: Sage.

Beck, U. and Beck-Gernsheim, E. (1995) *The Normal Chaos of Love.* Cambridge: Polity Press.

Beechey, V. (1979) 'On patriarchy', *Feminist Review*, 3, pp. 66–82.

Beechey, V. (1987) *Unequal Work.* London: Verso.

Bem, S. L. (1974) 'The measurement of psychological androgeny', *Journal of Consulting and Clinical Psychology*, 42, pp. 155–62.

Bergman, H. and Hobson, B. (2002) 'Compulsory fatherhood: The coding of fatherhood in the Swedish welfare state', in B. Hobson (ed.) *Making Men into Fathers: Men, Masculinities and the Social Politics of Fatherhood.* Cambridge: Cambridge University Press.

Berman, M. (1983) *All That is Solid Melts into Air: The Experience of Modernity.* London: Verso.

Bernstein, A. (2002) 'Is it time for a victory lap?: Changes in the media coverage of women in sport', *International Review for the Sociology of Sport*, 37, 3–4, pp. 415–28.

Bertoia, C. E. and Drakich, J. (1995) 'The fathers' rights movement: Contradictions in rhetoric and practice', in W. Marsiglio (ed.) *Fatherhood: Contemporary Theory, Research and Social Practice.* London: Sage, pp. 43–52.

Beynon, J. (2002) *Masculinities and Culture.* Buckingham: Open University Press.

Bhabha, H. (1990) *Nation and Narration.* London: Routledge.

Bhatt, C. (1997) *Liberation and Purity: Race, New Religious Movements and the Ethics of Postmodernity.* London: University College Press.

Biagi, S. (1996). *Media Impact: An Introduction to Mass Media.* Belmont, CA: Wadworth.

Bingham, C. (2001) *Schools of Recognition: Identity Politics and Classroom Practices.* Boulder, CO: Rowman and Littlefield.

Birrell, S. and Cole, C. L. (1994) 'Double fault: Renee Richards and the construction and naturalization of difference', in S. Birrell and C. L. Cole (eds) *Women, Sport, and Culture.* Champaign, IL: Human Kinetics, pp. 393–97.

Bjornberg, U. (ed.) (1992) *European Parents in the 1990s: Contradictions and Comparisons.* New Brunswick, NJ: Transaction Publications.

Bleys, R. (1996) *The Geography of Perversion: Male to Male Behaviour Outside of the West.* London: Cassell.

Bly, R. (1990) *Iron John: A Book about Men.* Reading, MA: Addison-Wesley.

Bocock, R. (1993) *Consumption.* London: Routledge.

Bolotin, S. (1982) 'Voices from the "post-feminist" generation', *New York Times Magazine*, 17 October.

Bordo, S. (1993a) 'Feminism, Foucault and the politics of the body', in C. Ramazanoglu (ed.) *Up Against Foucault: Explorations of Some of the Tensions between Foucault and Feminism.* London: Routledge.

Bordo, S. (1993b) *Unbearable Weight: Feminism, Western Culture and the Body.* Berkeley, CA: University of California Press.

Bourdieu, P. (1984) *Distinction: A Social Critique of the Judgement of Taste.* London: Routledge.

Bourdieu, P. (1990) *In Other Words: Essays Towards a Reflexive Sociology*. Cambridge: Polity.

Bourdieu, P. (2001) *Masculine Domination*. Cambridge: Polity Press.

Bowlby, R. (1985) *Just Looking, Consumer Culture in Dreiser, Gissing and Zola*. London: Macmillan.

Bradley, H. (1989) *Men's Work, Women's Work*. Cambridge: Polity.

Bradley, H. (1996) *Fractured Identities: Changing Patterns of Inequality*. Cambridge: Polity Press.

Bradley, H. (1997) 'Gender and changing employment: feminization and its effects', in R. Brown (ed.) *The Changing Shape of Work*. London: Macmillan.

Bradley, H. (1999) *Gender and Power in the Workplace*. London: Macmillan.

Brah, A. (1992) 'Difference, diversity, differentiation', in J. Donald and A. Rattansi (eds) *'Race', Culture and Difference*. Buckingham: Open University Press.

Brah, A. (1996) *Cartologies of Diaspora: Contesting Identities*. London: Routledge.

Brah, A., Hickman, M. J. and Mac an Ghaill, M. (eds) (1999) *Global Futures: Migration, Environment and Globalization*. London: Macmillan.

Breugel, I. (1996) 'Whose myths are they anyway?: A comment', *British Journal of Sociology*, 47, 1, pp. 175–7.

Breugel, I. (2000) 'No More Jobs for the Boys? Gender and Class in the Restructuring of the British Economy', *Capital and Class*, 71, pp. 79–102.

Briggs, A. and Burke, P. (2002) *A Social History of the Media*. Cambridge: Polity.

Bristow, J. (1997) *Sexuality*. London: Routledge.

Bristow, J. and Wilson, A. R. (eds) (1993) *Activating Theory: Lesbian, Gay and Bisexual Politics*. London: Lawrence and Wishart.

Brittan, A. (1989) *Masculinity and Power*. New York: Blackwell.

Brooks, A. (1997) *Postfeminisms*. London: Routledge.

Brown, W. (1988) *Manhood and Politics*. Totowa, NJ: Rowman and Littlefield.

Brunsdon, C. (1997) *Screen Tastes*. London: Routledge.

Brunt, R. (1989) 'The politics of identity', in S. Hall and M. Jacques (eds) *New Times: The Changing Face of Politics in the 1990s*. London: Lawrence and Wishart.

Bryson, L. (1994) 'Sport and the maintenance of masculine hegemony', in S. Birrell and C. Cole (eds) *Women, Sport and Culture*. Champaign, IL: Human Kinetics.

Bryson, V. (1999) *Feminist Debates: Issues of Theory and Political Practice*. London: Macmillan.

Bulbeck, C. (1988) *One World Women's Movement*. London: Pluto Press.

Burman, E. (1995) 'What is it? Masculinity and femininity and the cultural representation of childhood', in S. Wilkinson and C. Kitzinger (eds) *Feminism and Discourse*. London: Sage

Burstyn, V. (1999) *The Rites of Men: Manhood, Politics, and the Culture of Sport*. Toronto, ON: University of Toronto Press.

Butler, J. (1990) *Gender Trouble: Feminism and the Subversion of Identity*. London: Routledge.

Butler, J. (1993) *Bodies that Matter; On the Discursive Limits of 'Sex'*. London: Routledge.

Butler, J. (1999) *Gender Trouble: Feminism and the Subversion of Identity*. London: Routledge.

Butler, J. (2004) *Undoing Gender*. London: Routledge.

Buysse, J. M., and Embser-Herbert, M. W. (2004) 'Construction of gender in sport: An analysis of intercollegiate media guide cover photographs', *Gender & Society*, 18, 1, pp. 66–81.

Cairns, D. and Richards, S. (1988) *Writing Ireland: Colonialism, Nationalism and Culture*. Manchester: Manchester University Press.

Callinicos, A. (1999) 'Social theory put to the test of politics: Pierre Bourdieu and Anthony Giddens', *New Left Review*, 23, pp. 77–102.

Capranica, L. and Aversa, F. (2002) 'Italian television sport coverage during the 2000 Sydney Olympic Games: A gender perspective', *International Review for the Sociology of Sport*, 37, pp. 337–49.

Carby, H. V. (1998) *Race Men*. Cambridge: Harvard University Press.

Carlsen, S. and Larsen, J. E. (1994) (eds) *The Equality Dilemma: Reconciling Working Life and Family Life, Viewed in an Equality Perspective: The Danish Example*. Copenhagen: Munksgaard International Publishers.

Carrington, B. (1998) 'Sport, masculinity and Black cultural resistance', *Journal of Sport and Social Issues*, 22, pp. 275–98.

Carter, E., Donald, J. and Squires, J. (eds) (1993) *Space and Place: Theories of Identity and Location*. London: Lawrence and Wishart.

Casey, C. (1995) *Work, Self and Society: After Industrialism*. London: Routledge.

Casey, C. (2002) *Critical Analysis of Organizations: Theory, Practice, Revitalization*. London: Sage.

Cashmore, E., and Parker, A. (2003) 'One David Beckham? Celebrity, Masculinity and the Soccerati', *Sociology of Sport Journal* 20, 3, pp. 214–31.

Castells, M. (1996) *The Rise of Network Society*. Oxford: Blackwell.

Central Statistical Office (2001) *Social Trends*. London: Stationery Office.

Chang, K. and Ling, L.H.M. (2000) 'Globalization and its intimate other: Fillipina domestic workers in Hong Kong', in M. H. Marchand and A. S. Runyan (eds) *Gender and Global Restructuring: Sightings, Sights and Resistances*. London: Routledge.

Chapman, R. and Rutherford, J. (eds) (1988) *Male Order: Unwrapping Masculinity*. London: Lawrence and Wishart.

Chari, S. (2004) *Fraternal Capita: Peasant-Workers, Self-made Men, and Globalization in Provincial India*. Stanford, CA: Stanford University Press.

Cheal, D. (1991) *Family and State Theory*. Hemel Hemstead: Harvester Wheatsheaf.

Cherlin, A. J. (ed.) (1988) *The Changing American Family and Public Policy*. Washington, DC: Urban Institute Press.

Choi, P. Y. L. (2000) *Femininity and the Physically Active Woman*. London: Routledge.

Chow, E. N. (2003) 'Studying globalization and social change in the 21st century', *International Sociology*, 18, 3, pp. 443–60.

Chowdhry, G. (1995) 'Engendering development? Women in development (WID) in international development regimes', in M. H. Marchand and J. L. Parpart (eds) *Feminism, Postfeminism and Development*. London: Routledge.

Clare, A. (2000) *On Men: Masculinity in Crisis*. London: Chatto and Windus.

Clayman, S. and Heritage, J. (2002) *The News Interview: Journalists and Public Figures in the Air*. New York: Cambridge University Press.

Cockburn, C. (1983) *Brothers: Male Dominance and Technological Change*. London: Pluto Press.

Cockburn, C. (1991) *In the Way of Women: Men's Resistance to Sex Equality in Organizations*. London: Macmillan.

Cockburn, C. K. (1987) *Two-Track Training: Sex Inequalities and the YTS*. London: Macmillan.

Collier, R. (1998) *Masculinities, Crime and Criminology: Men, Corporeality and the Criminal(ised) Body*. London: Sage.

Collier, R. (2001) 'Dangerousness, popular knowledge and the criminal law: a case study of the paedophile as socio-cultural phenomenon', in P. Alldridge and C. Brants (eds) *Personal Autonomy, the Private Sphere and the Criminal Law: A Comparative Study*. Oxford and Portland, OR: Hart Publishing.

Collinson, D. and Hearn, J. (1996) ' "Men" at "work": Multiple masculinities/multiple workplaces', in M. Mac an Ghaill (ed.) (1996) *Understanding Masculinities: Social Relations and Cultural Arenas*. Buckingham: Open University Press.

Connell, R. W. (1983) *Which Way is Up?* London: Allen and Unwin.

Connell, R. W. (1987) *Gender and Power*. Cambridge: Polity Press.

Connell, R. W. (1995) *Masculinities*. Cambridge: Polity Press.

Connell, R. W. (1998) 'Masculinities and globalization', *Men and Masculinities*, 1, 1, pp. 49–62.

Connell, R. W. (2000) *The Men and The Boys*. Cambridge: Polity.

Connell, R. W. (2002) *Gender*. Cambridge: Polity.

Coppock, V., Haydon, D. and Richter, I. (1995) *The Illusions of 'Post-feminism': New Women, Old Myths*. London: Taylor and Francis.

Corner, J. (1983) 'Textuality, communication and power', in H. Davis and P. Walton (eds) *Language, Image, Media*. Oxford: Basil Blackwell.

Cornwall, A. and Lindisfarne, N. (1994) (eds) *Dislocating Masculinities Comparative Ethnographies*. London: Routledge.

Coward, R. (1999) *Sacred Cows*. London: HarperCollins.

Cowburn, M. and Dominelli, L. (2001) 'Masking hegemonic masculinity: reconstructing the paedophile as the dangerous stranger', *British Journal of Social Work*, 31, pp. 399–415.

Craig, S. (1992) (ed.) *Men, Masculinity and the Media*. London: Sage.

Craik, J. (1994) *The Face of Fashion: Cultural Studies in Fashion*. London: Routledge.

Cranny-Francis, A., Waring, W., Stavropoulos, P. and Kirkby, J. (2003) *Gender Studies: Terms and Debates*. Basingstoke: Palgrave Macmillan.

Creedon, P. J. (1994) 'Women, media and sport: Creating and reflecting gender values', in P. J. Creedon (ed.) *Women, Media and Sport*. Thousand Oaks, CA: Sage.

Cronin, A. (2000) *Advertising and Consumer Citizenship: Gender, Images and Rights*. London: Routledge.

Croteau, D. and Hoynes, W. (2000) *Media/Society: Industries, Images and Audiences*. London: Pine Forge Press.

Cully, M., Woodland, S., O'Reilly, A. and Dix, G. (1999) *Britain at Work: As Depicted by the 1998 Workplace Relations Survey*. London: Routledge.

Cunningham, K. (2003) 'Cross-regional trends in female terrorism', *Studies in Conflict and Terrorism*, 26, 3, pp. 171–95.

Dally, A. (1982) *Inventing Motherhood: The Consequences of an Ideal*. London: Burnett Books.

Davis, K. (1991) 'Critical sociology and gender relations', in K. Davis, M. Leijenaar and J. Oldersma. (eds) *The Gender of Power*. London: Sage.

Davis, K. (2002) 'A dubious equality: Men, women and cosmetic surgery', *Body and Society*, 8, 1, pp. 49–65.

Davis, K., Leigenaar, M. and Oldersma, J. (eds) (1991) *The Gender of Power*. London: Sage.

Davis, L. (1994) 'A Post-modern paradox? Cheerleaders at women's sporting events', in P. J. Creedon (ed.) *Women, Media and Sport*. Thousand Oaks, CA: Sage.

de Lauretis, T. (1987) *Technologies of Gender: Essays on Theory, Film and Fiction*. Bloomington, IN: Indiana University Press.

Delamont, S. (2001) *Changing Women, Unchanging Men? Sociological Perspectives on Gender in a Post-Industrial Society*. Buckingham: Open University Press.

Delmonico, D. L. (2003) 'Cybersex: Changing the way we relate', *Sexual and Relationship Therapy*, 18, 3, pp. 259–60.

Dench, G. (1996) *Transforming Men*. New Brunswick, NJ: Transaction Books.

Denfeld, R. (1995) *The New Victorians: A Young Woman's Challenge to the Old Feminist Order*. New York: Simon and Schuster.

Dennis, N. and Erdos, G. (1993) *Families without Fathers*. London: IEA Health and Welfare Unit.

Denzin, N.K. (1990) 'Harold and Agnes: A Feminist Narrative Undoing', *Sociological Theory*, 8, 2, pp. 198–216.

Denzin, N. K. (1994) 'Evaluating qualitative research in the post-structural moment: the lessons James Joyce teaches us', *International Qualitative Studies in Education*, 7, pp. 64–88.

Derne, S. (2002) Globalization and the reconstitution of local gender arrangements, *Men and Masculinities*, 5, 2, pp. 144–64.

Derrida, J. (1978) *Writing and Difference*. Chicago, IL: University of Chicago Press.

Derrida, J. (1987) *The Truth in Painting*. Chicago, IL: Chicago Press.

Desai, M. (2002) 'Transnational solidarity: Women's agency, structural adjustment and globalization', in N. A. Naples and M. Desai (eds) *Women's Activism and Globalization: Linking Struggles and Transnational Politics*. London: Routledge.

Diamond, I. and Quinby, L. (1988) 'Intoduction', in I. Diamond and L. Quinby (eds) *Feminism and Foucault: Reflections on Resistance*. Boston, MA: Northeastern University Press.

Diawara, M. (1998) 'Homeboy cosmopolitan: Manthia Diawara interviewed by Silvia Kolbowski', *October*, 83, pp. 51–70.

Dibbell, J. (1993) 'A rape in cyberspace: How an evil clown, a Haitian trickster spirit, two wizards, and a cast of dozens turned a database into a society', *The Village Voice*, pp. 36–42. Retrieved 13 August 1999 from http://www.mixolydian.org/goliard/library/dibbell.html

Dicken, P. (1998) *Global Shift: Transforming the World Economy*. London: Paul Chapman.

Digby, T. (ed.) (1998) *Men Doing Feminism*. London: Routledge.

Diprose, R. (1994) *The Bodies of Women: Ethics, Embodiment and Sexual Difference*. London: Routledge.

Dobash, R. E., Dobash, R. and Harry Frank Guggenheim Foundation (1998) *Rethinking Violence Against Women*. Thousand Oaks, CA: Sage.

Dollimore, J. (1991) *Sexual Dissidence: Augustine to Wilde, Freud to Foucault*. Oxford: Clarendon Press.

Dollimore, J. (1997) 'Desire and difference: Homosexuality, race, masculinity', in Stecopoulos, H. and Uebel, M. (eds) (1997) *Race and the Subject of Masculinities*. Durham, NC and London: Duke University Press.

Donald, S. and Lee, C. (2001) 'Mulan illustration? Ambiguous women in contemporary Chinese cinema', in S. Munshi (ed.) *Images of the 'Modern Woman' in Asia: Global Media, Local Meanings*. Surrey: Curzon Press.

Doring, N. (2000) 'Feminist Views of Cybersex: Victimization, liberation and empowerment', *Cyber psychology and Behavior*, 3, 5, pp. 863–84.

Douglas, A. (1977) *The Feminization of American Culture*. New York: Alfred A. Knopf.

Douglas, M. (1966) *Purity and Danger: An Analysis of Concepts of Pollution and Taboo*. London: Routledge.

Dozier (2005) 'Beards, breasts and bodies: Doing sex in a gendered world', *Gender and Society*, 19, 3, pp. 297–316.

du Gay, P. (1996) *Consumption and Identity at Work*. London: Sage.

Dunbar, M. D. (2000) 'Dennis Rodman – do you feel feminine yet? Black masculinity, gender transgression and reproductive rebellion on MTV', in J. McKay, M. Messner and D. Sabo (eds) *Masculinities, Gender Relations, and Sport*. London: Sage.

Duncan, M.D. (1990). Sports photographs and sexual difference: Images of women and men in the 1984 and 1988 Olympic Games. *Sociology of Sport Journal*, 7, 22–43.

Duncan, M. C and Messner, M. A. (1998). 'The media image of sport and gender', in L. A. Wenner (ed.) *Media/Sport*. Boston, MA: Routledge and Kegan Paul.

Duncan, M. C., Messner, M. A., Williams, L., Jensen, K. and Wilson, W. (1994) 'Gender stereotyping in televised sport', in S. Birrell and C. Cole (eds) *Women, Sport, and Culture*. Champaign, IL: Human Kinetics.

Dunch, R. (2002) 'Beyond cultural imperialism: Cultural theory, Christian missions, and global modernity', *History and Theory*, 41, 3, pp. 301–25.

Dunne, G. A. (1999) A passion for 'sameness'? Sexuality and gender accountability, in E. B. Silva, and C. Smart (eds) *The 'New' Family?* London: Sage.

Dunne, G. A. (2001) 'The Lady Vanishes? Reflections on the Experiences of Married and Divorced Gay Fathers', *Sociological Research Online*, 6, 3, (November). Retrieved from http: www.socresonline.org.uk/6/3/dunne.html, pp. 1–17.

Dunphy, R. (2000) *Sexual Politics: An Introduction*. Edinburgh: Edinburgh University Press.

Dworkin, A. (1981) *Pornography: Men Possessing Women*. London: Women's Press.

Dyer, R. (1989) 'Don't look now', in A. McRobbie (ed.) *Zoot Suits and Second Hand Dresses: An Anthology of Fashion and Music*. London: Macmillan.

Easthope, A. (1990) *What a Man's Gotta Do: The Masculine Myth in Popular Culture*. London: Routledge.

Eastman, S. T. and Billings, A. C. (1999) 'Gender parity in the Olympics: Hyping women athletes, favoring men athletes ', *Journal of Sports and Social Issues* 23, 2, pp. 140–70.

Edelman, L. (1994) *Homographesis: Essays in Gay Literary and Cultural Theory*. London: Routledge.

Edwards, T. (1994) *Erotics and Politics: Gay Male Sexuality, Masculinity and Feminism*. London: Routledge.

Edwards, T. (1997) *Men in the Mirror: Mens' Fashion, Masculinity and the Consumer Society*. London: Cassell.

Edwards, T. (1998) 'Queer fears: Against the cultural turn', *Sexualities*, 1, 4, pp. 47–84.

Elam, D. (2000) 'Gender or sex?', in A. Tripp (ed.) *Gender*. Basingstoke: Palgrave.

Elias, N. (1978) *The Civilising Process*. Oxford: Basil Blackwell.

Enloe, C. (1989) *Bananas, Beaches and Bases: Making Feminist Sense of International Politics*. London: Pandora.

Epstein, C. F. (1988) *Deceptive Distinctions*. New Haven, CT: Yale University Press.

Epstein, D. (1997) 'Boyz' own stories: Masculinities and sexualities in schools', *Gender and Education*, 9, 1, pp. 105–15.

Epstein, D. and Johnson, R. (1998) *Schooling Sexualities*. Buckingham: Open University Press.

Epstein, J. and Straub, K. (eds) (1991) *Body Guards: The Cultural Politics of Gender Ambiguity*. London: Routledge and Kegan Paul.

Erikson, E. H. (1968) *Identity: Youth and Crisis*. New York: Norton.

Eshcle, C. (2004) 'Feminist studies of globalisation: beyond gender, beyond economism?', *Global Studies*, 18, 2, pp. 97–125.

Esping-Andersen, G. (ed.) (1993) *Changing Classes*. London: Sage.

European Commission Network on Childcare (1993) *Men as Carers: Report of an International Seminar in Ravenna*. Brussels: European Commission Network on Childcare.

Evans, D. (1993) *Sexual Citizenship: The Material Construction of Sexualities*. London: Routledge.

Fairhurst, E. (1998) ' "Growing old gracefully" as opposed to "mutton dressed as lamb": The social construction of recognising older women', in S. J. Nettleton and S. J. Watson (eds) *The Body in Everyday Life*. London: New York.

Falk, P. (1994) *The Consuming Body*. London: Sage.

Faludi, S. (1992) *Backlash*. London: Chatto and Windus.

Faludi, S. (1999) *Stiffed: The Betrayal of Modern Man*. London: Chatto and Windus.

Fanon, F. (1970) *Black Skins, White Masks*. London: Paladin.

Farrell, W. (1974) *The Liberated Man*. New York: Random House.

Farrell, W. (1994) *The Myth of Male Power: Why are Men the Disposable Sex?* New York: Fourth Estate.

Favell, A. (2001) 'Multi-ethnic Britain: An exception in Europe?', *Patterns of Prejudice*, 35, 1, pp. 35–57.

Featherstone, M. (1991a) 'The body in consumer culture', in M. Featherstone, M. Hepworth and B. S. Turner (eds) *The Body: Social Process and Cultural Theory*. London: Sage.

Featherstone, M. (1991b) *Consumer Society and Postmodernism*. London: Sage.

Featherstone, M., Hepworth, M. and Turner, B. S. (eds) (1991) *The Body, Social Process and Cultural Theory*. London: Sage.

Fendler, L. (1998) 'What is it impossible to think? A genealogy of the educated subject', in T. S. Popkewitz and M. Brennan (eds) *Foucault's Challenge: Discourse, Knowledge and Power in Education*. New York: Teachers College Press.

Ferguson, K. (1984) *The Feminist Case Against Bureaucracy*. Philadelphia, PA: Temple University Press.

Ferguson, K. E. (1993) *The Man Question: Visions of Subjectivity in Feminist Theory*. Berkeley, CA and Oxford: University of California Press.

Fetveit, A. (1999) 'Reality TV in the digital era: A paradox in visual culture?', *Media, Culture & Society*, 21, pp. 787–804.

Finch, J. and Mason, J. (1993) *Negotiating Family Responsibilities*. London: Routledge.

Firestone, S. (1979) *The Dialectic of Sex*. London: Women's Press.

Fishman, M. (1980) *Manufacturing the News*. Austin, TX and London: University of Texas Press.

Fiske, John (1987) *Television Culture*. London: Routledge.

Flax, J. (1990) 'Postmodernism and gender relations in feminist theory', in L. J. Nicholson (ed.) *Feminism/Postmodernism*. London: Routledge.

Fletcher, R. (1984) *Education in Society: The Promethean Fire*. Harmondsworth: Penguin.

Foucault, M. (1978) *The History of Sexuality*. Vol. 1, *An Introduction*. New York: Pantheon.

Foucault, M. (1980) *History of Sexuality*. London: Vintage Books.

Foucault, M. (1981) *The History of Sexuality*, Vol. 1, *An Introduction*. Harmondsworth: Penguin.

Foucault, M. (1988) 'Technologies of the self', in L. H. Martin., H. Gutman. and P. H. Hutton (eds) *Technologies of the Self: A Seminar with Michel Foucault*. London: Tavistock.

Foucault, M. (1994) *Ethics: Essential Works of Foucault 1954–1984*. London: Penguin.

Fox, K. (2000) 'Time to commit', *The Pink Paper*, 5 December, pp. 31–6.

Francis, B. (1998) *Power Plays: Primary School Children's Construction of Gender, Power and Adult Work*. Staffordshire: Trentham Books.

Francis, B. (2000) *Boys, Girls and Achievement: Addressing Classroom Issues*. London: Falmer Press.

Frank, B. (1987) 'Hegemonic heterosexual masculinity', *Studies in Political Economy*, 24, pp. 159–70.

Frank, A. (1990) 'Bringing bodies back in: A decade review', *Theory, Culture and Society*. 7, pp. 1131–62.

Frank, A. (1991) 'For the sociology of the body: An analytical review', in M. Featherstone, M. Hepworth, and B. S. Turner, (eds) *The Body: Social Process and Cultural Theory*. London: Sage.

Frank, B., Davison, K. and Lovell, T. (2003) 'Tangle of trouble: Boys, masculinity and schooling, future directions', *Educational Review*, 55, 2, pp. 119–133.

Fraser, N. (1989) *Unruly Practices: Power, Discourse and Gender in Contemporary Social Theory*. Cambridge: Polity Press.

Fraser, N. (1998) 'From redistribution to recognition? Dilemmas of justice in a post-socialist age', in A. Phillips (ed.) *Feminism and Politics*. Oxford: Oxford University press.

French, M. (1992) *The War Against Women*. London: Hamish Hamilton.

French, S. (1995) 'The fallen idol', in P. Moss (eds) *Father Figures: Fathers in the Families of the 1990s*. Edinburgh: HMSO.

Furstenberg, F. F., Jr (1988) 'Good dads–bad dads: Two faces of fatherhood', in A. J. Cherlin (ed.) *The Changing American Family and Public Policy*. Washington, DC: Urban Institute Press.

Fuss, D. (1991) *Inside/Out: Lesbian Theories, Gay Theories*. New York: Routledge.

Gagnon, J. and Simon, W. (1974) *Sexual Conduct*. London: Hutchinson.

Galambos, N. L. and Tilton-Weaver, L. C. (2000) 'Adolescents' psychosocial maturity, subjective age, and problem behavior: In search of the adultoid', *Applied Developmental Science*, 4, pp. 178–92.

Gamson, P. (1995) 'Must identity problems self destruct? A queer dilemma', *Social Problems*, 42: 390–407.

Gannon, L. R. (1999) *Women and Aging: Transcending the Myths*. New York: Routledge.

Garbarino, J. (1999) *Lost Boys: Why Our Sons Turn Violent and How We Can Save Them*. New York: Ballantine Books.

Garfinkel, H. (1967) *Studies in Ethnomethodology*. Englewood Cliffs, NJ: Prentice-Hall.

Garlick, S. (2003) 'What is a man?: Heterosexuality and the technology of masculinity', *Men and Masculinities*, 6, pp. 156–72.

Garrett, P. (1998) 'Notes from a diaspora: Anti-discriminatory social work practice, Irish people and the practice curriculum', *Social Work Education*, 17, 4, pp. 435–48.

Gatens, M. (1990). 'A Critique of the Sex/Gender Distinction', in S. Gunew (ed.) *A Reader in Feminist Knowledge*. London: Routledge, pp. 139–57.

Gatens, M. (1992) 'Power, bodies and difference', in M. Barrett and A. Phillips (eds) *Destabilizing Theory: Contemporary Feminist Debates*. Cambridge: Polity Press.

Gatens, M. (1996) *Imaginary Bodies; Ethics, Power and Corporeality*. London: Routledge.

Gavanas, A. (2002) 'The fatherhood responsibility movement: The centrality of marriage, work and male sexuality in the reconstruction of masculinity and fatherhood', in B. Hobson (ed.) *Making Men into Fathers: Men, Masculinities and the Social Politics of Fatherhood*. Cambridge: Cambridge University Press.

Gergen, K. J. (1999) *An Invitation to Social Construction*. London: Sage.

Gherardi, S. (1995) *Gender, Symbolism and Organizational Cultures*. London: Sage.

Giddens, A. (1984) *The Constitution of Society*. Cambridge: Polity Press.

Giddens, A. (1990) *The Consequences of Modernity*. Cambridge: Polity Press.

Giddens, A. (1991) *Modernity and Self-identity: Self and Society in the Late Modern Age*. Cambridge: Polity Press.

Giddens, A. (1992) *The Transformation of Intimacy: Sexuality, Love and Eroticism in Modern Societies*. Cambridge: Polity Press.

Giles, D. (2003) *Media Psychology*. Mahwah, NJ: Lawrence Erlbaum.

Gillis, J. R. (1997) *A World of Their Own Making: Myth, Ritual and the Quest for Family Values*. Oxford: Oxford University Press.

Gilman, S. L. (1985) *Difference and Pathology: Stereotypes of Sexuality, Race and Madness*. Ithaca, NY: Cornell University Press.

Gilroy, P. (1993) *The Black Atlantic: Modernity and Double Consciousness*. London: Verso.

Ginn, J., Arber, S., Brannen, J. and Arber, S. (1996) 'Feminist fallacies: A reply to Hakim on women's employment', *British Journal of Sociology*, 47, 1, pp. 167–74.

Gittens, D. (1993) *The Family in Question: Changing Households and Familial Ideologies*. Basingstoke: Macmillan.

Glick Schiller, N., Basch, L. and Blanc-Szanton, C. (1992) *Toward a Transnational Perspective on Migration: Race, Class, Ethnicity and Nationalism Reconsidered*. New York: New York Academy of Science.

Goffman, E. (1963) *Stigma: Notes on the Management of the Spoiled Identity*. London: Penguin.

Goffman, E. (1969) *The Presentation of Self in Everyday Life*. London: Allen Lane.

Goodwin, J. (1999) *Men's Work and Male Lives: Men and Work in Britain*. Aldershot: Ashgate.

Gorman, L. and McLean, D. (2003) *Media and Society in the Twentieth Century: A Historical Introduction*. Melbourne: Blackwell.

Goss, R. E. and Strongheart, A. A. S. (eds) (1997) *Our Families, Our Values: Snapshots of Queer Kinship*. New York: Haworth Press.

Graber, D. A. (2002) *Mass Media & American Politics*. 6th edn, Washington, DC: Congressional Quarterly Press.

Gramsci, A. (1971) *Selections from the Prison Notebooks*. London: Lawrence and Wishart.

Greer, C. (2003) *Sex Crime and the Media: Sex Offending and the Press in a Divided Society*. Cullompton: Willan.

Grewal, I. and Kaplan, C. (1994) *Scattered Hegemonies: Postmodernity and Transnational Feminist Practices*. Minneapolis, MN: University of Minnesota Press.

Griffin, C. (1993) *Representations of Youth: The Study of Youth and Adolescence in Britain and America*. Cambridge: Polity Press.

Griswold, R. (1992) *Fatherhood in America: A History*. New York: Basic Books.

Grosz, E. (1989) *Sexual Subversions: Three French Feminists*. London: Routledge.

Grosz, E. (1994a) 'Identity and difference: A response', in P. James (ed.) *Critical Politics*. Melbourne: Arena Publications, pp. 29–33.

Grosz, E. (1994b) *Volatile Bodies: Toward a Corporeal Feminism*. Bloomington, IN: Indiana University Press.

Grosz, E. (1999) 'Space, time and bodies', in J. Wolmark (ed.) *Cybersexualities: A Reader on Feminist Theory, Cyborgs and Cyberspace*. Edinburgh: Edinburgh University Press.

Grumet, M. (1988). *Bitter Milk: Women and Teaching*. Amherst, MA: University of Massachusetts Press.

Gullette, M. (1997) *Declining to Decline: Cultural Combat and the Politics of the Midlife*. Charlottesville, VA: University Press of Virginia.

Haiken, E. (2000) 'Does medicine make the man?', *Men and Masculinities*, 2, 4, pp. 388–409.

Hakim, C. (1995) 'Five feminist myths about women's employment', *British Journal of Sociology*, 46, 3, pp. 429–55.

Halberstam, J. (1998) *Female Masculinity*. Durham, NC: Duke University Press.

Halberstam, J. and Livingston, I. (eds) (1995) *Posthuman Bodies*. Indianapolis, IN: Indiana University Press.

Hall, S. (1980) 'Encoding/decoding', in Centre for Contemporary Cultural Studies (eds) *Culture, Media, Language*. London: Hutchinson, pp. 128–38.

Hall, S. (1988) 'The toad in the garden: Thatcherism among the theorists', in C. Nelson and L. Grossberg (eds) *Marxism and the Interpretation of Culture*. London: Macmillan Education.

Hall, S. (1991) 'Old and new ethnicities', in A. D. King (ed.) *Culture, Globalization and the World System*. London: Macmillan.

Hall, S. (1992) 'The question of cultural identity', in S. Hall, D. Held and T. McGrew (eds) *Modernity and Its Futures*. London: Polity/The Open University.

Hall, S. (1996) 'Who needs "identity"?', in S. Hall and P. du Gay (eds) *Questions of Cultural Identity*. London: Sage, pp. 1–17.

Hall, S. (ed.) (1997a) *Representation: Cultural Representations and Signifying Practices*. London: Sage.

Hall, S. (1997b) 'Introduction', in S. Hall (ed.) *Representation: Cultural Representations and Signifying Practices*. London: Sage.

Hall, S. and Gieben, B. (1992) *Formations of Modernity*. Cambridge: Polity Press and The Open University.

Hall, S., Held, D. and McGrew, T. (1992) *Modernity and Its Futures*. Cambridge: Polity Press and The Open University.

Hall, S., Critcher, C., Jefferson, T., Clarke, J. and Roberts, B. (1978) *Policing the Crisis: Mugging, The State and Law and Order*. London: Macmillan.

Hanmer, J. and Maynard, M. (eds) (1987) *Women, Violence and Social Control*. Atlantic Highlands, NJ: Humanities Press International.

Haraway, D. (1990) *Simians, Cyborgs and Women: The Reinvention of Nature*. New York: Routledge.

Harding, S. (1991) *Whose Science? Whose Knowledge? Thinking from Women's Lives*. Ithaca, NY: Cornell University Press.

Hardt, M. and Negri, A. (2000) *Empire*. Cambridge, MA: Harvard University Press.

Hargreaves, J. (1997) 'Women's boxing and related activities: Introducing images and meanings', *Body & Society*, 3, 4, pp. 33–49.

Hargreaves, J. (2001) Women's boxing and related activities: Introducing images and meanings, *InYo: Journal of Alternative Perspectives*. Retrieved on 26 June 2006 from http://ejmas.com/jalt/jaltart_hargreaves_0901.htm

Harris, A. (2004) *Future Girl: Young Women in the Twenty-first Century*. London: Routledge.

Harris, J. and Clayton, B. (2002) 'Femininity, masculinity, physicality and the English tabloid press: The case of Anna Kournikova', *International Review for the Sociology of Sport*, 37, 3/4, pp. 397–413.

Hartley, J (1998) 'Juvenation: News, girls and power', in C. Carter, G. Branston and S. Allan (eds) *Gender, News and Power*. London: Routledge.

Hartmann, H. (1994) 'The unhappy marriage of marxism and feminism: Towards a more progressive union', in D. B. Grusky (ed.) *Social Stratification: Class, Race and Gender in Sociological Perspective*. Boulder, CO: Westview Press.

Harvey, D. (1989) *The Condition of Postmodernity: An Enquiry into the Origins of Cultural Change*. Oxford: Basil Blackwell.

Hausman, B. L. (1995) *Changing Sex: Transsexualism, Technology, and the Idea of Gender*. Durham and London: Duke University Press.

Hawkes, G. (1996) *A Sociology of Sex and Sexuality*. Buckingham: Open University Press.

Haywood, C. (1993) Using Sexuality: An Exploration into the Fixing of Sexuality to Make Male Identities in a Mixed Sex Sixth Form. Unpublished MA Dissertation, University of Warwick.

Haywood, C. (2006) *Schooling, Sexuality and the Politics of Desire*. Unpublished PhD Thesis, University of Newcastle–upon–Tyne.

Haywood, C. and Mac an Ghaill, M. (1996) 'Schooling masculinities', in M. Mac an Ghaill (ed.) *Understanding Masculinities: Social Relations and Cultural Arenas*. Buckingham: Open University Press.

Haywood, C. and Mac an Ghaill, M. (1997a) 'Materialism and deconstructivism: Education and the epistemology of identity', *Cambridge Journal of Education*, 27, 2, 261–73.

Haywood, C. and Mac an Ghaill, M. (1997b) 'A man in the making: sexual masculinities within changing training cultures', *The Sociological Review*, 45, 4, pp. 576–90.

Haywood, C. and Mac an Ghaill, M. (2001) 'The significance of teaching English boys: Exploring social change, modern schooling and the making of masculinities', in W. Martino and B. Meyenn (eds) *What About the Boys?* Buckingham: Open University Press.

Haywood, C. and Mac an Ghaill, M. (2003) *Men and Masculinities: Theory, Research and Social Practice*. Buckingham: Open University Press.

Hearn, J. (1987) *The Gender of Oppression: Men, Masculinity and the Critique of Marxism*. Brighton: Harvester Wheatsheaf.

Hearn, J. (1992) *Men in the Public Eye*. London: Routledge.

Hearn, J. (1995) 'Imaging the aging of men', in M. Featherstone and A. Wernick (eds) *Born Dying: Images of Aging*. London: Routledge.

Hearn, J. and Parkin, W. (2001) *Gender, Sexuality and Violence in Organizations*. London: Sage.

Hennessy, R. (2000) *Profit and Pleasure: Sexual Identities in Late Capitalism*. London: Routledge.

Hepworth, M. (1999) 'In Defiance of An Ageing Culture', *Ageing and Society*, 19, pp. 139–48.

Hepworth, M. and Featherstone, M. (1998) 'The male menopause: Lay accounts and the cultural construction of midlife', in S. Nettleton and J. Watson (eds) *Lay Perceptions of The Body*. London: Routledge.

Herdt, G. (ed.) (1994) *Third Sex, Third Gender: Beyond Sexual Dimorphism in Culture and History*. New York: Zone Books.

Hester, J. D. (2004) 'Intersex(es) and informed consent: How physicians' rhetoric constrains choice', *Theoretical Medicine*, 25, pp. 21–49.

Hey, V. (1997) *The Company She Keeps: An Ethnography of Girls' Friendship*. Buckingham: Open University Press.

Hickman, M. J. and Walter, B. (1995) 'Deconstructing whiteness: Irish women in Britain', *Feminist Review*, 50, pp. 5–19.

Hirsch, M. and Fox Keller, E. (eds) (1990) *Conflicts in Feminism*. London: Routledge.

Hobson, B. and Morgan, D. (2002) 'Introduction', in B. Hobson (ed.) *Making Men into Fathers: Men, Masculinities and the Social Politics of Fatherhood*. Cambridge: Cambridge University Press.

Hockey, J. and James, A. (1993) *Growing Up and Growing Old: Ageing and Dependency in the Life Course*. London: Sage.

Hodson, D. L. (1999) 'Once intrepid warriors': Modernity and the production of Massai masculinities, *Ethnology*, 38, 2, pp. 121–51.

Hollands, R. G. (1990) *The Long Transition: Class, Culture and Youth Training*. London: Macmillan.

Hollway, W. (1996) 'Masters and men in the transition from factory hands to sentimental workers', in D. Collinson and J. Hearn (eds) *Men as Managers, Managers as Men: Critical Perspectives on Men, Masculinities, and Managements*. London: Sage.

Hollway, W. (1998) 'Gender difference and the production of subjectivity', in J. Henriques, W. Hollway, C. Urwin, C. Venn and V. Walkerdine (eds) *Changing the Subject: Psychology, Social Regulation and Subjectivity*., 2nd edn, London: Routledge.

Hooper, C. (2001) *Manly States: Masculinities, International Relations, and Gender Politics*. New York: Columbia University Press.

Horne, J., Tomlinson, A. and Whannel, G. (1999) *Understanding Sport*. London: Routledge.

Horrocks, R. (1994) *Masculinity in Crisis*. London: Macmillan.

Hughes, C. (2002) *Women's Contemporary Lives: Within and Beyond the Mirror*. London: Routledge.

Huhndorf, S. M. (2001) *Going Native: Indians in the American Cultural Imagination*. Ithaca, NY and London: Cornell University Press.

Ilcan, S and Phillips, L. (1998) *Transgressing Boundaries: Critical Perspectives on Gender, Household and Culture*. London: Bergin and Garvey.

Irigaray, L. (1985) *This Sex which Is Not One*. New York: Cornell University.

Isaksen, L.W. (2002) 'Masculine dignity and the dirty body', *Nora: Nordic Journal of Women's Studies*, 10, 3, pp. 137–46.

Jackson, S. and Jones, J. (eds) (1998) *Contemporary Feminist Theories*. Edinburgh: Edinburgh University Press.

Jackson, S. and Scott, S. (2002) *Gender: A Sociological Reader*. London: Routledge.

Jameson, F. (1983) 'Postmodernism and consumer society', in H. Foster (ed.) *Post-modern Culture*. London: Pluto Press.

Jameson, F. (1991) *Postmodernism or the Cultural Logic of Late Capitalism*. London: Sage.

Jamieson, L. (1998) *Intimacy: Personal Relationships in Modern Societies*. Cambridge: Polity Press.

Jansen, S. C. and Sabo, D. (1994) 'The sport/war metaphor: hegemonic masculinity, the Persian Gulf War, and the new world order', *Sociology of Sport Journal*, 11, pp. 1–17.

Jardine, A. and Smith, M. (eds) (1992) *Men in Feminism*. New York: Methuen.

Jeffreys, S. (1994) *The Lesbian Heresy: Feminist Perspectives on the Sexual Revolution*. London: The Women's Press.

Jeffreys, S. (1999) 'Globalizing sexual exploitation: Sex tourism and the traffic in women', *Leisure Studies*, 18, pp. 179–96.

Jeffreys, S. (2003) 'Sex tourism: Do women do it too?', *Leisure Studies*, 22, pp. 223–38.

Jenson, J., Hagen, E. and Reddy, C. (eds) (1988) *Feminization of the Labour Force*. Polity: Cambridge.

Johansson, P. (2001) 'Selling the 'modern woman': Consumer culture and Chinese gender politics,' in S. Munshi (ed.) *Images of the 'Modern Woman' in Asia: Global Media, Local Meanings*. Surrey: Curzon Press.

Johnson, M. (1988) *Strong Mothers, Weak Wives: The Search for Gender Equality*. Berkeley, CA: University of California Press.

Johnson, M. (2003) 'Anomalous bodies: Transgenderings and cultural transformations', in J. Weeks, J. Holland and M. Waites (eds) *Sexualities and Society: A Reader*. Cambridge: Polity.

Joinson, A. (1998). 'Causes and implication of disinhibited behavior on the Internet', in J. Gackenbach (ed.) *Psychology and the Internet: Intrapersonal, Interpersonal, and Transpersonal Implications*. San Diego, CA: Academic Press.

Jones, G. and Wallace, C. (1992) *Youth, Family and Citizenship*. Buckingham: Open University Press.

Jones, O. (1999) Tomboy tales: 'The rural, nature and the gender of childhood', *Gender, Place and Culture*, 6, 2, pp. 117–36. Joyrich (1996) *Re-viewing Reception: Television, Gender, and Postmodern Culture*. Bloomington, IN: Indiana University Press.

Kane, M. J., and Greendorfer, S. L. (1994) 'The media's role in accommodating and resisting stereotyped images of women in sport', in P. J. Creedon (ed.) *Women, Media, and Sport: Challenging Gender Values*. Thousand Oaks, CA: Sage.

Kanter, R. M. (1997) *Men and Women of the Organization*. New York: Basic Books.

Kaplan, E. A. (1992) *Motherhood and Representation: The Mother in Popular Culture and Melodrama*. London: Routledge.

Karam, A. (1997) *Women, Islamisms, and State: Contemporary Feminisms in Egypt*. New York: St. Martin's Press.

Katz, J. (1999) *Video: Tough Guise: Violence, Media and the Crisis in Masculinity*. Northampton, MA: Media Education Foundation.

Kearney, R. (1988) *Across the Frontiers: Ireland in the 1990s*. Dublin: Wolfhound Press.

Keating, M. (2002) 'Media Most Foul–Fear of Crime & Media Distortion', in A. Boran (ed.) *Crime: Fear or Fascination?'* Chester: Chester Academic Press.

Kennedy, E. (2000) 'Bad boys and gentlemen: Gendered narrative in televised sport, *International Review for the Sociology of Sport*, 35, 3, pp. 59–73.

Khan, F., Ditton, J., Elliott, L., Short, E., Morrison, A., Farrall, S. and Gruer, L. (2000) 'EscapeEs: What sort of ecstasy do package tour ravers seek?', in S. Cliff and S. Carter (eds) *Tourism and Sex: Culture, Commerce and Coercion*. Kings Lynn: Biddles.

Kimmel, M. (1994) 'Consuming manhood: the feminization of American culture and the recreation of the male body, 1832–1920', in L. Goldstein (ed.) *The Male Body: Features, Destinies, Exposures*. Ann Arbor, MI: University of Michigan Press.

Kimmel, M. and Messner, M. (1989) *Men's Lives*. New York: Macmillan.Kimmel, M. and Mosmiller, T. (1992) *Against the Tide: Profeminist Men in the United States, 1776–1990. A Documentary History*. Boston, MA: Beacon.

Kimmel, M. S. (1987a) 'The contemporary "crisis" of masculinity in historical perspective', in H. Brod (ed.) *The Making of Masculinities: The New Men's Studies*. London: Allen and Unwin.

Kimmel, M. S. (1987b) 'Rethinking "masculinity": New directions in research', in M. S. Kimmel (ed.) *Changing Men: New Directions on Men and Masculinity*. London: Sage.

Kimmel, M. S. (2003) 'Globalization and its mal(e) contents: The gendered moral and political economy of terrorism,' *International Sociology*, 18, pp. 603–20.

Kirsch, M. H. (2000) *Queer Theory and Social Change*. London: Routledge.

Klein M. (1946) Notes on some schizoid mechanisms. *International Journal of Psycho-analysis*, 27, pp. 99–110.

Knoppers, A. and Elling, A (2004) ' "We do not engage in promotional journalism": Discursive strategies used by sport journalists to describe the selection process', *International Review for the Sociology of Sport*, 39, 1, pp. 57–73.

Knowles, C. and Mercer, S. (1992) 'Feminism and anti-racism: An exploration of the political possibilities', in J. Donald and A. Rattansi (eds) *'Race', Culture and Difference*. Buckingham: Open University Press.

Kramsch, C. (1998) *Language and Culture*. Oxford: Oxford University Press.

Ku, L., Sonenstein, F. L. and Pleck, J. H. (1993) 'Neighbourhood, family and work: Influences on the pre–marital behaviours of adolescent males', *Social Forces*, 72, 2, pp. 479–503.

Kumar, K. (1995) *From Post-industrial to Post-modern Society*. Oxford: Blackwell.

Kunneman, H. (1997) 'The relevance of postmodern and feminist philosophy for the study of aging', *Journal of Ageing Studies*, 11, 4, pp. 273–82.

Laclau, E. (1990) *New Reflections on the Revolution of our Time*. London: Verso.

Lakoff, G. and Johnson, M. (1980) *Metaphors We Live By*. Chicago, IL: University of Chicago Press.

Laquer, T. (1990) *Making Sex: Body and Gender from the Greeks to Freud*. Harvard: Harvard University Press.

Lash, S. (1993) 'Reflexive modernization: the aesthetic dimension', *Theory, Culture and Society*, 10, 1, pp. 1–23.

Lash, S. (1994) 'Reflexivity and its doubles: structure, aesthetics, community', in U. Beck, A. Giddens and S. Lash *Reflexive Modernization: Politics, Tradition and Aesthetics in the Modern Social Order*. Cambridge: Polity Press.

Lash, S. and Urry, J. (1994) *Economies of Signs and Spaces*. London: Sage.

Lasswell, H. D. (1948) 'The structure and function of communication in society', in L. Bryson (ed.), *The Communication of Ideas: A Series of Addresses*. New York: Harper and Brothers.

Lawler, S. (2000) *Mothering the Self: Mothers, Daughters, Subjectivities*. London: Routledge.

Lawrence, F. (2005) 'The third way's dirtiest secret', *The Guardian*, 3 February, p. 24.

Lazreg, M. (1988) 'Feminism and difference: The perils of writing as a woman on women in Algeria', *Feminist Studies*, 14, 1, pp. 87–107.

Lee, D. (2000) 'Hegemonic masculinity and male feminization: The sexual harassment of men at work', *Journal of Gender Studies*, 9, 2, pp. 47–65.

Lees, S. (1994) *Sugar and Spice: Sexuality and Adolescent Girls*. Harmondsworth: Penguin.

Lewis, A. (2004) Gender swapping on the Internet: Do boys really want to be girls and girls be boys? *Counselling Australia*, 4, 3. Retrieved http://www.angelalewis.com.au/PDFs/Gender%20Swapping.pdf.

Ling, L. H. M. (1999) 'Sex machine: Global hypermasculinity and images of the Asian woman in modernity', *Positions: East Asia Cultures Critique* 7, 2, pp. 277–306.

Ling, R. (2004) *The Mobile Connection: The Cell Phone's Impact on Society*. San Francisco, CA: Morgan Kaufmann.

Lingard, B. and Douglas, P. (1999) *Men Engaging Feminisms: Pro-feminism, Backlashes and Schooling*. Buckingham: Open University Press.

Lipman-Blumen, J. (1992) 'Connective leadership: Female leadership styles in the 21st century workplace', *Sociological Perspectives*, 35, 1, pp. 183–203.

Lloyd, J. (1995) 'Fathers in the media: The analysis of newspaper coverage of fathers', in P. Moss (ed.) *Father Figures: Fathers in the Families of the 1990s*. Edinburgh: HMSO.

Lull, J. and Hinerman, S. (1997) 'The search for scandal.' in J. Lull, and S. Hinerman (eds) *Media Scandals*. New York: Columbia University Press.

Luttwak, E. (1998) *Turbo-capitalism: Winners and Losers in the Global Economy*. London: Weidenfield and Nicolson.

Lyndon, N. (1992) *No More Sex War: The Failures of Feminism*. London: Mandarin.

Lyotard, J. F. (1984) *The Postmodern Condition: A Report on Knowledge*. Minneapolis, MN: University of Minnesota Press; Manchester: University of Manchester Press.

Lyotard, J.-F. (1988) *The Differend: Phrases in Dispute*. Minneapolis, MN: University of Minnesota Press.

Mac an Ghaill, M. (1994a) *The Making of Men: Masculinities, Sexualities and Schooling*. Buckingham: Open University Press.

Mac an Ghaill, M. (1994b) '(In)visiblity: Sexuality, masculinity and "race" in the school context', in D. Epstein (ed.) *Challenging Lesbian and Gay Inequalities in Education*. Buckingham: Open University Press.

Mac an Ghaill, M. (1996) *Understanding Masculinities: Social Relations and Cultural Arenas*. Buckingham: Open University Press.

Mac an Ghaill, M. (1999) *Contemporary Racisms and Ethnicities: Social and Cultural Transformations*. Buckingham: Open University Press.

Mac an Ghaill, M. and Haywood, C. (2003) 'Young Irelanders: Post-colonial ethnicities-expanding the nation and Irishness', *European Journal of Cultural Studies*, 6, 3, pp. 386–403.

Mac an Ghaill, M., Hanafin, J. and Conway, P. F. (2003) *Gender Politics and Exploring Masculinities in Irish Education*. Dublin: National Council for Curriculum and Assessment.

Maccoby, E. and Jacklin, C. (1974) *The Psychology of Sex Differences*. Oxford: Oxford University Press.

MacKinnon, C. A. (1982) 'Feminism, Marxism, method, and the state: An agenda for theory', *Signs: Journal of Women in Culture and Society*, 7, 3, pp. 515–44.

MacKinnon, C. A. (1987) *Feminism Unmodified: Discourses on Life and the Law*. London: Harvard University Press.

MacKinnon, K. (2003) *Representing Men: Maleness and Masculinity in the Media*. London: Arnold.

MacNeill, M. (1994) 'Active women, media representations and ideology', in S. Birrell and C. L. Cole (eds) *Women, Sport and Culture*. Champaign, IL: Human Kinetics.

Mamo, L. and Fishman, J. R. (2001) 'Potency in all the right places: Viagra as a technology of the gendered body', *Body & Society*, 7, 4, pp. 13–35.

Markson, E. W. and Taylor, C. A. (2000) 'The mirror has two faces', *Ageing and Society*, 20, 2, pp. 137–60.

Marshall, B. L. (1994) *Engendering Modernity: Feminism, Social Theory and Social Change*. Cambridge: Polity Press.

Marshall, B. L and Katz, S. (2002) 'Forever functional: Sexual fitness and the ageing male body', *Body & Society*, 8, 4, pp. 43–70.

Marshall, J. (1981) 'Pansies, perverts and macho men: Changing conceptions of male homosexuality', in K. Plummer (ed.) *The Making of the Modern Homosexual*. London: Hutchinson.

Marsland, D. (1993) *Understanding Youth: Issues and Methods in Social Education*. St Albans: Claridge Press.

Martin, E. (1987) *The Woman in the Body: A Cultural Analysis of Reproduction*. Boston, MA: Beacon Press.

Martin, E. (1994) *Flexible Bodies: Tracking Immunity in American Culture from the Days of Polio to the Age of AIDS*. Boston, MA: Beacon Press.

Martin, L. H., Gutman, H. and Hutton, P. H. (eds) (1988) *Technologies of the Self: A Seminar with Michel Foucault*. London: Tavistock.

Marx, K. (1972) *Karl Marx: Economy, Class and Social Revolution*. London: Nelson.

Mason, J. (1996) 'Gender, care and sensibility in family and kinship relationships', in J. Holland and L. Adkins (eds) *Sex, Sensibility and the Gendered Body*. London: Macmillan.

Mayo, E. (1933) *The Human Problems of Industrial Civilisation*. Boston, MA: Harvard University.

McDonald, M. (1981) 'Schooling and the reproduction of class and gender relations', in R. Dale, G. Esland, R. Ferguson and M. MacDonald (eds) *Politics, Patriarchy and Practice*. Lewes: Falmer and Open University Press.

McDowell, L. (1991) 'Life without father and Ford: The new gender order of post-Fordism', *Transactions, Institute of British Geographers*. 16, pp. 400–19.

McDowell, L. (1997) *Capital Culture: Gender at Work in the City*. Oxford: Blackwell.

McFarland, P. (2002) Hyper-Masculine and Misogynist Violence in Chicano Rap. Retrieved on 22 August 2005 from http://bad.eserver.org/issues/2002/61/mcfarland.html.

McInnes, J. (1998) *The End of Masculinity*. Buckingham: Open University Press.

McIntosh, M. (1981) [1968] 'The homosexual role', in K. Plummer (ed.) *The Making of the Modern Homosexual*. London: Hutchinson.

McIntosh, M. (1993) 'Queer theory and the war of the sexes', in J. Bristow and E. Wilson (eds) *Activating Theory: Lesbian, Gay and Bisexual Politics*. London: Lawrence and Wishart.

McIntosh, M. (unpub.,) 'Notes on gender', in Segal, L. (1990) *Slow Motion: Changing Masculinities, Changing Men*. London: Virago.

McLuhan, M. (2001) *The Medium is the Massage: An Inventory of Effects*. Corte Madera, CA: Gingko Press.

McNair, B. (2002) *Striptease Culture*. London: Routledge.

McNay, L. (2000) *Gender and Agency: Reconfiguring the Subject in Feminist and Social Theory*. Cambridge: Polity.

McRae, S. (ed.) (1999a) *Changing Britain: Families and Households in the 1990s*. Oxford: Oxford University Press.

McRae, S. (1999b) 'Introduction: Family and household change in Britain', in S. McRae (ed.) *Changing Britain: Families and Households in the 1990s*. Oxford: Oxford University Press.

McRobbie, A. (1991) *Feminism and Youth Culture: From 'Jackie' to 'Just Seventeen'*. London: Macmillan.

McWhorter, L. (1999) *Bodies and Pleasures: Foucault and the Politics of Sexual Normalization.* Bloomington, IN: Indiana University.

Mead, H. G. (1967) *Mind, Self and Society.* Chicago, IL: Chicago University Press.

Mead, M. (1935) *Sex and Temperament in Three Primitive Societies.* New York: Dell.

Melas, N. (2005) 'Forgettable vacations and metaphor in ruins: Walcott's *Omeros', Callaloo*, 28, 1, pp. 147–68.

Mercer, K. (1990) 'Welcome to the jungle: identity and diversity in post-modern politics, in J. Rutherford (ed.) *Identity, Community and Difference.* London: Lawrence and Wishart.

Mercer, K. (1991) 'Skin head sex thing: racial differences and homoerotic imagery', in Bad Object Choices (eds) How Do I Look? *Queer Film and Video.* Seattle, WA: Bay Press.

Merck, M., Segal, N. and Wright, E. (eds) (1998) 'Introduction', *Coming Out of Feminism.* London: Blackwell, pp. 1–10.

Merleau-Ponty, M. (1962) *The Phenomenology of Perception.* London: Routledge.

Mermin, J. (1999) *Debating War and Peace.* Princeton, NJ: Princeton University Press.

Messner, M. A. (1992) *Power at Play: Sports and the Problem of Masculinity.* Boston, MA: Beacon Press.

Messner, M. A. (1997) *The Politics of Masculinities: Men in Movements.* Thousand Oaks, CA: Sage.

Messner, M. A., Dunbar, M. and Hunt, D. (2000) 'The Televised Sports Manhood Formula', *Journal of Sport and Social Issues*, 24, 4, pp. 380–94.

Messner M. A., Duncan, C. and Cooky, C. (2003) 'Silence, sports bras, and wrestling porn: Women in televised sports news and highlights shows', *Journal of Sport and Social Issues*, 27, 1, pp. 38–51.

Metcalf, A. and Humphries, M (eds) (1985) *The Sexuality of Men.* London: Pluto Press.

Meyers, D. T. (ed.) (1997) *Feminist Social Thought: A Reader.* London: Routledge.

Middleton, P. (1989) 'Socialism, feminism and men', *Radical Philosophy*, 53, pp. 8–19.

Middleton, P. (1992) *The Inward Gaze: Masculinity, Subjectivity and Modern Culture.* London: Routledge.

Milkie, M. A. (2002) 'Contested images of femininity: An analysis of cultural gatekeepers' struggles with the "real girl" critique', *Gender & Society*, 16, pp. 839–59.

Millar, S. (1997) 'Here comes trouble', *The Guardian*, 13 February.

Miller, J. (1996) *School for Women.* London: Virago.

Miller, T. (1998) 'American exceptionalism', *Journal of Sport and Social Issues*, 12, 4, pp. 347–9.

Miller, Toby. (2005) 'A metrosexual eye on queer guy', *GLQ: A Journal of Lesbian and Gay Studies*, 11, 1, pp. 112–17.

Mirande, A. (1997) *Hombres y Machos: Masculinity and Latino Culture.* Boulder, CO: Westview Press.

Modeleski, T. (1991) *Feminism without Women: Culture and Criticism in a 'Postfeminist' Age.* London: Routledge.

Mohanty, C. T. (1988) 'Under western eyes: Feminist scholarship and colonial discourses', *Feminist Review*, 30, pp. 61–88.

Mohanty, C. T. (1992) 'Feminist encounters: Locating the politics of experience', in M. Barrett and A. Phillips (eds) *Destablizing Theory: Contemporary Feminist Debates.* Cambridge: Polity Press.

Morgan, D. H. J. (1992) *Discovering Men.* London: Routledge.

Morgan, D. H. J. (1996) *Family Connections: An Introduction to Family Studies.* Cambridge: Polity Press.

Morgan, D. H. J. (1999) 'Risk and family practices: Accounting for change and fluidity in family life', in E. B. Silva and C. Smart (eds) *The New Family.* London: Sage.

Morgan, R. (1984) (ed.) *Sisterhood is Global.* New York: Anchor Press/Doubleday.

Morland (2001)'Is intersexuality real?', *Textual Practice*, 15, 3, pp. 527–47.

Morrell, R. (2002) 'Men, movements, and gender transformation in South Africa', *The Journal of Men's Studies*, 10, 3, pp. 309–27.

Mort, F. (1988) 'Boys own? Masculinity, style and popular culture', in R. Chapman and J. Rutherford (eds) *Male Order: Unwrapping Masculinity.* London: Lawrence and Wishart.

Mort, F. (1996) *Cultures of Consumption: Masculinities and Social Space in Late Twentieth-century Britain.* London: Routledge.

Morton, D. (1995) 'Birth of the cyberqueen', *PMLA*, 110, 3, pp. 369–81.

Moss, P. (ed.) (1995) *Father Figures: Fathers in the Families of the 1990s*. Edinburgh: HMSO.

Moss, P. and Brannen, J. (1987) 'Fathers and employment', in C. Lewis and M. O'Brien (eds) *Reassessing Fatherhood: New Observations on Fathers and the Modern Family*. London: Sage.

Mosse, G. L. (1996) *The Image of Man: The Creation of Modern Masculinity*. Oxford: Oxford University Press.

Mowforth, M. and Munt, I. (1998) *Tourism and Sustainability: New Tourism in the Third World*. New York: Routledge.

Mulvey, L. (1975) 'Visual pleasure and narrative cinema', *Screen*, 16, 3, pp. 6–18.

Mulvey, L. (1989) *Visual and Other Pleasures*. Basingstoke: Macmillan.

Nandy, A. (1983) *The Intimate Enemy: Loss and Recovery of Self Under Colonialism*. Oxford: Oxford University Press.

Nash, C. (1993) 'Remapping and renaming: New cartologies of identity, gender and landscape in Ireland', *Feminist Review*, 44, pp. 39–57.

Nayak, A. and Kehily, M. J. (1997) 'Masculinities and schooling: Why are young men so homophobic?', in D. L. Steinberg, D. Epstein and R. Johnson (eds) *Border Patrols: Policing the Boundaries of Heterosexuality*. Cassell: London.

Nichols, J. (1975) *Men's Liberation*. New York: Penguin.

Nicholson, L. J. (ed.) (1990) *Feminism/Postmodernism*. London: Routledge.

Nixon, S. (1992) 'Have you got the look? Masculinities and shopping spectacle', in R. Shields (ed.) *Lifestyle Shopping: The Subject of Consumption*. London: Routledge.

Nixon, S. (1996) *Hard Looks: Masculinities, Spectatorship and Consumption*. London: UCL Press.

Nixon, S. (1997) 'Exhibiting masculinity', in S. Hall (ed.) *Representation: Cultural Representations and Signifying Practices*. London: Sage.

Oakley, A. (1972) *Sex, Gender and Society*. London: Temple Smith.

Oakley, A. (1974) *The Sociology of Housework*. London: Martin Robertson.

Oakley, A. (1979) *Becoming a Mother*. London: Martin Robertson.

O'Brien, Johnson and Cairns, D. (1991) *Gender in Irish Writing*. Milton Keynes: Open University Press.

O'Callaghan, M. (1995) 'Continuties in imagination', in Jan N. Pieterse and B. Parekh (eds.) *Decolonization of the Imagination: Culture, Knowledge and Power*. London and Atlantic Highlands, NJ: Zed Books.

O'Connell, Davidson, J. and Sanchez Taylor, J. (1994) *Child Prostitution and Sex Tourism: Thailand*. Leicester: ECPAT.

Ohi, K. (2000) 'Molestation 101: Child abuse, homophobia, and the boys of St. Vincent.' *GLQ: A Journal of Lesbian and Gay Studies*, 6, 2, pp. 195–248.

Ong, A. (1988) 'Colonialism and modernity: Feminist re-presentation of women in non-western societies', *Inscriptions*, 3, 4, pp. 79–93.

Ong, A. (1999) *Flexible Citizenship: The Cultural Logics of Transnationality*. Durham, NC: Duke University Press.

Opperman, M. (1999) 'Sex tourism', *Annals of Tourism Research*, 26, 2, pp. 252–66.

O'Sullivan, D. (1999) 'Gender equity as policy paradigm in the Irish educational policy process', *Economic and Social Review*, 30, 3, pp. 309–36.

O'Sullivan, J. (1996) 'If you're hip, you must be Irish', *The Independent*, 1 July.

O'Sullivan, P. B. and Flanagan, A. J. (2003) 'Reconceptualizing "flaming" and other problematic messages', *New Media and Society*, 5, 1, pp. 69–94.

Oudshorn, N. (1994) *Beyond the Natural Body: An Archaeology of Sex Hormones*. Routledge: London.

Owen, M. (2004) 'Cutting up': making sense of self-harm', in A. Boran and B. Murphy (eds) *Gender in Flux*. Chester: Chester Academic Press, pp. 151–71.

Paetcher, C. (1998) *Educating the Other: Gender, Power and Schooling*. London: Falmer Press.

Paglia, C. (1992) *Sexual Personae*. London: Penguin Books.

Paglia, C. (1993) *Sex, Art and American Culture*. London: Penguin Books

Pahl, R. (1995) *After Success*. Cambridge: Polity Press.

Pajaczkowska, C. and Young, L. (1992) 'Racism, representation, psychoanalysis', in J. Donald and A. Rattansi (eds.) *Race, Culture and Difference*. London: Sage.

Parsons, T. (1955) 'The American father: Its relation to personality and to social structure', in T. Parsons and R. F. Bales (eds) *Family Socialization and Interaction Process*. New York: The Free Press.

Parsons, T. and Bales, R. F. (eds) (1955) *Family Socialization and Interaction Process*. New York: The Free Press.

Pateman (1989) *The Disorder of Women: Democracy, Feminism and Political Theory*. Cambridge: Polity Press.

Paterson, A. (1998) *Unmasking the Masculine: 'Men' and 'Identity in a Sceptical Age*. London: Sage.

Payne, J. (1995) *England and Wales Youth Cohort Study*. Sheffield: Department for Education and Employment.

Pearson, R. (2000) 'All Change? Men, Women and Reproductive Work in the Global Economy', *European Journal of Development Research* 12, 2, pp. 19–237.

Pease, B. (2000) *Recreating Men: Postmodern Masculinity Politics*. London: Sage.

Pease, B. and Pringle, K. (eds) (2001) *A Man's World? Changing Men's Practices in a Globalized World*. London: Zed Books.

Peterson, V. S. and Runyan, A. S. (1993) *Global Gender Issues*. Boulder, CO: Westview Press.

Pettman, J. J. (1997) 'Body politics: International sex tourism', *Third World Quarterly*, 18, 1, pp. 93–108.

Phillips, A. (1992) 'Universal pretensions in political thought', in M. Barrett and A. Phillips (eds) *Destablizing Theory: Contemporary Feminist Debates*. Cambridge: Polity Press.

Phillips, A. (1998a) 'Introduction', in A. Phillips (ed.) *Feminism and Politics*. Oxford: Oxford University Press.

Phillips, A. (1998b) 'Democracy and representation: Or, why should it matter who our representatives are?', in A. Phillips (ed.) *Feminism and Politics*. Oxford: Oxford University Press.

Phillips, J. L. (1999) 'Tourist-oriented prostitution in Barbados: The case of the beach boy and the white female tourist', in K. Kempadoo (ed.) *Sun, Sex, and Gold: Tourism and Sex Work in the Caribbean*. Lanham, MA: Rowman and Littlefield.

Phizacklea, A. (1990) *Unpacking the Fashion Industry: Gender, Racism and Class in Production*. London: Routledge.

Phizacklea, A. and Wolkowitz, C. (1995) *Homeworking Women*. London: Sage.

Pile, S. and Thrift, N. (1995) *Mapping the Subject: Geographies of Cultural Transformation*. London: Routledge.

Plummer, K. (1975) *Sexual Stigma*. London: Routledge.

Plummer, K. (ed.) (1981) *The Making of the Modern Homosexual*. London: Hutchinson.

Plummer, K. (1992) *Modern Homosexualities*. London: Routledge.

Plummer, K. (1995) *Telling Sexual Stories: Power, Change and Social Worlds*. Lomdon: Routledge.

Polivka, L. (2000) 'Postmodern aging and the loss of meaning', *Journal of Aging and Identity*, 5, 4, pp. 225–35.

Pollack, W. (1996) *Real Boys: Rescuing Our Sons From The Myths of Boyhood*. New York: Henry Holt & Company.

Pollert, A. (1981) *Girls, Wives, Factory Lives*. London: Macmillan.

Potts, A. (2004) 'Deleuze on Viagra (or, what can a 'Viagra-body') do?, *Body & Society*, 10, 1, pp. 17–36.

Powell, J. L. and Longino, C. F., Jr (2002) 'Postmodernism versus modernism: rethinking theoretical tensions in social gerontology', *Journal of Aging and Identity*, 7, 4, pp. 219–26.

Prideaux, B., Agrusa, J., Donlon, J. and Curran, C. (2004) 'Exotic or erotic: Contrasting images for defining destinations', *Asia Pacific Journal of Tourism Research*, 9, 1, pp. 5–17.

Pringle, R. (1989) *Secretaries Talk: Sexuality, Power and Work*. London: Verso.

Pringle, R. (1992) 'Absolute sex? Unpacking the sexuality/gender relationship', in R. W. Connell and G. W. Dowsett (eds) *Rethinking Sex: Social Theory and Sexuality Research*. Melbourne: Melbourne University Press.

Pronger, B. (1990) *The Arena of Masculinity: Sports, Homosexuality and the Meaning of Sex*. London: Gay Men's Press.

Prosser J. (1998) *Second Skins: The Body Narratives of Transsexuality*. New York: Columbia University Press.

Pruitt, D. and LaFont, S. (1995) 'For Love and Money: Romance Tourism in Jamaica'. *Annals of Tourism Research*, 22, 2, pp. 422–40.

Quicke, J. (1999) *A Curriculum for Life: Schooling for a Democratic Learning Society*. Buckingham: Open University Press.

Rail, G. (1998) *Sport and Postmodern Times*. Albany, NY: State University of New York Press.

Rainbow, P. (ed.) (1984) *The Foucault Reader*. Harmondsworth: Penguin.

Rapoport, R. N., Fogarty, M. and Rapoport, R. (1982) *Families in Britain*. London: Routledge and Kegan Paul.

Real, M. (1998) 'Media-sport: Technology and the commodification of postmodern sport', in L. Wenner (ed.) *Media Sport*. London: Routledge.

Redman, P. (2001) 'The discipline of love: Negotiation and regulation in boys' performance of a romance-based heterosexual masculinity', *Men and Masculinities*, 42, 2, pp. 186–200.

Redman, P. and Mac an Ghaill, M. (1996) 'Schooling sexualities: Heterosexual masculinities, schooling, and the unconscious', *Discourse*, 17, 2, pp. 243–56.

Rees, T. L. (1999) *Women and Work*. Cardiff: University of Wales Press.

Reeve, J. (1992) 'Future Prospects for Hormone Replacement Therapy', *British Medical Bulletin* 48, 2, pp. 458–68.

Renan, E. (1990) 'What is a nation?', in H. Bhabha (ed.) *Nation and Narration*. London: Routledge.

Renold, E. (2000) ' "Coming out": Gender, (hetero) sexuality and the primary school', *Gender and Education*, 12, 3, pp. 309–26.

Reynaud, E. (1983) *Holy Virility: The Social Construction of Masculinity*. London: Pluto Press.

Richardson, D. (ed.) (1996) *Theorising Heterosexuality*. Buckingham: Open University Press.

Richardson, D. (2000) *Rethinking Sexuality*. London: Sage.

Riley, D. (1988) *Am I that Name? Feminism and the Category of 'Woman' in History*. Basingstoke: Macmillan.

Roberts, C. (2004) 'Sex, race and 'unnatural' difference: Tracking the chiastic logic of menopause-related discourses', *European Journal of Women's Studies*, 11, 1, pp. 27–44.

Rodríguez, M. G. (2005) 'The place of women in Argentinian football', *The International Journal of the History of Sport*, 22, 2, pp. 231–45.

Roiphe, K. (1994) *The Morning After: Sex, Fear and Feminism*. London: Hamish Hamilton.

Roper, M. (1994) *Masculinity and the British Organization Man since 1945*. Oxford: Oxford University Press.

Roper, M. and Tosh, J. (eds) (1991) *Masculinities in Britain since 1800*. London: Routledge.

Rose, N. (1991) *Governing the Soul: The Shaping of the Private Self*. London: Routledge.Roulson, C. (1997) 'Women on the margin: The women's movements in Northern Ireland, 1973–1995', in L. A. West (ed.) *Feminist Nationalism*. London: Routledge.

Rowan, J. (1987) *The Horned God*. London: Routledge and Kegan Paul.

Rowan, J. (1997) *Healing the Male Psyche: Therapy as Initiation*. London: Routledge.

Rowe, D. (1999) *Sport, Culture and the Media: The Unruly Trinity*. Buckingham: Open University Press.

Rowe, D., McKay, J. and Miller, T. (2000) 'Panic sport and the racialized masculine body', in J. McKay M. A. Messner and D. Sabo (eds) *Masculinities, Gender Relations, and Sport*. Thousand Oaks, CA: Sage.

Rubin, Gayle (1984). 'Thinking Sex: Notes for a Radical Theory of the Politics of Sexuality' in Carole S. Vance (ed.), *Pleasure and Danger: exploring female sexuality*. Boston: Routledge & Kegan Paul, pp. 267–319.

Rubin, G. (1975) 'The traffic in women: notes on the "political economy" of sex', in R. R. Reiter (ed.) *Toward an Anthropology of Women*. London: Monthly Review Press.

Rubin, G. (1993) 'Thinking sex: Notes for a radical theory of the politics of sexuality', in H. Abelove, M. Barale and D. Halperin (eds) *The Lesbian and Gay Studies Reader*. London: Routledge.

Rubin, G. with Butler, J. (1998) 'Sexual traffic', in M. Merck., N. Segal and E. Wright (eds) *Coming Out of Feminism*. London: Blackwell.

Russell, G. (1983) *The Changing Role of Father*. London: University of Queensland Press.

Rutherford, J. (1988) 'Who's that man', in R. Chapman and J. Rutherford (eds) *Male Order: Unwrapping Masculinity*. London: Lawrence and Wishart.

Rutherford, J. (1997) *Forever England: Reflections on Masculinity and Empire*. London: Lawrence and Wishart.

Sabo, D. and Jansen, S. C. (1998) 'Prometheus unbound: Constructions of masculinity in the sports media', in Werner, L. A. (ed.) *MediaSport*. London: Routledge.

Salvation Army International (2005) 'Global Sexual Trafficking', Retrieved on 24 February 2006 from http://www1.salvationarmy.org/ihq%5Cwww_sa.nsf/0/B5DD72A243A1150B 80256E49006C621E?openDocument.

Salzinger, L. (2003) *Genders in Production: Making Workers in Mexico's Global Factories*. Berkeley and Los Angeles, CA: University of California Press.

Sanchez Taylor, J. (2001) 'Dollars are a girls' best friend? Female tourists' sexual behaviour in the Caribbean ' *Sociology*, 35, 3, pp. 749– 64.

Sassen, S. (1998) *Globalization and its Discontents*. New York: the New Press.

Savage, M., Barlow, J., Dickens, P. and Fielding, T. (1992) *Property, Bureaucracy and Culture: Middle Class Formation in Contemporary Britain*. London: Routledge.

Sawicki, J. (1991) *Disciplining Foucault: Feminism, Power and the Body*. New York: Routledge.

Scheer, S. and Palkovitz, R. (1994) 'Adolescents-to-adults: Social status and cognitive factors,' *Sociological Studies of Children*, 6, pp. 125–40.

Scheurich, J. J. (1995) 'A postmodernist critique of interviewing', *International Journal of Qualitative Studies in Education*, 8, 3, pp. 239–52.

Schiller, H. I. (1976) *Communication and Cultural Domination*. New York: International Arts and Sciences Press.

Schiller, H. I. (1991) 'Not yet the post-imperialist order', *Cultural Studies in Mass Communcation*, 8, pp. 13–28.

Schlesinger, P. (1978) *Putting 'Reality' Together*. London: Routledge.

schraefel, m. c. (1999) 'Jacking in to the virtual self', in S. Brodribb (ed.) *Reclaiming the Future: Women's Strategies for the 21st Century*. Charlottetown, PEI: Gynergy Press.

Scott, J. (1999) 'Family change: revolution or backlash in attitudes?', in S. McRae, (ed.) *Changing Britain*. Oxford: Oxford University Press.

Scott, J. W. (1988a) *Gender and the Politics of History*. New York: Columbia University Press.

Scott, J. W. (1988b) 'Deconstructing equality versus difference: Or, the uses of poststructuralist theory for feminism', *Feminist Studies*, 14, pp. 33–50.

Scott, J. W. (1997) 'Deconstructing equality – versus – difference: or, the uses of poststructuralist theory for feminism', in D. T. Meyers (ed.) *Feminist Social Thought: A Reader*. London: Routledge, pp. 757–71.

Scott, J. W. (2000) *Feminism and History*. Oxford: Oxford University Press.

Sedgwick, E. K. (1991) *Epistemology of the Closet*. Hemel Hempstead: Harvester Wheatsheaf.

Sedgwick, E. K. (1994) *Tendencies*. London: Routledge.

Segal, L. (1990) *Slow Motion: Changing Masculinities, Changing Men*. London: Virago.

Segal, L. (1999) *Why Feminism? Gender, Psychology and Politics*. New York: Columbia University Press.

Segal, L. (2001) 'Back to the boys? Temptations of the good gender theorist', *Textual Practice*, 15, 12, pp. 231–50.

Seidler, V. J. (1992) *Men, Sex and Relationships: Writings from Achilles Heel*. London: Routledge.

Seidman, S. (1993) 'Identity and politics in a "postmodern" gay culture: Some historical and conceptual notes', in M. Warner (ed.) *Fear of a Queer Planet: Queer Politics and Social Theory*. Minneapolis, MN: University of Minnesota Press.

Shakespeare, T., Gillespie-Sells, K. and Davies, D. (1996) *The Sexual Politics of Disability: Untold Desires*. London: Cassell.

Sherlock, J. (1999) 'Globalisation: Western culture and *Riverdance*', in A. Brah, M. J. Hickman and M. Mac an Ghaill (eds) *Thinking Identities: Ethnicity, Racism and Culture*. London: Macmillan.

Shilling, C. (2003) *The Body and Social Theory*. 2nd edn, London: Sage.

Shire, C. (1994) 'Men don't go to the moon: Language, space and masculinities in Zimbabwe', in A. Cornwall and N. Lindisfarne (eds) *Dislocating Masculinity: Gender, Power and Anthropology*. London: Routledge.

Shurmer-Smith, P. and Hannan E. K. (1994) *Worlds of Desire. Realms of Power: A Cultural Geography*. London: Edward Arnold.

Silva, E. B. and Smart, C. (eds) (1999) *The New Family?* London: Sage.

Silverman, M. (1992) *Deconstructing the Nation: Immigration, Racism and Citizenship in Modern France*. London: Routledge.

Simpson, B. (1998) *Changing Families: An Ethnographic Approach to Divorce and Separation*. Oxford: Berg.

Simpson, M. (ed.) (1996) *Anti-Gay*. London: Cassell.

Sinfield, A. (1998) *Gay and After*. London: Serpents's Tail.

Sivanandan, A. (1989) 'New circuits of imperialism', *Race and Class*, 30, 4, pp. 1–19.

Skeggs, B. (1997) *Formations of Class and Gender: Becoming Respectable*. London: Sage.

Skeggs, B. (2004a) 'Context and background: Pierre Bourdieu's analaysis of class, gender and sexuality', in L. Adkins and B. Skeggs (eds) *Feminism After Bourdieu*. Oxford: Blackwell.

Skeggs, B. (2004b) *Class, Self, Culture*. London: Routledge.

Skelton, C. (2001) *Schooling the Boys: Masculinities and Primary Education*. Buckingham: Open University Press.

Smart, C. and Neale, B. (1999) *Family Fragments?* Cambridge: Polity Press.

Smith, B. G. (ed.) (2000) *Global Feminisms since 1945*. London: Routledge.

Smith, D. (1987) *The Everyday World as Problematic: A Feminist Sociology*. Milton Keynes: Open University Press.

Smith, M. K. (2003) *Issues in Cultural Tourism Management*. Routledge: New York.

Smyth, G. (2001) *Space and the Irish Cultural Imagination*. London: Palgrave Press.

Snodgrass, J. (ed.) (1977) *For Men Against Sexism*. New York: Times Change Press.

Sontag, S. (1978) 'The Double Standard of Ageing', in V. Carver and P. Liddiard (eds.) *An Ageing Population*, London: Hodder and Stoughton, pp. 72–80.

Spargo, T. (1999) *Foucault and Queer Theory*. Cambridge: Icon Books

Spike Peterson, V. and Sisson Runyan, A. (1993) *Global Gender Issues*. Oxford: Westview Press.

Spivak, G. (1988a) 'Can the subaltern speak?', in C. Nelson and L. Grossberg (eds) *Marxism and the Interpretation of Culture*. Urbana-Champaign, IL: University of Illinois Press.

Spivak, G. (1988b) *In Other Worlds: Essays in Cultural Politics*. New York: Routledge.

Sport England (1999) 'The participation of women in sport', Retrieved on 3 January 2006 from http://www.stats4schools.gov.uk/images/SP_Women_sportparticipation_tcm86-13168.pdf

Squires, J. (1999) *Gender in Political Theory*. Cambridge: Polity Press.

Stacey, J. (1991) 'Promoting normality; Section 28 and the regulation of sexuality', in S. Franklin, C. Lury and J. Stacey (eds) *Off-Centre: Feminism and Cultural Studies*. London: Routledge.

Stacey, J. (1996) *In the Name of the Family: Rethinking Family Values in the Postmodern Age*. Boston, MA: Beacon Press.

Stanworth, M. (ed.) (1987) *Reproductive Technologies*. Cambridge: Polity Press.

Stecopoulos, H. and Uebel, M. (eds) (1997) *Race and the Subject of Masculinities*. London: Duke University Press.

Stein, A. and Plummer, K. (1994) ' "I can't even think straight": Theory and the missing revolution in sociology', *Sociological Theory*, 12, 2, pp. 178–87.

Steinman, C. (1992) 'Gaze out of bounds', in S. Craig (ed.) *Men, Masculinity and the Media*. London: Sage.

Stienstra, D. (1994) *Women's Movements and International Organizations*. London: Macmillan.

Stienstra, D. (2000) 'Dancing resistance from Rio to Beijing: Transnational women's organizing and United Nations conferences, 1992–6', in M. H. Marchand and A. S. Runyan (eds) *Gender and Global Restructuring*. London: Routledge.

Stoller, R. (1968) *Sex and Gender: On the Development of Masculinity and Femininity*. London.

Stoller, R. (1979) *Sexual Excitement: Dynamics of Erotic Life*. New York: Pantheon.

Stoltenberg, J. (1989) *Refusing to Be a Man*. New York: Meridian.

Stranack, J. (2002) 'Are we all trash', *Blueboy*, 10, pp. 26–7.

Suler, J. (1999) [1996] *The Psychology of Cyberspace*, Accessed on 25 November, 2005 from <http://www.rider.edu/~suler/psycyber/genderswap.html>.

Sullivan, A. (ed.) (1997) *Same Sex Marriage: Pro and Con – A Reader*. New York: Vintage Books.

Sweetman, C. (1997) *Men and Masculinity*. Oxford: Oxfam.

Talbot, R. (2001) 'Myths in the Representations of Women Terrorists', *Eire-Ireland: Journal of Irish Studies*, 25, 3–4, pp. 1–10.

Tarchert (2002) 'Fuzzy gender: Between female-embodiment and intersex', *Journal of Gender Studies*, 11, 1, pp. 29–38.

Taylor, F. W. (1947) *Scientific Management*. New York: Harper and Row.

Therberge, N. and Cronk, A. (1994) 'Work routines in newspaper sports departments and the coverage of women's sports', in S. Birrell and C. Cole (eds) *Women, Sport and Culture*. Champaign, IL: Human Kinetics.

Thomas, D. (1993) *Not Guilty: In Defence of the Modern Man*. London: Weidenfeld and Nicholson.

Thomas, M. (2000) 'Exploring the contexts and meanings of women's experiences of sexual intercourse on holiday', in S. Clift and S. Carter (eds) *Tourism and Sex: Culture, Commerce and Coercion*, The Cutting Edge of Tourism Series. London: Pinter.

Thompson, J. B. (1995) *Media and Modernity: A Social Theory of the Media*. Cambridge: Polity with Blackwell.

Thorne, B. (1993) *Gender Play: Girls and Boys in School*. New Brunswick, NJ: Rutgers University Press.

Thrift, N. (1989) 'Images of social change', in C. Hamnett, L. McDowell and P. Sarre (eds) *The Changing Social Structure*. London: Sage.

Thurlow, C. and Brown, A. (2003) 'Generation Txt? The sociolinguistics of young people's text-messaging', *Discourse Analysis Online*. Accessed on 4 December 2005 from http://www.shu.ac.uk/daol/articles/v1/n1/a3/ thurlow2002003–01.html

Tilly, C. (1996) *Half a Job: Bad and Good Part-time Jobs in a Changing Labour Market*. Philadelphia, PA: Temple University Press.

Tolson, A. (1977) *The Limits of Masculinity*. London: Tavistock.

Tomlinson, A. (2002) 'Editorial', *International Review for the Sociology of Sport*, 37, pp. 275–7.

Troupe, Q. (1989) *James Baldwin: The Legacy*. New York: Simon and Schuster/Touchstone.

True, J. (2003) *Gender, Globalization, and Post-Socialism. The Czech Republic after Communism*. New York: Columbia University Press.

Tuchman, G. (1978), 'Introduction: The symbolic annihilation of women by the mass media', in G. Tuchman, Arlene Daniels and James Benet (eds) *Hearth and Home: Images of Women in the Mass Media*. New York: Oxford University Press.

Tuggle, C. A., and Owen, A. (1999) 'A descriptive analysis of NBC's coverage of the Centennial Olympics: The "games of the women"?' *Journal of Sport and Social Issues*, 23, 2, pp. 171–82.

Turkle, S. (1995). *Life on the Screen: Identity in the Age of the Internet*. New York: Simon and Schuster.

Turner, B. S. (1984) *The Body and Society*. Oxford: Basil Blackwell.

Turner, B. S. (1991) 'Recent developments in the theory of the body', in M. Featherstone, M. Hepworth and B. S. Turner (eds) *The Body: Social Process and Cultural Theory*. London: Sage.

Turner, B. S. (1992) *Regulating Bodies: Essays in Medical Sociology*. London: Routledge.

Urry, J. (1990) 'Work, production and social relations', *Work, Employment and Society*, 4, 2, pp. 271–80.

Urry, J. (2000) *Sociology Beyond Societies: Mobilities for the Twenty-first*. London: Routledge.

Urry, J. (2003) *Global Complexity*. Cambridge: Polity.

Urry, J. (2004) *Globalising the Tourist Gaze*. Lancaster: Lancaster University.

Van Zoonen, L. (2002) 'Gendering the internet: claims, controversies and cultures', *European Journal of Communication*, 17, 1, pp. 5–23.

Vance, C. (1989) 'Social construction theory: problems in the history of sexuality', in D. Altman, C. Vance, M. Vicinus and J. Weeks (eds) *Homosexuality, Which Homosexuality*. Amsterdam and London: Uitgeverij An Dekker/Schorer.

Vance, C. (1995) 'Social construction theory and sexuality', in M. Berger, B. Wallis, and S. Watson (eds) *Constructing Masculinity*. New York: Routledge, pp. 37–48.

VanEvery, J. (1995) *Heterosexual Women Changing the Family: Refusing to Be a Wife*. London: Taylor and Francis.

Varney, W. (1998) 'Barbie Australis: The commercial reinvention of national culture', *Social Identities*, 4, 2, pp. 161–76.

Velu, C. (1999) 'Faut – il "practiser" avec l'universalisme? A short history of the PACS', *Modern and Contemporary France*, 7, 4, pp. 429–42.

Von Der Lippe, G. (2002) 'Media image: sport, gender and national identities in five European countries', *International Review for the Sociology of Sport*, 37, 3–4, pp. 371–95.

Walby, S. (1990) *Theorizing Patriarchy*. Oxford: Blackwell.

Walby, S. (1997) *Gender Transformations*. London: Routledge.

Walby, S. (2002) 'Feminism in a global age', *Economy and Society*, 31, 4, pp. 533–57.

Walby, S. (ed.) (1992) *Gender Segregation at Work*. Milton Keynes: Open University Press.

Walby, S. (ed.) (1999) *New Agendas for Women*. London: Macmillan.

Walkerdine, V. (1990) *Schoolgirl Fictions*. London: Verso.

Walkerdine, V. and Lucey, H. (1989) *Democracy in the Kitchen: Regulating Mothers and Socialising Daughters*. London: Virago.

Walkerdine, V., Lucey, H. and Melody, J. (2001) *Growing Up Girl: Psycho-Social Explorations of Gender and Class*. London: Palgrave.

Walshe, E. (1997) 'Introduction: Sex, Nation and Dissent', in E. Walshe (ed.) *Sex, Nation and Dissent in Irish Writing*. Cork: Cork University Press.

Walter, B. (1995) 'Irishness, gender and space', *Society and Space*, 13, pp. 35–50.

Walter, B. (2001) *Outsiders Inside: Whiteness, Place and Irish Women*. London: Routledge.

Walter, N. (1998) *The New Feminism*. London: Little Brown.

Walter, N. (1999) (ed.) *On The Move: Feminism for a New Generation*. London: Virago.

Walter, N. (2004) 'The silence of the fathers is what really harms families', *The Guardian*, 1 September, p. 20.

Warner, M. (ed.) (1993) *Fear of a Queer Planet: Queer Politics and Social Theory*. Minneapolis, MN: University of Minnesota Press.

Watney, S. (1987) *Policing Desire*. London: Methuen.

Weaver-Hightower, M. (2002). 'The gender of terror and heroes? What educators might teach about men and masculinity after September 11, 2001', *Teachers College Record*, 12 August 2002. Retrieved 1 January 2005 from http://www.tcrecord.org/content.asp?contentid=11012

Weber, M. (1958) *The Protestant Ethic and the Spirit of Capitalism*. New York: Charles Scribner's Sons.

Weeks, J. (1986) *Sexuality*. London: Tavistock Publications.

Weeks, J. (1977) *Coming Out: Homosexual Politics in Britain from the Nineteenth Century to the Present*. London: Quartet.

Weeks, J. (1990) 'Post–modern AIDS?', in T. Boffin and S. Gupta (eds) *Ecstatic Antibodies: Resisting the AIDS Mythology*. London: Rivers Oram Press.

Weeks, J. (1995) *Invented Moralities: Sexual Values in an Age of Uncertainty*. Cambridge: Polity Press.

Weeks, J. (1998) 'The sexual citizen', *Theory, Culture and Society*, 15, 3–4, pp. 35–52.

Weeks, J., Heaphy, B. and Donovan, C. (1999) 'Families of choice: Autonomy and mutuality in non-heterosexual relationships', in S. McRae (ed.) *Changing Britain: Families and Households*. Oxford: Oxford University Press.

Weeks, J., Heaphy, B. and Donovan, C. (2001) *Same Sex Intimacies: Families of Choice and Other Life Experiments*. London: Routledge.

Weeks, J., Holland, J. and Waites, M. (eds) (2003) *Sexualities and Society: A Reader*. Cambridge: Polity.

Wensig, E. H. and Bruce, T. (2003) 'Bending the rules: Media representations of gender during an international sporting event', *International Review for the Sociology of Sport*, 38, pp. 387–96.

Westwood, S. (1990) 'Racism, black masculinity and the politics of space', in J. Hearn and D. H. J. Morgan (eds) *Men, Masculinities and Social Theory*. London: Unwin Hyman.

Westwood, S. (1996) ' "Feckless fathers": Masculinities and the British state', in M. Mac an Ghaill (ed.) *Understanding Masculinities: Social Relations and Cultural Arenas*. Buckingham: Open University Press.

Whannel, G. (2001) 'Punishment, redemption and celebration in the popular press: The case of David Beckham', in D. L. Andrews and S. J. Jackson (eds) *Sport Stars: The Cultural Politics of Sporting*. Celebrity. London: Routledge.

Wharton, A. S. (2005) *The Sociology of Gender: An Introduction to Theory and Research*. Malden: Blackwell.

Whitehead, S. M. (2002) *Men and Masculinities: Key Themes and New Directions*. Cambridge: Polity.

Whittock, M. (2000) *Feminising the Masculine? Women in Non-traditional Employment*. Aldershot: Ashgate.

Wilbush, J. (1994) 'Confrontation in the climacteric', *Journal of the Royal Society of Medicine*, 87, pp. 342–7.

Wilkinson, H. (1999) 'The Thatcher legacy: Power of feminism and the birth of girl power', in N. Walter (ed.) *On the Move: Feminism for a New Generation*. London: Virago.

Williams, C. L. (1993) 'Introduction', in C. L. Williams (ed.) *Doing 'Women's Work': Men in Non-traditional Occupations*. London: Sage.

Williams, H. (2003) 'New Labour is Older than it Thinks', *The Guardian*, 11 September, p. 25.

Williams, S. L. (2002) 'Trying on gender, gender regimes, and the process of becoming women', *Gender & Society*, 19, 1, pp. 29–52.

Willis, P. (1977) *Learning to Labour: How Working Class Kids Get Working Class Jobs*. Hants: Saxon House.

Willis, P. (2000) *The Ethnographic Imagination*. Cambridge: Polity Press.

Wilton, T. (1996) 'Which one's the man? The heterosexualisation of lesbian sex', in D. Richardson (ed.) *Theorising Heterosexuality*. Buckingham: Open University press.

Winn, M. (1983) *Children Without Childhood*. New York: Pantheon Books.

Winterich, J. A (2003) 'Sex, menopause, and culture: Sexual orientation and the meaning of menopause for women's sex lives', *Gender & Society*, 17, 4, pp. 627–42.

Wolffensperger, J. (1991) 'Engendered structure: Giddens and the conceptualization of gender', in K. Davis, M. Leijenaar and J. Oldersma (eds) *The Gender of Power*. London: Sage.

Wolmark, J. (ed) (1999) *Cybersexualities: A Reader on Feminist Theory, Cyborgs and Cyberspace*. Edinburgh: Edinburgh University Press.

Wolpe, A. M. (1988) *Within School Walls: The Role of Discipline, Sexuality and the Curriculum*. London: Routledge.

Women's Sport Foundation (2003) *Transexuality and Sport–Women's Sports Foundation (WSF) Response to the Department for Culture, Media and Sport*. Retrieved on 20 November 2004 from http://www.wsf.org.uk/docs/Transsexuality.doc.

Wood, S. (1989) 'New wave management', *Work, Employment and Society*, 3, 3, pp. 379–402.

World Trade Organisation (2000) *International Trade Statistics*. Geneva: WTO Publications.

Wray, S. (2003) 'Women growing older: Agency, ethnicity and culture', *Sociology*, 37, 3, pp. 511–27.

Wright, J. E, and Clarke, G. (1999) 'Sport, the media and the construction of compulsory heterosexuality: A case study of women's rugby union', *International Review for the Sociology of Sport*, 34, pp. 227–43.

Yeatman, A. (1994) *Postmodern Revisionings of the Political*. London: Routledge.

Young, I. M. (1993) 'Together in difference: transforming the logic of group political difference', in J. Squires (ed.) *Principled Positions: Postmodernism and the Rediscovery of Value*. London: Lawrence and Wishart.

Yuval-Davis, N. (1997) *Gender and Nation*. London: Sage.

Name Index

Subject Index